Carnivalizing Reconciliation

Worlds of Memory

Editors:
Jeffrey Olick, University of Virginia
Aline Sierp, Maastricht University
Jenny Wüstenberg, Nottingham Trent University

Published in collaboration with the Memory Studies Association

This book series publishes innovative and rigorous scholarship in the interdisciplinary and global field of memory studies. Memory studies includes all inquiries into the ways we—both individually and collectively—are shaped by the past. How do we represent the past to ourselves and to others? How do those representations shape our actions and understandings, whether explicitly or unconsciously? The "memory" we study encompasses the near-infinitude of practices and processes humans use to engage with the past, the incredible variety of representations they produce, and the range of individuals and institutions involved in doing so.

Guided by the mandate of the Memory Studies Association to provide a forum for conversations among subfields, regions, and research traditions, Worlds of Memory focuses on cutting-edge research that pushes the boundaries of the field and can provide insights for memory scholars outside of a particular specialization. In the process, it seeks to make memory studies more accessible, diverse, and open to novel approaches.

Volume 8
Carnivalizing Reconciliation: Contemporary Australian and Canadian Literature and Film beyond the Victim Paradigm
Hanna Teichler

Volume 7
Nordic War Stories: World War II as History, Fiction, Media, and Memory
Edited by Marianne Stecher-Hansen

Volume 6
The Struggle for the Past: How We Construct Social Memories
Elizabeth Jelin

Volume 5
The Mobility of Memory: Migrations and Diasporas across European Borders
Edited by Luisa Passerini, Milica Trakilović, and Gabriele Proglio

Volume 4
Agency in Transnational Memory Politics
Edited by Jenny Wüstenberg and Aline Sierp

Volume 3
Resettlers and Survivors: Bukovina and the Politics of Belonging in West Germany and Israel, 1945–1989
Gaëlle Fisher

Volume 2
Velvet Retro: Postsocialist Nostalgia and the Politics of Heroism in Czech Popular Culture
Veronika Pehe

Volume 1
When Will We Talk about Hitler? German Students and the Nazi Past
Alexandra Oeser

Carnivalizing Reconciliation

*Contemporary Australian and Canadian
Literature and Film beyond the Victim Paradigm*

Hanna Teichler

berghahn
NEW YORK · OXFORD
www.berghahnbooks.com

First published in 2021 by
Berghahn Books
www.berghahnbooks.com

© 2021, 2025 Hanna Teichler
First paperback edition published in 2025

All rights reserved. Except for the quotation of short passages
for the purposes of criticism and review, no part of this book
may be reproduced in any form or by any means, electronic or
mechanical, including photocopying, recording, or any information
storage and retrieval system now known or to be invented,
without written permission of the publisher.

Library of Congress Cataloging-in-Publication Data
A C.I.P. cataloging record is available from the Library of Congress
Library of Congress Cataloging in Publication Control Number: 2021034481

British Library Cataloguing in Publication Data
A catalogue record for this book is available from the British Library

ISBN 978-1-80073-172-1 hardback
ISBN 978-1-80539-749-6 paperback
ISBN 978-1-80539-926-1 epub
ISBN 978-1-80073-173-8 web pdf

https://doi.org/10.3167/9781800731721

Sigelziffer D.30

Contents

Acknowledgments	vi
Introduction. Carnivalizing Reconciliation	1
Chapter 1. Justice through Storytelling? Australian and Canadian Reconciliation and the Victim Paradigm	22
Chapter 2. Carnivalizing Reconciliation: Beyond the Victim Paradigm	59
Chapter 3. Beyond the Partisan Divide: Transcultural Recalibrations of National Myths in Joseph Boyden's *Three Day Road* and Gail Jones's *Sorry*	88
Chapter 4. "Double Visions": Intimate Enemies and Magic Figures in Kim Scott's *Benang* and Tomson Highway's *Kiss of the Fur Queen*	136
Chapter 5. From Victimology to Empowerment? Zacharias Kunuk's *Atanarjuat* and Baz Luhrmann's *Australia*	185
Conclusion. Fictions of Reconciliation	227
Bibliography	235
Index	262

Acknowledgments

John Lennon is said to have coined the phrase "Life is what happens while you are busy making other plans." As I write these lines in preparation of the publication of my first book, nothing seems to be able to capture the nature of pursuing a PhD project more aptly. The project, with its constantly shifting nature and the frequent erosion of plans, schedules, convictions, and (identity) positions is exactly what happened while I was busy making other plans. It may have taken some (a long!) time from the first thoughts to this publication, but I made it past the finish line. And this section is my opportunity to thank those who guided, helped, pushed, dragged or cheered me on and along.

First and foremost, this book would not have been possible without the unwavering support of my two advisors, Frank Schulze-Engler and Astrid Erll. This book went through many stages and shed its skin several times, yet Frank and Astrid never ceased to encourage me, to cheer me on, or to identify flaws in my writing, and for that I am forever grateful. Karin Ikas' teachings and input at the early stages of this book set the foundations unto which this PhD thesis could eventually build, and for that I am thankful.

I am also indebted to the series editors, Jeffrey Olick, Aline Sierp, and Jenny Wüstenberg for not only providing the venue to publish my work, but also for being my friends, support network, and sources of wisdom.

My gorgeous friends and dear peers Magdalena Pfalzgraf, Rebekah Vince, Johanna Vollmeyer, Jenny Wüstenberg, Silvia Anastasijevic, and Karsten Levihn-Kutzler were and are integral, if not *the* most important companions on this journey, and have become "partners-in-crime" to other exciting post-doc adventures. Here's to the next ten years!

Last but not least, the pursuit of a PhD puts a strain on social relationships, especially towards the finish line. I am grateful that my family and my friends have stood by me and tolerated manic as well as depressive episodes, total seclusion, and a certain wise guy attitude. They all supported me through bouts of my occasional snarkiness and need for reclusiveness to be able to balance the multiple demands of this professional field (Mama, Papa, Paul, Angelika, Nikolai, Annabelle). A special thanks goes out to my dear friend Dr. Dussel, as he knows, very few of the adventures that I was privy to would have been possible without him!

Lastly, my appreciation goes out to the Berghahn team who enabled the publication of this monograph.

Introduction

Carnivalizing Reconciliation

On 11 June 2008, Canadian prime minister Stephen Harper addressed the House of Commons and the Canadian nation at large to issue an apology on behalf of the Canadian government. This apology formed part of a larger process of reconciliation between the nation of Canada and its Indigenous peoples. Before Harper actually spoke, several "distinguished guests" were announced and entered the House.[1] Some of them were visibly excited and delighted; others wiped their faces, and tears were shed. They were representative leaders of Canada's First Nations, welcomed with standing ovations that lasted several minutes. Among the delegates was Marguerite Wabano, 104 years old on the day of the apology and Canada's oldest survivor of a residential school.[2] She very visibly wore a silver Christian cross on her blue dress as Harper guided her to her seat. First Nations chief Phil Fontaine and his colleagues were directed to a circular arrangement of chairs in the center of the solemn hall. Against the impressive backdrop of the House of Commons, Fontaine's traditional headdress appeared even more iconic. Wooden carved benches and liveried government officials surrounded the representatives of Canada's Indigenous peoples as they listened to Harper's apology. The message sent out, as symbolized by this circle of chairs, was powerful, iconic, and far-reaching: after decades of fighting for recognition, Canada's Indigenous populations, with this gesture from the government, were effectively brought from society's margins to the discursive center, to the heart of the democracy, and to the root locus of governmental power. In reply to the prime minister's words of apology, Phil Fontaine stated triumphantly: "For our parents, our

grandparents, indeed for all of the generations which have preceded us, this day testifies to nothing less than the achievement of the impossible."[3] The impressive architecture of the House, Marguerite Wabano's silver cross, and Phil Fontaine's iconic headdress, however, also testify to the fact that Indigenous and non-Indigenous Canada are, inevitably, culturally and historically entangled. The colonial encounter and subsequent attempts to culturally assimilate Canada's Indigenous peoples has left a lasting imprint not only on Indigenous identities but also on the Canadian society at large. These Indigenous leaders symbolize the many facets of Indigenous modernities and their central position within a contemporary Canadian national narrative.

The Canadian apology was predated by Prime Minster Kevin Rudd's gesture of atonement to Australia's Aboriginal peoples, and both formed an integral part of what Jeffrey Olick has termed the "politics of regret":[4] understood here as a set of processes and practices to reframe the past in the spirit of promoting human rights, "politics of regret" seem to appeal to contexts where societies struggle with the remainders of governmental abuse of power, racial segregation, and colonialism. These proceedings come with a lot of symbolic capital, for example, the promise of providing a stage to address these legacies and from which to break the structural silence that oftentimes surrounds historical injustices. Such "politics of regret" both create and use "commemorative tropes [that] work to inform the representation of diverse events and traumas beyond national and cultural boundaries, bridging—but not negating—spatial, temporal and ideational differences."[5] Such differences are turned into "matters of apology and healing" with their own discursive rules and performative conventions:[6] makeshift court proceedings, the facilitation of storytelling and testimony in a safe space, public apologies by institutions and governments, and final reports as the attempt to narrativize suffering are all key elements of these "politics of regret." The (hi)stories of the margins become the center of public attention for a specific period of time.

The presence of the Indigenous leaders within the House of Commons thus represents the promise that is a key part of the identity-political performances of such public apologies—during a specific time frame, discursive hierarchies and social positions can be temporarily reversed. Law scholar Teresa Godwin Phelps interprets this notion of reversed discursive hierarchies as carnivalesque and establishes a link to a mode of literary representation that literary theorist and philosopher Mikhail Bakhtin described as destabilizing or reversing power structures.[7] Derived from Bakhtin's literary theory, Phelps distills properties that, in her view, aptly describe the mechanisms of real-world truth and reconciliation commissions. Through the temporal and elite-licensed reversal of—in particular discursive and representational—hierarchies that structure a transitioning society, a sense of justice can be achieved. For Phelps, the notion of reversal is not connected with reversing actual regimes of power—like political regimes, for example—but with contesting monolithic historical representation or the complete lack thereof, with raising awareness and giving voice to the formerly marginalized and silenced—in short, with narrative activity. The carnivalesque, in Phelps's terms, is thus a figure of thought that can describe the mechanisms of alternatives to criminal justice: truth and reconciliation commissions.

Yet both variations of the carnivalesque—Bakhtin's literary aesthetics and Phelps's alternative justice through narrative action—are in themselves not able to accommodate identities, narratives, and histories that point beyond neatly arranged identity categories that structurally are the product of reconciliation. As will become obvious in the course of this study, reconciliation operates with binary models of cultural and historical identities, and while a carnivalesque perspective akin to especially Phelps's conception may reverse power hierarchies, it also reproduces these binary schemata.

Phelps's understanding of the carnivalesque fails to account for the inconsistencies and problematic aspects that reconciliation entails and produces, such as an extraordinary emphasis on victimhood. The notion of the carnivalesque, I argue, requires an opening up toward nonbinary systems of representing cultural encounters and entanglements. Therefore, in this study, I will set the carnivalesque with its central mechanisms of reiteration and reversal in relation to a transcultural perspective on collectives and identities. In this manner, a carnivalesque research perspective takes neither containers and compartments nor normative historical representations for granted and instead strives to highlight frictions, processes of mutual construction and exchange, and subversive identities that run against the official grain of reconciliation reproducing victimhood on a public stage. More precisely, it is through the analysis of fiction that more complex cultural encounters in the Australian and Canadian context become visible, that Indigenous modernities are explored, and that the moral impetus of "just remembrance" is creatively tackled. In the course of the present study, I develop the notion of the carnivalesque into a research perspective that highlights and captures ambiguity, and not essences and essentials. Moreover, the carnivalesque not only lends a specific expression to identity politics in transcultural contexts but also functions as an aesthetics of transcultural encounters. Through the analysis of a representative body of fictional engagements with the discourses, histories, and identities that reconciliation produces, a more ambiguous picture of Australian and Canadian (national) identities can be worked out. In summary, my carnivalesque perspective on contemporary Australian and Canadian literature and film highlights the subversive as well as empowering potential reconciliation, potential that is located within the sphere of the imaginary.

While the present study engages with two examples of "politics of regret," it can neither provide an exhaustive analysis of either transitional politics or restorative justice nor contribute to the field of Bakhtin research. This analysis will draw connections to other cases of reconciliation processes and hint at similarities and differences, yet it does not offer a conclusive evaluation of the international discourse of reconciliation. In this context, this study does not lay claim to practicing political or legal science but puts literary studies' concepts and methodologies to use in order to approach and analyze Australian and Canadian reconciliation.

Michael Rothberg's fervent call for us to broaden our analytical toolboxes and critical vocabulary, however, resonates profoundly within this study. Rothberg believes that our understanding of power, privilege, violence, and injustice suffers from an underdeveloped vocabulary. In particular, we lack adequate concepts for describing what Hannah Arendt called "this vicarious responsibility for things we have not done": that is, the manifold indirect, structural, and collective forms of agency that enable injury, exploitation, and domination but frequently remain in the shadows.[8]

While the processes of reconciliation in Australia and Canada are vitally important as tokens of recognition of Indigenous suffering and survival, and are as such tributes to both countries' Indigenous peoples, it is my contention that they are also invested in narrowing down the vocabulary, subject positions, and identity templates available to the discourses and practices of reconciliation. Instead of providing a stage to analyze the colonial practices of forcible removal and cultural reeducation and how they linger in the present, a collective reworking of Indigenous trauma as the result of these practices is "mandated"—to borrow a term from Lea David—to achieve a sense of reconciliation and, perhaps most controversially, justice.[9] As such, I argue, these processes are bound to disappoint, and to conflate the plurifold agents and positions to one very prominent victim paradigm that allows the state to reposition itself as a benevolent enabler of "new beginnings."

It is the realm of the fictional, the imaginary, where a broadening of perspective and vocabulary that Rothberg calls for is achieved. My reading of a selection of contemporary Australian and Canadian literature and film show that these "fictions of reconciliation" are by no means unproblematic, nor are they in the position to achieve social justice, but the authors and directors discussed here show a vested interest in exploring the past and its impact in more ambiguous ways than the official rhetoric, practice, and frameworks of reconciliation.

The Presence of the Absent: Memory, Identity, and the "Politics of Regret"

"The presence of the absent"—with this catchy phrase, Paul Ricoeur aptly refers to the influence that the past and its representations exert on the present, and thus describes the paradoxical nature of processes that venture into the past to lay claim to a specific present.[10] The past comes to bear on the here and now only to be related to imaginations of futures. If the past is reframed in a strategic manner, by political and civil agents and with a specific agenda in mind, such performances can be regarded as memory politics. Such orchestrated engagements with the past oftentimes supplant actual political action, as will be analyzed in this study.

The Australian and Canadian prime ministers' efforts to express remorse refer to systems of forcible cultural assimilation and reeducation that were in place during colonial rule and in its aftermath. Australian prime minister Kevin Rudd's apology was the result of a controversial decade-long debate whether or not to offer a gesture of atonement to Australia's Indigenous population—he had advocated for an apology during his election campaign. The Aboriginals and Torres Strait Islanders of Australia had been subject to enforced relocation to reserves, whereas their children—the ones of mixed descent in particular—were taken from their family and kin.[11] This foster system designed to culturally reeducate Aboriginal children into an ultimately European image was in place until the mid-1970s. In a similar manner, the weight of a specific episode of Canada's past came to bear fully on the present: Prime Minister Stephen Harper apologized for the systematic mistreatment of Canada's First Nations under colonial rule and in its aftermath. In Canada, the First Nations, Inuit, and Métis people were forcibly relocated, whereas their children were brought to residential schools.[12] These schools were run by churches and funded by the government, and it was their designated aim to oversee the children's "(re)education" as citizens of the commonwealth and members of the Anglo-Canadian society, thereby eradicating all notions of indigeneity. The last residential school for Indigenous children was closed in the late 1990s.[13]

In recent years, victims and survivors of both systems have forcefully claimed public attention by filing lawsuits and pressing governments for land titles and compensation. Australia witnessed a heated public debate, the so-called "history wars" during the early 2000s, with a powerful discourse emerging with regard to the origins of the Australian nation as a penal and settler colony, and the fate of the Indigenous population who posed an obstacle to colonial advancements. On 20 November 2005, Canada's Indian Residential Schools Settlement Agreement was reached in order to merge all looming claims and to designate a clear path on how to proceed with the legacy of the past.[14] This Settlement Agreement envisaged the establishment of the Canadian Truth and Reconciliation Commission (TRC). The implementation of such a commission to publicly rework the legacies of forcible cultural reeducation constitutes a victory for Canada's Indigenous peoples: "Residential school survivors demanded that Canada open up, listen, learn and start taking responsibility for the damage caused. The Commission is their victory and tribute."[15] Contrary to Australia, the Canadian public has maintained a high degree of ignorance with regard to the Indian residential school system.[16] It was thus one of the designated aims of the Canadian commission to inform the public. Robyn Green describes the commission's task as an utter conundrum: "[T]he TRC strives to balance the painstaking tasks of obtaining and recording survivor stories, advancing a national pedagogical project, and creating a space for celebratory exhibitions of cultural resilience."[17]

The Australian National Inquiry into the Separation of Aboriginal and Torres Strait Islanders Children from Their Families operated from 1995 to 1997 and published the famous *Bringing Them Home Report* in 1997. Among several recommendations directed at compensation and reimbursement, the key finding of the *Bringing Them Home Report* was that the system of forcible removal was genocidal in its intent and effect. This evaluation of the system of cultural reeducation and its effects led to a heated public debate about the appropriateness of such claims. Danielle Celermajer notes a "backlash of resistance, provoking some Australians to protest what they saw as an unjust accusation, an imputation of guilt and responsibility for actions they did not personally commit."[18] The self-image of Australia as a liberal and inclusive nation was under attack: the construction of a new national narrative that included Indigenous resistance and suffering posed a threat to well-established notions of national identity.

Thus, in order to engage with reworking colonial legacies, many different claims, interests, and viewpoints have to be included and satisfied.[19] The Canadian TRC and the Australian inquiry were supposed to provide the framework to negotiate these different identity-political positions. Their common denominators are mandates to inform the public, to raise awareness of Indigenous suffering and continuous social disadvantage as a result of these systems, and to serve as spaces of Indigenous self-empowerment through voicing out.[20] In both cases, the emphasis was not placed on forensic and expert-centered reworking of colonial violence with a tangible juridical and political outcome; the focus rested on enabling storytelling and on eliciting emotional responses to the stories told in the context of the two commissions.[21]

Teresa Godwin Phelps analyzes this shift from legal justice to alternative conceptions of redress. She looks at various truth commissions and cases where processes of reconciliation were implemented after periods of state-sanctioned violence and oppression, and she highlights how these alternatives elevate storytelling and narrative activity to become the central principles of their understandings of justice:[22]

The formal choice that a country makes to collect personal stories and to publish them, perhaps as a part of a larger, more general story, reflects a view of life, of politics, of what it means to be a government, of who citizens are and should be. Clearly, a country's examination of an oppressive past need not include personal stories at all. A country could employ political scientists and philosophers to write a general, abstract rendering of what occurred and why.[23]

The urge to find alternatives to criminal justice recognizes the impact that unresolved conflicts have on communities, and it acknowledges that new forms of dealing with "economic, social, cultural, and humanitarian issues" are required.[24] An advancing system of international jurisdiction in response to the atrocities of World War II and an increasingly worldwide demand for the promotion of human rights are significant for this paradigmatic shift in conceptions of justice.[25]

Regret and atonement have become central elements of memory politics; reconciliation has been "elevated to a general principle" in postwar and postcolonial identity politics.[26] Memory work has become a mechanism to obtain social justice. The Australian and Canadian processes of reconciliation are just two examples of such "politics of regret." In recent decades, various commissions with distinct purposes and in diverse historical and geographical contexts have been implemented. As such, the search for "truths" in relation to national histories, and to performatively reintegrate painful legacies into national identity and narratives, experienced a boom. In many cases, as in Australia and Canada, criminal justice was not an option, and additional approaches to and different understandings of "justice" were thus required.[27]

The commission that Desmond Tutu and Nelson Mandela conceptualized for South Africa became one of the most prominent and globally visible examples of an institutionalized truth and reconciliation process. After the effective breakdown of the apartheid state, alternative notions of justice were expected to enable South Africa's transition from authoritarian rule to democracy by including the legacies of apartheid into the newly formed national consciousness. The Truth and Reconciliation Commission of South Africa (TRC South Africa) had a distinct outline: it initiated its proceedings immediately after the end of the apartheid regime, was equipped with amnesty and subpoena powers, fostered democracy, and intertwined victim and perpetrator narratives through its amnesty-for-testimony structure.[28] Although its fundamental setting is quite simple—victims are the antagonists of perpetrators, black stands against white—the workings of the TRC South Africa precisely blurred these neatly erected boundaries. It produced a South African national narrative that represented how difficult it is to maintain such lines of division—victim, perpetrator, even bystander—in these contexts. While it is arguably still debatable whether the South African TRC can be regarded as an outright success, its international prominence and prototypical character contributed to providing truth and reconciliation commissions with a traveling framework. The TRC South Africa has in any case established the notions and rhetoric of (self-)empowerment of formerly marginalized groups through storytelling, and it has given the reworking of the past a specific mode or mechanism that appealed to other contexts of native empowerment.

Inquiries into the past carry the potential to fundamentally disrupt the "dominant narratives of the state," yet the "politics of regret" in Canada and Australia fortify the nation-frame and exclude claims of Indigenous self-government because they presuppose national cohesion as the goal.[29] Reconciliation remains curiously connected with the nation as the framework in which and through which new relations with Indigenous populations can be imagined. Hence, reconciliation processes are indicative of an altered perception of what a national container "is made of" and how it can be discursively reinforced. The production of national narratives, of national memories, is one of the key features of constructing national belonging and national identity. Homi Bhabha characterizes the complex connections between nation and narration in the following manner:

> If the ambivalent figure of the nation is a problem of its transitional history, its conceptual indeterminacy, its wavering between vocabularies, then what effect does it have on narratives and discourses that signify a sense of "nationness": the *heimlich* pleasures of the hearth, the *unheimlich* terror of the space or race of the Other; the comfort of social belonging, the hidden injuries of class; the customs of taste, the powers of political affiliation; the sense of social order, the sensibility of sexuality; the blindness of bureaucracy, the straight insight of institutions, the quality of justice, the common sense of injustice; the *language* of the law, and the *parole* of the people.[30]

Australian and Canadian reconciliations are centrally engaged with (re)defining the "narratives and discourses" that display and negotiate this "sense of 'nationness'": where to feel "at home" in the national fabric, what to reject as un-belonging, and what to fear as the "other." While this emphasis on constructing a national space makes complete sense in relation to the South African case, reconciliation is not at all about political change in Canada and Australia. It is about reconfiguring national history and national identity in the process. More precisely, the "politics of regret" in these contexts are about struggling with reconciling (at least) two competing national selves that have come to meet through reconciliation: both countries pride themselves on what they became after independence, in particular given their "humble origins" as British settler colonies.[31] Australia and Canada are both immigrant nations and ultimately understand themselves as multicultural.[32] Canada, in particular, self-represents and is regarded as an international bastion of human and minority rights—it was among the first nations to ratify the Genocide Convention in 1948. However, the fact that this Genocide Convention effectively banned the politics of forcible cultural reeducation and relocation of native peoples did not keep Canada from continuing its racist policies toward its Indigenous peoples, and in both countries, the practices were maintained well into the twentieth century. These two competing narratives—benevolent Canada and Australia versus the systems of forcible removal—collided within and through the framework of the "politics of regret."

Reconciliation processes enable us as researchers to describe how two societies seek to reinvent themselves. Australian and Canadian "sorry politics" such as the government apologies and the two commissions are mnemonic practices and seek to institutionalize the remembrance of forcible cultural reeducation. The painful memories of the systems of forcible removal shake the foundations of Australian and Canadian national identity and force their reevaluation and reorganization. Individual remembrance—the testimony of the victim—is rendered a collective experience, highly politicized through their public performance, and a public narrative to be put to strategic use. Ann Rigney cautions us to further analyze the possibilities as well as the limitations and pitfalls of reconciliation.[33] She writes:

> The challenge for memory studies is to analyze from a multidirectional perspective the narratives and discourses underlying the reconciliation scenario, the repertoire of mnemonic practices that have accompanied its emergence and the political mechanisms at work in its application.[34]

The scripted framework of reconciliation, I argue, strategically limits the identity templates available. Despite all the rhetoric of empowerment, change, and revision, reconciliation is ambiguous in nature and scope: the performances of reconciliation tend to generate what Amartya Sen calls "singular identities":[35] The "politics of regret" structurally invite people to perceive their identity in a singular form, because one aspect—native identity, for example—requires and effectively undergoes a strategic emphasis. Reconciliation, accordingly, produces the illusion of unambiguous identity templates. Hence, advocates for cultural essentialism and authenticity can rely on the rather simplistic identity schemes that form the structural basis of reconciliation; a neat division into binaries like "us" and "them," superior and inferior, seems entirely possible and, as my analysis shows, *necessary* to come to terms with these specific pasts. The promise of the TRC—to guide a nation toward reconciliation—may appeal to those who see Australia's and Canada's future in the abandonment of difference, and in buying in to the narrative of a reconciled general public that encounters "the other" on equal terms. Charles Taylor specifically alerts us to the "inauthentic and homogenizing demand for recognition of equal worth, on the one hand, and the self-immurement within ethnocentric standards, on the other," that is both tempting and misleading.[36] Notions of cultural authenticity, as well as the conception of cultures and identities as containers, are structurally present within the framework that truth and reconciliation provides.

One example of such a "singular identity" is the category of the victim that is, as I show in my analysis, prominently reproduced in the context of Australian and Canadian "politics of regret." The notion of empowerment through voicing out is closely associated with the performative recalibration of social hierarchies, but this renegotiation starts with marking victims as such. Matt James remarks in this regard, that

> [a]lthough they have many different emphases and dimensions, victim-centered approaches treat truth as multifaceted and deeply experiential reality that is best approached by hearing the diverse voices of survivors of state-inflicted trauma on their own terms. The question of victim-centeredness is above all a question of how a commission approaches the business of gathering and conveying truth.[37]

This connection between regaining representational and discursive power is a remnant of the South African TRC and its quasi-legal powers. Victims were actually in power, because they could facilitate perpetrators receiving amnesty. As chapter 2 outlines, these quasi-legal capacities were not part of the reconciliation package that emerged in Canada and Australia. Because of the absence of legal powers and the centering on the voice of the victim, the notion of victimhood and the identity template of the victim are very prominently visible. In the process of reconciling, the "issue of the forced removal of children is framed specifically and characteristically as an Indigenous experience."[38] Consequently, the forcibly removed child becomes the primary framework through which to perceive Indigenous identity. To emphasize and center the residential school experience and the forcible removal of the "stolen generations" reduces Indigenous identity to a comprehensible, emotionally and ethically condemnable "stolen children" narrative. This reconciliation narrative suddenly ties in with the colonial discourse of native inferiority and resonates within the idea that Indigenous peoples rarely reach beyond a status of inferior childishness. It is precisely this conundrum that is characteristic of reconciliation: such processes and performances counter structural silences and raise awareness, but they also perpetuate Indigenous victimhood.

Beyond the Victim Paradigm

Teresa Godwin Phelps appropriates Mikhail Bakhtin's notion of the carnivalesque in order to work out how this emphasis on victim and victimhood is eventually productive and empowering.³⁹ Bakhtin imagines the marketplace as the venue where carnivalesque reversals of existing power structures occur. Because the carnivalesque emphasizes the polyphonic, playful exploration of several identities, norms, and roles during carnival, Bakhtin posits the sternness of feudal, official festivities—which are also hosted to further disseminate and vindicate the dominant ideology—against the playful, humorous, and at times grotesque character of the carnivalesque space. Mimicry and mockery function as diversion and temporary relief. Through its citational mechanism, carnival produces a counterideology to the prevailing one.

Bakhtin's carnivalesque highlights how the imaginative and descriptive space that literary fiction provides can challenge existing patterns of social hierarchies and predetermined roles. He established a theory of literary criticism in which he describes how new aesthetics—that of the bodily, the hedonist, the humorous, and the grotesque—found their way into (Renaissance) literary representation. Accordingly, the carnivalesque also describes a stylistic resistance to existing patterns, structures, and conventions of literary aesthetics and worldmaking. Bakhtin holds that the boundaries between art and life, between representation, perception, and these very formative structures under whose yoke the "low cultures" performed their carnivalesque resistance are permeable. Consequently, Bakhtin not only describes a cultural practice—carnival—but also the style in which, in his example, Rabelais subverted canonical procedures of representation and literary aesthetics. In order for these roles to come into being, and to subvert them, normative structures, formative patterns, and their respective agency have to be identified.

In alignment with this carnivalesque ideology, Phelps considers the "politics of regret" as ultimately carnivalesque in nature, and to a certain extent they are. This carnivalesque space is sanctioned by "elites," the political agents and institutions involved in these processes. These performances create a space where resistance to formative patterns, roles, and identities is temporarily—precisely for the duration of these performances—possible. The "politics of regret" by default rely on the reiteration of antagonisms, identity containers, and monolithic, simplified identity portfolios. The distinction between Indigenous and non-Indigenous, between victim (or survivor) and "the rest," between colonizer and colonized is programmatic. Whether these simplistic dichotomies live up to social realities of contact, intermingling, and exchange is not the issue of discussion in Phelps's study. On the contrary, the strong element of play and exploration within Bakhtin's conception is reduced to the fact that elevating the survivors' stories above all other possible narratives is a temporal reversal of narrative power regimes.

In chapter 3 of this study, the limits of Phelps's notion of the carnivalesque become evident when applied to the two apologies of the former prime ministers of Australia and Canada. In effect, the translation of Phelps's carnivalesque to the context of performative politics in Canada and Australia shows how Phelps's carnivalesque is unable to accommodate the frictions, inconsistencies, and ambiguities that accompany identity negotiations and transcultural encounters. When the "carnival of reconciliation" is over, the playful exploration of resistance to elites ends, and the social hierarchy returns to the status quo ante.

Consider the apology scene that I described at the beginning of this introduction: the arrangement of Indigenous leaders receiving the apology firsthand in the very center of the Canadian state is an ultimately carnivalesque gesture. Stephen Harper adopts the rhetoric and habitus of humility, remorse, and recognition. The state performatively bends the knee. Consequently, power hierarchies are temporarily reversed, and the Indigenous leaders are literally moved from the margins to the center. While the Harper apology is especially powerful in terms of images that were created through this specific arrangement, Kevin Rudd's apology is more interesting in terms of its wording. Through the apologies, the state reinvents itself as an agent of redemption and remorse.

Yet, upon closer scrutiny, it becomes clear that these apologetic performances only function because they rely on very schematic identity portfolios beyond which they rarely reach. The two apologies resurrect simplistic containers like a singular national history in which forcible reeducation is only one "sad chapter." They rely on a construction of collectives that are composed of the "Indigenous," or even "Indigenous victims," on the one hand, and an amorphous settler community on the other. In this vein, there is no playful exploration of identities and hierarchies that is so central to Bakhtin's carnivalesque, no imagination of contemporary realities and Indigenous modernities. Akin to Bakhtin's notion, however, the reversal of power hierarchies through the apology performances comes to an end once the processes are finished. The scripted framework of reconciliation strategically limits the identity templates available and presupposes the outcome: a reconciled society.

Hence I propose to reconsider what is at the core of Bakhtin's idea of carnivalesque reversal: the (playful) exploration of "the other" by fools and tricksters who paint outside the lines that dominant structures—here, Australian and Canadian reconciliation—provide. The carnivalesque mechanisms after all are not limited to reversal but also entail contestation and exploration. The latter lose their grit when remaining limited to exploring Indigenous trauma and being preconditioned as victim-centered.

A carnivalesque lens that is sensitive to transcultural dynamics not only helps to identify simplistic binary identity templates such as victim/perpetrator, Indigenous/non-Indigenous, but also exposes them as strategic fictions, or "lies that bind," as Kwame Anthony Appiah would have it.[40] Bakhtin's carnivalesque has always been both, an aesthetic and an identity-political concept, but it is also complicit in perpetuating the upper-lower binaries. My carnivalesque, I argue, remains attentive to aesthetics and politics in fiction, yet it pays attention to and helps describe how cultures cut across each other, become entangled, and leave behind scripted realities.

The carnivalesque I develop in this study is particularly powerful when it comes to describing and analyzing processes of transcultural encounters. Monolithic conceptions of nation and culture are still part of the "national romantic," as Dagmar Brunow reminds us.[41] Yet, the end of (British) imperialism and the advance of globalization processes have fundamentally contributed to understanding that these simplistic notions of the connection between culture and nation (both in the singular) are no longer valid instruments to describe postcolonial realities and societies. Decolonization and its accompanying struggles for reframing cultural encounters as acts of violence perpetrated by one dominant culture on others demanded the introduction of a research and descriptive category that would accommodate the fact that "target cultures refuse to sit still for pedagogic purposes."[42]

Transcultural research, consequently, perceives cultures not as essential but as performative.[43] In a similar vein to the carnivalesque, a transcultural perspective looks for moments when cultures escape their own compartmentalization through and within their representations. Cultures, thus imagined, cannot be understood as fixed, stable, and profoundly distinct from others but rather as effects of borrowing, imitation, encounters, and exchange, and also of oppression, colonialism, and social hierarchies. This constant process of evocation enables renewal and thus precludes any system from moving in a circle of ceaseless repetition.[44] This means that each performance of cultural inventory, every citing of a cultural framework, delimits the range of what is fictionalized into "belonging" to this specific framework. Astrid Erll highlights the power of perspective in this regard:

> [W]hile it may be true that members of a family, residents of a city, or citizens of a nation can establish a memory culture and will usually conceive of it as pure, holistic, and discrete (this is the actors' perspective), an analytical observer's point of view on the people, contents, media, forms and practices of such memory cultures will always reveal their inherent transcultural nature. All memories produced in culture are transcultural. They are borrowed from elsewhere, inspired by neighbours, stolen from strangers. They are co-constructed and amalgamated.[45]

The notion of playful explorations, radical transgressions, and reformulations of social hierarchies and norms that Bakhtin so prominently highlights are hence also characteristic of transcultural dynamics. As the reader will see in more detail in chapters 2 and 3, the spaces that processes of truth and reconciliation open up cannot provide this liberating quality. These processes are highly scripted and dependent on the execution of certain roles—the victim, for example—and these roles are *not* meant to be imaginatively explored and humorously contested.

Notwithstanding their temporariness, the "politics of regret" profoundly resonate within the Australian and Canadian societies and have sparked cultural productions and fictional explorations of national narratives and historical truths. Artistic engagements with memory politics form part of the larger processes of reconciliation that outlive the strategic temporariness of public apologies and truth commissions. They may venture further and dig deeper into the entanglements that historical legacies hold ready. Carnival produces a counterideology to the prevailing one. Literature and art provide alternative spaces where the negotiations of identities, histories, and truths may be continued or taken into radically different directions.

Carnivalizing Reconciliation in Literature and Film

Young settler daughter Perdita, the main narrative voice in the historical novel *Sorry* (2008), looks back on her childhood trauma and tells the reader how difficult it was for her to find her words, to regain her voice, again:

> A whisper: sssshh. The thinnest vehicle of breath. This is a story that can only be told in a whisper. There is a hush to difficult forms of knowing, an abashment, a sorrow, an inclination towards silence. My throat is misshapen with all it now carries. My heart is a sour, indolent fruit.[46]

Australian author and scholar Gail Jones published her novel as an intervention in the controversies surrounding a governmental apology in Australia. As she states in the acknowledgments, it is personally important to Jones to display "solidarity" with Australia's Indigenous peoples and their fight for recognition and land titles, and her novel is "written in the hope that further native title grants will be offered in the spirit of reconciliation."[47] *Sorry* is just one example where authors and directors have made it their task to comment on and engage with the discourses of reconciliation, forcible removal, cultural reeducation and (trans)cultural identities by means of fiction. These artistic explorations attest to the impact that reconciliation processes in Canada and Australia had on their respective (artistic) communities, and to the capacity of literature and film to further explore identities, histories, and futures in this context. As will be analyzed on the basis of a select corpus of fiction—from both Indigenous and non-Indigenous authors and directors—the carnivalesque as a figure of thought and a literary aesthetic can be encountered in these works with a hitherto unknown power for aesthetic transgression.

The carnivalesque, as will be analyzed in chapters 4–6, proves a valuable category to approach identity politics in fiction once it is supplemented with a transcultural perspective on collectives and narratives. My carnivalesque viewpoint has the power to leave behind this tight framework of political constraints, of discursive regimes and confining normative structures, that official discourses of reconciliation in Australia and Canada provide. Through narrative fiction it becomes possible to venture further along the slippery slopes of politically sanctioned identity formations, of further exploring truths and fictions, discourses and histories, and, most importantly, identities. Fictional narratives can be understood as "referential constructs projecting fictional worlds,"[48] and as powerful means to enable "imaginary extensions to the scope of knowledge."[49] This scope of "knowledge" refers to fiction's capacity—in the present context of Australian and Canadian reconciliation—to try out, picture, mimic, mock, or envision national narratives, histories, identities, and social orders. Thus conceived, the nature of fiction can be described as ultimately carnivalesque.

Essential to this understanding of the mechanisms of fiction as carnivalesque is that explorative narrative activity is the primary human capacity of constructing a self, a sense of existence in time and space, as well as a historical consciousness.[50] The self is constructed through

> the interconnection of events constituted by emplotment[, which] allows us to integrate with permanence in time what seems to be its contrary in the domain of sameness-identity, namely diversity, variability, discontinuity, and instability.[51]

In this manner, fictional narratives are by default able to leave behind the identity political constraints and simple container mentalities that, through reconciliation, are validated on a public platform. They can delve into identities and truths that run against the political grain and venture where no politician, activist, lobbyist, or lawyer could go. Historical "knowledge" that is often invoked as being revised by reconciliation processes becomes appropriated "knowledge" to readers and viewers; it is simulated, mediated, inevitably secondary experience that is transmitted through narrative fiction.[52] Its secondary nature resonates within the idea of carnival and marketplace that Bakhtin describes as central to carnivalesque explorations: in a specific framework, the rules, norms, and truths of dominant groups are taken up, appropriated, transformed, and ultimately contested. It is its penchant for nonconformity and creativity that makes the undermining, subversive character of carnival, and thus can be set in fruitful relation to the mechanisms of narrative fiction. Narration, thus conceived, is "the fundamental condition of our representation of experience and explanatory mode for our ways of representing experience."[53]

In chapters 4–6, a selected body of fictional works will be explored and analyzed in terms of their carnivalesque mechanisms and aesthetics. All works discussed here were conceived by prominent and quite visible creative artists who are very engaged in identity politics in the Canadian and Australian context. Joseph Boyden, for example, was regarded as Canada's most successful Indigenous author. A controversy over Boyden's fraudulent native identity flared up in recent months, rendering him a mnemonic imposter.[54] Tomson Highway (Canada) is known for his dedication to promoting Indigenous cultural heritages and traditions, and he has publicly discussed his experience as a survivor of an Indian residential school. Zacharias Kunuk (Canada) sets out to retrace a notion of Inuit historical identity in order to reiterate and preserve it for contemporary Inuit people, and his feature film made it all the way to the Cannes Film Festival. Gail Jones's Australian aforementioned "sorry novel"—a generic ascription that will be analyzed in more detail in chapter 4—was published only months before Kevin Rudd actually delivered the public apology. Baz Luhrmann (Australia) tasked himself with creating an Australian national epos that interrelates settlement, the Stolen Generations, as well as the historic achievements of British settlement in Australia. His movie, although it is not his most successful one, reached a wide audience across the globe. Kim Scott is a prominent author in Australia, yet his works are probably best known among specialists.

Some of the cultural productions analyzed within this study are bestsellers and blockbusters, having attracted and reached a vast reader- and viewership, while others are niche products with less success in terms of revenue and readership. Nonetheless, all examples have become available to international audiences and traversed several cultural and national boundaries. Some of them have won prestigious prizes—Zacharias Kunuk's *Atanarjuat* (2001) was, for example, awarded the Golden Camera in Cannes; Kim Scott's novel *Benang* (1999) was bestowed with the Miles Franklin Literary Award in 2001. Accordingly, the fictional explorations of the discourses and identities of Australian and Canadian reconciliation have certainly impacted these negotiations. All of the works discussed here employ some version of the carnivalesque in order to make their political points regarding memory. The latter can be identified through the subversion of social hierarchies (victim versus perpetrator) or historical representations ("the nation forged in fire" paradigm), or by contesting fixed notions of cultural identities and belonging by conceiving protagonists that freely oscillate between cultural boundaries (the persona of the trickster-fool, for example). Yet there is a major difference in quality and scope perceivable with regard to the primary works, and these discrepancies are reflected in the structure of this study.

In chapter 4, a fictional work that is particularly innovative and imaginative in writing "against the official reconciliation grain" is juxtaposed with an example where the carnivalesque in a Phelpsian manner reproduces fixed, compartmentalized identities and narratives. Joseph Boyden's *Three Day Road* (2005) pursues the agenda of overturning representational hierarchies with regard to Canada's mythicized "birth of the nation" in the European theaters of the Great War. Beyond that, Boyden's text is especially powerful with regard to imagining a transcultural identity, employing a trickster-fool character that in a carnivalesque manner transgresses all the ultimately fictional cultural boundaries. This transcultural protagonist is not a victim, although he went through a residential school, but uses his mixed cultural background to his advantage. Boyden's novel is juxtaposed with Gail Jones's attempt (2007) to explore Australian settler guilt, but *Sorry*'s uniquely manieristic narrative makeup and the strategic lack of a viable Aboriginal perspective reverse-carnivalizes Jones's well-meaning intentions and instead produces a case of settler navel-gazing rather than an intervention into the apology discourse.

As discussed in chapter 5, Kim Scott's *Benang* (1999) impressively pushes the Australian cultural boundaries by imagining a protagonist who literally "floats" between the cultural poles: Harley is imagined as a powerful transcultural protagonist who, having turned the tables on his molesting grandfather whose breeding project he is, presents a uniting force instead of a vengeful, divisive one. The character of victim and perpetrator and their cultural makeup is taken up very prominently in Tomson Highway's *Kiss of the Fur Queen* (1998). From his autobiographical background, Highway set out to personalize the abstract perpetrator force and employs, akin to Boyden's text, traditional Indigenous mythological characters (the *windigo*, the fur queen as a trickster figure) to represent raping priests and native cultural heritage. Contrary to the explorative force of *Benang*, Highway's *Kiss of the Fur Queen* remains curiously stuck in this binary system.

The two feature films analyzed in chapter 6 both consider themselves as representing Canada's and Australia's national history in an epic manner. Zacharias Kunuk's feature film *Atanarjuat* (2001) remediates the Inuit oral myth of the fast runner and seemingly sets out to imagine an Inuit identity that is untethered by colonialism. Yet, upon closer investigation, *Atanarjuat* innovatively carnivalizes the notion of cultural authenticity by the use of intertextual references to other filmic investigations of Inuit identity. Thus conceived, Kunuk's film carnivalizes not only the notion of cultural containment but also of the "colonial gaze," a formative tradition of derogatively representing indigeneity in Canadian feature film and documentary history. Baz Luhrmann's colorful filmic epos *Australia* (2008) also attempts to diversify Australian national identity by representing a (hi)story whose narrative agency seems to be firmly placed in Aboriginal hands. In a similar manner to Jones's *Sorry*, Luhrmann's film strives to empower Aboriginals, yet it appropriates their voice, speaks for them instead of with them: ultimately *Austra-*

lia practices "enforced" reconciliation because it lets an Australian history of settlement and world war participation culminate in a central "Mother Australia" figure, a British settler wife who reconciles all rifts and inconsistencies in Australian history within herself. In the process, the self-set task to democratize and broaden Australian history and identity by relating it to the Aboriginals renders them as props and affords them minor roles in the overarching national narrative.

Through the discussion of the fictional works, it will become evident that a carnivalesque perspective and the analysis of carnivalesque aesthetics result in the discovery of highly productive ways of engaging with Canadian and Australian "politics of regret." These texts naturally go further and delve deeper into the spheres of identity politics than any commission or public apology could. The cultural productions analyzed in this study imagine transcultural identities that eventually might come closer to the experiences of cultural realities in Australia and Canada.

Before the analysis turns toward these fictions of reconciliation and their critical, subversive potentials and shortcomings, the two processes of reconciliation in Canada and Australia and their respective memory politics as "politics of regret" will be introduced and discussed. In the following chapter, I will shed light on how the notion of justice through storytelling—which is emblematic to Australian and Canadian reconciliation—harks back to the TRC South Africa and its proceedings. The specific outline of Canadian and Australian reconciliation also shows how the notion of "native empowerment" through such proceedings has cut across different contexts, and has discursively connected Indigenous histories, experiences, and identities across the globe. Despite the fact that, in Australia and Canada, Indigenous (hi)stories can no longer be ignored and have claimed a prominence unprecedented in scope and effect, mechanisms that were central to the South African context have been abandoned. This has led to a pointed emphasis on victims and victimhood, and thus creates its own identity-political drawbacks, as will be outlined in this next chapter. The analytical lens that a carnivalesque research perspective provides enables me to work out the potentials as well as the shortcomings of Australian and Canadian reconciliation that coexist in such curious proximity.

Notes

1. A video of the official apology is available on the website of the Government of Canada, "Indian Residential School Statement of Apology—Prime Minister Stephen Harper," n.d., retrieved 15 May 2015 from http://www.aadnc-aandc.gc.ca/eng/1100100015677/1100100015680.

2. See Aaron Wherry, "The Commons: The Apology," Macleans, 12 June 2008, retrieved 4 March 2018 from http://www.macleans.ca/uncategorized/the-commons-the-apology/.
3. Phil Fontaine as quoted by Wherry, "The Commons: The Apology."
4. Jeffrey K. Olick, *The Politics of Regret: On Collective Memory and Historical Responsibility* (New York: Routledge, 2007).
5. Lucy Bond and Jessica Rapson, eds., *The Transcultural Turn: Interrogating Memory between and beyond Borders*, 1st ed., Media and Cultural Memory/Medien Und Kulturelle Erinnerung, vol. 15 (Boston: De Gruyter, 2014), 18.
6. Jennifer Henderson and Pauline Wakeham, "Introduction," in *Reconciling Canada: Critical Perspectives on the Culture of Redress*, ed. Jennifer Henderson and Pauline Wakeham (Toronto: University of Toronto Press, 2013), 14–15.
7. Teresa Godwin Phelps, *Shattered Voices: Language, Violence, and the Works of Truth Commissions* (Philadelphia: University of Philadelphia Press, 2004), and Mikhail M. Bakhtin, *Rabelais and his World* (Bloomington: Indiana University Press, 1984).
8. Michael Rothberg, *The Implicated Subject: Beyond Victim and Perpetrators* (Stanford, CA: Stanford University, 2019), 1.
9. Lea David, *The Past Can't Heal Us. The Dangers of Mandating History in the Name of Human Rights*, Human Rights in History (New York: Cambridge University Press, 2020).
10. Paul Ricoeur, *History, Memory, Forgetting* (Chicago: University of Chicago Press, 2004), 97.
11. For further reading, see, e.g., Justin Healey, ed., *The Stolen Generations* (Rozelle: Spinney Press, 2001).
12. For further reading, see J. R. Miller, *Shingwauk's Vision: A History of Native Residential Schools* (Toronto: University of Toronto Press, 1996).
13. See Truth and Reconciliation Commission of Canada, *Interim Report*, 10 December 2014, retrieved 4 March 2018 from http://www.trc.ca/websites/trcinstitution/index.php?p=580.
14. "The Indian Residential School Settlement Agreement" is available online at http://www.residentialschoolsettlement.ca/settlement.html, retrieved 4 March 2018.
15. Matt James, "A Carnival of Truth? Knowledge, Ignorance and the Canadian Truth and Reconciliation Commission," *International Journal of Transitional Justice* 6 (2012): 184.
16. See Julie McGonegal, "The Great Canadian (and Australian) Secret: The Limits of Non-Indigenous Knowledge and Representation," *English Studies in Canada* 35, no. 1 (March 2009): 67–83.
17. Robyn Green, "Unsettling Cures: Exploring the Limits of the Indian Residential School System Settlement Agreement," *Canadian Journal of Law and Society* 27, no. 1 (2012): 131.
18. Danielle Celermajer, "The Apology in Australia: Re-covenanting the National Imaginary" in *Taking Wrongs Seriously: Apologies and Reconciliation*, ed. Elazar Barkan and Alexander Karn (Palo Alto, CA: Stanford University Press, 2006), 153.
19. See, e.g., Priscilla Hayner, *Unspeakable Truths: Transitional Justice and the Challenge of Truth Commissions* (New York: Routledge, 2011).
20. See Olick, *Politics of Regret*.
21. See James, "Carnival of Truth?" and Anne-Marie Reynaud, "Dealing with Difficult Emotions: Anger at the Truth and Reconciliation Commission of Canada," *Anthropologica* 56, no. 2 (2012): 369–82.
22. Phelps analyzes the cases of the Argentinian, Chilean, and Salvadoran Truth Commissions as well as the South African example. See Phelps, *Shattered Voices*, in particular chapters 5 and 6.
23. Phelps, *Shattered Voices*, 75.

24. Truth and Reconciliation Commission of Canada, *Honouring the Truth, Reconciling for the Future*, final report, n.d., retrieved 4 March 2018 from http://www.trc.ca/websites/trcinstitution/File/2015/Honouring_the_Truth_Reconciling_for_the_Future_July_23_2015.pdf.
25. See, e.g., Scott Veitch, ed., *Law and the Politics of Reconciliation* (Aldershot: Ashgate, 2007), and Jennifer Lind, *Sorry States: Apologies in International Politics* (Ithaca, NY: Cornell University Press, 2010).
26. Olick, *Politics of Regret*, 14.
27. See, e.g., Sarah Keenan, "Moments of Decolonization: Indigenous Australia in the Here and Now," *Canadian Journal of Law and Society* 29, no. 2 (2014): 163–80, for an overview of attempts by Indigenous claimants to attain justice through the Australian legal system. She writes: "Indigenous law and practice is the foundation of native title, but Indigenous Australia is constructed as an almost mythical place located in the distant past and only capable of being rescued by (settler) law in limited circumstances." Keenan concludes that not only is the Australian legal system unable to address colonial legacies through its frameworks, but Australian law is also complicit in historicizing and discriminating the Indigenous. For Canada, Leslie Thielen-Wilson states a similar case by emphasizing that Canadian law is an inept tool to further decolonization, because "colonial power continues to operate through law in the present." Leslie Thielen-Wilson, "Troubling the Path to Decolonization: Indian Residential School Case Law, Genocide, and Settler Illegitimacy," *Canadian Journal of Law and Society* 29, no. 2 (2014): 184.
28. The TRC South Africa will be introduced in more detail in chapter 2.
29. Ronald Niezen, *Truth and Indignation: Canada's Truth and Reconciliation Commission on Indian Residential Schools* (Toronto: University of Toronto Press, 2013), 10.
30. Homi K. Bhabha, "Introduction: Narrating the Nation," in *Nation and Narration*, ed. Homi K. Bhabha (London: Routledge, 1990), 2, emphasis in the original.
31. This aspect will be taken up again in chapter 2.
32. For further reading in the Australian context, see David Goodman, ed., *Multicultural Australia: The Challenges of Change* (Newham: Scribe, 1991). For the Canadian context, see Tridafilos Tridafilopoulos, *Becoming Multicultural: Immigration and the Politics of Membership in Canada and Germany* (Vancouver: UBC Press, 2013).
33. Ann Rigney, "Reconciliation and Remembering: (How) Does It Work?" *Memory Studies* 5, no. 3 (2012): 251–58.
34. Rigney, "Reconciliation and Remembering," 252.
35. Amartya Sen, *Identity and Violence: The Illusion of Destiny* (London: Penguin, 2006), xii.
36. Charles Taylor, *Multiculturalism and the Politics of Recognition* (Princeton, NJ: Princeton University Press, 1994), 72.
37. James, "Carnival of Truth?" 185.
38. Denise Cuthbert and Marian Quartly, "Forced Child Removal and the Politics of National Apologies in Australia," *American Indian Quarterly* 37, no. 1 (2013): 185.
39. See Bakhtin, *Rabelais and his World*.
40. Kwame Anthony Appiah, *The Lies that Bind: Creed, Country, Colour, Class, Culture* (London: Profile Books, 2016).
41. Dagmar Brunow, *Remediating Transcultural Memory: Documentary Filmmaking as Archival Intervention* (Berlin: De Gruyter, 2015), 25.
42. Frank Schulze-Engler and Sissy Helff, "Introduction," in *Transcultural English Studies: Theories, Fictions, Realities*, ed. Frank Schulze-Engler and Sissy Helff (Amsterdam: Rodopi, 2009), x.
43. See Andreas Lagenohl, Ralph J. Poole, Manfred Weinberg, eds., *Transkulturalität. Klassische Texte* (Bielefeld: transcript, 2015), 13.

44. Anne Enderwitz, "Ereignis und Wiederholung als Koordinaten von Geschlecht und Gedächtnis," in *Iterationen: Geschlecht im kulturellen Gedächtnis*, ed. Anja Schwarz (Göttingen: Wallstein Verlag, 2008), 37.
45. Astrid Erll, "Travelling Memory in European Film: Towards a Morphology of Mnemonic Relationality," *Image & Narrative* 18, no. 1 (2017): 6.
46. Gail Jones, *Sorry: This Is a Story That Can Only Be Told in a Whisper* (London: Vintage, 2008), 1.
47. Jones, *Sorry*, 217.
48. Richard Walsh, *The Rhetoric of Fictionality: Narrative Theory and the Idea of Fiction* (Columbus: Ohio State University Press, 2007), 159.
49. Walsh, *Rhetoric of Fictionality*, 161.
50. See, e.g., Paul Ricoeur, *Time and Narrative*, vols. 1–3 (Chicago: University of Chicago Press, 1984–85), and Paul Ricoeur, *Oneself as Another* (Chicago: University of Chicago Press, 1992).
51. Ricoeur, *Oneself as Another*, 140.
52. See Alison Landsberg, *Prosthetic Memory: The Transformation of American Remembrance in the Age of Mass Culture* (New York: Columbia Press, 2007).
53. Kristin Veel, *Narrative Negotiations: Information Structures in Literary Fiction* (Göttingen: Vandenhoeck & Ruprecht, 2009), 15.
54. This aspect will be taken up again in chapter 4.

Chapter 1

JUSTICE THROUGH STORYTELLING?

Australian and Canadian Reconciliation and the Victim Paradigm

In 2015, the Truth and Reconciliation Commission of Canada (TRC Canada) published its long-awaited final report. In its executive summary, the report describes the mandate of this commission:

> The Commission heard from more than 6,000 witnesses, most of whom survived the experience of living in the schools as students. The stories of that experience are sometimes difficult to accept as something that could have happened in a country such as Canada, which has long prided itself on being a bastion of democracy, peace, and kindness throughout the world. Children were abused, physically and sexually, and they died in the schools in numbers that would not have been tolerated in any school system anywhere in the country, or in the world. But, shaming and pointing out wrongdoing were not the purpose of the Commission's mandate. Ultimately, the Commission's focus on truth determination was intended to lay the foundation for the important question of reconciliation.[1]

The commission's task was twofold: it sought (1) to provide a stage for victims and survivors of the Indian residential school system to tell their stories, and (2) to educate the Canadian public about the forcible relocation of its native populations. It pays tribute to the victims and survivors of a specific historical atrocity and simultaneously mobilizes the residential school legacy "as a symbol of broader 'human values.'"[2] Canada is the first "established democracy" and the first G8 nation to initiate a truth and reconciliation commission.[3] As the work of this TRC has since brought to light, six thousand children did not survive their stay at a residential school. The odds of dying at such an institution almost equaled those faced by the Canadian Expeditionary Forces during the World War II.[4] As this institutionalized reeducation program has left its imprint on many survivors, TRC Canada is the result of political mobilization, Indigenous lobbyism, and longstanding legal quarrels about reimbursement and a proper management of this specific historical legacy. One outcome of this process is that 2.8 billion Canadian dollars were paid as compensation to former students. On occasion of the publication of the abovementioned report, the Canadian Truth and Reconciliation Commission retrospectively accepted Stephen Harper's public apology.[5]

The Canadian efforts were preceded by Australian reconciliation initiatives, which span across decades and cut through the Australian community. In 1997, the now famous *Bringing Them Home Report* was issued by the Australian National Inquiry into the Separation of Aboriginal and Torres Strait Islander Children from their Families. This publication arguably marked a culmination point in the history of Australian reconciliation, yet the struggle for reconciliation had still stretched on for years. The final report of Australia's version of a truth and reconciliation commission, however, remains the most successful government publication to this day.

The Australian and Canadian commissions are showcases of what Jennifer Henderson and Pauline Wakeham—with a nod to Jacques Derrida—described as "forgiveness gone global."[6] To varying degrees, both case studies situate themselves within the discourse of reconciliation, which has become a signifier of transitional justice within the international community as this next chapter outlines. The notion of truth and reconciliation relates back to the South African model, which very prominently claimed the international stage in the late 1990s. Nelson Mandela and Desmond Tutu's famous Truth and Reconciliation Commission of South Africa (TRC South Africa) centrally contributed to establishing the paradigms of TRCs, and it is regularly regarded as the prototype of such a process. The Canadian TRC in particular establishes a link to its South African predecessor and refers to it as its role model. The purpose of such investigations into a nation's troubled past is as clear as it is arguably unattainable: to harvest the past in order to better understand the demands of the present, and to eventually develop a vision of the future.[7] The South African TRC's image of having facilitated a change of power hierarchies rendered it an appealing format to other contexts of empowering marginalized peoples, as will be argued in what follows. Truth and reconciliation commissions seem able to (re)establish "[t]he human right to have the otherness of the past acknowledged through the creation of symbolic and cultural acts, utterances and expressions."[8] Thus conceived, reconciliation is both a discourse and a practice that cuts across marginalized histories and identities on a global scale, thus attesting to the attention that particularly Indigenous voices and agents have rightfully claimed.[9] Contrary to the South African TRC, however, the Canadian commission and the Australian inquiry were not designed to guide the nations' political transition or negotiate, for example, alternative forms of governing Indigenous peoples; both examples focus on storytelling, giving testimony and rewriting national narratives as forms of justice and performances of redress. As will become apparent, the stories of victims, in this context, become reconciliation's primary narrative, a prominent framework through which to perceive indigeneity in Australia and Canada.

The Traveling Framework of Reconciliation

In 2009 the General Assembly of the United Nations announced the International Year of Reconciliation as an act of recognizing that reconciliation has gained momentum in the twenty-first century:

> The declaration of an international year of reconciliation at the end of the first decade of the new millennium will provide the international community with the opportunity to pursue, with the active involvement of all stakeholders, efforts to develop reconciliation processes, which are necessary to and a condition for the establishment of firm and lasting peace.[10]

The resolution recognizes the impact that unresolved conflicts have on communities and acknowledges that new forms of dealing with "economic, social, cultural, and humanitarian issues" are required.[11] Regret and atonement have become central elements of engaging with historical legacies, and reconciliation has been "elevated to a general principle" in postwar and, as referenced by the Australian and Canadian example, particularly postcolonial identity politics.[12] Reconciliation has become the primary discursive and performative framework to come to terms with (ongoing) violent conflicts and civil wars, and it is used to address historical injustices and systematic oppression of marginalized groups by governments and their institutions. Reconciliation has become a global practice.[13] Will Kymlicka and Bashir Bashir explain this proliferation:

> Most countries around the world exhibit a long history of exclusion and discrimination directed against particular groups, often defined along ethnic, racial, religious, or ideological lines. Members of these groups have been treated as second-class citizens, if not as slaves, enemies, traitors, aliens, or barbarians unworthy of even second-class citizenship. The underlying justifications for these forms of exclusion have been increasingly discredited by the post-war

human rights revolution, decolonization, and by contemporary norms of liberal-democratic constitutionalism, with their firm commitments to norms of equal rights and non-discrimination, and their repudiation of older ideologies of racial, ethnic, and religious hierarchies.[14]

Reconciliation processes and performative "politics of regret," understood here as a set of processes and practices to reframe the past in the spirit of promoting human rights, seem to appeal to contexts where contemporary social hierarchies struggle with the remainders of racial segregation and colonialism. These proceedings come with a lot of symbolic capital—for example, the promise of providing a stage to address these legacies and break the structural silence that oftentimes surrounds historical injustices. Such "politics of regret" both create and use "commemorative tropes [that] work to inform the representation of diverse events and traumas beyond national and cultural boundaries, bridging—but not negating—spatial, temporal and ideational differences."[15] Such differences are turned into "matters of apology and healing," with their own discursive rules and performative conventions[16]: makeshift court proceedings, the facilitation of storytelling and testimony in a "safe space," public apologies by institutions and governments, and final reports as the attempt to narrativize suffering are all key elements of these "politics of regret."

First examples of truth and reconciliation commissions were established in South America, yet they largely remained invisible to international audiences.[17] Commissions operated, for instance, in Argentina, Uruguay, Chile, and El Salvador—a list that testifies to proliferation, or "globalization," of the demand for processes that facilitate national reckonings with historical legacies.[18] While the Argentinean commission was concerned with uncovering "truths" about disappeared victims of civil war and was initially "intended as a preparatory stage for forthcoming criminal prosecutions," others were designed to facilitate the transition from authoritarian rule to democracy.[19]

> In societies as disparate as Argentina, Bosnia, Cambodia, Cyprus, El Salvador, Guatemala, Haiti, Nigeria, South Africa, and Sri Lanka, and now in Sierra Leone and Kosovo, there is a natural, consuming desire to elicit as complete an accounting as possible of how people disappeared, how they were assassinated, how and why they were flung from airplanes above the Atlantic Ocean, and how and why they were slaughtered in groups and tossed into unmarked graves.[20]

In light of the manifold issues to address, these commissions led a hybrid existence.[21] The mandates of these truth commissions oscillated between fact-finding missions and mock trials as attempts to uncover the "truth," to negotiate blame and guilt under the public gaze, and to fundamentally alter the historical record of the respective country. In many cases, criminal prosecutions did not result, and the commissions remained the only platform on which human rights violations could be openly addressed. Ben Michal Hirsch describes how "[t]hese truth commissions were forged as political compromises between the constraining power of the former regime and the international demands for justice and accountability."[22]

To this day, arguably, one specific commission remains paradigmatic in the "global economy of forgiveness"[23]: in 1995 the TRC South Africa not only powerfully claimed international attention but also furthered the idea that narrative action—storytelling—is a central component and mechanism of reconciliation.[24] South Africa was forced to become aware of the historical burdens and present injustices that were the result of the apartheid regime. The commission operated after the end of this regime and was designed to guide South Africa's transition from the politics of racial segregation to democracy. This TRC was implemented to facilitate a nationwide acknowledgment of the cruelty of the apartheid regime as well as its enduring effects on the population. It set out to shed light on how deep (the legacies of) apartheid cut into the South African social fabric. In this spirit, one of the proclaimed aims was to involve several voices in the creation of a new South African public record; former apartheid representatives as well as democratic activists, victims, and survivor representatives were heard. Extensive reworking and reprocessing of the past, the inclusion of the "old regime" and the multiple perpetrator voices in the process, and the attempt to overcome the internal division of South Africa's society were the major paradigms under which truth and reconciliation were traded. Reconciliation was framed as a bottom-up approach to create a new society on and with the legacies of the old, and with altered power relations.

The structure of TRC South Africa resembled a court: commissioners presided over the processes through which testimonies by victims and perpetrators were collected.[25] Reconciliation in South Africa thus involved a "post-conflict investigative phase" of discovery, of uncovering the "truth," and of negotiating guilt, redemption, and forgiveness and imagining a vision of South Africa's future.[26] Desmond Tutu and his fellow commissioners attempted to satisfy the individual as well as collective desire for justice, and to guide the transition from a regime of terror to a democratic rule.[27]

> The people who conceptualized and designed the South African TRC introduced two types of unique features in the design, goals, and framing of the commission. The first type is institutional, including quasi-legal powers, scope of mandate, and transparency and publicity. The second type of unique features is those of content; specifically, the idea of aligning the truth-seeking process with the goals of reconciliation and healing. These unique features of the South African TRC along with the widespread perception of success even

before its operation was completed made South Africa an ideal-type model for all subsequent TRCs.[28]

Because of its specific rendering and its relative success in the eyes of particularly the international community, TRC South Africa was then and later regarded as a prototype, an exemplary case of such a commission.[29] Revenge and punishment as mechanisms to obtain justice were replaced by establishing a new form of power balance: full amnesty was offered to perpetrators who were willing to testify, and their testimony was rewarded with forgiveness by the victim.[30] It was the designated aim of this commission to find the middle ground between blanket amnesty and criminal prosecution. Amnesty for perpetrators became a possibility and a means to overcome the victim-perpetrator deadlock, but rigid guidelines of when to grant it were applied.[31] This truth-for-amnesty-trade was one of the points that triggered harsh criticism; TRC South Africa was accused of selling social justice cheaply, and of overriding (demands for) criminal justice.[32] In effect, TRC South Africa ultimately pushed its own conceptual envelope, as its proceedings revealed that neat categories and attributions (perpetrator = white, victim = black) did not live up to social realities. South African reconciliation brought to light the fact that, among the perpetrators, there were native people—neighbors, friends, even family—while some non-native South Africans were victimized by the apartheid regime.[33] The structure of the TRC South Africa also did not allow for the recognition of the South African (postapartheid) national community as diverse or that a postapartheid national narrative represents transcultural entanglements beyond the colonizer-colonized rationale.[34]

However, it was precisely this "uniquely South African innovation"—the possibility of amnesty in exchange for testimony—that has been translated into a discursive "framework of reconciliation," and that has profoundly furthered an international discourse of restorative[35] and transitional justice as alternatives to criminal justice.[36] South African reconciliation was evaluated not in terms of how it effectively blurred ethnically motivated victim-perpetrator boundaries, and thus complicated the creation of a postapartheid national narrative, but with regard to its potential of empowering the marginalized, the victims. In the aftermath of the work of TRC South Africa, "[t]he framing of the truth-seeking process's relative merits has shifted from emphasizing what TRCs can achieve in comparison with trials, to emphasizing what TRCs can achieve that is different from and better than trials."[37]

> In the debates that followed the South African Truth Commission, truth and reconciliation commissions shifted from being seen as a political compromise to being regarded as a "holistic" tool for social and political reconstruction and came to be associated with multiple democratizing effects.[38]

TRC South Africa inspired the proliferation of truth and reconciliation commissions, becoming a template on whose basis several other commissions were established.[39] Such commissions were seen as the manifestation of a desire and necessity to deal with the past, and of how to arrive at a sense of justice while at the same time strengthening the position of victims.[40] The conception of this South African commission not only allowed formerly marginalized and oppressed social groups to be a part of the truth-seeking and transitional process that South Africa engaged in, it also enabled the (temporal) reversal of power hierarchies. Precisely the possibility of granting amnesty to perpetrators gave significant power to former victims, as they now had a say in how perpetrators were dealt with as well as with regard to how their story was told. Voices of victims were no longer marginalized or silenced; on the contrary, they at best received recognition at home as well as media coverage and attention globally.

What remained internationally visible of the struggle to come to terms with apartheid is this discursive legacy of the TRC South Africa's proceedings: the agency of coming to terms with colonialism was firmly placed in native hands. Yet the structure of Tutu and Mandela's commission was much more complicated than that, because TRC South Africa's characteristic features were its immediacy (the TRC operated after the breakdown of the apartheid regime), its ability to enable political transition (it guided South Africa's transition to democracy), its quasi-legal character (e.g., subpoena and amnesty powers), and its fabrication of a national narrative that included the voices of both victims *and* perpetrators. Arguably, the South African "politics of regret" lent an official framework to grassroots initiatives and (international) claims to eventually deal with apartheid and find ways to move beyond it. However, it is primarily the image, the *idea* of South African reconciliation as ultimately empowering the powerless that began to travel to other contexts, appealing to other political and historical constellations. The inconsistencies and frictions within the South African process itself were smoothed over by this reading and were translated into in this narrowly defined narrative of native empowerment.

The Danger of a "Single Story": Locating Reconciliation in Australian National Discourse

Conceptually, processes of reconciliation seek to challenge the persistence of what Nigerian author Chimamanda Ngozi Adichie has termed "a single story."[41] Adichie refers to the sustained discursive dominance of master narratives. Such representations of national identity relate back to a certain interpretation of a nation's historical inventory: a "single story" tends to blank out narratives that run against an overarching discursive framing of national history in service of its dominant, oftentimes glorified interpretation. Reconciliation, it may seem, holds out the promise of being a corrective to such monodimensional narratives, of being able to rewrite the "grands récits," as Jennifer Henderson and Pauline Wakeham so poignantly remark.[42] Australian novelist, playwright, essayist, and poet Mudrooroo describes what it means for Aboriginal peoples to break with Australia's "single story."[43] Here he envisions an Australian national identity that is not

> constructed for [Australians] as a historical continuity beginning two hundred odd years ago with the arrival of the first wave of European invaders, so pregnant with contradictions and constant rewritings, inscriptions, rubbings out and pencillings in of what, after all, are perhaps mundane events in the history of European imperialism. To Us Indigenous Mobs, the arrival of the first wave of invaders (those who came to settle, take up land, dispossess and deprive us of our inheritance, so that what we once owned, what had passed down to us from our ancestors, no longer belonged to us) is but an interlude in our long possession of Australia.[44]

Mudrooroo refers to Australia's "single story" of prosperity, democracy, and multiculturalism that is difficult to reconcile with Aboriginal dispossession and assimilation. The processes of reconciliation and the "politics of regret" set out to inscribe Indigenous (hi)stories into Australia's national narrative, and thus seek to pluralize historical representations. In the process, a sense of justice derives from this act of revising Australia's national narrative. David A. Crocker postulates that "[r]estorative justice emerges from the desire to create a new nation,"[45] while Teresa Godwin Phelps emphasizes that "justice is not a single event that occurs once and for all . . . but is instead an ongoing, dynamic process, of which storytelling is a vital part."[46] Storytelling in itself becomes a means to obtain justice, for the stories of victims of forcible removal that have been formerly unheard, that may even remain unclaimed, have the power to "correct" unilateral depictions of national histories. A national narrative that reflects Australia's successful emancipation from its colonial "mother" Great Britain, its current identity as a multiethnic immigration country, falls short of acknowledging that much of Australia's success story only became possible at the expense of its Indigenous populations. The process of reconciliation in Australia, as will become evident, marks precisely the attempt to "correct" this national imaginary by opening it toward Indigenous histories and representations.

What, then, are the historical legacies that came under scrutiny in both countries? More precisely: which reading of Australian and Canadian (post) colonial histories can provide a sense of justice to their respective Indigenous populations? As has been well established in the public consciousness, Australia and Canada are both former British settler colonies and have controversial colonial histories. The situation in both countries can be characterized as a double colonial dynamic: English immigrants settled on Australian and Canadian soil, and they came to stay. In the centuries that passed, these immigrants subsequently developed a sense of Australian- and Canadianness.[47] In the process, the two settler colonies strategically and continuously displaced their native populations, effectively rendering them homeless in their country of origin. The question of Indigenous landownership was never raised: *Terra nullius* was the term of reference to indicate that Australia had never belonged to anyone else other than the British crown. Indeed, Indigenous people found "in possession of land" were declared trespassers, and land titles were not granted to Aboriginal populations. This practice of law did not change until 1992.[48] Nineteenth-century Australia could be described as being dominated by violent battles for the right of land ownership, food and water resources, and ethnic riots. From the very beginning of Australian colonization, the Indigenous workforce was exploited by European settlers:

> The greatest advantage of young Aboriginal servants was that they came cheap and were never paid beyond the provision of variable quantities of food and clothing. As a result, any European on or near the frontier, quite regardless of their own circumstances, could acquire and maintain a personal servant.[49]

The abduction of young Aboriginal children was quite common among settlers. Random kidnappings to secure the supply of servants led to the systematic removal of children from their families. The issue was traded under the sign of missionary programs to "inculcate European values and work habits in children, who would then be employed in service to the colonial settlers."[50] Particularly in the late nineteenth and early twentieth centuries, the Australian colonial government established guidelines to "breed out" Aboriginality in order to achieve biological assimilation and absorption within settler society.[51] During its execution, the system enabled the removal of between seventeen and fifty thousand Indigenous children.[52] Coral Dow speaks of "between one in three and one in ten" "stolen" Indigenous children.[53] They often lived a life of duress and abuse, both sexual and psychological. A survivor recounts the following:

> The thing that hurts the most is that they didn't care about who they put us with. As long as it looked like they were doing their job, it just didn't matter. They put me with one family and the man of the house used to come down and use me whenever he wanted to. . . . Being raped over and over and there was no-one I could turn to. They were supposed to look after me and protect me, but no-one ever did.[54]

Driven by the idea of the "self-extinction" of Aboriginality, special laws were passed, and children were forcibly removed from their parents and kin.[55]

> The underlying assumption of the biological rationale was the existence of racial affinity between the Aborigine and the European. According to this view a controlled breeding program, over the course of three to four generations, had every success with a negligible chance of so-called "atavism" or "throwbacks."[56]

These children of mixed descent were labeled "half-castes," "quadroons," or "octoroons" in reference to the degree of Aboriginal heritage. Governmental education provided different "curricula" for the children—boys were supposed to become farmhands and workers; girls were trained as domestic servants.[57] The term "Stolen Generation" was coined for these forcibly removed children,[58] and this practice was allowed until 1985.[59]

During the late 1990s, anthropologist W. E. H. Stanner directed public attention to a curious phenomenon that he referred to as the "Great Australian Silence": Aboriginal suffering was frequently omitted from historical records, and knowledge of the fate of the Stolen Generations was scarce.[60] Historical representations that would have shed light on the Stolen Generations, Indigenous displacement, and resistance had been nonexistent within Australia's national narratives of the twentieth century.[61] "Stanner also . . . first identified the oddness of the Australian yearning for an unblemished history in which no crimes had been committed and no innocent blood shed."[62] With his very publicly voiced stance on Australia's misguided identity-politics, Stanner inaugurated a controversy that was unprecedented in scope and publicity. In the years to follow, these "history wars" underwent different phases and were represented by alternating spokesmen.[63] These "wars" speak to the fact that

> [i]n many places in the world today, the past is very much present on the public agenda, but it is more often a horrible, repulsive past than the heroic golden ages so often part of public discourse in previous centuries. Political legitimation depends just as much on collective memory as it ever has, but this collective memory is now often one disgusted with itself, a matter of "learning the lessons" of history more than fulfilling its promise or remaining faithful to its legacy.[64]

The Australian "history wars," in short, were about renegotiating discursive power over representations of Australian history: the common Euro-Australian self-perception as being rightfully Australian due to the successful colonizing enterprise was well nourished.[65] Right-wing historian Keith Windshuttle, for example, proclaimed that rewriting Australian history to promote the representation of Indigenous histories, thus turning Aboriginals into victims of colonization and settler descendants into perpetrators, would only serve populist purposes, support dubious multicultural agendas, and affront Anglo-Australian identity severely.[66] Stuart Macintyre further explains:

> [Windshuttle] suggested that the discipline and practice of history was suffering a potentially mortal attack from pernicious theorists who asserted that it was impossible to tell the truth about the past, who were hostile to the idea of an objective, knowable past.[67]

An "objective, knowable" past, in Windshuttle's terms, cannot but legitimize the settlement in Australia, and cannot but establish the idea of righteous settlement to begin with. Robert Manne summarizes this arguably questionable stance on Australian identity that certainly had its supporters:

> [T]he law-abiding Christian gentlemen who colonized Australia were incapable of savage deeds; and that, in the infamous case of Tasmania, Indigenous society was destroyed by a combination of disease, the deep dysfunctionality of a social system that had survived by luck for 35,000 years, the willingness of Indigenous men to sell their womenfolk to whites, and the wave of murderous criminality the Indigenous people foolishly unleashed against the well-meaning and peaceful British colonists, who had rightfully settled on lands to which the Indigenous nomads had no particular attachment of a sentimental or spiritual kind.[68]

This notion of Australian identity as settler identity, albeit rendered here in polemic terms, was nourished and disseminated by popular fiction: the *Bulletin*, the "Bushman's Bible," provided authors like Henry Lawson or Banjo Patterson the space to perpetuate the myth of the hardened but righteous bushman or drover who cultivated the barren and hostile outback, thus effectively laying the foundation to Australian civilization.[69] This idea of Australianness was vividly attacked by its opponents who advocated for Indigenous representation in Australian historiography, in school and university curricula.[70] On many occasions, Aboriginal and other protesters displayed their resistance to this enthusiastic stance on Australia's *grand récit* by wearing black armbands or clothes to public protests. A symbol for this struggle over Australian history was found; the Black Armband. Wearing such an armband obviously denotes grief, loss, and mourning over Indigenous suffering.[71] Initially used as a derogatory term, as the "'Black Armband' tag was a strategic conservative swipe at histories that revealed Australia's past as racist and violent" and "[i]ts application served to present critical history as unbalanced, a misrepresentation of our national heritage," it became emblematic of a discourse that the different parties could rally around.[72]

Indeed, politicians did not refrain from taking sides and putting the matter on their respective party agenda, with the trench between them running along well-established ideological frontiers: the political left, as represented by (former) prime ministers Paul Keating and Kevin Rudd (both Labor Party), were in favor of integrating Aboriginal histories into national historical representations. Keating famously advertised for Indigenous inclusion into the image of Australia in his "Redfern Speech."[73] Opponents of this position held the view that such rewritings fundamentally misrepresent Australian history and exert a constant and unwarranted moral pressure on Australian society. John Howard, Keating's successor from 1996 to 2007, personified the obduracy of the "voices of dissent" to Keating's acknowledging approach.[74] He considered it particularly disturbing and unsettling for the vast majority of Australians to perceive their national history as racist and cruel, and their nation as built on the misery of others. Howard emphasizes the importance

> to ensure that our history as a nation is not written definitively by those who take the view that we should apologize for most of it. This black armband view of our past reflects a belief that most Australian history since 1788 has been little more than a disgraceful story of imperialism, exploitation, racism, sexism and other forms of discrimination. I take a very different view. I believe that the balance sheet of our history is one of heroic achievement and that we have achieved much more as a nation of which we can be proud than of which we should be ashamed. In saying that I do not exclude or ignore specific aspects of our past where we are rightly held to account. Injustices were done in Australia and no-one should obscure or minimize them. But in understanding these realities our priority should not be to apportion blame and guilt for historic wrongs but to commit to a practical program of action that will remove the enduring legacies of disadvantage.[75]

This attempt to pursue a window dressing approach to Australian history, and to elevate the national settler success story to the primary source of Australian identity, remained the paradigms of conservatism.[76] Reflecting this, John Howard adamantly refused to issue an official apology to the Indigenous population of Australia.[77]

Since the 1980s, and notwithstanding Howard's fundamental refusal, Australian reconciliation movements gradually gained momentum, and several, at times state-sanctioned, reconciliation initiatives were established.[78] As a culmination point of these various reconciliation initiatives, an inquiry about the procedures of forced removal during the twentieth century in Australia was launched. It was the aim of the commission to "trace the past laws which resulted in the separation of children from their families by compulsion" and to try to determine a justification for reimbursement and compensation."[79] The inquiry set out to rework this system of forcible removal by accessing it through public hearings, by collecting testimonies of survivors, and by producing the final report. The first hearings were held at the end of 1995; its final analysis, the famous *Bringing Them Home Report*, was issued in 1997.[80] The tone of the report and its structure bear the markings of legal discourse; its text is interspersed by the testimonies given by survivors. The recommendations of the closing report "are directed to healing and reconciliation for the benefit of all Australians."[81] The report concluded that, under international law, the forcible removal system and its objective "amount to genocide."[82] Furthermore, it recommends a public apology from the federal government; the wording should be agreed upon in negotiation with the Aboriginal and Torres Strait Islanders Commission, stem from the official acknowledgment of "responsibility of [the Australian Parliaments'] predecessors for the laws, policies, and practices of forcible removal," and result in reparation and reimbursement.[83]

Given this background, the initiation of a nationwide engagement with the fate of the Indigenous populations of Australia and Canada is the success of continuous Indigenous lobbyism and increasing pressure on acting institutions and individuals. "The National Inquiry [in Australia] opened a debate unprecedented in its breadth and continuity, engaging a huge cross section of Australians and sustaining interest far beyond the five minutes of fame which human rights issues are lucky to win."[84] In this sense, Australian reconciliation testifies to the general developments with regard to the promotion of minority rights, which have been discussed in the previous section. The increasing visibility of Aboriginal mistreatment in the public sphere led to the creation of a body, an institution, that was tasked to shed light on this underrepresented part of Australian history. The histories and stories of a population that nowadays represents 2.8 percent of the entire civic body became a matter of public engagement, and of controversial debate. The Australian Inquiry was conceptualized and put to work right around the time South Africa's "miracle" of transitioning to democracy took place. As will become clearer in the course of this analysis, the Australian Inquiry strongly resembles a truth and reconciliation commission, and thus forms part of the general tendency to listen to, to engage with, and to come to terms with native histories and colonial legacies.

However, most of the key recommendations of the report were not supported by the federal government. The establishment of a reparations tribunal "with the comprehensive jurisdiction and extensive powers suggested would neither guarantee a less stressful consideration of matters nor less expense for either party than court proceedings."[85] Twenty years after its publication, the Aboriginal and Torres Strait Islander Healing Foundation reports that the majority of the *Bringing Them Home* recommendations have not yet been implemented. For many Stolen Generations members, this has created additional trauma and distress. Failure to act has caused a ripple effect in current generations. We are now seeing an increase in Aboriginal people in jails, suicide is on the rise, and more children are being removed.[86] It seems as if the process of reconciliation in Australia has yet to arrive at a point of closure. The question remains whether that is at all possible.

The Canadian Roadmap to Reconciliation

Quite similar to the struggle of coming to terms with Australia's (post)colonial legacy of forcibly reeducating its Aboriginals is the situation in Canada: Canada was also forced to reevaluate its historical inventory and national identity in light of its own processes of reconciliation. During the 1990s, former students of the so-called Indian residential schools took action against the churches and the federal government, which resulted in a class-action suit. The court ruled that compensation must be provided for former students and that a "roadmap" to deal with this particular historical legacy must be developed.[87] This ruling arguably marked the birth of Canadian memory politics, as one of these prerequisites envisaged the establishment of TRC Canada. Matt James highlights the following aspect with regard to the genesis of the Canadian TRC: "Residential school survivors demanded that Canada open up, listen, learn and start taking responsibility for the damage caused. The Commission is their victory and tribute."[88] The commission commenced its work in 2008, equipped with a $60 million budget and a five-year mandate to reveal the truths and legacies.

In the introductory part of the preliminary report, TRC Canada locates itself within the discourse of reconciliation and truth commissions.[89]

> The Commission determined early on that the work of the Truth and Reconciliation Commission of Canada has an international importance. This was underscored when the United Nations proclaimed 2009 as the International Year of Reconciliation. . . . The Commissioners also recognize it is important to place Canada's residential school system within the international context.[90]

The report further states that "many countries around the world established boarding schools as part of the colonial process" and have thus "shared many common elements and left a common legacy."[91] This "common legacy" refers to the forcible removal of Indigenous children in order to reeducate them as Euro-Canadians. During 1830–50, imperial policy had already begun to marginalize the native population, depriving them of any juridical, legislative, regulatory, or constitutional influence and obliterating the idea of self-governing Indigenous entities.[92] Missionaries were deployed to inculcate European values and ways of life. Several treaties had envisaged self-governing native states, but crucially differing lifestyles—hunters/gatherers versus the "modern" agricultural settler—contributed to the idea to provide the Indigenous with skills to obtain self-sufficiency on the basis of European economy.[93]

Directed by the Department of Indian Affairs, the churches fostered the establishment of a boarding school system in order to achieve these goals.[94] Native children were taken from their families and forcibly placed into the custody of residential schools. Resistance from Canada's Indigenous communities was limited, since these schools were a powerful tool of social control.[95] Elizabeth Furniss speaks of

> a dream shared by the Roman Catholic Missionaries and the Canadian government: to see Native people, through Residential Schooling, abandon their cultural heritage and their nomadic hunting and fishing lifestyle, and adopt the presumably civilized ways of Europeans. With Native people living as whites, wearing European dress, speaking the English language, and working as farmers or laborers within the colonial economy, the "Indian problem," government and church agents believed, would no longer exist: Indians would melt seamlessly into the mainstream society.[96]

Eventually, it became clear that the civilizing mission of the settlers and the idea of "self-government" for the Indigenous population were incompatible. In 1867 the responsibility for all "Indian affairs" was transferred from the British crown to the colony.[97] This year marked the creation of the Dominion of Canada, which resulted in the transfer of more and more legislative power from London to the colonial government.[98] This development led to the passing of several Aboriginal acts in order to further British-Canadian influence on First Nations people, successively regulating every aspect of Indigenous life.[99] The colonial government regarded it as their "duty towards the red man" to turn them into worthy citizens in their own image.[100] In the beginning, the provision of education was not entirely declined by Canada's natives; some of them saw a chance to ameliorate their living conditions and gain access to settler society by way of learning how to read and write.[101] "Agricultural technique was a bridge from the old world to the new, but so were schools and teachers."[102] Miller refers to the schooling project as a joint endeavor, a "product of both Indian initiative and European cultural aggression," and highlights that the system has only "gradually become the vehicle of newcomer's attempts to refashion and culturally eliminate" indigeneity.[103]

> Not all societies have schools, but all human communities possess educational systems. This is so because education, as distinct from schooling, has clear purposes whose achievement is essential for any collectivity to survive and to prosper. Education aims, first, to explain to the individual members of a community who they are, who their people are, and how they relate to other peoples and the physical world around them.[104]

Behind each school stood the federal government, which had created an educational collaboration with the churches.[105] The system was designed by the state, but the children were in immediate care of the churches. The proclaimed aim was the "elevation of Indigenous people from their savagery" through cultural reeducation.[106] It was common belief among Anglo-Canadians that

> Europeans have taken it upon themselves, to varying degrees, in different historical periods, to transform Native peoples, both physical and culturally, into an image more acceptable to European sensibilities. This effort has been legitimized by a fundamental conviction that Native people require the guidance of Europeans to live successful lives, and that European intervention in Native peoples' lives, even when forcefully applied, is ultimately in Native peoples' "best interests."[107]

The situation within most of the schools may be described as heinous: rapid deterioration of buildings, overcrowding, and chronic underfunding shaped school facilities; sexual abuse, neglect, and violent oppression characterized the relationship between teachers and students.[108] The beginning of the twentieth century was marked by epidemics of white plague and tuberculosis that broke out in the schools. An unknown number of residential school pupils did not survive their stay. In 1973, 71 schools were still operating, housing and teaching 5,347 children.[109] More than 150,000 Indians, Inuit, and Métis children were placed in these schools; an estimated 80,000 former students are still alive today.[110] The Canadian residential school system officially operated from 1879 until 1986.[111]

The schools were certainly among the most damaging effects of colonization on Canada's Indigenous populations. In the years following the closure of these schools, more and more claims of abuse were brought to public attention as the claimants depicted how school staff had sexually and physically abused their students.[112] Consequently, the system that had formerly "operated largely out of sight and mind of the Euro-Canadian public" came under scrutiny.[113] From the very beginning, one of the major obstacles Canadian reconciliation faced was the apparent disinterest of the general public. While the "history wars" in Australia led many people to become aware of the matter of forcible removal, Canada did not engage in a general reevaluation of the colonial past prior to the workings of the TRC.

> In the public discourse that has emerged in response to Canada's Truth and Reconciliation Commission, the residential school legacy is frequently referred to as Canada's "dark secret," as an occluded and oppressed form of knowledge that the reconciliation process promises to "reveal" or to "expose." But despite the prevalence of this rhetoric of secrecy and revelation, . . . the legacy of residential schooling has not entered the public consciousness of non-Indigenous Canadians to nearly the same extent that the legacy of the Stolen Generations, as it is called, has entered that of non-Indigenous Australians.[114]

In this setting, to generate a public reaction and to ignite controversial debates about the origins of the Canadian nation were highly dependent on the public performance of the TRC Canada and the publication of the (final) report. As Julie McGonegal remarks, "Non-Indigenous Canadians have not accepted the burden of speaking about their relation to colonialism or confessing their complicity."[115]

This deliberate silence on the colonial past stems from the clash of two opposing national narratives:

> Current struggles to contain the meaning of residential schooling point to colonialism's uneasy status as a purportedly finished project. Indigenous claims to land, natural resources, and self-determination threaten to take the open secret of ongoing colonial oppression and reconstitute it as an outright scandal for a self-proclaimed liberal democracy.[116]

Through the works of the TRC, Canadian society was forced to realize that the atrocities committed under colonial rule continued well into the twentieth century and that the structural disadvantage of Canada's Indigenous populations is a result of the system of forcible removal. The refusal to engage with the results of European settlement might be rooted in a particular self-understanding: Canada sees itself as a liberal democracy, a community that was built on certain inalienable and exemplary values. It was among the first states to publicly ratify the Genocide Convention, which was the result of the Holocaust and the Nuremberg trials, and has since engaged in quite a number of conciliatory processes.[117] In 1988, the government apologized to Canada's Japanese community for their internment during World War II, and this gesture of remorse was also directed at Canada's Italian community in 1990 for the same historical mistreatment. In 2006, a formal apology was issued to Chinese Canadians for the infamous Head Tax. As one can gather from this far-from-comprehensive enumeration, Canada has quite the track record of human rights abuses, but it has also offered its share of conciliatory gestures of recognition and remorse. Canada has taken and takes pride in its status as a multicultural society, promoting multiculturalism with its "emphasis on the value of cultural diversity and the sense of horizontal relationships between the superficially differentiated tiles of a national cultural mosaic" to state reason.[118] "[I]ndividual ethnicity does not replace Canadian identity, rather it defines Canadians and their position in the world."[119] This nation prides itself on being open-minded and tolerant toward foreigners, and after World Wars I and II it became "one of the world's main immigrant-receiving societies"[120] Yet, Canada forcibly reeducated its native populations well into the twentieth century. The narrative of forcible removal thus runs counter to the image of "benevolent Canada."

The TRC could have brought about a clash of these contradictory narratives. In order to disseminate the experiences of Canada's Stolen Generations, the commission held several national events, collected statements and documents relating to residential schools and their former attendants, and initiated several community events with the support of government funding. These communal events were envisaged to produce local narratives relating to the residential school experience, whereas the national events were designed to draw national attention.[121] According to the report, 155,000 people visited the seven national events, among which were an estimated 9,000 former residential school attendants and survivors.[122] The report lists 238 days on which hearings were held and statements were gathered and heard. Yet, the goal and the scope of Canada's TRC lay beyond assigning blame or engaging in a through reworking of persisting structures and legacies of oppression.

Toothless Tigers or Acts of Empowerment?

While deliberating over the structure and shape of the Canadian model, Indigenous activists in particular argued for the implementation of a truth and reconciliation commission like the South African example. Although all representatives agreed on taking up the "brand name" from the South African predecessor, the "uniqueness" of the Canadian situation had to be taken into account.[123] TRC Canada was established in reference to and reverence for TRC South Africa, but on Canadian terms. "As one member explains, the more they talked about what a people's inquiry would look like, the more the image of South Africa and a truth and reconciliation kind of process came out."[124] The commission's primary concern was in "reveal[ing] to Canadians the complex truth about the history and the ongoing legacy of the church-run residential schools" and to "guide and aspire a process of truth and healing."[125] The educative and pedagogical impetus were central to the undertaking. Rosemary Nagy retells the genesis of the Canadian TRC:

> Within a year, however, this informal group [composed of representatives of Indigenous organizations such as the National Residential School Survivor Society (NRSSS) AFN, Métis National Council, the churches, law commissions, and the federal government] began a shift in language from "public inquiry" to "national community inquiry" to "a People's Commission for Truth, Hope, and Reconciliation."[126]

As Nagy further delineates, the Indigenous representatives initially argued for a close resemblance to the South African model—subpoena powers and the possibility to name culprits—yet the churches and federal government representatives were against such legal powers.[127] Hence, TRC Canada had no legal or political power whatsoever, and was furthermore prohibited from naming any names of perpetrators or suspects. In comparison with the South African model, not only was the Canadian Truth Commission *not* equipped with any power to tackle and resolve matters legally, but, paradoxically, the process of truth and reconciliation as provided by TRC Canada precluded all participants from filing any legal claims regarding the Indian residential school system in the future. Accordingly, there was no need for any provisions of amnesty for perpetrators. As a consequence, TRC Canada only represented the "spirit" of previous, famous truth commissions that I outlined earlier:

> While in some cases the establishment of a TRC is the result of international conditionality or direct imposition, often it is the *idea* of a truth commission, as typified by the South African TRC, which provides inspiration for actors seeking to deal with legacies of human rights abuse.[128]

Key features of the South African commission were abandoned, but the "promise" of native empowerment and changed power relations that was derived from TRC South Africa's proceedings made its way to the Canadian context. In the end, TRC Canada turned into a "blame-free structure," becoming a victim-centered, nonjudicial, and nonforensic body that provided a stage to listen to the stories of former students and survivors.[129]

This shift from amnesty powers to narrative and testimonial activity within the framework of "truth and reconciliation" has a fundamental impact on what such a process can actually achieve. Clearly defined aspects of national and colonial history are called upon to validate Indigenous suffering and displacement on a public level, and to render part and parcel of a "proper" Australian and Canadian national narrative, one that is decidedly attentive to human rights violations against their Indigenous peoples.[130] The Canadian commission thus sought to facilitate the production of a specific kind of decontextualized knowledge: TRC Canada could not address ongoing conflicts (oil pipelines, land rights, questions of citizenship, and treaty politics, etc.), but it could make citizens access the past in a different manner:

> Commissions of Inquiry, in their basic form, investigate an issue by gathering a broad spectrum of information in order to see the larger context that gave rise to the problem. Then they make policy recommendations to prevent a recurrence of the problem. . . . Sometimes a commission, in addition to these essential functions, also performs a social function. This involves a process whereby the commission involves the wider public than those people directly affected by the issue at hand, openly acknowledges the harm done, fosters a sense of societal identification with the victims, establishes an incontrovertible record, and makes recommendations to prevent the injustice's recurrence.[131]

Here, Stanton describes an important paradigmatic change in Australian and Canadian reconciliation: discourses of judicial and legal reworking of (structural) human rights abuses, of obtaining legal justice, have been replaced by "narrative justice," a morally immaculate memorialization of and the elicitation of emotional responses to historical injustice.[132]

In order to find a language to deal with past atrocities and to integrate them into a contemporary (national) identity, reconciliation weaves together the subjective experiences of victims. A specific semantic field emerges, one that does not prominently feature legal (quasi-)terms and concepts such as "accountability," "reparation," or "penalty" but is firmly referencing trauma discourse with "self-empowerment through voicing-out," "self-empowerment through forgiveness," "survivor," "healing," etc. Such catchphrases also framed the reception of TRC South Africa's work, but they have become even more central to Canadian and Australian reconciliation. The central mechanism at work here comes close to what Teresa Godwin Phelps and others have argued, that a victim's identity as a human can be reconstituted by the act of (public) storytelling.[133] The Canadian and Australian commissions, consequently, were not structured with a view to establishing legal justice but with empowering former victims through storytelling:

> The next group of benefits can be seen more clearly from the perspective of the social fabric, the state in which the victim is claiming a voice, an identity, and the power to speak the truth. . . . [S]tories can communicate the experience of pain and suffering between people who normally cannot understand each other. Stories can "translate" events and emotions in a way that other forms of discourse cannot, can overcome the *différend* (the lack of a shared language in which a person can express an injury) that bars both justice and understanding.[134]

Victims are invited to use the space that TRCs provide to profoundly transform their subject position and to move from the silent margins to the discursive center. Storytelling, in this vein, is understood as a mode to redistribute discursive power—power over one's voice and power over one's representation.[135]

> A practical consensus that emerged was that TRCs may achieve multiple and important psychological, political, and legal goals, including many of the goals of criminal prosecutions. A second, normative consensus that emerged was that finding the truth is in itself a form of justice. This ideational shift elevated the normative status of the truth-seeking process. Finally, . . . TRCs increasingly came to be seen as distinct from trials and as a complementary rather than an alternative tool for dealing with the past.[136]

What is more, there is a moral dimension to the collection and publication of victims' accounts: if the "right" and "proper" stories were only told, collectives could supposedly be prevented from repeating the mistakes of the past. Traumatic experiences become stories with the potential to mobilize, and they are assigned a new role as foundational narratives to a newly developed sense of national self post-reconciliation. The TRC model of justice through "correcting national history" has instead become a "morally desirable practice" than a means to bring about tangible change to former victims.[137] Jennifer Henderson and Pauline Wakeham succinctly argue that

> [t]he [Canadian] culture of redress entails a specific form of justice seeking that interprets social relations in distinctive ways: with a historical orientation, highlighting intentionality, and with a view to pursuing the settlement of grievance in a form that involves an affective component such as the validation of grief.[138]

Such victim-centered processes are thus Janus-faced in nature: these inquiries into the past are powerful mnemonic nodal points, because they make social inequalities visible by focusing on marginalized voices and (hi)stories that have been left out of canonical representations of national identity. Such commissions operate under the assumption, and hand out the promise, that they can harvest the past to better understand the demands of the present, without, however, being able to facilitate a credible vision for the future. Through their proceedings, TRCs reflect the power structures of production and reception of memory discourses, and how their dynamics and relations are changed by the desire to facilitate the discourse of "moral remembrance."[139] Wulf Kansteiner describes the entanglements of agents and narratives engaged in the production of memories and conceives collective memory as

> the result of the interaction among three types of historical factors: the intellectual and cultural traditions that frame all our representations of the past, the memory makers who selectively adopt and manipulate these traditions, and the memory consumers who use, ignore, or transform such artifacts according to their own interests.[140]

Through reconciliation, the voices of the marginalized claim center stage, thus challenging well-established representational hierarchies in Australian and Canadian national narratives and effectively working toward a state of reconciliation. The words of Australian author and activist Mudrooroo concerning the reclamation of Indigenous histories, as quoted earlier, resonates within Kansteiner's description of power dynamics, which accompany struggles over rewriting the past, and David's emphasis on a moral impetus: Aboriginal (hi)stories have in the pre-reconciliation past been left out, "adapted to fit," and "re-fashioned" in order to legitimate settlement in Australia:[141]

Our story, our history, will query what has been written by the dominant society, as the true record of a sequence of events along the timeline. From this re-writing of what was once considered an official or "true" narrative, an equally "true" revisionist version may result, which seeks to replace what is now seen as an outmoded narrative. This is the stage, especially with the efforts of the Reconciliation Council behind it, that the process of rewriting history in Australia has now reached.[142]

The crucial mechanism at work in Australian and Canadian "politics of regret" are not punitive in nature but seek to "balance the books" of history as an act of empowerment. Processes of truth and reconciliation are indicative of how a particular understanding of a nation's past can be challenged, and of how history is performatively "rewritten" to gain a specific identity-political significance for the present. In other words, the potential of the TRC to bring about change in relations does not entail a strategic and systematic dismantling of oppressive structures, politics, and mindsets that influence Indigenous communities today but much rather focuses on rendering remorse for past Indigenous mistreatment as part of what Matt James calls "the national brand."[143]

The framework of reconciliation as practiced in Australia and Canada is the attempt to exert control over this highly ambiguous process of remembering the systems of cultural "e-education." It enables the government to reinvent itself as the enabler of reconciliation and new beginnings without the potentially dire consequences of court proceedings and constitutional changes. The difficult legacies of the past, in this sense, have now been tackled on a very public scale, and their performative reworking becomes part of the national myth and gets incorporated into national identity. Undeniably, the silence on the issues of forcible removal and cultural reeducation in the Canadian public sphere was heavy and impermeable for many decades. With this in mind, Paulette Regan, director of research of the TRC of Canada, perceived this commission as a chance for non-Indigenous Canada to listen and learn:

> We [Canadians] do not categorize the residential school system and other assimilationist strategies as acts of violence, yet their caustic effects are evident. In the seismic wake of destruction left by the public policy experiment that was the Indian residential schools, Indigenous communities struggle with poverty, poor health, and education outcomes, economic disadvantage, domestic violence, abuse, addiction, and high rates of youth suicide. It is easy, from the safety of our relatively comfortable lives, to judge the apparent inability of Native people to rise above such conditions, thus pathologizing the victim of our well-intended actions. It is equally easy to think that we know what is best for them—hence our persistence to solve the Indian problem.[144]

Regan calls for a reframing of what the Canadian non-Indigenous majority understands as (colonial) violence and draws a direct connection between the "public policy experiment" and the still disadvantageous position of Canada's First Nations. Regan emphasizes the need to educate the wider Canadian public about the residential school system in order to ensure that the settler community learns something about *itself*. For Regan, this is the strongest decolonizing power of the work of the Canadian Commission: through storytelling and listening, through exchanging a limited form of "knowledge," a decolonizing space is supposedly constructed.

There is, however, an important distinction that Roger I. Simons recognizes: the fundamental difference between "learning about and learning from history."[145] In this setting, it is the task of the settler community to change its perspective on the Indigenous by bearing witness to the stories unfolding. It is a veritable conundrum that such victim-centered approaches construct: the reworking of colonial history brings painful memories, stories of abuse, and violence to the fore but ultimately renders its acknowledgment an act of navel-gazing into the past and does not necessarily prompt "non-Indigenous Canada"—whatever that is—to engage with the structures that continue to disenfranchise Canada's Indigenous peoples.[146] On the contrary, the Canadian TRC ostensibly centered on Indigenous voices and histories, but in the process these legacies can also be actively integrated into the national narrative of "benevolent multicultural Canada." The "politics of regret" may challenge established national narratives—settler success stories and muted Indigenous agency—and empower the marginalized at the moment of their performance, but the very existence of reconciliation discourses and processes can be productively reframed as characteristic for a "philanthropic" Canadian national identity.

Jennifer Henderson and Pauline Wakeham argue that, through reconciliation, the Canadian image of the national self has already been altered, and that this reoriented knowledge about the past has been smoothly integrated into Canada's idealized national image: "Knowledge of these state-inflicted group injuries, and Canada's proclaimed regret for them, now forms part of the hegemonic understanding of Canada."[147] The Canadian example of a truth and reconciliation process highlights that renegotiating national history is a symbolic, but highly strategic, reorientation toward and resignification of the past.[148] Roland Chrisjohn and Tanya Wasacase argue that Canadian reconciliation

> is an attempt to insinuate a revised and bogus history of Indian/non-Indian relations in Canada. It implies that, once upon a time, Indigenous peoples and settlers lived in peace and harmony, working collaboratively towards shared longterm goals, only to have residential schooling (which began with only the best of intentions) rear its ugly head and drive a wedge between Canadians and

Indigenous peoples. The job of the Truth and Reconciliation Commission, like that of a good marital therapist or (more appropriately in this instance) a concerned priest, is to mend the rift, heal the split, and make two conjoin again as one.[149]

Through reconciliation, the state and its institutions are enabled to reframe themselves as agents of reconciliation and thus reframe this difficult historical legacy as attesting to, for example, Canada's tolerance, open-mindedness, and respect toward its Indigenous populations. Polemically speaking, the fallacy embedded in "politics of regret" is located in their ability to "snatc[h] triumph from disaster" and to make these memory politics about "settler Canada" again.[150]

Australian and Canadian "politics of regret," thus conceived, are at risk of becoming self-serving endeavors, because they primarily enable a reconciliation of settler societies with their colonial past.[151] To engage in processes of exchanging attitudes and narratives enables the non-Indigenous majority to "retain an illusion of innocence" in the present and of "settler futurity" with the residential school legacy neatly contained and filed under "reconciled."[152] What is more, the notion of learning about the Stolen Generations and the Indian residential school system can result in a non-Indigenous introspection that does not entail or recognize other sections of Canada's or Australia's "multicultural" society. The binary arrangement of settler descendant/Indigenous is by no means representative of both multifaceted societies. As Jennifer Henderson and Pauline Wakeham so poignantly enunciate, Canadian redress "has a history" with an "ever-accumulating list of reconciliatory gestures" toward other historically shunned minorities. The experiences and agency of migrants, their sense of displacement, homelessness, and perhaps also arrival, do not feature at all. Reconciliation, thus conceived, resurrects the category of the settler, revolving around the (settler) majority and their attitude toward the Indigenous, while the stories of suffering and abuse become requisites to this introspection.

Moreover, Anne-Marie Reynaud points toward the fact that the "TRC's efforts to create a master narrative that insists on suffering and healing is bound to shape and control the emotional expressions it encourages and discourages."[153] She argues that TRCs are expected

> [to play] host to a fundamental tension between two competing imperatives: the imperative of fidelity to legitimate emotions stemming from injustice (such as anger, rage or sorrow), and the countervailing imperative to overcome these emotions for the sake of reconciliation.[154]

Seen in this light, commissions such as the Australian Inquiry and the TRC of Canada generate templates defining which narratives and performances are central to the undertaking of reconciliation and ways to appropriately respond to these stories. The very nature of such commissions channels the way in which a society approaches its own past and provides "toolboxes" (structures, rituals, mechanisms, scopes) of how to do that. Along with these "scripts" to tackle the past come certain templates that ultimately define the position that people are confined to by implication.[155]

The Pitfalls of Good Intentions I: Toward the Victim Paradigm

Central to both reconciliation endeavors discussed here are the stories of the victims and survivors, but this centrality is also complicit in fostering a specific identity template in relation to the Stolen Generations and Indian residential school survivors: continuous victimhood.

This emotional turn in conflict solution discourses—as exemplified by TRC Canada and the Australian inquiry—should be identified as the imminent problem, and the most pertinent. With regard to TRC South Africa, Heidi Grunebaum strongly highlights the responsibility that comes with it—the burden and the pain of voicing-out rests on the victim.[156] To achieve reconciliation might easily result in mechanisms where victims feel compelled to speak up, to represent themselves as victims and survivors.[157]

Consider, for example, the Australian conundrum. The inquiry strongly and successfully contributed to "indigenizing" identity politics, yet it also contributed to unintentionally producing a very powerful identity template: the Indigenous (child) in need of healing and, possibly, state intervention.[158] In the context of Australian reconciliation, other narratives of "Stolen Children" surfaced in the context of the inquiry, and the Australian nation was forced to look back on a "tradition" of child removal. There have been many cases of state-ordered forcible adoptions of children who were labeled as living under intolerable circumstances, and those children were mostly non-Indigenous. The British government, for example, had shipped orphans to the Australian colony in order to lessen the strain on British orphanages. To witness the reworking of the Stolen Generations issue sparked an engagement with these matters; lobbies and claimants of "Forgotten Australians" and "Mothers of the White Stolen Generation" came into being, both as a reaction to and an engagement with the Indigenous "Stolen Generations" narrative.[159] The forcibly removed child became a topos and a symbol that dominated the public debate, and Australians were thus able to form an "appropriate" emotional response.[160] Reconciliation renders forcibly removed Aboriginal peoples the poster children for reworking colonial legacies:[161]

> For many non-Indigenous Australians, vexed and divided on issues such as land rights, alcoholism, and law and order in Indigenous communities, the issue of

the Stolen Generations, while hard to confront, appeared more straightforward. This was not a matter of politics. It was about the suffering of *innocent* children and their removal from their families.¹⁶²

This framing of indigeneity is closely aligned with the narrative of the forcibly removed child; the idea of the damaged native has become a formative identity template that governs how the Indigenous are perceived.¹⁶³ The conundrum of these post–South Africa reconciliation endeavors, it may seem, lies within the limitation of the focus: through the fixation on the systems of forcible removal (in opposition to evaluating colonial history in its breadth) and on the narratives of victimization, the image of the victim becomes more central than that of the perpetrator, or the bystander and enabler.¹⁶⁴

Moreover, there is another problematic aspect to victim-centeredness. Indigenous scholar Jo-Ann Episkenew takes a stand against how the notion of "healing" and "trauma" marks Canada's Indigenous peoples as deficient, and furthers a paternalistic stance on indigeneity and Canadian history:

> Healing does not imply that Indigenous people are sick. . . . Colonialism is sick; under its auspices and supported by its mythology, the colonizers have inflicted heinous wounds on the Indigenous population that they set out to civilize. Although Indigenous people understand their need to heal from colonial trauma, most settlers deny that their society is built on a sick foundation and, therefore, deny that it requires a cure.¹⁶⁵

In the context of the "politics of regret," native communities are presented as being unable or reluctant to move beyond victimhood as indigeneity implies victimhood by default. As Denise Cuthbert and Marian Quartly convincingly argue, the Stolen Generations complex has become the designating narrative for all indigeneity:

> During the course of the inquiry from 1995 to 1997, and following the tabling of its final report, forced Indigenous child removal became the most popularly recognized issue for Indigenous Australia and the one on which the reconciliation project would come to hinge. . . . In a much belated response to one of the recommendations of the HREOC's final report and signaling the rise to preeminence of the Stolen Generations as symbolic of all wrongs done "by us" to Indigenous people, the terms of Rudd's apology are both an apology to the Stolen Generations and an apology to all Indigenous Australians through consideration of the Stolen Generations.¹⁶⁶

The heralded decolonizing pedagogical space, in Paulette Regan's terms, thus produces a very dominant designating narrative for Indigenous communities. As a result, the Stolen Generations discourse has been the formative template through which indigeneity has been constructed in the wake and aftermath of the Australian processes of reconciliation:

> The progressive Indigenization of forced child removal and the concomitant sidelining of other political claims of Australia's Indigenous peoples in the period between 1992 and 2008 has perversely allowed for the replacement of politics by sentiment around the issue of child removal.[167]

The performance of national reckoning, national regret, and ultimately a post-reconciliation national identity was and is inextricably linked with the forcibly removed Indigenous child, and has potentially drawn attention away from actual claims made by Australia's and Canada's Aboriginal peoples. Matt James observes a similar tendency of pathologizing the Indigenous in Canada. He writes with regard to the powerful and formative discourse of the so-called "residential schools syndrome,"[168] which surfaced (again) through the works of the Canadian TRC, that

> the highly partial nature of the "residential schools syndrome" framing, combined with a range of prevailing anti-indigenous stereotypes and biases, pathologizes Aboriginal people as helpless therapeutic subjects who need externally administered healing in order to unburden themselves of their anger and become conventionally productive citizens.[169]

Media coverage of Prime Minister Harper's apology, which was supposed to be "a historic act that should have been an occasion for settler society introspection," led to a wide range of "paternalistic commentary about the damaged state of Indigenous individuals and communities."[170] Instead of promoting the notion of Indigenous resilience and strength, the forcibly removed child narrative and the image of the helpless, invalid native claimed its own stage. Similar to the Australian example, the grand narrative of the forcibly removed child ran the risk of occupying the center stage of reconciliation, brushing aside questions of the possibility of true political change for Indigenous communities. What was meant to be a gesture of respect—centering on experiences and representations of Indigenous suffering—may eventually have reenacted the entirely colonial trope of the childish native, and the native as child. Liz Conor argues in this context:

> This discursive conception of the Aboriginal child as repossessed inheritor—by which I mean their inheritance becomes repossessed by whites who wish to claim them as of their blood, and therefore of Aboriginal children's land—has a long history in the trans-colonially and trans-nationally circulated figure of the "piccaninny." The piccaninny-as-image fulfilled a distinctly British acquisitive impulse over the colonized, racialized child, through slavery, missionary work,

child removal and immigration programmes, and, on the level of representation . . . as ornaments and souvenirs.[171]

Thus conceived, the "politics of regret" as endeavored by Canada and Australia are complicit in reiterating this derogatory image of their respective native populations and render it a very publicly performed identity template. As Conor suggests, the forcibly removed child becomes an "ornament" to the nation, because the reconciliation processes so poignantly center the narrative of forcible removal and its effects on individual and collective. This time, however, the Indigenous child is repatriated and reconnected to the national frame.

Notes

1. Truth and Reconciliation Commission of Canada, *Honouring the Truth, Reconciling for the Future*. Final report. N.d. http://www.trc.ca/websites/trcinstitution/File/2015/Honouring_the_Truth_Reconciling_for_the_Future_July_23_2015.pdf, n.p.
2. See Lucy Bond and Jessica Rapson, eds., *The Transcultural Turn: Interrogating Memory between and beyond Borders*, 1st ed. Media and Cultural Memory/Medien Und Kulturelle Erinnerung, vol. 15. (Berlin: De Gruyter 2014), 4.
3. Jennifer Henderson and Pauline Wakeham, "Introduction," in *Reconciling Canada: Critical Perspectives on the Culture of Redress*, ed. Jennifer Henderson and Pauline Wakeham (Toronto: University of Toronto Press, 2013), 3.
4. See the interview with commissioner Murray Sinclair, "Truth and Reconciliation Commission: By the Numbers," CBC News, 3 June 2015, retrieved 2 March 2018 from http://www.cbc.ca/news/indigenous/truth-and-reconciliation-commission-by-the-numbers-1.3096185. The chance of dying during World War II was 1:25, to meet one's end in a residential school was 1:26.
5. Sinclair, "Truth and Reconciliation Commission."
6. Henderson and Wakeham, "Introduction," 3. See also Lea David, *The Past Can't Heal Us: The Dangers of Mandating Memory in the Name of Human Rights*, Human Rights in History (New York: Cambridge University Press, 2020).
7. See David, *Past Can't Heal Us*.
8. Anna Reading, quoted in Bond and Rapson, *Transcultural Turn*, 17.
9. See Chadwick Allen, *Trans-Indigenous: Methodologies for Global Native Literary Studies* (Minneapolis: University of Minnesota Press, 2012).
10. United Nations General Assembly, International Year of Reconciliation, A/Res/61/17, 23 January 2008, retrieved 6 February 2015 from http://www.un.org/en/ga/search/view_doc.asp?symbol=A/RES/61/17.
11. TRC Canada, *Honouring the Truth*.
12. Jeffrey K. Olick, *Politics of Regret: On Collective Memory and Historical Responsibility* (London: Routledge, 2007), 14.
13. For a general overview of cases of truth and reconciliation commissions, see, for example, Amy Benson Brown and Karen Poremski, eds., *Roads to Reconciliation: Conflict and Dia-*

logue in the Twenty-First Century (Armonk, NY: M. E. Sharp Publishers, 2004); Priscilla B. Hayner, *Unspeakable Truths: Transitional Justice and the Challenge of Truth Commissions* (New York: Routledge, 2011).
14. Will Kymlicka and Bashir Bashir, eds., *The Politics of Reconciliation in Multicultural Societies* (Oxford: Oxford University Press, 2009), 1.
15. Bond and Rapson, *Transcultural Turn*, 18.
16. Henderson and Wakeham, "Introduction," 14–15.
17. See Amy Gutmann and Dennis Thompson, "The Moral Foundations of Truth Commissions," in *Truth versus Justice: The Morality of Truth Commissions*, ed. Robert I. Rotberg and Dennis Thompson (Princeton, NJ: Princeton University Press, 2000), 23–43.
18. Henderson and Wakeham, "Introduction," 3.
19. Michal Ben-Josef Hirsch, "Ideational Change and the Emergence of the International Norm of Truth and Reconciliation Commissions," *European Journal of International Relations* 20, no. 3 (2014): 817.
20. Dennis Frank Thompson and Robert I. Rotberg, *Truth versus Justice: The Morality of Truth Commissions* (Princeton, NJ: Princeton University Press, 2000), 3-4.
21. Rotberg, *Truth versus Justice*, 6.
22. Hirsch, "Ideational Change," 817.
23. Henderson and Wakeham, "Introduction," 3.
24. For further reading, see Dorothy Shea, who describes the tension between the demand for juridical power (subpoena and investigative powers) and the granting of amnesty, which weakened, in her view, the impact of the TRC's work: Dorothy Shea, *The South African Truth Commission: The Politics of Reconciliation* (Washington, DC: United States Institute of Peace Press, 2000). See also Deborah Posel and Graeme Simpson, eds., *Commissioning the Past: Understanding South Africa's Truth and Reconciliation Commission* (Johannesburg: Witwatersrand University Press, 2002). For an evaluation of Christian theological concepts at work within the TRC South Africa, see, e.g., Megan Shore, *Religion and Conflict Resolution: Christianity and South Africa's Truth and Reconciliation Commission* (Burlington: Ashgate, 2009). Heidi Grunebaum explores the institutionalization of collective memory through the works of the TRC South Africa, emphasizing the creation of a new "language" of memory and transition: Heidi Grunebaum, *Memorializing the Past: Everyday Life in South Africa after the Truth and Reconciliation Commission* (New Brunswick, NJ: Transaction Publishers, 2011). Antije Krog follows a similar trajectory when she describes how an entirely new vocabulary to describe atrocities, human rights violations, shame, and guilt emerged as a result of the commission's work: Antjie Krog, *Conditional Tense: Memory and Vocabulary after the South African Truth and Reconciliation Commission* (London: Seagull Books, 2013). Adam Sitze convincingly argues that the most important aspect to evaluating the works of the TRC South Africa is how it undermined colonial jurisprudence by innovatively adapting it and translating it to decolonize South Africa: Adam Sitze, *The Impossible Machine: A Genealogy of South Africa's Truth and Reconciliation Commission* (Ann Arbor: University of Michigan Press, 2013).
25. For a discourse analysis, see Annelies Verdoolaege, *Reconciliation Discourse: The Case of the Truth and Reconciliation Commission* (Amsterdam: John Benjamin, 2008).
26. See Verdoolaege, *Reconciliation Discourse*.
27. See Desmond Tutu, *No Future without forgiveness* (London: Rider, 1999).
28. Hirsch, "Ideational Change," 817–18.
29. See Catherine M. Cole, *Performing South Africa's Truth Commission: Stages of Transition* (Bloomington: Indiana University Press, 2010); Charles Villa-Vicencio, *Walk with Us and Listen: Political Reconciliation in Africa* (Washington, DC: Georgetown University Press, 2009); and Michael Boesch, ed., *Suedafrikas Inszenierung der Wahrheit: Die politische*

Erinnerungskultur nach der Apartheid (Schwerte: Katholische Akademie Schwerte, 2010), 7.
30. See Cole, *Performing*, x–xii; Boesch, *Suedafrikas Inszenierung*, 9-10.
31. See Villa-Vicencio, *Walk with Us*; Ernesto Verdeja, *Unchopping a Tree: Reconciliation in the Aftermath of Political Violence* (Philadelphia: Temple University Press, 2009).
32. Elizabeth Kiss writes: "With no prospect of a decisive victory over the minority white regime, the ANC was compelled to acquiesce in the amnesty guarantees demanded by the National Party leaders, both to secure a settlement and to stave off a direct threat by the security forces to disrupt the 1994 democratic elections. On this view, the amnesty granted by the TRC did indeed sacrifice justice. Or, at best, it salvaged "certain essential elements" of justice by virtue of the uniquely South African innovation of making amnesty individual and conditional on public disclosure of specific misdeeds." Elizabeth Kiss, "Moral Ambitions within and beyond Political Constraints," in *Truth versus Justice: The Morality of Truth Commissions*, ed. Robert I. Rotberg and Dennis Thompson (Princeton, NJ: Princeton University Press, 2000), 70.
33. See Antije Krog, *Country of My Skull* (Johannesburg: Random House Struik, 2009).
34. See Krog, *Country of My Skull*.
35. Restorative justice focuses on the restoration to unity of a divided collective. See, e.g., Kiss, "Moral Ambitions."
36. See David A. Crocker, "Truth Commissions, Transitional Justice, and Civil Society," in *Truth versus Justice: The Morality of Truth Commissions*, ed. Robert I. Rotberg and Dennis Thompson (Princeton, NJ: Princeton University Press, 2000), 99–121. See also André du Toit, "The Moral Foundations of the South African TRC: Truth as Acknowledgement and Justice as Recognition," in *Truth versus Justice: The Morality of Truth Commissions*, ed. Robert I. Rotberg and Dennis Thompson (Princeton, NJ: Princeton University Press, 2009), 122–40.
37. Hirsch, "Ideational Change," 825.
38. Hirsch, "Ideational Change," 810.
39. See Astrid Erll, "Travelling Memory," *Parallax* 17 (2011): 4–18, and Astrid Erll, "From 'District 6' to District 9 and Back: The Plurimedial Production of Travelling Schemata," in *Transnational Memory: Circulation, Articulation, Scales*, ed. Chiara DeCesari and Ann Rigney (Berlin: De Gruyter, 2014), 29–50.
40. See Gutmann and Thompson, "Moral Foundations."
41. Chimamanda Ngozi Adichie, "The Danger of a Single Story," TEDGlobal, 2009, retrieved 5 February 2018 from https://www.ted.com/talks/chimamanda_adichie_the_danger_of_a_single_story.
42. Henderson and Wakeham, "Introduction," 15.
43. Mudrooroo Narogin or Colin Johnson was brought up in a Roman Catholic orphanage and considers himself to be Aboriginal. His Indigenous heritage was called into question in the late 1990s, and his case became a public controversy. He left Australia in 2001.
44. Mudrooroo Narogin, *Us Mob: History, Culture, Struggle; An Introduction to Indigenous Australia* (Sydney: Angus & Roberston, 1995), iv.
45. Crocker, "Truth Commissions," 111.
46. Teresa Godwin Phelps, *Shattered Voices: Language, Violence and the Work of Truth Commissions* (Philadelphia: University of Pennsylvania Press, 2004), 9.
47. The first records of overseas enterprises to discover new territories give the date of 1606 as the first encounter with the country Australia and its Indigenous inhabitants. Between 1606 and 1770, approximately fifty-four ships from different countries landed on the Australian coast. In 1770, Lieutenant James Cook claimed the East Coast in the name of King George III as property of the British crown; it was given the name New South

Wales. Eleven ships with 1,350 people arrived in Australia to settle in 1788. Captain Arthur Phillip had instructions to establish the first British colony. Australia the new acquisition was mainly used as a penal colony from 1788 to 1823, with the next free settlers only arriving in 1793. Since this analysis looks at transcultural Anglophone literatures and films, the French Canadian history and involvement in colonial rule will not be addressed.

48. *Mabo v. Queensland* (commonly known as *Mabo*) was a decision of the High Court of Australia recognizing native rights of property for the first time. The status *Terra nullius* was abolished.
49. Damien Short, *Reconciliation and Colonial Power: Indigenous Rights in Australia* (Aldershot: Ashgate, 2008), 87. See also Michelle Grattan, ed., *Essays on Australian Reconciliation* (Melbourne: Bookman Press, 2000).
50. Short, *Reconciliation*, 87.
51. Eugenics refers to a scientific construct that believes in the possibility of improving the quality of the human species by either the extinction of "inferior" genetic material or the encouragement of reproduction of exclusive material. Short comments: "A central pillar of its thought concerned the responsibility of the modern state to improve a nation's racial stock via positive breeding programs." Short, *Reconciliation*, 89.
52. Short, *Reconciliation*, 92.
53. Coral Dow, "Sorry: The Unfinished Business of the Bringing Them Home Report," Background Note, Parliamentary Library Western Australia, February 2008, retrieved 27 May 2021 from https://www.aph.gov.au/About_Parliament/Parliamentary_Departments/Parliamentary_Library/pubs/BN/0708/BringingThemHomeReporthttp://www.aph.gov.au/About_Parliament/Parliamentary_Departments/Parliamentary_Library/pubs/BN/0708/BringingThemHomeReport, p. 1.
54. Aboriginal and Torres Strait Islander Healing Foundation. "Bringing Them Home 20 Years On: An Action Plan for Healing," 2017. Retrieved 20 October 2020 from https://healingfoundation.org.au/app/uploads/2017/05/Bringing-Them-Home-20-years-on-FINAL-SCREEN-1.pdf.
55. After 1940 the removal of children was governed by the General Child Welfare Law. All that was needed to take a child away from its family was a statement that it was in a state of neglect or destitution, with its future well-being unforeseeable. While the parents were left on the margins of society, their children were brought to institutions or schools, later even to (mainly white) foster families. Following the successful 1967 constitutional referendum, the commonwealth obtained concurrent legislative power over Aboriginal affairs with the states. In 1967, the Federal Office of Aboriginal Affairs was founded to support another change of tenor. Since the word "assimilation" had gained some unpopular connotation in recent years, the Aboriginal enterprise was from then on labeled under the umbrella term "integration." However, it was only a matter of renaming; the policy applied to the Aboriginal community did not change. Children were still removed from their families, although the Whitlam Labor Government elected in 1972 allowed removal applications and supported the establishment of Aboriginal legal services. In the aftermath, the family tracing and reunion agency Link-up (NSW) Aboriginal Corporation was founded. Although this agency has reunited many families up to the present day, it seems impossible to state the precise number of removed children.
56. Short, *Reconciliation*, 92.
57. Bringing them Home—report, 151.
58. Dow, "Sorry," 4.
59. The Victorian police were empowered to remove children until 1985. *Bringing Them Home Report*, 54.

60. See W. E. H. Stanner, *After the Dreaming* (Sydney: Australian Broadcast Commission, 1969).
61. See Stuart Macintyre and Anna Clark, *The History Wars*, new updated ed. (Carlton: Melbourne University Press, 2004), 171–91. They describe how the history wars found another "battleground" in schools and classrooms: anxiety toward which impression of the past should be conveyed to schoolchildren and students expanded the impact of the discussion about Australian history from the academic/political realm to history teaching and education as a "national concern" (173). The child was turned into a "symbol of the future" (172) of the nation, the youth into "a collective empty vessel waiting to be taught 'the Australian history'" (182).
62. Robert Manne, "Comment: The History Wars," *The Monthly*, November 2009, retrieved 21 March 2013 from http://www.themonthly.com.au/nation-reviewed-robert-manne-comment-history-wars-2119.
63. See Macintyre and Clark, *History Wars*.
64. Olick, *Politics of Regret*, 14.
65. Bain Attwood, *Telling the Truth about Aboriginal History* (Crow's Nest: Allen & Unwin, 2005), 15.
66. See Robert Manne, *Whitewash: On Keith Windshuttle's Fabrication of Aboriginal History* (Melbourne: Schwartz, 2003).
67. Macintyre and Clark, *History Wars*, 11.
68. Manne, *Whitewash*, 85.
69. See the National Museum of Australia, "The Bulletin," retrieved 10 September 2019 from https://www.nma.gov.au/defining-moments/resources/the-bulletin.
70. Henry Reynolds, *The Other Side of the Frontier: Aboriginal Resistance to the European Invasion of Australia* (Sydney: University of New South Wales Press, 1981), and Henry Reynolds, *Why Weren't We Told? A Personal Search for the Truth about our History* (Sydney: Viking, 1999).
71. See Mark McKenna, "Different Perspectives on Black Armband History," Parliament of Australia, No. 5, Research Papers, retrieved 21 March 2013 from http://www.aph.gov.au/About_Parliament/Parliamentary_Departments/Parliamentary_Library/pubs/rp/RP9798/98RP05#BLACK.
72. Anna Clark, "History in Black and White: A Critical Analysis of the Black Armband Debate," *Journal of Australian Studies* 26, no. 75 (2002): 1.
73. "This is perhaps the point of this Year of the World's Indigenous People: to bring the dispossessed out of the shadows, to recognize that they are part of us, and that we cannot give indigenous Australians up without giving up many of our own most deeply held values, much of our own identity—and our own humanity." See Paul Keating, "Redfern Speech," n.d., retrieved 12 February 2018 from https://www.creativespirits.info/aboriginalculture/politics/paul-keatings-redfern-speech. This speech was the closest to an apology to the Indigenous population of Australia that Australia witnessed until 2008. Keating's national story entailed images of Australian "triumph over . . . tribulations and prejudices to embrace diversity" and was faithful to Australia "flourish[ing] in the open, globalized economy." McKenna, "Different Perspectives," n.p.
74. McKenna quoting John Howards' Sir Thomas Playford lecture at Adelaide Town Hall on 5th July 1996. McKenna, "Different Perspectives."
75. McKenna, "Different Perspectives."
76. The Royal Commission into Aboriginal Deaths in Custody, for example, had published its final report on 15 April 1991. The commission was established to scrutinize the too common and too numerous deaths of Aboriginals in custody, and their findings and analyses suggested that the poor condition of the most part of Indigenous Australia

was a direct effect of colonization and its assimilation systems. For further information about this commission, see, e.g., http://www.naa.gov.au/collection/fact-sheets/fs112.aspx (retrieved 21 March 2013).
77. John Howard has recently critiqued the school history curriculum, which had been established by the Labor government led by Julian Gillard. His remarks are directed at the attempt to consider and serve Aboriginal representation and appreciation within history curricula in schools. *The Australian*, admittedly a pro Black Armband newspaper, quotes Howard in an online article: "The curriculum does not properly reflect the undoubted fact that Australia is part of Western civilization; in the process, it further marginalizes the historic influence of the Judeo-Christian ethic in shaping Australian society and virtually purges British history from any meaningful role." Dennis Shanahan, "John Howard Revives History Wars in Attack on Labor Curriculum," *The Australian*, 28 September 2012, retrieved 21 March 2013 from http://www.theaustralian.com.au/nation al-affairs/education/john-howard-revives-history-wars-in-attack-on-labor-curriculum/ story-fn59nlz9-1226482959782.
78. Historian Peter Read was one of the first academics to document the policies of forcible removal during the 1980s. In the volume's fourth reprint in 2006, he writes: "When I wrote 'The Stolen Generations' in 1981, child separation was scarcely talked about. Non-Aborigines said it couldn't have happened. The victims of separation thought it shameful to talk about their removal. They believed that maybe their parents hadn't been able to care for them properly, or worse still, didn't want them." Peter Read, *The Stolen Generations: The Removal of Aboriginal Children in New South Wales 1883 to 1969* (Sydney: Department of Aboriginal Affairs, 2006), available online at http://www.daa.nsw.gov.au/publications/StolenGenerations.pdf, 2.
79. *Bringing Them Home Report*, 1.
80. The report was presented to the Parliament on 26 May 1997. Up to this present day, it is the most successful government publication in Australian history. Short, *Reconciliation*, 93.
81. *Bringing Them Home Report*, 5.
82. "The assimilation policy persisted until the early 1970's and continues to influence public attitudes and some official practices today. Yet within a few years of the end of the Second World War, Australia, together with many other nations, had pledged itself to standards of conduct which required all governments to discontinue immediately a key element of the assimilation policy, namely the wholesale removal of Indigenous children from Indigenous care and their transfer to non-Indigenous institutions and families. . . . The Australian practice of Indigenous child removal involved both systematic racial discrimination and genocide as defined by international law." *Bringing Them Home Report*, 230–31, see also Dow, "Sorry."
83. *Bringing Them Home Report*.
84. Danielle Celermajer, "The Apology in Australia: Re-covenanting the National Imaginary," in *Taking Wrongs Seriously: Apologies and Reconciliation*, ed. Elazar Barkan and Alexander Karn (Palo Alto, CA: Stanford University Press, 2006), 156.
85. Dow quotes a response of the Commonwealth government under Prime Minister John Howard; Dow, "Sorry," 3.
86. Aboriginal and Torres Strait Islander Healing Foundation, "Bringing Them Home 20 Years On: An Action Plan for Healing," 2017, retrieved 20 October 2020 from https://healingfoundation.org.au/app/uploads/2017/05/Bringing-Them-Home-20-years-on-FINAL-SCREEN-1.pdf.
87. The conditions have been defined within the Indian Residential School Settlement Agreement, retrieved 15 February 2018 from http://www.thecanadianencyclopedia.ca/en/article/indian-residential-schools-settlement-agreement/.

88. Matt James, "A Carnival of Truth? Knowledge, Ignorance and the Canadian Truth and Reconciliation Commission," *International Journal of Transitional Justice* 6 (2012): 184.
89. In 2015, the Canadian TRC published its final report. It is available online at http://www.trc.ca/assets/pdf/Honouring_the_Truth_Reconciling_for_the_Future_July_23_2015.pdf (retrieved 11 September 2019).
90. TRC Canada, Truth and Reconciliation Commission of Canada. *Interim Report*. 10 December 2014. Retrieved 4 March 2018 from http://www.trc.ca/websites/trcinstitution/index.php?p=580, section "The International Context."
91. TRC Canada, *Interim Report*, section "The International Context."
92. As early as 1754, the *Department of Indian Affairs* for the British territory was founded. At first, it was established to support military and trade alliances that became even more common after 1763 and lasted until approximately 1820. The increasing immigration of settlers and decreasing food resources put pressure on the living conditions of both Indigenous and non-Indigenous inhabitants. Struggles for and over land possession characterized the relationship between settlers, governments, and the Native peoples in the following decades. See John S. Milloy, "A National Crime: The Canadian Government and the Residential School System," *Manitoba Studies in Native History* 11 (2014): 9.
93. Elizabeth Furniss, *Victims of Benevolence: The Dark Legacy of the Williams Lake Residential School* (Vancouver: Arsenal Pulp Press, 1995), 20.
94. Two initial forms of school were erected: "boarding schools" were supposed to teach basic skills like reading, writing, and mathematics, and they were located in proximity to the reserves of First Nations. The second type was made in the image of British "industrial schools," which were in fact trade schools. The latter were more centrally located. These two school forms targeted children from the age of seven onward. By 1890, the vast majority of schools were "industrial schools," since one idea had become even more persistent: progress of native communities could only be achieved if they adapted to a world of industry and agriculture. By 1830, school attendance was not yet mandatory for the First Nations, but this situation changed when problems with runaways and a decreasing number of enrollments threatened the "success" of the entire educational project. Another problematic aspect was that graduates immediately (re)turned to their initial culture and habits as soon as they left school, so the federal government offered land to graduates if they refrained from returning to their kin. However, all those measurements did not result in more Indigenous pupils attending schools. As a consequence, attendance became mandatory.
95. Resistance from within the schools was quite common. Many cases of fleeing pupils have been documented; some of these cases ended tragically. Elizabeth Furniss describes two examples: eight boys tried to escape the William Lake Residential School, seven of which were captured on their way. One boy, Duncan Sticks, managed to run into the forest, where his body was found shortly afterward thirteen kilometers away from the school. On another occasion, again eight boys arranged for a group suicide by eating poison. Seven survived; one boy, Augustine Allan, died. Although investigations were launched in the aftermath of these two incidents, the public interest was very limited. Furniss, *Victims of Benevolence*, 14–15.
96. The study quoted here is focused on the situation in British Columbia, namely on the Williams Lake Residential School, run by the oblates of St. Joseph's Mission. Since the quotation might suggest that the Catholic Church was the main partner of the government with regard to the schooling system, it is necessary to state that other churches have also been involved in the establishment and management of the schools, as this chapter will continue to show. Furniss, *Victims of Benevolence*, 13.
97. Milloy, *National Crime*, 19.

98. This development was stipulated in the British North American Act, Section 91:24. See Milloy, *National Crime*, 20.
99. Most Aboriginal acts were passed during the years 1867 to 1884.
100. Milloy, *National Crime*, 6.
101. Furniss, *Victims of Benevolence*, 21.
102. Milloy, *National Crime*, 54.
103. J. R. Miller, *Shingwauk's Vision: A History of Native Residential Schools* (Toronto: University of Toronto Press, 2011), 10.
104. Miller, *Shingwauk's Vision*, 15.
105. The federal government was mainly represented by the Department on Indian Affairs. Anglicans, Catholics, Presbyterians, and United Churches were running the schools for the most part. For further information, see Agnes Grant, *No End of Grief: Indian Residential Schools in Canada* (Winnipeg: Pemmican Publishing, 1992); and Miller, *Shingwauk's Vision*.
106. Milloy, *National Crime*, 37.
107. Furniss, *Victims of Benevolence*, 16.
108. Furniss mentions two figures that shed light on the circumstances in most of the schools: in fifteen schools in remote areas, 24 percent of the (ex-)students had died; in another, 69 percent of the inmates had died of tuberculosis. Furniss, *Victims of Benevolence*, 29. For a more precise account of the situation within the schools, see, e.g., TRC Canada, *Interim Report*; Grant, *No End of Grief*; and Miller, *Shingwauk's Vision*. Geoffrey Carr discusses the relationship between the very architecture and shape of the residential schools with the purported goal, namely, of segregation and assimilation. Geoffrey Carr, "Atopoi of the Modern: Revisiting the Place of the Indian Residential School," *English Studies in Canada (ESC)* 35, no. 1 (March 2009): 109–35.
109. See TRC Canada, *Interim report*, 1.
110. See TRC Canada, *Interim report*, 1.
111. Furniss, *Victims of Benevolence*, 30.
112. Furniss, *Victims of Benevolence*, 30.
113. Furniss, *Victims of Benevolence*, 30.
114. Julie McGonegal, "The Great Canadian (and Australian) Secret: The Limits of Non-Indigenous Knowledge and Representation," *English Studies in Canada* 35, no. 1 (March 2009): 67.
115. McGonegal, "Great Canadian," 70.
116. Jennifer Henderson and Pauline Wakeham, "Colonial Reckoning, National Reconciliation? Aboriginal Peoples and the Culture of Redress in Canada," *English Studies in Canada* 35, no. 1 (2009): 5.
117. For a comprehensive list and analysis of Canada's reconciliation initiatives, see Jennifer Henderson and Pauline Wakeham, eds., *Reconciling Canada: Critical Perspectives on the Culture of Redress* (Toronto: University of Toronto Press, 2013).
118. Henderson and Wakeham, "Introduction," 13.
119. The Canadian Encyclopedia, "Multiculturalism," retrieved 2 March 2018 from http://www.thecanadianencyclopedia.ca/en/article/multiculturalism/.
120. The Canadian Encyclopedia, "Multiculturalism."
121. TRC Canada, *Final Report*, chapter "Commission Activities."
122. See TRC Canada, *Final Report*, 29.
123. Rosemary Nagy, "The Truth and Reconciliation Commission of Canada: Genesis and Design," *Canadian Journal of Law and Society* 29, no. 2 (2014): 212.
124. Nagy, "Truth and Reconciliation Commission of Canada," 210.
125. TRC Canada, *Final Report*, 27.

126. Nagy, "Truth and Reconciliation Commission of Canada," 210.
127. Nagy, "Truth and Reconciliation Commission of Canada," 211.
128. Nagy, "Truth and Reconciliation Commission of Canada," 211, emphasis in the original.
129. Nagy, "Truth and Reconciliation Commission of Canada," 211.
130. David, *Past Can't Heal Us*, 1.
131. Kim Stanton, "Looking Forward, Looking Back: The Canadian Truth and Reconciliation Commission and the Mackenzie Valley Pipeline Inquiry," *Canadian Journal of Law and Society* 27, no. 1 (2012): 84.
132. See James, "Carnival of Truth"; Nagy, "Truth and Reconciliation Commission of Canada"; Robinder Kaur Sehdev, "Introduction: Residential Schools and Decolonization," *Canadian Journal of Law and Society* 27, no. 1 (2012): 67–73; Paulette Regan, *Unsettling the Settler Within: Indian Residential Schools, Truth-Telling and Reconciliation in Canada* (Vancouver: UBC Press, 2010); Sarah Keenan, "Moments of Decolonization: Indigenous Australia in the Here and Now," *Canadian Journal of Law and Society* 29, no. 2 (2014): 163–80.
133. Anne-Marie Reynaud, "Dealing with Difficult Emotions: Anger at the Truth and Reconciliation Commission of Canada," *Anthropologica* 56, no. 2 (2012): 57–59.
134. Reynaud, "Dealing with Difficult Emotions," 55.
135. Alfred Allan, "The South African Truth and Reconciliation Commission as a Therapeutic Tool," *Behavioral Sciences & the Law* 18, no. 4 (2000): 459–77; and Grunebaum, *Memorializing the Past*. Allan focuses on the effect that storytelling enables the transfer from object to subject by telling, voicing, and mourning, for after having gone through all the three stages, forgiving may be possible. In Allan's terms, forgiving is in this context the ultimate act of regaining subjectivity. Grunebaum discusses the (im)possibility of integrating excessive violence into a society's narrative. She analyzes places and rituals of memory with regard to South Africa and stresses time as an important factor when trying to rework the past.
136. Hirsch, "Ideational Change," 818.
137. Hirsch, "Ideational Change," 821.
138. Henderson and Wakeham, "Introduction," 17.
139. David, *Past Can't Heal Us*, 4.
140. Wulf Kansteiner, "Finding Meaning in Memory: A Methodological Critique of Collective Memory Studies," *History & Theory* 41 (May 2002): 180.
141. Mudrooroo, *Us Mob*, 175.
142. Mudrooroo, *Us Mob*, 176.
143. Matt James, "Neoliberal Heritage Redress," in *Reconciling Canada: Critical Perspectives on the Culture of Redress*, edited by Jennifer Henderson and Pauline Wakeham (Toronto: Toronto University Press, 2013), 44.
144. Regan, *Unsettling the Settler Within*, 11.
145. Roger I. Simons, "Towards a Hopeful Practice of Worrying: The Problematics of Listening and the Educative Responsibilities of Canada's Truth and Reconciliation Commission," in *Reconciling Canada: Critical Perspectives on the Culture of Redress*, ed. Jennifer Henderson and Pauline Wakeham (Toronto: University of Toronto Press, 2013), 130.
146. The final report of the TRC Canada remarks that there are some sparse occasions when former residential school attendants tell a different story about their experience in school. At times, former students give accounts of caring teachers, staff, and government or church representatives, expressing that they have enjoyed their stay. These accounts, however, are by far outweighed by negative experiences. See TRC Canada, *Final Report*.
147. Henderson and Wakeham, "Colonial Reckoning," 3.

148. See Peter Burke, "History as Social Memory," in *Memory, History, Culture and the Mind*, ed. Thomas Butler (New York: Blackwell, 1989), 97–113. See also Astrid Erll, *Kollektives Gedächtnis und Erinnerungskulturen: Eine Einführung. 3., aktualisierte und erweiterte Auflage* (Stuttgart: J. B. Metzler, 2017), 39.
149. Quoted in Henderson and Wakeham, "Colonial Reckoning," 14.
150. Stuart Hall, *The Fateful Triangle: Race, Ethnicity, Nation* (Cambridge, MA: Harvard University Press, 2017), 139.
151. See Ronald Niezen, *Truth and Indignation: Canada's Truth and Reconciliation Commission on Indian Residential Schools* (Toronto: University of Toronto Press, 2013); Regan, *Unsettling the Settler Within*; and James, "Carnival of Truth"; or Short, *Reconciliation*.
152. Keenan, "Moments of Decolonization," 169.
153. Reynaud, "Dealing with Difficult Emotions."
154. Reynaud, "Dealing with Difficult Emotions," 370.
155. Michael Rothberg, *Implicated Subjects: Beyond Victims and Perpetrators* (Stanford, CA: Stanford University Press, 2019).
156. Grunebaum, "Talking to Ourselves," 307.
157. Sam Boris Garkawe, "The South African Truth and Reconciliation Commission: A Suitable Model to Enhance the Role and Rights of the Victims of Gross Violations of Human Rights?" *Melbourne University Law Review* 27 (2003): 334–80. http://epubs.scu.edu.au/cgi/viewcontent.cgi?article=1020&context=law_pubs.
158. See Garkawe, "South African."
159. See Denise Cuthbert and Marian Quartly, "Forced Child Removal and the Politics of National Apologies in Australia," *American Indian Quarterly* 37, no. 1 (Winter/Spring 2013): 181–82.
160. See also Shurlee Swain and Margot Hillel, eds., *Child, Nation, Race and Empire: Child Rescue Discourse in England, Canada, Australia, 1850–1915* (Manchester: Manchester University Press, 2010).
161. Cuthbert and Quartly, "Forced Child Removal," 185.
162. Cuthbert and Quartly, "Forced Child Removal," 185, emphasis in the original.
163. See Cuthbert and Quartly, "Forced Child Removal," and Niezen, *Truth and Indignation*.
164. For further reading on the complex figure of the perpetrator, see Jonathan Dunnage, "Perpetrator Memory and Memory about Perpetrators," *Memory Studies* 3, no. 2 (2010): 91–94; Michael Rothberg, *The Implicated Subject: Beyond Victims and Perpetrators* (Stanford, CA: Stanford University Press, 2019).
165. Quoted in Henderson and Wakeham, "Colonial Reckoning," 16.
166. Cuthbert and Quartly, "Forced Child Removal."
167. Cuthbert and Quartly, "Forced Child Removal," 180.
168. The notion of "residential school syndrome" considers the traumatic effect that residential school attendance has had not only on its pupils but also on the communities. For a critical analysis of the "residential school syndrome" in terms of its structural racism, see Roland David Chrisjohn, Sherri Lynn Young, and Michael Maraun, *The Circle Game: Shadows and Substance in the Indian Residential School Experience in Canada* (Madison: Theytus Books, 2006).
169. James, "Carnival of Truth?" 197.
170. James, "Carnival of Truth?" 197.
171. Liz Conor, "A 'Nation so Ill-Begotten': Racialized Childhood and Conceptions of National Belonging in Xavier Herbert's *Poor Fellow My Country* and Baz Luhrmann's *Australia*," *Studies in Australasian Cinema* 4, no. 2 (2010): 97–113.

Chapter 2

CARNIVALIZING RECONCILIATION

Beyond the Victim Paradigm

Reconciliation discourses in Australia and Canada are at the same time enabling and problematic. They are empowering because they move memories and discourses in relation to forcible child removal and cultural reeducation from a marginalized position toward the discursive center. They offer the possibility for discussing previously undermined, subverted, forgotten, or oppressed narratives of colonial dominance. These processes inscribe Indigenous suffering and resilience into the national narratives of Canada and Australia. They have become central to an agenda and a discourse of new beginnings and mutual relations between the Indigenous and non-Indigenous populations of both countries. Truth commissions and official inquiries into colonial pasts indeed have the power to address some of the still prevailing imbalances and social hierarchies that have left their traces on contemporary, democratic societies such as Canada and Australia. Victims regain power over their story and locate themselves and their fates firmly within the national framework.

Yet, it is also true that there are no alternatives to the Euro-Australian and Euro-Canadian nation frame, and "sorry politics" instead reinforce national cohesion rather than facilitating discussion of versions of Indigenous independence and self-governance. It stands to reason that truth and reconciliation commissions and public inquiries are perceived as instances of collective therapy, healing and redemptive testifying rather than enablers of new beginnings and reconciliation. Because of the abandonment of legal procedures and the centering on the voice of the victim, the notion of victimhood and the identity template of the victim are prominent, and they become the primary framework of how to perceive indigeneity in both countries.

In order to tackle the disadvantageous aspects of victim-centeredness, law scholar Teresa Godwin Phelps offers an enticing perspective on such commissions and their paradigms.[1] Phelps reinvigorates Mikhail Bakhtin's notion of the carnivalesque in order to approach the vexed issue of victim-centeredness.[2]

> Considering the potential of the carnivalesque helps us to grasp the importance of a victim-centered approach in the Canadian context. Changing Canada's colonial relationship with the Indigenous communities—a relationship that has deprived those communities to pursue their own destinies—requires not just standard, elite driven methods that, in their design and operation, repudiate colonial assumptions. A victim-centered truth commission could be an important instance of this kind of purpose and focus.[3]

According to Phelps's view, reconciliation processes offer the possibility to radically reframe previously undermined, subverted, forgotten, or oppressed narratives of colonial dominance. Phelps describes the discursive spaces that reconciliation processes provide as instances where social and representational hierarchies are temporarily reversed. In Phelps's terms, they are carnivalesque, for they are short-lived, licensed instances of contesting well-established historical truths, national narratives, and political identities. Phelps's argument thus harks back to the canonical understanding that truth commissions are spaces of resistance to dominant understandings of historical truths and identities, but it also explains the lack of tangible outcomes at the end, as I will outline in this analysis.

Phelps revealingly introduces her analysis of the carnivalesque through a scene from Chilean writer Ariel Dorfman's play *Death and the Maiden*.[4] This play features a female protagonist, Paulina, who was raped and tortured by the very man who—years later—helps Paulina's husband with a broken tire. She gains control over the perpetrator, Dr. Miranda, and dwells on what she is able to do to and with him, now that the tables have turned. Paulina finally abandons thoughts of revenge and murder, yet she forcefully claims that her story (and many others) must be heard.

Phelps engages with what she describes as the empowering and subversive potentials of truth commissions and storytelling and, in response to that, carves out a carnivalesque perspective on alternative conceptions of justice. She firmly holds that these commissions enable a temporal reversal of power balances, of normative and formative frameworks of historical representation, and of constraints that history, society, and the law places on (formerly) marginalized people.[5] It is precisely this rhetoric of resistance and celebrating difference within a previously negotiated time frame that has made Bakhtin's concept so interesting for and applicable to contexts where national narratives and (trans)cultural identities are negotiated on a public platform.

Toward the end of the twentieth century, Mikhail M. Bakhtin proposed a model to describe how language constructs and controls the world around us, the roles we assume, and the position we hold within the social fabric. More precisely, Bakhtin explored the notion that language is a viable tool of social control, often being used as a vehicle of dominance and oppression. French Renaissance writer François Rabelais, as analyzed by Bakhtin, was able to use language's regulatory potential in a manner of resistance and treated the imaginative and descriptive power of literature as spaces to challenge existing patterns of social hierarchies and predetermined roles. The system of language thus is complicit in establishing norms and exerting control, but it also provides the means for resistance.

Bakhtin opens up a plausible dichotomy:[6] he posits an ecclesiastical and feudal culture—in his terms the dominant, normative, and formative culture—against a culture of resistance, subversion, and explorative contestation.[7] The latter is located within the sphere of carnival.

> Laughter and its forms represent . . . the least scrutinized sphere of the people's creation. . . . There was no room in this concept [of Romanticism] for the peculiar culture of the marketplace and of folk laughter with all its wealth of manifestations. Nor did the generations that succeeded each other in that marketplace become the object of historic, literary or folkloristic scrutiny. The element of laughter was accorded the least place of all in in the vast literature devoted to myth, to folk lyrics, and to epics.[8]

Bakhtin perceives the world as being composed of two antagonizing sides—an upside and a downside, one that is official, powerful, and impacts the daily life and social position of its subjects, the other that "of man, of human relations," and as such connected with "low culture."[9] The binary logic of this world, however, can be temporarily turned upside-down. He further elaborates as follows:

> A boundless world of humorous forms and manifestations opposed the official and serious tone of medieval ecclesiastical and feudal culture. In spite of their variety, folk festivities of the carnival type, the comic rites and cults, the clowns and fools, giants, dwarfs, and jugglers, the vast and manifold literature of parody—all these forms have one style in common: they belong to one culture of folk carnival humor.[10]

Carnival is to be understood as the expression of a countermovement to official formative rituals, rites, proceedings, and the normative frameworks that enable their performance. In Bakhtin's terms, a dominant social group, an elite, uses rituals and performances to strengthen their dominance, to disseminate their truths, frameworks of thinking, and hierarchical structures.

Carnival, accordingly, offers a space to play with these formative and normative conventions, to alter their meaning and explore their shape. Culture, in Bakhtin's sense, does not refer to racial, ethnic, or geographical collective units that share cultural inventory and engage in exchange, but rather to class and social status.

> All these forms of protocol and ritual based on laughter and consecrated by tradition . . . were sharply distinct from the serious official, ecclesiastical, feudal, and political cult forms and ceremonials. They offered a completely different, non-official, extraecclesiastical and extrapolitical aspect of the world, of man, and of human relations; they built a second world outside officialdom, a world in which all medieval people participated more or less, in which they lived during a given time of year.[11]

The carnivalesque is a mode of expressing, a style of language, of images, of settings that again counter what the leading classes hold dear and precious. Carnival belongs to the "world of ideals" and offers a secondary social space: "[Marketplace festivals] are the second life of the people, who for a time entered the utopian realm of community, freedom, equality, and abundance."[12] Carnival meant the temporal suspension of hierarchical precedence and dominance, while at the same time it celebrated inequality, difference, and reversals. Bakhtin's notion of the carnivalesque blurs the boundaries between literature (as fiction) and life (as "reality"):

> [T]he basic carnivalesque nucleus of the [folk] culture is by no means a purely artistic form nor a spectacle and does not, generally speaking, belong to the sphere of art. It belongs to the borderline between art and life. In reality, it is life itself, but shaped according to a certain pattern of play.[13]

The carnivalesque is a concept that describes carnival itself as a set of rituals, spectacles, narratives and identities that exist *alongside* and *in resistance* to the "feasts" of the feudal, dominant social group. These performances are resistances, contestations of existing patterns of social dominance.

Bakhtin further carves out a carnivalesque aesthetic, its particular linguistic qualities and specificities, for instance by highlighting that carnival relies on humor.[14] Laughter, in his understanding, is the quintessential capacity on which the enacting of carnival, of temporally reversed power structures, builds. The carnivalesque aesthetic is also characterized by the different personas on whose shoulders carnival unfolds. It is the clowns and fools, giants, dwarfs, and jugglers who embody carnival. These personas offer the possibility to explore resistance and renewal, to counter the existent, and to defy the superiors. It is through their eyes that we might see a world turned upside-down, it is through their voice that we can witness resistance to existing social structures and formative patterns, and it is through their stories that we can exchange positions, identities, and worldviews. Finally, it is through their laughter and the laughter they cause that self-empowerment unfolds, but only for a given period of time.

Bakhtin effectively established a theory of literary criticism in which he describes how new aesthetics—that of the bodily, the hedonist, the humorous, and the grotesque—have found their way into literary representation. Accordingly, the carnivalesque also describes a stylistic resistance to existing patterns, structures, and conventions of literary aesthetics and world-making. He emphasizes that the boundaries between art and life, between representation, perception, and these very formative structures under whose yoke the "low cultures" performed their carnivalesque resistance, are permeable. Consequently, Bakhtin not only describes a cultural practice—carnival—but also the style in which Rabelais and his contemporaries subverted canonical procedures of representation and literary aesthetics.

Carnival, the Carnivalesque, and Temporary Reversals

Teresa Godwin Phelps appropriates Bakhtin's notion of the carnivalesque in order to discern a vocabulary and describe the mechanisms of truth commissions and processes of reconciliation. She employs literary theory to derive a research perspective on victim-centered truth commissions. In her view, the act of storytelling framed by truth and reconciliation processes entails the possibility of a transitory reversal of social hierarchies and leads to empowerment through countering hegemonial understandings of national narratives and identities. In other words, Bakthin's carnivalesque and Phelps's reframing presuppose that the social space consists of norms that are reenacted, reiterated and reexperienced.

Such a perspective on society hinges on understanding the latter as a space that is constructed and held together by certain normative frameworks, collective norms that delimit this social realm, and the possibility to subvert these norms creatively through reiterating them.[15] Hence, collective and collectivized performances such as processes of reconciliation render these codes and contexts of communication visible and subversible.[16] Phelps's contextualization of the carnivalesque as an alternative conception of justice works by identifying reiteration and reversal as the fundamental principles of victim-centered processes of reconciliation.[17] The central figures of thought within particularly Phelps's carnivalesque are thus reiteration and reversal.[18]

The social realm consists of countless regulatory norms that "materialize" through the formation of identities. Identity portfolios (victim, Indigenous, non-Indigenous, etc.) that come with and are used by "politics of regret" are generated and contested through performance.[19] Against the backdrop of an overarching social hierarchy that is grounded in language and narrative, subjectivity is (also) constructed through discursive formations and image-making. With reference to Judith Butler, the body is the site where discursive practices and their effects on subjects become viable and visible. Discourse produces norms and regulations, and the markers that signify a compliance with discursive norms become ascribed to the body. In other words, the normative structures that produce social categories such as gender and race become perceivable and, thus, intelligible when they "manifest" on the body: clothing, habitus, and manners, for example, (re)present a statement of belonging or exclusion, of compliance with the normative structures or a defiance of them.

To assume an identity is thus defined by how compliant with the "law" the individual performs his or her assumed identity.[20] The "reiterative and citational practice" by which "discourse produces the effects that it names" evokes a normative framework that operates through inclusion and exclusion.[21] A failure to assume a social norm accordingly results in the production of an outside, a sphere of nonbelonging that, in turn, helps to reinforce categories of belonging, of complying with the "law."[22] It is precisely the shifting between compliance and failing to comply where the possibility of resistance is located. Although identity formations tend to "conceal the conventions" of which they are "a repetition," the force and power of those social norms depend on the incessant citation and reiteration of the latter.[23] Every citation bears the possibility of a change, of a different reproduction of the norm that it seeks to (re)construct.[24]

Performativity thus denotes a possibility of a resignification of the regulatory forces that shape identity formations and define belonging and exclusion. If the discursive formations that determine subject positions are, hence, sources of power *over* individuals, then their productive resignification by means of citation and iteration "with a twist" enables a person or a collective to gain power *for* someone: they open up a space for recalibrating power imbalances.[25] This space, in Butler's terms, is the social sphere itself. Phelps follows this trajectory and conceives the framework of truth and reconciliation commissions and their final reports as this space of contestation. It is in this manner that Phelps understands the empowering potential in victim-centered commissions.

A research perspective derived from Bakhtin's carnivalesque hence understands identities as ultimately performative. In the context of this study, social hierarchies (colonizer, colonized; Indigenous, non-Indigenous) are defined by historical representations and hard facts (colonization), but they are also linguistically and performatively constructed alongside social frameworks.[26] According to Phelps's carnivalesque, the "politics of regret," with their very visible publicity, enable the reversal of social and representational hierarchies through their reiteration and rededication in the process. Hence, a carnivalesque performance is a (re-)creation of reality that has undergone a change of paradigms that govern top and bottom, but not so much the in-between, of social hierarchies.[27] The "politics of regret," according to Phelps, shed a light on which values and positions in the social fabric a collective perceives as given, existent, collectively agreed on, or even hereditary in a sense, and how these categories have changed as a result of engaging with difficult historical legacies. These rather abstract descriptions of social forces and discursive formations will become more tangible when they are brought to bear on the two public apologies in Australia and Canada and—later in this study—on fictional explorations of reconciliation. As it has been established, the iterability, performativity, and contestability of identities is fundamental to carving out the mechanisms of a carnivalesque perspective on "sorry politics" in Australia and Canada.

I argue that there are, however, fundamental problems to Phelps's conception of empowerment through carnivalization in the context of Australian and Canadian reconciliation processes. For one, Bakhtin imagines the space of carnival to be one that enables its participants to counter how elites live and think. Thus conceived, it opens up a space where other identities, histories, and stories can be explored, experienced, mocked, and contested. In essence, carnival produces a counterideology to the prevailing one. Yet reconciliation in Canada and Australia is also complicit in actually strengthening discourses of national benevolence, because an apologizing state produces a counterideology to forcible removal and cultural reeducation. The temporary empowerment of Indigenous peoples unfolds alongside a state that reinvents itself as an agent of reconciliation, as will be outlined in more detail in the course of this work.

Moreover, Bakhtin emphasizes the polyphonic, the lively, at times mischievous, exploration of several identities, norms, and roles during carnival. He posits the sternness of feudal, official festivities—which are also hosted to further disseminate and vindicate the dominant ideology—against the playful, humorous, and occasionally grotesque character of the carnivalesque space. Mimicry and mockery function as diversion and temporary relief. Yet the "politics of regret" in Canada and Australia exist in their own solemnity, which can arguably be attributed to the traumatic nature of the matters discussed. Phelps translates the carnivalesque into a context that is characterized by suffering, guilt, trauma, and recognition, thus missing the lightheartedness of Bakhtin's grotesque, humorous, or mischievous temporal reversals. Truth and reconciliation processes also demand a certain attitude toward the stories told, toward the atrocities committed. There is no space in which to—lightheartedly or otherwise—*explore* the role of the victim, or of the survivor, or of the perpetrator whose story is by default excluded from the Canadian and Australian processes of reconciliation. Such at times painful but ultimately empowering forays into other identities and their entanglements will be reserved for literature and film, as will be shown in chapters 5–7.

What is more, Bakhtin imagines the marketplace as the venue where carnivalesque reversals of existing power structures occur. Within this space, true democracy appears to reign: there is, in Bakhtin's terms, no difference between spectators and participants, between actors and audiences:

> This temporary suspension, both ideal and real, of hierarchical rank created during carnival a special type of communication impossible in everyday life. This led to the creation of special forms of marketplace speech and gesture, frank and free, permitting no distance between those who came in contact with each other and liberating from norms of etiquette and decency imposed at other times.[28]

Accordingly, the space of the carnival does not know any "footlights," referring to the almost normative distinction between audience and actors in classical drama. Translated to our scenarios in Canada and Australia, this marketplace becomes the stage that the two commissions have provided to former victims and survivors. By extension, the entire public realm of Canada and Australia would fall under the category of the marketplace, since both processes of reconciliation claim to involve the general public. Furthermore, Phelps sees the narrative of the respective truth commission reports as spaces that resemble the notion of the marketplace.

This central place that Bakhtin envisages, however, appears to differ fundamentally from the enclosed and safe space that TRCs and their like provide. The marketplace is a spot where everyday life unfolds alongside artistic spectacles. The hearings conducted in Canada and Australia were public by definition, which means that the interested and concerned public was allowed and encouraged to come and bear witness. But they were also highly orchestrated and important to a certain political agenda. Media coverage assured that the stagings of the politics of redress were available to a large audience, but the emphasis on suffering and victimhood to an extent presupposed the roles that are available to Indigenous peoples. This public platform, the marketplace of alternative notions of justice, if we follow Phelps, was specifically designed for these processes, thus introducing its own norms to comply with. These spaces of truth-telling are emotionally and symbolically charged and resemble court structures rather than a common marketplace. Bakhtin understands the marketplace as the space where difference can be—at least temporarily—reversed and overcome. Truth commissions and inquiries, however, by default rely on dichotomies and antagonisms and their repeated reiteration. It does not become clear to which extent

Phelps engages with the notion of the marketplace; her emphasis solely rests on asserting the public-ness and performativity of processes of truth and reconciliation.

Moreover, a carnivalesque perspective on the processes of truth and reconciliation is certainly incomplete without taking into consideration what Amartya Sen calls "social identities":[29]

> And yet history and background are not the only way of seeing ourselves and the groups to which we belong. There are a great variety of categories to which we simultaneously belong. I can be, at the same time, an Asian, an Indian citizen, a Bengali with Bangladeshi ancestry. . . . This is just a small sample of diverse categories to each of which I may simultaneously belong. . . . Belonging to each one of the membership groups can be quite important, depending on the particular context. When they compete for attention and priority over each other . . ., the person has to decide on the relative importance to attach to the respective identities, which will, again, depend on the exact context.[30]

Here Sen describes the structural diversity of identities that we hold in ourselves. Identities do not simply exist in a singular form, and a "person has to make choices . . . about what relative importance to attach" to certain identities.[31] Particularly in the two contexts discussed here, the rhetoric of reconciliation draws on a reiteration of difference; of binary oppositions like Indigenous and non-Indigenous (settler) majority. These oppositions are, in Sen's words, "singular identities": they pretend to be monolithic, schematic, intelligible, but they appear in this manner only because they are discursively constructed to serve a certain identity-political agenda.[32] Reconciliation processes come with the promise of granting recognition to the formerly marginalized through their public mechanisms, and a neat division between Indigenous and non-Indigenous seemingly enables such recognition in the first place. As a consequence, the notion of absolute (cultural) difference is translated into the discursive space that reconciliation provides. Thus conceived, difference is validated on a public scale but at the cost of simplifying cultural realities. Charles Taylor writes that

> [t]he demand for recognition [on behalf of minority or "subaltern" groups, in some forms of feminism, and in what is today called the politics of "multi-culturalism"] is given urgency by the supposed links between recognition and identity, where this latter term designates something like a person's understanding of who they are, of their fundamental defining characteristics as a human being. The thesis is that our identity is partly shaped by recognition or its absence, or by the *mis*recognition of others, and so a person or group of people can suffer real damage, real distortion, if the people or society around them mirror back to them a confining or demeaning or contemptible picture of themselves.[33]

Processes of reconciliation are dependent on performances of identities, and in order to connect the questions of identity formation to the issues under scrutiny—forcible relocation, cultural reeducation—these identities are essentialized. Identities that were formerly excluded, marginalized, and misrepresented, as Taylor argues, receive recognition within the overarching narrative and performative framework of the national. Following Phelps's argument, through the "politics of regret" and their public performance of reconfiguring national history, such recognition can be temporarily granted. The latter, however, occurs in fictions of fixed identity portfolios.

In this manner, reconciliation processes cater to advocates of cultural essentialism and authenticity, and they rely on the rather simplistic identity schemes that form the structural basis for reconciliation. A neat division into binaries like "us" and "them," superior and inferior, seems entirely possible and necessary. As a result of the temporal foregrounding of and emphasis on certain identities—Indigenous, non-Indigenous, victim—the illusion of solitary, singular identities arises. Individual and collective identities are by default mutually constructed and transculturally entangled, in particular in postcolonial contexts such as Canada and Australia, yet Phelps's carnivalesque—or Bakhtin's, for that matter—cannot accommodate the shiftiness of identities beyond the notion of empowerment through reversal. Temporary reversals in Phelps's conception may for a given time upend social hierarchies and identities, but they result in equally schematic reversed identities, predicated on victim and victimhood.

Consequently, reconciliation as described by Phelps does not engage in problematizing essentialized identities constructed in the wake of reconciliation, and Phelps's carnivalesque is unable to account for cultural realities that point at their intrinsic entanglements. In order to render the carnivalesque a more productive category to analyze reconciliation, I propose that its mechanisms and aesthetics need to be set in productive dialogue with a transcultural research perspective. The carnivalesque can enable us to describe the entanglements and constructed-ness of cultural identities and provide the perspective through which to analyze the potpourris and entanglements rather than essences that were invoked at the beginning of this chapter. A transcultural perspective does not understand culture and related identities as fixed and stable, and the carnivalesque provides us with the means to describe these processes that cut across received cultures and identities. Transcultural theory devaluates models of describing cultures as homogenous and unambiguous, for a transcultural analysis seeks to carve out what renders them nuanced and heterogeneous.[34] A transcultural lens attempts to describe processes of negotiation and conflict, of exchange between, across, and within cultures, and strives to highlight the dynamics of cultural production.[35] Transcultural research perceives culture not as essential but as an articulation, and it can thus in most productive ways correspond with the performativity of identity that is at the heart of Bakhtin's carnivalesque.[36] What we delineate as cultures are ensembles of images, symbols, signs, and signifiers that are historically constructed and performed in the present, and thus are constantly undergoing reformulations and resignifications.[37]

The public apologies of 2008 were emotionally charged political performances designed to signal a change of paradigms, acts of resignifying the discourse position of both countries' Indigenous populations and politics. If carnival is to be perceived as a countermovement to official rituals, rites, and proceedings, it can be argued that a government apology is a ritual, a political rite with the potential to suspend hierarchies for a specific time frame and to performatively take responsibility for state-sanctioned crimes.[38] In the following, I undertake a close reading of both apologies through a carnivalesque lens, as such a reading prepares the ground for my subsequent analyses of a selection of fictions of reconciliation.

Enchanted National Solipsisms: The Public Apologies in Canada and Australia

Harboring restorative and performative power, at least theoretically, government apologies have become part of political repertoires and "politics of regret." The act of apologizing has increasingly become a viable tool of memory and identity politics, since such a gesture is an effective display of emotions that comes without any binding provisions or legal requirements. Apologies are performances through which identification with the nation frame, composed of stories and images that demarcate "what makes one nation different from all other nations," can be renegotiated and reoriented.[39] This specific ritual chimes with a nation's "spiritual" quality, its organic structure that comes into being and becomes visible through the performance of its underlying narratives and structures.[40]

It is not surprising that, in what we call the era of human rights, public apologies have been issued in a variety of political and historical contexts.[41] Deeply embedded in the postwar international consciousness is the famous *Kniefall* of Willy Brandt, which honored victims of and signaled responsibility for the atrocities committed during the Third Reich. Lending expression to a change of political paradigms, the rise to economic prominence and political stability of (Western) Germany in the aftermath of World War II can also be attributed to Brandt's iconic gesture and performance of humility and responsibility.[42] In 1995, Queen Elizabeth II signed a Royal Assent to an Act of Parliament that recognized the harm brought upon the Maori people of New Zealand as a result of the Treaty of Waitangi. With this act, Queen Elizabeth II indirectly apologized for the injustices committed.[43] In 2006, the Canadian government under Prime Minister Stephen Harper offered a full apology for the so-called Chinese Head Tax. This tax was implemented to keep Chinese families from immigrating into Canada after the completion of the Canadian Pacific Railway.[44] As of today, Aboriginal Australians have received several apologies from "state governments, police forces, and churches for the . . . policy of child removal," but to grant a government apology was an issue of controversial debates, as the discussion of Australia's "history wars" in this study has shown.[45] The current Canadian prime minister Justin Trudeau and his Liberal government issued a plethora of apologies since being in office. Trudeau apologized to the descendants of Asian passengers who were denied entry into Canada in 1914. He further demanded that Pope Francis apologize for the involvement of the Catholic Church in the Canadian residential school scheme, but to no avail. Trudeau granted posthumous exonerations to six Indigenous chiefs who were hanged by the colonial government.[46] In 2018 he asked members of the Inuit community to accept his apology for "the colonial, purposeful mistreatment of Inuit people with tuberculosis."[47] However, some governments adamantly refrained from issuing any apology, notwithstanding political pressure from the international community. The Howard government in Australia had managed to refuse to deliver an apology for decades. The Turkish government still abstains from offering a statement of regret for the genocide of Armenian people around time of World War I.[48]

In the following, the Australian and Canadian public apologies will be introduced in more detail: Canada, as we have already seen, chose a specific and very memorable rendering of the apology speech, while public life in Australia virtually came to a halt when Kevin Rudd's gesture of atonement was broadcast. Both apologies pursue a similar rhetorical strategy with regard to Australian and Canadian memory politics; they frame the systems of cultural reeducation as "sad chapters" in an otherwise positive account of national history. Both governments apologized for the harm done and promised to create a climate that would prevent repetition, yet the apology gestures come with no political or legal concessions. An analysis of these apology performances through a carnivalesque lens brings their shortcomings to the fore: while the apologies temporarily reverse power hierarchies, they rely on overly schematic identity portfolios—an "us and them" logic—that simplify the complex and ambiguous interrelation of historical and contemporary transcultural identities.

When Saying Sorry Must Be Enough

The governmental apologies issued by Kevin Rudd (Australia) and Stephen Harper (Canada) formed instrumental parts of both countries' "politics of regret":[49]

Those who might have thought that after years of feet-dragging the moment would have passed could not have been more wrong; even people who had expressed cynicism about the apology or who were not sympathetic to the new government found themselves profoundly involved and affected, often despite themselves. Over the following days and weeks, the press, radio and face-to-face conversations were filled with ordinary Australians' deeply emotional responses to hearing the words, "I say sorry" given the pride of place by the national government and an unprecedented hope that this indeed might be a turning point in Australia's political culture.[50]

When properly staged, the use of formal yet empathetic language and the almost formalistic sincerity that an apology issued by the head of government promises has, renders an apology a popular gesture. In Butlerian jargon, an apology works through the citation and simultaneous recalibration of political culture—what was once accepted practice (forcible removal and cultural reeducation) is now deemed outrageous and harmful. "[T]hose who apologize," as Eva Mackey provocatively argues, are supposed to "emerge after the apology ritual as washed clean and innocent, feeling redeemed, future-looking and unified."[51] An apology, hence, signals a performative reversal of paradigms with regard to the political relation to the (formerly) oppressed:

> The relationship between the state and Indigenous groups has been and continues to be an interconnected but profoundly unequal one, with each successive generation negotiating terms of association on an uneven and seemingly overdetermined political field. Apologies, in their own specific ways, can help to reorient that field, as political actors recognize.[52]

Apologies are "performative summar[ies] of the character of a nation" through which a community is invited to recognize how its collective norms formed the necessary conditions for wrongs to occur, and then expresses shame for those laws and practices.[53] Indeed, for a specific period of time, such rituals affect the political landscape and reorient it: as part of the reconciliation package, Canadian prime minister Stephen Harper's gesture of atonement was agreed upon after the settlement of 2007. The timing had to be sorted out, as did the nature and content of this apology, but after some deliberation across party lines and with Phil Fontaine, national chief of the Assembly of the First Nations (Harper exchanged letters with Fontaine to get a grasp of how the apology should look and sound in the eyes and ears of those addressed), the speech was finally delivered on 11 June 2008.[54] The Great Canadian Silence had been temporarily lifted.

To further emphasize the importance of this gesture, Harper's apology performance was meticulously choreographed: Indigenous leaders entered the parliament, and they were greeted with several minutes of standing ovations.[55]

They were placed in the middle of the parliament; their chairs were arranged to form a circle.[56] This image of Canada's natives in the center of the House of Commons, awaiting and receiving the apology firsthand, is very powerful, as it signaled that the government in general, and Stephen Harper in particular, assigned great importance to this performance. Moreover, through this arrangement, Indigenous peoples were visually rendered *central* to Canada and its national identity. Harper thereby pulled off a veritable political stunt, and set a precedent: this venerable place is usually not open to the public once in session, and it is not government business as usual to have Indigenous leaders reply to government policies and performances. The presence of non-members required consent, and a motion was drafted to ensure

> [t]hat, notwithstanding any standing or special order or usual practices of the House, after statements by ministers today, the House resolve itself into committee of the whole to allow Phil Fontaine, National Chief of the Assembly of First Nations, Patrick Brazeau, National Chief of the Congress of Aboriginal Peoples, Mary Simon, President of the Inuit Tapiriit Kanatami, Clem Chartier, President of the Métis National Council, and Beverley Jacobs, President of the Native Women's Association of Canada to make a statement in response to the ministerial statement of apology to former students of Indian residential schools; that the Speaker be permitted to preside over committee of the whole; after these statements, the Chairman shall leave the chair and the House shall adjourn to the next sitting day.[57]

It passed unanimously, and as a result, Indigenous representatives were very effectively placed in the middle of Canada's House of Commons and at the "heart" of the nation. At the end of Harper's speech, the audience and parliament once again gave standing ovations. For almost fifteen minutes, Stephen Harper had apologized in English and French, and said "we are sorry" in Ojibway, Cree, and Inuktitut.

Canadian prime minister Harper delivered this very special apology performance only a few weeks after his Australian colleague, Kevin Rudd, issued his apology to the Indigenous populations of Australia. On 13 February 2008, the day had finally come for Australia's Indigenous peoples: Prime Minister Rudd apologized publicly to the Indigenous populations of Australia in general, and to the members of the Stolen Generations in particular. "Some have asked—why apologize?" queries Kevin Rudd five minutes into his speech, immediately providing an answer:[58] the apology marked a powerful attempt to address the "past mistreatments" of Aboriginal people on a public scale, and to atone for their effects. Rudd's speech was praised as a "masterful piece of political rhetoric,"[59] with this particular apology setting out to represent the "inner transformation" that Australia had gone through in recent years, a change largely due to the process of reconciliation.[60]

This apology was the culmination of a long-lasting struggle of dealing with and acknowledging Australia's historical legacies in relation to its Aboriginals.[61] It marked a preliminary end to a collective endeavor to evoke and facilitate what Lea David calls "proper, morally driven remembrance."[62] The climate for offering apologies and being supported in doing so had thus significantly changed, and Kevin Rudd had introduced the matter of apologizing into his election campaign. Rudd honored the apology—or understood that this was the right time to deliver it—such that he made it his primary order of government business. Rudd's gesture of atonement was his first act as newly elected prime minister, and of the forty-second Australian parliament. The visitor's gallery was crowded on the day he delivered his apology, and as the camera moved over this gallery, one could see that many Indigenous people were present. A few chairs were placed at the outer walls of the hall, and due to the enormous interest in Rudd's apology, every last one was taken. Contrary to the Canadian setting, however, Indigenous representatives were confined to the galleries, which, like balconies, hover over the heads of the politicians.[63] As a result, Australia's Aboriginals, although central to the apology performance as recipients, and in total contrast to the Canadian setting, remained an abstract mass at the outskirts of the room. This setting triggers an interpretation that Australia's Indigenous now represent a part of the nation but still occupy a marginalized position within the national framework.

Publicity was guaranteed, in any case. Rudd's speech was broadcast nationally, and without interruption, by all major TV networks. Public viewings were held all over Australia, and thousands attended these gatherings. Companies and schools organized mass screenings, while 1.3 million Australians watched from home, resulting in record-breaking viewership.[64] To underline the importance that this gesture carried, Catherine Philpott quotes a member of the Australian Indigenous community who witnessed Rudd's apology:

> And I watched and I had tears in my eyes, 'cause I reckon, all those people, all those people who are now vindicated by that sorry. It means that we weren't lying about our own history, or what we went through, it wasn't a lie, we didn't dream it, it wasn't a nightmare.[65]

In a similarly contemplative mood, First Nations leader Phil Fontaine remarked in response to Stephen Harper's apology:

> Our peoples, our history, and our present being are the essence of Canada. The attempt to erase our identities hurt us deeply, but it also hurt all Canadians and impoverished the character of this nation. We must not falter in our duty now. Emboldened by this spectacle of history, it is possible to end our racial nightmare together. The memories of residential schools sometimes cut like merciless knives at our souls. This day will help us put that pain behind us.[66]

In the wake of the apology, the traumatic historical experiences of Australia's and Canada's respective Indigenous populations were narrativized and validated on a public platform. These apologies, alongside the processes of both commissions, mandated history to effectively validate Indigenous suffering under the regime of forcible cultural reeducation. By means of this gesture, the attempts to eradicate indigeneity not only became public knowledge but were also set in relation to the Australian and Canadian present. The two apologies discussed here entail a carnivalesque, an empowering moment, because they, as Fontaine puts it, "embolden" Indigenous peoples, because this "spectacle of history" temporarily renders them the center of attention.

Sad Chapters Turn New Beginnings?

How can we speak of empowerment through a simple act of validating the historical experience of a certain group? Within a limited time frame, Indigenous histories and suffering are most inherent to the Australian and Canadian national fabric and are addressed in the very spaces where democracy is performed. Through highly scripted performances that are aimed at triggering affect, Indigenous histories are paraded in front of the nation for didactic purposes, as a critical engagement with traumatic pasts supposedly renders collectives less prone to repeat the "mistakes of the past."[67] In reference to Fontaine's statement quoted above, apologies are spectacles, because they are meticulously staged and orchestrated events designed to temporarily reverse power hierarchies and shift the relevance of Indigenous histories from being at best marginalized to forming part of the respective national narratives:

> Australians are a passionate lot. We are also a very practical lot. For us, symbolism is important but, unless the great symbolism of reconciliation is accompanied by an even greater substance, it is little more than a clanging gong. It is not sentiment that makes history; it is our actions that make history. Today's apology, however inadequate, is aimed at righting past wrongs. It is also aimed at building a bridge between Indigenous and non-Indigenous Australians—a bridge based on a real respect rather than a thinly veiled contempt.

Rudd adumbrates his understanding of "changed paradigms" and "new beginnings," but I argue that he endows this apology with powers that it does not have because it remains a rhetorical gesture. Past wrongs cannot be righted with one speech, especially as the framing of the apology decontextualizes the Stolen Generations from larger questions pertaining to treaty rights, land ownership, and self-government. What is even more problematic here is the binary opposition of the "us and them" logic: Rudd paints a picture of an Australian society that is divided along the lines of ethnic belonging, of indigeneity and "the rest," obviously the majority. This particular framing of Australian society is indicative of one of the pitfalls of the "politics of regret." Two broadly distinguished groups are called upon through the apologies, and the utterly heterogeneous and by its own definition multicultural composition of Australian society is simply referred to as "Australians," or subdivided according to the qualifiers "Indigenous" and "non-Indigenous." This broad division caters to noncomplex antagonisms and oversimplifies the identity-political landscape. Indigeneity in general, and Aboriginality in particular, are reduced to mnemonic referents, to signal words in the nation's grand historical exercise of reconciliation. For rhetorical purposes, these categories are resurrected, yet these neat divisions ignore collective realities:

> Not all Indigenous cultures are the same, even within the Australian context. . . . Yet non-Indigenous Australians and media implicitly assume that Indigenous Australians all hold the same views. . . . These assumptions of homogeneity serve to further marginalize the Indigenous minority.[68]

Apologies run the risk to in fact present homogenized ideas of collectivity as given, even as desirable, and blank out other cultural forces and identities that are also involved in the negotiations and performances of Australian and Canadian national identity. What is more, the two apologies invoke the idea that Australian and Canadian societies were homogenous and united even in their desire to reeducate the native. Kevin Rudd speaks of a "settler society" when referring to Australia, and although this qualification is historically accurate, it renders reconciliation solely a matter to be solved between "black" and "white" Australia. Stephen Harper remains nebulous when he addresses "all Canadians" and refers to "our life as a country," thus introducing group schemata that cope over the internal heterogeneity of "immigrant nation" Canada. Harper's apology also opens up a dichotomy between First Nations, Inuit, and Métis on the one hand and the government of Canada on the other. Eva Mackey even argues that this rhetoric of the compartmentalization "reproduces colonial relational structures in powerful and subtle ways" instead of fundamentally changing existing obstacles to improved relationships, such as the recognition of treaties.[69] In this setting, the Canadian government becomes an abstract perpetrator force, as do the churches that were centrally involved in carrying out the system of assimilation and cultural reeducation:

> Most schools were operated as joint ventures with Anglican, Catholic, Presbyterian and United churches. The Government of Canada built an educational system in which very young children were often forcibly removed from their homes and often taken far from their communities. Many were inadequately fed, clothed and housed. All were deprived of the care and nurturing of their parents, grandparents and communities. First nations, Inuit and Métis lan-

guages and cultural practices were prohibited in these schools. Tragically, some of these children died while attending residential schools, and others never returned home.[70]

The repetitive use of passive constructions such as "were taken" or "were deprived" renders perpetrator involvement structural, not personal, and to some extent frames it as a natural force that came over Canada's Indigenous peoples. The purpose of this rhetorical move is quite clear: the practices enabling the systems to operate are unequivocally condemned and marked as inappropriate while simultaneously being transferred into an abstract past. The wording of the speeches refers to the categories "nation" and "culture" as solipsistic and auto-reinforcing frameworks of imagining the collective, constructing, as Melissa Nobles suggests, national "membership."[71] Apologies are hence "at worse cynically self-serving":[72]

> To the extent that we understand identity-claims as rallying points for political mobilization, they appear to hold out the promise of unity, solidarity, universality. As a corollary, then, one might understand the resentment and rancor against identity as signs of a dissention and dissatisfaction that follow the failure of that promise to deliver.[73]

Moreover, the scope of the apology is strategically limited, arguably in order *not* to bring about tangible political change but to reframe the national narrative in a specific manner:

> By limiting the apology and redress to residential schools, the official apology carved out a very small part of a much broader process of cultural genocide that was ... deeply interconnected with the theft of land that was pivotal to building the nation-state.[74]

Also to be considered in this context is the suggestion Kevin Rudd makes that it would be possible to envisage a "future where all Australians, whatever their origins, are truly equal partners, with equal opportunities and with an equal stake in shaping the next chapter in the history of this great country, Australia."[75] Rudd relishes his vision of a community of Australians that is no longer characterized by internal racial division—an outright utopia that is reduced to absurdity by the implementation of political programs such as the Australian Intervention or the Canadian refusal to honor treaties with its First Nations population.[76] He foresees a future of mutual partnership and understanding, a goal that is as unlikely as it is absolute. Rudd concludes his apology by emphasizing that, with this performance of regret, "we might transform the way the nation thinks about itself."[77] Noel Pearson, an Aboriginal leader, is quoted as having summed up his stance on the historical act of saying sorry as follows: "Blackfellas will get the words, the whitefellas keep the money."[78]

These performative politics are thus indicative of a different understanding of the functions and modalities of remembering national pasts. The gesture of atonement helps to "identif[y] the past as a major, if not only source of harm" on a collective scale, and thus furthers an understanding why the legacies of the past still have a powerful bearing on the present but effectively excludes any explorations of how this present can be changed for Aboriginal people.[79] As Australia "wrestl[es] with our soul," and Rudd's gesture of remorse expresses the "mood of the nation," the apology seeks to restore "moral capital" on behalf of the apologizing group.[80] Apologies thus are an integral aspect of "politics of regret," of constructing a new national narrative, and "[t]his official narrative suggests that although founded on colonial violence, the nation is at last moving towards its logical conclusion—a fair, open, and tolerant society."[81]

Yet the creation of such a new narrative can be detrimental to any attempts of Indigenous claims to political agency, because it is the state that facilitates reconciliation and decides on its agenda. It is necessary to consider how the Australian apology is used as an opportunity to represent the state and the nation as agents of nonrepetition, of new beginnings and reversed representational hierarchies in relation to Indigenous histories. Rudd unequivocally emphasizes that

> [t]here is a further reason for an apology as well: it is that reconciliation is in fact an expression of a core value of our nation—and that value is a fair go for all. There is a deep and abiding belief in the Australian community that, for the stolen generations, there was no fair go at all. There is a pretty basic Aussie belief that says that it is time to put right this most outrageous of wrongs. It is for these reasons, quite apart from concerns of fundamental human decency, that the governments and parliaments of this nation must make this apology—because, put simply, the laws that our parliaments enacted made the stolen generations possible.[82]

In this manner, Kevin Rudd frames the systems of forcible removal as "fully lawful" at the time of their exertion, yet Australians "must face the facts" that assimilation policies were not implemented for the benefit of Australia's Indigenous peoples:

> We, the parliaments of the nation, are ultimately responsible, not those who gave effect to our laws. And the problem lay with the laws themselves. As has been said of settler societies elsewhere, we are the bearers of many blessings from our ancestors; therefore we must also be the bearer of their burdens as well. Therefore, for our nation, the course of action is clear: that is, to deal now with what has become one of the darkest chapters in Australia's history.

Pursuing a similar strategy, Canadian cultural reeducation and strategic assimilation policies are contained and rendered a "sad chapter" of national history in Harper's statement of atonement:

> Therefore, on behalf of the government of Canada and all Canadians, I stand before you, in this chamber so central to our life as a country, to apologize to aboriginal peoples for Canada's role in the Indian residential school system. To the approximately 80,000 living former students, and all family members and communities, the government of Canada now recognizes that it was wrong to forcibly remove children from their homes, and we apologize for having done this. We now recognize that it was wrong to separate children from rich and vibrant cultures and traditions, that it created a void in many lives and communities, and we apologize for having done this.[83]

Both apologies thus pursue the same strategy in order to mark the two systems as wrongful and unlawful practices.[84] Harper as well as Rudd frame both systems as "wrongs of the past,"[85] "inflicting profound grief, suffering and loss"[86] and "ha[ving] caused great harm."[87] In the process and through such a rhetorical framing, decades-long and state-sanctioned mistreatment of Indigenous peoples is condensed to the narrative of forcible removal, compartmentalized as a "thing of the past" and used as a platform to reinvent the state.[88] Akin to a carnivalesque logic deprived of its revolutionary momentum, the legacies of forcible removal are performatively lived out on a public stage—"the carnival of reconciliation"—brought to the attention of "the people" and subsequently relegated to the past. The carnivalesque aspect of these apologies—the fact that they are politically sanctioned and temporarily granted instances of reversed hierarchies—in the Canadian context leads to the conclusion that, once carnival is over, histories, identities, and truths are reverse-engineered to once again become part of Canada's inventory of "glaring omissions" and "celebratory rewritings."[89] Jennifer Henderson and Pauline Wakeham unearth the following telling remark by Stephen Harper:[90]

> Harper asserted: "We are one of the most stable regimes in history. There are very few countries that can say for nearly 150 years they've had the same political system without any social breakdown, political upheaval or invasion. We are unique in that regard. We also have no history of colonialism." . . . While Harper's claims regarding the absence of any "social breakdown" or "invasion" in Canada alone offer a whitewashing of the foundational imperialist invasion upon which the nation is predicated as well as the state's long-standing policies of race-based discrimination, his outright denial of the "history of colonialism" punctuated the speech with a particularly remarkable form of erasure.[91]

Harper stated this in 2009, one year after his apology. Yves Frenette recognizes a specific strategy that the conservative Harper government pursued during its time in office, and which was arguably employed within the apology as well. Harper's apology is part of the "conservative programme to reinvent the nation" and is complicit in the quest to "disentangle national identity from multicultural values."[92] Through the phrasing of the apology, Canada's troubled history with its native peoples is by no means "hot, controversial, of burning concern and in the making"; the apology is more interested in maintaining the illusion of a stable, coherent and benevolent national identity.[93] As Mathew Dorrell further outlines, the Canadian nation and its nationals as imagined by the Harper government "require the continual production of others on whom we 'practice' benevolence."[94] Accordingly, the narrative of "benevolent" Canada is by no means reframed or attacked, it is instead brought to its seemingly (teleo)logic conclusion within the Canadian nation frame.

In a similar vein, Kevin Rudd romanticizes the power of apologizing and simultaneously reconciles the legacies of the "Stolen Generations" with the image of "benign Australia":

> Let [the apology] not become a moment of mere sentimental reflection. Let us take it with both hands and allow this day, this day of national reconciliation, to become one of those rare moments in which we might just be able to transform the way in which the nation thinks about itself, whereby the injustice administered to the stolen generations in the name of these, our parliaments, causes all of us to reappraise, at the deepest level of our beliefs, the real possibility of reconciliation . . . : reconciliation across all Indigenous Australia; reconciliation across the entire history of the often bloody encounter between those who emerged from the Dreamtime a thousand generations ago and those who, like me, came across the seas only yesterday; reconciliation which opens up whole new possibilities for the future.[95]

Rudd calls upon an Australian national identity that encompasses settler identities and histories as well as First Australians:

> Let us turn this page together: Indigenous and non-Indigenous Australians, government and opposition, Commonwealth and state, and write this new chapter in our nation's story together. First Australians, First Fleeters, and those who first took the oath of allegiance just a few weeks ago. Let's grasp this opportunity to craft a new future for this great land: Australia. I commend the motion to the House.[96]

Here he weaves together the stories of Aboriginal Australians, settlers and their descendants, as well as multicultural Australia as represented by those who recently became Australian citizens. State apologies evidently are performances of what can be termed—in reference to Frank Schulze-Engler's "enchanted solidarities" with formerly oppressed groups on the part of academic, intellectual, and political communities—enchanted national solipsism.[97] On the one hand, apologies do indeed signal a fundamental reversal of power hierarchies—the state becomes the vicarious repentant for crimes committed in national history and thus empowers the formerly marginalized with this gesture of atonement and recognition. On the other hand, the state gets to temporarily reinvent itself as the agent of reconciliation, while it can continue to hinder the actual processes (in the Canadian case) by withholding documents, ignoring treaties, or passing racially discriminatory laws (the Intervention in Australia). The nation—in the Australian and Canadian cases—can reconcile itself with its assimilationist legacy because the nation is able to appease itself and its seemingly changed paradigms through an apology. Thus conceived, national apologies are only at a first glimpse empowering to Australia's and Canada's Indigenous peoples. They are instead instances where forcible cultural reeducation can be mended with national imaginaries of benevolence, human rights bastions, and multiculturality, thus carnivalizing their good intentions. In their specific framing, these apologies do not allow for explorations of perpetrators and perpetration, structural or individual. On the contrary, they relegate power imbalances and persistent political disadvantage to a distant past, as it has already been argued, thus precluding a fundamental reworking of the historical complex of colonialism itself, as well as its enduring practices.

The "politics of regret" seem to be built on the notion of two opposing cultures that seek to find common ground to form new relationships. Diana Taylor observes two facets of culture: one that creates the illusion of semantic stability and "self-reinforcing" cultural identities, and one that is inherently political, even "politiciz[ed]," and characterized by the "strategic use of cultural symbols."[98] The processes of reconciliation and the public apologies of Stephen Harper and Kevin Rudd are characterized by a specific, namely reductive, use of symbolic action and political rhetoric in order to create precisely this illusion of stable identities. A carnivalesque perspective on reconciliation akin to Phelps's notion picks up on these schematic identities and identifies the empowering potential as embedded in the binary reversal—margin becomes the center, the voiceless receive a voice, the powerful display gestures of remorse. The roles, as we have seen, are also predetermined, the binary reversal licensed by the state of the facilitator of reconciliation. In this manner, reconciliation is state sanctioned and effectively not a bottom-up initiative. This carnivalesque reconciliation is very static. Instead, I propose to reconsider what is at the core of Bakhtin's idea of carnivalesque reversal: the (playful) exploration of the other by fools and tricksters who paint outside the lines that reconciliation provides, providing their audience with imaginations of perpetrators and perpetration, of victims who turned the tables on those who harmed them, or bring to our attention the plurifold transcultural entanglements that a nuanced engagement with Indigenous cultural reeducation ultimately bear witness to. The carnivalesque mechanisms after all are not limited to reversal but also entail contestation and exploration. The latter lose their grit when remaining confined to and being preformed as victim-centered.

In the following analyses of literary texts and feature films, Bakhtin's notion of the carnivalesque will be reconnected to narrative fictions and their creative ways of world-making and exploring identities. As has been cautioned, to ascribe an ultimately liberating and empowering quality to processes of reconciliation is to ignore the pitfalls of essentialism that they bring with them. The ambiguous nature of truth commissions and the settings they provide result in monoliths, yet they can work as catalysts for processes of negotiation that are unavailable to political settings. Schulze-Engler states the following with regard to world war literature in former colonies:

> Representations of experiences of global war in Indigenous literature are more than just mnemonic minority reports: Indigenous literature negotiates these challenges [of globalized modernities and war memory as a contested site], explores issues that have not been voiced in public discourse yet and wrestles with myths of national identity and Indigenous warriorhood that continue to shape Indigenous and non-Indigenous perceptions of contemporary indigenality alike.[99]

Translated into our scenario of Australian and Canadian reconciliation processes, this means that the national container within which reconciliation is constructed and perceived, as well as the corresponding identities and frameworks of representation, are limited by ethics and politics, whereas the artistic space allows the artist to venture further, to dig deeper, and to foresee identities, histories, and truths unavailable to official, institutionalized processes.

The fictional narrative itself holds a specific position within (trans)cultural processes. More precisely, one can describe a "coherently distinct cultural role" that is attributed to fiction.[100] This mode of imagination is framed by culturally embedded frameworks of representation, such as culturally "specific" arrangements, encoding, and representation, and is in turn an important part of *doing* culture: fictional narratives draw on these seemingly preestablished conventions, but at the same time have the power and possibilities to alter these conventions. Cultural processes—such as reconciliation—become visible through the analysis of formative narrative structures that govern these narratives, as well as formative "master narratives" and seminal discourses that are further explored by fictional narratives. They are, in this sense, the "counting out . . . of the contents of accumulated wisdom" of a given collective, a "thesaurus of resources" and "shared treasures."[101] Seen in this light, fictions are attributed with a certain "exploratory power."[102] They unfold "possible worlds" and impossible ones; these worlds are evoked as narratively constructed yet intelligible possibilities as well as contestations, mockeries, and reversals.[103] Narratives and discourses of the past are also able to form alliances and instigate group cohesion across boundaries:[104] the production and articulation of narratives about the past construct discursive spaces. Within these spaces, groups construct themselves and their relation to others through narrating their past.

Although it may seem indeed trivial and self-evident to reconnect Bakhtin's carnivalesque to textual analysis, such an analytical lens applied to a highly contested identity-political (con)text offers new critical insights. As it has been shown, the scripted framework of reconciliation strategically limits the identity templates available and presupposes the outcome: a reconciled society. This reconciliation is achieved through reconciling with Australian and Canadian history of forcible removal, and not through fundamental political changes. The carnivalesque lens that I carve out is sensitive to transcultural dynamics, and helps to identify not only simplistic binary identity templates such as victim/perpetrator and Indigenous/non-Indigenous but exposes them as strategic fictions, or "lies that bind" as Kwame Anthony Appiah would have it.[105] My carnivalesque, I argue, remains attentive to aesthetics and politics in fiction, yet it pays attention to and helps describe how cultures cut across each other, become entangled, and leave behind scripted realities.

This study will now venture into the artistic space of narrative fiction in order to further analyze what reconciliation might look like to Indigenous and non-Indigenous artists. The victim paradigm that reconciliation structurally produces plays an important part in the discussion of fictional takes on and engagements with reconciliation. Indeed, as will become clear, the victim takes on several roles: Joseph Boyden's (2005, Canada) and Gail Jones's (2007, Australia) historical novels undertake a revisionist writing of history, thus countering the notion of Indigenous peoples as excluded from national narratives and marking histories and identities as subject to negotiation and imagination. Kim Scott's *Benang* (1999, Australia) and Tomson Highway's *Kiss of the Fur Queen* (1998, Canada) translate perpetrators into protagonists and highlight the intimacy of violence and cultural reeducation. Perpetrators as well as their victims do not remain abstract forces and misguided policies but are represented in their closeness to home. All the sources discussed in what follows employ the carnivalesque in some form, either as a figure of thought and a means to counter schematic histories and identities or as an aesthetics of resistance.

Notes

1. Teresa Godwin Phelps, *Shattered Voices: Language, Violence, and the Work of Truth Commissions* (Philadelphia: University of Philadelphia Press, 2006).
2. Mikhail M. Bakhtin, *Rabelais and His World* (Bloomington: Indiana University Press, 1984).
3. Matt James, "A Carnival of Truth?" *International Journal of Transitional Justice* 6, no. 2 (2012): 188.
4. Ariel Dorfman, *La Muerte y la Doncella* (Madrid: Ollero & Ramos, 1995).
5. See Phelps, *Shattered Voices,* in particular chapter 4.
6. Bakhtin, *Rabelais and His World*, 3.
7. Bakhtin, *Rabelais and His World*, 4.
8. Bakhtin, *Rabelais and His World*, 4.
9. Bakhtin, *Rabelais and His World*, 6.
10. Bakhtin, *Rabelais and His World*, 4.
11. Bakhtin, *Rabelais and His World*, 5–6.
12. Bakhtin, *Rabelais and His World*, 9.
13. Bakhtin, *Rabelais and His World*, 7.
14. Bakhtin, *Rabelais and His World*, 5, 8, 9.
15. See Milton Singer, "Search for a Great Tradition in Cultural Performances," in *Performance: Critical Concepts in Literary and Cultural Studies*, ed. Philip Auslander (London: Routledge, 2003), 57–71.
16. J. L. Austin and James O. Urmson, eds., *How to Do Things with Words* (Cambridge, MA: Harvard University Press, 1955), and John R. Searle, *Speech Acts: An Essay in the Philosophy of Language* (Cambridge: Cambridge University Press, 2012).
17. Language as (re)iteration is associated with poststructural philosophy and is in particular connected with Jacques Derrida. See Janelle Reinelt and Joseph R. Roach, "Introduction," in *Critical Theory and Performance*, ed. Janelle Reinelt and Joseph R. Roach (Ann Arbor: University of Michigan Press, 2007), 1–17; Stuart Hall and Paul du Gay, *Questions of Cultural Identity* (Los Angeles: Sage, 2011); and James Loxley, *Performativity* (London: Routledge, 2007).
18. See Anne Enderwitz, "Ereignis und Wiederholung als Koordinaten von Geschlecht und Gedächtnis," in *Iterationen: Geschlecht im kulturellen Gedächtnis*, ed. Sabine Lucia Müller and Anja Schwarz (Berlin: Wallstein Verlag, 2008), 37.
19. Judith Butler, *Bodies That Matter: On the Discursive Limits of "Sex"* (New York: Routledge, 1993). See also Chris Barker, *Cultural Studies: Theory and Practice* (Los Angeles: Sage, 2012), 90–95.
20. Barker, *Cultural Studies*, 2.
21. Barker, *Cultural Studies*, 2.
22. Barker, *Cultural Studies*, 14–15.
23. Barker, *Cultural Studies*, 13.
24. Barker, *Cultural Studies*, 13–14.
25. See Butler, *Bodies That Matter*, and Auslander, "Introduction," 15.
26. Theatricality offers a mode of understanding social interaction through performance, through its productive reiteration. Theater not only reproduces social (inter)action for the purpose of making it visible but also offers a vocabulary that allows us to describe aspects of social life, from cultural manifestations such as rituals and commemorations to everyday interaction, can be grasped in terms of a certain "vocabulary" that derives from drama studies. See Richard Schechner, *Performance Studies: An Introduction* (London:

Routledge, 2002), and Richard Schechner, *Performance Theory* (London: Routledge, 2009).
27. See Graham F. Thompson, "Approaches to Performance: An Analysis of Terms," in *Performance: Critical Concepts in Literary and Cultural Studies*, ed. Philip Auslander (London: Routledge, 2003), 138–52; and Elinor Fuchs, "Presence and Revenge of Writing: Re-thinking Theatre after Derrida" in Auslander, *Performance*, 109–18.
28. Bakhtin, *Rabelais and his World*, 10.
29. Amartya Sen, *Identity and Violence: The Illusion of Destiny* (London: Penguin, 2006), xii.
30. Sen, *Identity and Violence*, 19.
31. Sen, *Identity and Violence*, 19.
32. Sen, *Identity and Violence*, 20–21.
33. Charles Taylor, *Multiculturalism and the Politics of Recognition* (Princeton, NJ: Princeton University Press, 1994), 1.
34. See Andreas Lagenohl, ed., *Transkulturalität: Klassische Texte* (Bielefeld: Transcript, 2015), 12.
35. See Frank Schulze-Engler and Sissy Helff, eds., *Transcultural English Studies: Theories, Fictions, Realities* (Amsterdam: Rodopi, 2009).
36. See Lagenohl, *Transkulturalität*, 13.
37. See Erika Fischer-Lichte, *Performativität: Eine Einführung* (Bielefeld: Transcript, 2013).
38. For further reading, see Daniel Cuypers et al., eds., *Public Apology between Ritual and Regret: Symbolic Excuses on False Pretenses or True Reconciliation out of Sincere Regret?* (Amsterdam: Rodopi, 2013).
39. Neil Levi, "No Sensible Comparison? The Place of the Holocaust in Australia's History Wars." *History & Memory* 19, no. 1 (2007): 125. See also Benedict R. O.'G Anderson, *Imagined Communities: Reflections on the Origin and Spread of Nationalism* (New York: Verso, 2016).
40. Ernest Renan, "What Is a Nation?" in *Nation and Narration*, ed. Homi K. Bhabha (London: Routledge, 1990), 10.
41. For a concise account of various examples of apologies in international contexts, see Jennifer Lind, *Sorry States: Apologies in International Politics* (Ithaca, NY: Cornell University Press, 2008).
42. See Melissa Nobles, *The Politics of Official Apologies* (Cambridge: Cambridge University Press, 2008).
43. See Stephen Vines, "Queen to Say Sorry to the Maori People," *The Independent*, 2 July 1995, retrieved 1 December 2020 from http://www.independent.co.uk/news/queen-to-say-sorry-to-the-maori-people-1589370.html.
44. Each potential immigrant had to pay a head tax in order to receive permission to enter the country. Each spouse or sibling was charged with an even greater amount of money. This policy was in place from 1885 to 1923. See, for example, Prime Minister of Canada Stephen Harper, "PM Harper Offers Full Apology for the Chinese Head Tax," retrieved 1 December 2020 from http://pm.gc.ca/eng/news/2006/06/22/prime-minister-harper-offers-full-apology-chinese-head-tax.
45. See Nobles, *Politics of Official Apologies*, 7.
46. BBC News, "Does Trudeau Apologize Too Much?" 28 March 2019, retrieved 1 December 2020 from https://www.bbc.com/news/world-us-canada-43560817.
47. CBC News, "Trudeau Apologizes for Colonial, Purposeful Mistreatment of Inuit with Tuberculosis," 11 March 2019, retrieved 1 December 2020 from https://www.cbc.ca/news/canada/north/trudeau-apology-tuberculosis-iqaluit-1.5047805.
48. There is an ongoing discussion whether the massacre and forcible relocation of Armenians are to be regarded as genocidal in scope and nature. Whereas most countries clearly con-

sider it to fall under the category of genocide, the Turkish government adamantly refuses to recognize this claim.
49. For further reading, see, in particular, Nobles, *Politics of Official Apologies*; Thomas Cauvin, *Public History: A Textbook of Practice* (New York: Routledge, 2016); and Cuypers, *Public Apology*.
50. Danielle Celermajer, *The Sins of the Nation and the Ritual of Apologies* (New York: Cambridge University Press, 2009), 212.
51. Eva Mackey, "The Apologizer's Apology," in *Reconciling Canada: Crotocal Perspectives on the Culture of Redress*, ed. Jennifer Henderson and Pauline Wakeham (Toronto: University of Toronto Press, 2013), 49.
52. Nobles, *Politics of Official Apologies*, 37.
53. Danielle Celermajer, "The Apology in Australia: Re-covenanting the National Imaginary," in *Taking Wrongs Seriously: Apologies and Reconciliation*, ed. Elazar Barkan and Alexander Kern (Palo Alto, CA: Stanford University Press, 2009), 155.
54. For more background information, see Willow J. Anderson, "'Indian Drum in the House': A Critical Discourse Analysis of an Apology for Canadian Residential Schools and the Public's Response," *International Communication Gazette* 74, no. 6 (2012): 571–85.
55. The Australian Government, "Apology to Australia's Indigenous Peoples," retrieved 1 December 2020 from http://www.australia.gov.au/about-australia/our-country/our-people/apology-to-australias-indigenous-peoples; the Government of Canada, "Indian Residential School Statement of Apology—Prime Minister Stephen Harper," retrieved 1 December 2020 from http://www.aadnc-aandc.gc.ca/eng/1100100015677/1100100015680.
56. The text of the apology is available online; The Government of Australia, retrieved 1 December 2020 from https://www.australia.gov.au/about-australia/our-country/our-people/apology-to-australias-indigenous-peoples. The more interesting part of Rudd's apology can be seen on a version that is accessible via YouTube, retrieved 1 December 2020 from https://www.youtube.com/watch?v=MDvome0bCXs.
57. Stephen Harper, "Apology," available online as transcript and video at the homepage of the Government of Canada, retrieved 1 December 2020 from http://www.aadnc-aandc.gc.ca/eng/1100100015677/1100100015680.
58. There is a video of the apology on the official homepage of the government of Australia. However, this particular video is considerably shorter than the actual apology speech, and the transcript also omits a large part of Rudd's apology. The Government of Australia, retrieved 1 December 2020 from https://www.australia.gov.au/about-australia/our-country/our-people/apology-to-australias-indigenous-peoples. The more interesting part of Rudd's apology can be seen on a version that is accessible via YouTube, retrieved 1 December 2020 from https://www.youtube.com/watch?v=MDvome0bCXs.
59. Celermajer, *Sins of the Nation*, 210.
60. Celermajer, *Sins of the Nation*, 213.
61. To recapture: the very controversially debated *Bringing Them Home Report* had been published more than a decade before, and since then, many collective demonstrations of support for the Indigenous cause—the national Sorry Day with thousands walking the Sydney Harbor Bridge, for example—claimed public attention.
62. Lea David, *The Past Can't Heal Us: The Dangers of Mandating Memory in the Name of Human Rights* (Cambridge: Cambridge University Press, 2020), 4.
63. For a map of the Australian Parliament and House of Representatives, see https://www.aph.gov.au/About_Parliament/House_of_Representatives/House_of_Representatives_Seating_Plan (retrieved 1 December 2020).

64. Catherine Philpott, Nikola Balvin, David Mellor, and Di Bretherton, "Making Meaning from Collective Apologies: Australia's Apology to Its Indigenous Peoples," *Peace and Conflict: Journal of Peace Psychology* 19, no. 1 (2013): 35.
65. Philpot et al., "Making Meaning," 42. Philpott et al. have conducted a research inquiry into how an official apology changes the perception of the other group, and how it effects intergroup relationships. The focus lies on the responses to the Rudd apology by Indigenous people. They conducted interviews in order to obtain insights about how an apology may be truly meaningful to a specific group.
66. Phil Fontaine, quoted in the Encyclopedia of Canada, "Government Apology to Former Students of Indian Residential Schools," retrieved 1 December 2020 from http://www.thecanadianencyclopedia.ca/en/article/government-apology-to-former-students-of-indian-residential-schools/.
67. See David, *Past Can't Heal Us*, 6.
68. Nobles, *Politics of Official Apologies*, 35.
69. Mackey, "Apologizer's Apology," 49.
70. Harper, "Apology."
71. Nobles, *Politics of Official Apologies*, 36–37.
72. Nobles, *Politics of Official Apologies*, 302.
73. Butler, *Bodies That Matter*, 188.
74. Mackey, "Apologizer's Apology," 50.
75. Kevin Rudd, "Statement of Apology," retrieved 1 December 2020 from http://www.australia.gov.au/about-australia/our-country/our-people/apology-to-australias-indigenous-peoples.
76. For further reading on the Australian intervention, see, e.g., Australians Together, "The Intervention: A Controversial Policy Package," 7 October 2020, retrieved 1 December 2020 from https://australianstogether.org.au/discover/the-wound/the-intervention/.
77. Rudd, "Apology."
78. Noel Pearson, quoted by BBC News, "Australia Apology to Aborigines," 13 February 2008, retrieved 13 March 2018 from http://news.bbc.co.uk/2/hi/7241965.stm.
79. Nobles, *Politics of Official Apologies*, 27–28.
80. Philpott et al., "Making Meaning," 35.
81. Geoffrey Carr, "Atopoi of the Modern: Revisiting the Place of the Indian Residential School," *English Studies in Canada (ESC)* 35, no. 1 (March 2009): 109–35.
82. Rudd, "Apology."
83. Harper, "Apology."
84. Unlawful, in this context, refers not only to issues of law and jurisdiction but also to morally desirable and righteous behavior.
85. Rudd, "Apology."
86. Rudd, "Apology."
87. Rudd, "Apology."
88. See also Mackey, "Apologizer's Apology."
89. Mathew Dorrell, "From Reconciliation to Reconciling: Reading What 'We Now Recognize' in the Government of Canada's 2008 Residential School Apology," *English Studies in Canada* 35, no. 1 (2009): 29.
90. In the passage quoted here, Stephen Harper replied to a journalist's question if he would be concerned that the role of Canada in the world would further diminish in the future. Jennifer Henderson and Pauline Wakeham, "Colonial Reckoning, National Reconciliation? Aboriginal Peoples and the Culture of Redress in Canada," *English Studies in Canada* 35, no. 1 (2009): 3.
91. Henderson and Wakeham, "Colonial Reckoning," 1.

92. Yves Frenette, "Conscripting Canada's Past," *Canadian Journal of History* 49 (Spring 2014): 52–53.
93. Dorrell, "From Reconciliation to Reconciling," 30.
94. Dorrell, "From Reconciliation to Reconciling," 31.
95. Rudd, "Apology."
96. Rudd, "Apology."
97. Frank Schulze-Engler, "Once We Were Internationalists? Postcolonialism, Disenchanted Solidarity and the Right to Belong in a World of Globalized Modernity," *Reworking Postcolonialism: Globalization, Labour and Rights*, ed. Pavan Kumar Malreddy (Basingstoke: Palgrave Macmillan, 2015), 19–35.
98. Diana Taylor, "Transculturating Transculturation," *Performing Arts Journal* 13, no. 2 (May 1991): 91.
99. Schulze-Engler, "Once We Were Internationalists?" 19.
100. Richard Walsh, "The Pragmatics of Narrative Fictionality," in *A Companion to Narrative Theory*, ed. James Phelan and Peter J. Rabinowitz (Malden: Blackwell, 2005), 152.
101. Walsh, "Pragmatics of Narrative Fictionality," 101.
102. Walsh, "Pragmatics of Narrative Fictionality," 151.
103. For further reading, see, for example, John Divers, *Possible Worlds* (Florence: Taylor & Francis, 2014), or Rod Girle, *Possible Worlds* (Hoboken: Taylor & Francis, 2014).
104. Michael Rothberg, *Multidirectional Memory: Remembering the Holocaust in the Age of Decolonization* (Stanford, CA: Stanford University Press, 2009).
105. Kwame Anthony Appiah, *The Lies That Bind. Creed, Country, Colour, Class, Culture* (London: Profile Books, 2016).

Chapter 3

BEYOND THE PARTISAN DIVIDE

Transcultural Recalibrations of National Myths in
Joseph Boyden's *Three Day Road* and Gail Jones's *Sorry*

In 2005, writer Joseph Boyden—allegedly of Irish, Scottish, Ojibwe, and Nipmuk decent[1]—published a historical novel that instantly became a bestseller. *Three Day Road* tells the story of two young Cree friends who join the Canadian Expeditionary Force to fight in the theaters of the Great War. World War I was perceived as a great disaster in many participating countries. In Canada, however, there is a specific reason that it is referred to as the Great War.[2] The successful participation of the Canadian Expeditionary Force marked the beginning of its disengagement from England. The powerful national narrative of the Canadian "nation forged in fire," born in the trenches of Europe, relates back to this understanding of Canadian engagement in World War I.[3] Boyden's novel opens up this glorifying narrative of the birth of the Canadian nation toward Indigenous participation and thus "corrects" it, as Indigenous soldiers and their achievements in war did not play an important role in public perceptions of the Great War.[4]

Australian author and scholar Gail Jones has—at first sight—chosen a similar revisionist approach to Australia's national history. In her historical novel *Sorry*, Jones paints a gruesome picture of a British settler family that sets out to bring civilization to the "dark" continent. In lieu of a public apology—Kevin Rudd had not yet delivered his—Jones tasks historical fiction with the correction of Australia's sometimes celebratory national history. In an interview, she further elaborates:

> Each country negotiates its own highly specific history; however, the issue of remembering or forgetting is central to all. I am reminded of Milan Kundera's

famous statement: "The struggle of man against power is the struggle of memory against forgetting." The first responsibility is to remember what it serves the state to repress; the second to recall, to tell and to consider the recovered history through the lens of justice. My novel allegorizes the "forgetting" of the so-called Stolen Generations in Australia, those Aboriginal children forcibly removed from their families by order of state policy from about 1900 to 1970. The anguish and suffering of these people is the basis for a collection of heart-rending testimonies delivered to the Australian Parliament in May 1997. One of the recommendations of the report was that the government of the day offer a formal apology to Indigenous Australians for the wrongs done to them. The [Howard Liberal] government refused to say "sorry," a matter that was rectified [recently] when the new Labour government in Australia, under the leadership of Kevin Rudd, issued an apology at the opening of parliament. This did not necessarily atone or repair the hurt, but it did signal a new initiative for reconciliation and dialogue between Aboriginal and other Australians.[5]

Jones claims that it is imperative that Australians face their country's guilt and break their silence regarding the issue of the "Stolen Generations." *Sorry* is a literary intervention into the discourses relating to Australia's historical guilt, and it strives to be a literary apology itself.

Three Day Road and *Sorry* engage in the revision of formative national narratives, but with different outcomes. While Boyden's novel becomes an experimental and experiential site of negotiating historical representations and transcultural identities, Jones's text literally aches under the burden the author's "good intentions" place on the narrative. *Sorry* posits a wrecked settler family, adorned with an intertextual use of Shakespeare and a specific rendering of "high culture," against a voiceless and contourless Aboriginal community where true human dignity, in Jones's terms, resides. Contrary to Jones's good intentions, Aboriginal Australia is silenced by her text, because the novel does not feature any viable Aboriginal agency. While *Three Day Road* introduces carnivalesque characters into the text in order to highlight transcultural entanglements, thus pluralizing identity conceptions, *Sorry* frequently slips into stereotypical and schematic representations of identities and histories. Jones's novel is an example of how the imperative to correct, reverse, and contest may lead to the opposite effect. Before Jones's "sorry novel" is discussed in more detail, Joseph Boyden's novel will send the reader back to the trenches of World War I, where it makes a claim about Indigenous presence in and value to Canadian national narratives.

Mnemonic Imposters: Joseph Boyden's *Three Day Road*

While Canadian reconciliation was in full bloom, the so-called Boyden controversy ensued. As a highly visible public intellectual, Canadian Indigenous author Joseph Boyden had attracted a lot of attention in recent years. Serving as an honorary witness to the TRC Canada, he came to be represented as the "handsome, light-skinned media darling who told folkloric-sounding stories about his background and filled up so many column inches and so much airtime."[6] Eric Andrew-Gee, writer for the *Globe and Mail*, describes Boyden's transcultural identity-portfolio as highly beneficial to his acclaim as a writer and public persona:

> He was also, avowedly, of mixed ancestry—raised in suburban Toronto by Catholic parents amidst vague family lore of Indigenous blood. In an age of reconciliation, this mixed background was an asset: Boyden came to be seen as a "shining bridge," as one Indigenous scholar called him, able to mediate between white and Indigenous, at a time when that task seemed more urgent than ever.[7]

From this mixed background, Boyden has drawn a lot of his outspokenness, with his position as a Canadian aligning several cultural poles granting him authority as a commentator on colonial legacies and reconciliation.

Meanwhile, questions about his claimed Indigenous ancestry never lapsed into silence. In 2017, a controversy about his cultural origins arose as a result of an investigation launched by the Aboriginal Peoples Television Network (APTN).[8] Jorge Barrera initiated a nationwide inquiry into whether Joseph Boyden's claim to Indigenous ancestry was in fact fabricated. Studded with genealogical inquiries into Boyden's family records, Barrera's article represents Boyden's repeatedly voiced references to his indigeneity as fictitious, fraudulent, and simply baseless. An outrage accompanied these revelations, for Canada's most successful Indigenous writer, honorary witness to the TRC, was now suspected of being a fraud.[9] In an essay in his defense, Joseph Boyden outlines how he himself sees his connection to indigeneity:

> I'd also been especially vocal for the last years in speaking about Indigenous Canadian issues, all of them sacred, so many of them painful. . . . For the past few years, when the media came calling, whether it be the CBC or *Globe and Mail* or a tiny radio station in the rural North with a listenership of 50, I was more than willing to stand up and be vocal. As an honorary witness [to the TRC Canada,] my personal mandate is to speak in my role as a writer and public voice about the dark clouds and frightening basements of our shared history, and the abomination that was residential schools and the ongoing intergenerational tsunami of trauma. I look back now and I can see that I took to this role with the zealotry of a true believer.[10]

Here, Boyden insinuates that Indigenous identity is a question of identification, of believing, and not of blood relations or identity cards. He emphasizes the good intentions that motivated his actions and barely conceals his pride to have been considered a public voice of Canada's Indigenous peoples. What he does not say here, revealingly, is that he wrongfully laid claim to indigeneity by descent. Boyden was very versed in deflecting the occasional accusations, as Andrew McGee outlines:

> Boyden knew about the rumours, and even addressed them occasionally—but only in ad hominem fashion, playing the same identity politics others were playing with him. "It's never First Nations people who say I'm not Indian enough," Boyden told Charles Foran . . ., "Never a woman either. Always some white guy."[11]

To make these rumors an issue of his accusers, particularly with such a smug reference to the old white guy paradigm, certainly fueled the outrage that accompanied his fall from grace. McGee argues that Boyden was heavily criticized for accepting prize money—$5,000 for the McNally Robinson Aboriginal Book of the Year for *Three Day Road*—but also for the stellar publishing record of 500,000 sold copies, and for the speaking invitations and other literary prizes that followed. Boyden stood to gain significantly from posing as an Indigenous writer.

With his in all probability baseless claim to an Indigenous heritage, Joseph Boyden joined the ranks of other mnemonic imposters who laid claim to a cultural trauma that was not theirs: in the 1940s, it was revealed to Canada and the world that Grey Owl, potentially the first famed conservationist pursuing a First Nations lifestyle and strongly identifying as such, was born an Englishman.[12] From this scandal, the neologism "grey-owling" emerged to denote Indigenous identity fraud. Australia was rattled by the revelations that the 1995 winner of the Miles Franklin Award, Helen Demidenko, "falsified her family history" as a Ukrainian descendant who braved both Stalin's communists and the Nazi invasion.[13] Her novel *The Hand That Signed the Paper* (1994) was critically acclaimed and very successful before her deceit was uncovered. In 1996, Aboriginal canonical writer and lobbyist Mudrooroo's Indigenous identity was called out as fraudulent by his own sister, and in subsequent years he experienced a total exclusion from the literary and academic establishment.[14] Enric Marco, a Catalan mechanic, posed as a Holocaust survivor for many decades. In 2005, it was revealed that he was a fraud. Some Spanish newspapers at the time called for his suicide.[15]

Arguably most famously, however, Swiss journalist Daniel Ganzfried discovered that Benjamin Wilkomirski, the world-renowned author of the Holocaust memoir *Fragments: Memories of a Wartime Childhood*—published in German in 1995 and subsequently translated into twelve languages—was a fraud.[16] The publication of his memoir "had caused a sensation":

> It purported to be the story of a young Jewish child born in Latvia whose family was slaughtered in a massacre in Riga, and who was taken to the death

camps of Poland, where he somehow survived the war. Readers were horrified by the descriptions of the vile conditions in the camp, but they were also moved by his description of a child who could not understand that this was not how life was. The Binjamin in the book is so young that the camps are all he knows: hell is his only reality.[17]

Fragments quickly was labeled a masterpiece of Holocaust literature that derives its unique power from the innocent perspective of the child narrator trying to make sense of the horrors of concentration camps. Its author, called upon to give testimony as a victim and an expert, became a popular guest in radio and TV shows, embarking on book tours all over the world and moving audiences and "hard-bitten journalists to tears."[18]

Christopher Hope called it "achingly beautiful"; the *New York Times* said it was written "with a poet's vision; a child's state of grace"; Anne Karpf in this paper described it as "one of the great works about the Holocaust"; all agreed it was a masterpiece. There is just one problem—Binjamin Wilkomirski's memoir of surviving as a Jewish child alone in the Nazi concentration camps of Majdanek and Auschwitz was a fabrication, invented from beginning to end, one of the great hoaxes in publishing history.[19]

Through the investigative efforts of journalist Daniel Ganzfried, it came to light that Binjamin Wilkomirski was actually Bruno Doesseker, child of an "unmarried Protestant woman" who was later adopted by a Swiss couple. [20] While the Final Solution was set in motion, Doesseker allegedly enjoyed the comforts of his Swiss middle-class home. Part of the appeal of Wilkomirski as a public persona and of his writing was his claim to authenticity, to having directly experienced unspeakable acts of violence and humiliation. *Fragments* was written, marketed, and sold as an autobiographical rendition of the memories of a child. The fact that his narrative voice was that of a child is of particular importance because it only highlights the currency of the child-as-victim in memory politics. The outrage over Doesseker's real identity stemmed from the fact that both the text, *Fragments*, and its author intentionally lay claim to Holocaust trauma in general, and to child traumatization in particular. It was, after all, a fragmented autobiography that rendered child trauma palpable. Furthermore, this scandal lay bare the mechanisms of the cultural industry, as it welcomed and heralded Wilkomirski as a witness of Nazi terror, adorning his text with the label "authentic." As his tissue of lies was unraveled, it became clear how many institutions were involved in propping this text up as a classic in Holocaust literature. In the aftermath of this scandal, a consensus emerged to consider Bruno Doesseker a deeply disturbed individual who tragically came to believe in his own invention. While that might hold true, what is particularly interesting about this case is how a general public seems to have readily welcomed what many perceived to be an authentic representation of the unfathomable. One aspect of the drama is that people felt betrayed for trusting in its authenticity, in the existence of a "true" voice, in someone who "knows" what others cannot know. The discovery of Wilkomirski/Doesseker's actual identity naturally caused his fall from grace as a literary prodigy, just as it led to Boyden's downfall.

In an important regard, however, the Boyden controversy fundamentally differs from the Wilkomirski case (and others): *Three Day Road*, it must unequivocally be stated, was never written and classified as an autobiographical piece, but as historical fiction. To my knowledge, Boyden has never publically stated that he himself is a victim of the residential school system or has somehow suffered directly from its imposition. Arguably, he has never resisted the label Indigenous as it was placed on him, or as he frequently reiterated his Indigenous heritage. His esteem as an artist was tied to his indigeneity, but he never posed as a direct victim of colonial terror, as Wilkomirski for example had done. Canada, it seems, had willingly and gladly tapped into his Indigenous self-fashioning and incorporated this "media darling" into the processes and discourses of reconciliation. Much of the chagrin and anger that Boyden was met with is rooted in the overwhelming disappointment in Canada's beloved "Indigenous" artist, but it is also a result of realizing how welcome Boyden as a token and symbol of reconciliation had been.

The indignation that many felt and voiced upon the discovery of Boyden's questionable claims to indigeneity certainly was the result of a perceived betrayal. The imposter, after all, is the "antithesis of authenticity," as Maureen Clark poignantly remarks.[21] Boyden committed the ultimate sin of laying claim to a history that is not his, namely as a colonized, forcibly relocated, and culturally reeducated Indigenous person. By the same token, he inscribed himself and *was inscribed* into cultural trauma experiences and discourses that were not his for the taking. Thus, Boyden implicitly laid claim to and was readily incorporated into the victim narrative, representing this identity template that holds such a significant place in the logic of Canadian reconciliation. His fraudulent identity, or more precisely, his non-indigeneity all but denies him the right to explore cultural trauma from a fictional Indigenous vantage point.

To some Indigenous representatives, however, the invoking of such compartmentalized and unambiguous identity labels is not helpful or representative of Indigenous realities, with Robert Jago arguing that there is no such thing as *a* native identity and that this category is a colonial fiction perpetuated into the present:

> The concept of Native as its own identity (and not as a placeholder word for a specific tribal or nation identity), is a product of colonialism and the Indian Act. In the words of anti-colonial writer Frantz Fanon, "it is the settler who has brought the native into existence and who perpetuates his existence." There are Salish people, Haida, Cree, Ojibway, Métis, and Mi'kmaq among many

others, all three dimensional individuals you can walk up to on the street, and not one of which identifies with some culture called "Native." Still, we are told that a thing called the Native race exists, that Boyden is a member of it, that his disconnect from any community doesn't matter, and lastly that we have no say in this.[22]

Jago's statement elaborately problematizes compartmentalized identity conceptions. At the heart of the Boyden controversy lies the question of what and who defines indigeneity in Canada, and who is allowed to represent it. It is about the Indigenous perception of being silenced by discourses, well-intended or not, that continue to position indigeneity against non-indigeneity in a hierarchical manner, and of being paraded and labeled. Jago struggles with the fact that seemingly all-encompassing labels and ascriptions are used to group together the various and varying Indigenous identities of Canada. A native collective in a singular form, in this sense, is an identity-political fiction, but that does not diminish the power that such labels hold.

In recent years, Boyden seems to have disappeared from public view. Canadian scholar Darryl Leroux recently published a translation of an article that Boyden has apparently written for a French journal.[23] This essay is a remarkable documentation of incredulity, obstinacy, and the somewhat infantile defiance of the entire issue on Boyden's part. Boyden states that he indeed took a DNA test; it allegedly revealed "Native American" and "DNA from the Artic," without any specific details. He further alleges that despite his blood heritage, he was also "traditionally adopted" by "five Ojibwe or Cree communities" over the past two years "as a brother or son." This familial bond effectively renders Boyden what he claims he always has been—Indigenous. However, during my research, I was unable to find the original version of this essay, or any significant reaction to it.

In a nutshell, the Boyden controversy comes down to a simple formula: the explanans suddenly became the explanandum. With the advantage of hindsight it is certainly not without irony that his novel centers on a case of identity theft. Boyden, as one who stands accused of being a "shape-shifter" with regard to his Indigenous heritage, invents a shape-shifting character who easily crosses cultural boundaries, who is neither fully Indian nor fully Canadian. Xavier, framed as the "authentic" Indian, kills his volatile friend in the end. *Three Day Road* thus forms a timely commentary on the nonviability of transcultural identity portfolios.

A Nation Forged in Fire

Within *Three Day Road*, the reader (re)encounters the shape-shifter in the character of Elijah Weesageechak, one of Boyden's protagonists who has gone through a residential school education. In the novel, shape-shifting becomes a multifaceted metaphor: in Indigenous mythology, the trickster, a wily shape-shifter, is a connoisseur of the art of living. In the trenches of World War I, the art of living becomes the art of survival. Furthermore, in *Three Day Road*, shape-shifting represents cultural identities that colonialism has forcefully brought to interact. Both his fellow soldiers and his best friend Xavier always meet Elijah with suspicion, as to a certain extent he successfully oscillates between the cultural poles. Xavier and Elijah, the two young Cree boys Boyden sends into World War I, are childhood friends, and both have been subjected to colonial reeducation, albeit to varying degrees. Xavier escapes a longer education period, while Elijah remains there for several years. At some point, the two friends voluntarily join the Canadian Expeditionary Forces and excel as a sniper team, earning fame beyond their own regiment. As the war progresses, Elijah makes friends with the other Canadian soldiers and develops a taste both for killing and for morphine. Xavier is increasingly concerned about the state of Elijah's mental health and eventually murders his best friend. After the act, Xavier takes Elijah's dog-tags in order to secure some of Elijah's fame for himself. He loses a leg in battle and develops a morphine addiction as well.

On the eponymous three-day journey home, Xavier's aunt Niska tries to get through to her traumatized and silent nephew by telling him stories about their ancestors and communities. The reader only learns about the fate of the two Cree boys in retrospect, and through the narrative perspective of Xavier.

Returning injured and morphine-addicted from the trenches of Europe, Xavier travels with his aunt Niska back to his home community. Xavier frequently drifts in and out of consciousness and recalls his traumatic experiences of war. At times, the present (Xavier and Niska traveling) and the past (war in Europe) fuse and engage in a dialogue in Xavier's mind. He reminisces:

> "Do you want to know something, Auntie," I say, cupping my hand and taking a small sip from the river. "So many dead men lay buried over there that if the bush grows back the trees will hold skulls in their branches." I laugh, and it makes me feel worse. "I saw it already. We once left a place covered in our dead. When we came back a few months later flowers redder than blood grew everywhere. They covered the ground. They even grew out of rotting corpses." Knives of pain stab me low in the gut. My arm screams out high in the place where a bullet entered it. My head throbs with the cut of sunlight. She doesn't respond, but I know she listens. "Those flowers grew back, but that was all." I hurt so bad. "Useless things."[24]

A reader with a knowledge of World War I discourses, its symbols and representations, instantly pictures a specific kind of red flower while reading this passage. Red poppies have become the symbol of the horrors of World War I—a war that was only the beginning of decades of horrendous fighting and killing throughout the world.

In Canada, however, World War I narratives are closely connected to the birth of the Canadian nation. The myth of the "nation forged in fire" is both a narrative and a political construct, which, in the aftermath of this horrible war, led to a reevaluation of the significance of the war. Narratives of and on the Great War are almost tokenistically Canadian and are referenced in its canonical literature: Peregrine Acland inaugurated the Canadian war novel by publishing *All Else Is Folly* in 1929.[25] The war itself was depicted as a dreadful experience and was not glorified by romanticized notions of war. Yet this text already delineates the "emblematic" nature of Canadian attempts to make sense of its marginalized existence, both in a literal sense as existing at the geographical margins of the British Empire and in a metaphorical one as entering the war as a dominion.[26]

Timothy Findley's *The Wars* (1977) was another pivotal contribution to Canadian World War I fiction, as it significantly contributed to establishing the idea of Canada as born in the trenches of Belgium and France.[27] Canadian sacrifice in the Great War was framed to be a "transformative experience" and a ritual of "initiation."[28] Also embedded in the narrative was the stance that this alleged birth of the Canadian nation was rendered possible by bloodshed and death and hence was an ambiguous, but decisive, moment in Canadian history.[29] In the Canadian collective memory, participation in the Great War could at this point be archived and labeled under birth of the nation, as the coming of age story of Canada. Findley's novel marked the moment when the horrors of Great War were rebranded as the reason for Canada's emancipation from England.

There is a gap of twenty years between the publication of Findley's *The Wars* and Joseph Boyden's neo-Great-War-novel *Three Day Road*, arguably reflecting the fact that the foundations of the Canadian nation had recently been shaken, and formative narratives became subject to revision.[30] While World War I commemoration usually romanticizes Canada's losses in the trenches as the origin story of the nation's independence from Britain, it largely remains a settler Canadian mnemonic legacy, much to the exclusion of, for example, Indigenous voices. In other words, it is a site of "national monumentality" that seems to "belong" to non-Indigenous Canadians.[31] Joseph Boyden's novel *Three Day Road* successfully interweaves these specific strands of Canadian collective memories, and sources of ethnicized notions of national identity come to intersect. *Three Day Road* has since been received as an example of reinscribing Indigenous war participation into Canadian memory discourses.[32] Brigitte Glaser describes a second phase of Canadian writing about the Great War, in which recent Canadian World War I fiction sets out to include other perspectives on the war through "undercutting and destabilizing of fixed orders without dissolving them altogether."[33] Representing World War I becomes more ambiguous in the process. The Great War has thus once again become a site of identity negotiation:

> These imaginary "returns" to the Great War are strongly influenced by the current socio-political circumstances and contemporary versions of national history, telling and showing us as much about the period in which they were produced as about the reality and significance of the past military conflict.[34]

This new generation of World War I fiction in Canada re-politicizes Canadian participation by turning its focus toward the suppressed and marginalized: Frances Itani's novel *Deafening* (2003), for example, features a hearing-impaired woman who remains at the home front while her husband joins the army medical corps.[35] Jane Urquhart's novels *The Underpainter* (1997),[36] depicting the struggle of various highly traumatized protagonists to come to terms with life in peace, and *The Stone Carvers* (2001),[37] in which European immigrants to Canada return to the battlefields to participate in the creation of the Canadian War memorial at Vimy Ridge, shift from a direct making sense of the war to a different reading and contextualization of it.[38] This contemporary generation of writers has produced narratives within an allegedly postnational time, embarking on projects of revisionist history writing to reconfigure what national identity is composed of:

> The need to keep alive moments of the past and the wish to draw attention to those parts of history which seem to have been forgotten or have been suppressed most frequently range among the reasons given by authors when asked about their objectives in writing about World War I.[39]

The scope of historical and national consciousness is broadened by this new generation of writers by emphasizing narratives of the marginalized and the subaltern in the shape of women, Indigenous, and immigrants. Their chosen venue for this broadening of Canada's collective memory is historical fiction.

As part of this trend, *Three Day Road* reintroduces the "forgotten" participation of Indigenous soldiers into Canadian historical consciousness. In alignment with the tension between loss and victory, Boyden's text posits Canada's emergence against the backdrop of mass casualties, amputees, addicts, and mentally affected as the products of war on both sides of the trench line. As a representative of this second generation of war poets, and imbued with Indigenous identity politics, Boyden transfers his Indigenous protagonists into the context of Canada's coming of age. This refers to an actual fact: Indigenous enlisting became possible in nonfictional Canada at some point because casualties demanded further supplies of men capable of fighting. By the end of the war, around 35 percent of the Indigenous male population of Canada had enlisted.[40] Military service was not mandatory for the Indigenous, but

> the [Indian] Department receives testimonials of loyalty from Indian bands, and letters from individual Indians, which are fired with zealous and sincere patriotism and often display a highly intelligent interest in the progress of the war and a remarkably clear grasp of the principles at stake.[41]

Elijah and Xavier join the Canadian forces and gradually make a name for themselves as excellent trackers and snipers. Elijah, who had been brought up within a residential school, has to newly acquire these capacities that are framed to be typically, even stereotypically, Indian.[42] Xavier, who was able to leave residential school education at a very early stage, teaches his friend and revives Elijah's knowledge of traditional hunting and warfare. In Europe, they form a sniper team and excel in that regard. Boyden's novel effectively "personalizes"[43] this formative historical narrative and "reconstruct[s] a part of Canadian war history that has been suppressed":[44] *Three Day Road* offers a "reassessment of ways in which Canadians remember 1914–1918,"[45] functions as a "tribute" to Indigenous soldiers in particular,[46] includes a "native element into the most defining moment of Canadian history,"[47] and consequently destabilizes "Eurocentric accounts" of Canadian history:[48]

> Only personal narratives are *stories*: among memorial gestures only narratives happen along a line of time, in which meaning is not fixed but emergent. Stories deal with causality and change, and war-stories tell us processes of war: what happened to the teller and with what consequences.[49]

Collectivized myths are constructed through the plethora of voices, stories and narratives, "for what war stories construct is not a combining story that is told in any individual narrative, but takes its substance from the sum of many stories."[50] "The Prevalence of Native Canadian diegetic agency" throughout the novel centers the Indigenous voice, which itself constitutes an act of education and information to a seemingly indifferent public.[51] The text thus reintroduces the "forgotten" participation of Indigenous soldiers into Canadian historical consciousness.

Boyden's text posits the birth of the nation against the backdrop of mass casualties, amputees, addicts, and mentally affected that the war has produced on both sides of the trench line:

> Once the shelling has gone quiet, we make our way out and survey the damage. I'm surprised to see that very little looks different than it did before. There is the same mud and puddles and torn-up wagons and piles of bricks. The only real difference is the smell of cordite and the sweeter smell of blood that is as rich as the air, as if we'd just butchered a large moose. We do what we can to

help the wounded, and it is not long before stretcher-bearers appear to cart off the dead, and the living who can no longer walk.[52]

By producing an understanding of historical consciousness that temporarily reverses Euro-Canadian representational dominance in relation to the Great War, Boyden thus counters, enlarges, and creatively explores the myth of the birth of the nation. By means of the fictional, the text openly criticizes that the glory of World War I participation has not rubbed off on Indigenous Canadians even to this very day. "The novel thus stages the history of Indigenous participation in the 'Great War' as an act of transcultural memory and firmly embeds the two native soldiers' experiences of global war into local, Indigenous history, culture and mythology."[53] Frank Schulze-Engler further explains:

> At first sight, Joseph Boyden's historical novel on the role of Native Canadians in World War I is a book with a clear memory agenda: in the first paragraph of the "Acknowledgements" appended to the fictional text proper, Boyden invokes the heroism of Native Canadian soldiers and places his own novel unequivocally into a commemorative context. . . . One strand of Boyden's novel is thus centrally concerned with setting the historical record straight, with acknowledging the contribution of Native Canadian "forgotten heroes" to Canada's war efforts and with reinscribing Canada's Indigenous soldiers into a national narrative from which they have been unfairly excluded.[54]

As Samuel Hynes remarks in his landmark study on representations of World War I in English culture, "the First World War was the greatest military and political event of its time, but it was also the great imaginative event," and the events and narratives of the Great War are repurposed as framing three coming-of-age-narratives in *Three Day Road*.[55] On the one hand, the two friends venture into a foreign country, a foreign war, in order to become men, warriors. On the other hand, Canada experiences its own "rite of passage" when it detaches itself from England in the aftermath of the war. Thirdly, we might regard the three-day journey that Xavier and his aunt Niska undertake as Xavier's passage from the foreign into the secluded, the familiar, the seemingly unambiguous. In the end, Xavier and his aunt Niska travel back into the outback, where Xavier is supposed to recover physically and mentally from the experiences of the Great War.[56] During her journey home, Niska tries to revive Xavier's spirits and will to live by recounting stories about their cultural heritage, kin and family.

Transcultures Forged in Fire

The inner division of the Canadian Expeditionary Forces, as well as, by extension, the Canadian society into Euro-Canadians and Indians, remains integral to the narrative. The two Indigenous soldiers become an essential part of the war in the course of the novel but are constantly met with rejection and suspicion. In this regard, Schulze-Engler argues that

> *Three Day Road* is a complex, multi-layered text that cannot be reduced to one agenda only. If one of the strands running through Boyden's text is a revisionist reinscription of Native Canadians into one of Canada's most powerful myths of national identity, another—and arguably even more powerful—dimension of the novel relates to the debunking of this very myth by means of an assertive reinscription of the history of global war into a distinctly Indigenous narrative frame.[57]

Canadian national identity as represented by its armed forces is ambiguous by default, as the reader quickly learns. Among the Canadian troops, we encounter Canadian soldiers who are biased toward the Cree Elijah because he excels as a sniper. On the passage from Canada to Europe, Elijah enters the officer's mess to warn the other soldiers about an incident with the horses; they ignore the horse problem, however, and instead inquire about Elijah's hunting skills. "'That skill will come in handy,' another [officer] says. 'He'll make a fine scout. We need to recruit more Indians to our regiment.' The others laugh."[58] In this scene, Elijah is received as an "interesting new creature"[59] able to chase an animal through the forest, whereas the Canadian officers are "tall and look the same with their carefully groomed hair and moustaches."[60] Boyden posits "cultivated" Canadian soldiers against the "savages" Xavier and Elijah. This binary opposition is fortified as the scene continues, with Xavier ending the life of an injured horse, a deed for which he is almost arrested. While the other soldiers accuse Xavier of savagery and bloodlust, only Colonel McCaan identifies Xavier's actions as being among "the best traits of an officer" because he was able to come to a decision on his own.[61] The text invokes almost stereotypical identities and corresponding abilities: the natives succeed in hunting and have a taste for slaughter, whereas the civilized Canadian soldiers attempt to maintain a degree of cultivation in the midst of depravation.

Yet *Three Day Road* is a textual example of how identities point beyond themselves, although the reader encounters seemingly unambiguous representatives of the Indigenous population of Canada. On the other side of the identity-political spectrum, Boyden imagines two rather conservative Indians and places them in the midst of his coming-of-age narrative. Niska and Xavier represent a powerful, lively Indigenous culture and appear to function as the bearers of "true," authentic Indigenous identity. Niska's narrative strand circles around depicting Indigenous everyday life, their myths, skills, fears, and losses. She holds the firm belief that to tell one's story is the only possibility of healing and survival:

> I know that Xavier wants to talk to me. He goes as far as to let words come out of his mouth when he sleeps. He says very little when he's awake. I'm not able to make out more than the odd sentence when he is sleeping, though, and sometimes when he dreams he speaks aloud in English. I can't help but smile a bit when he does. As a child he was so proud that more than once he claimed he would never speak the *wemistikoshiw* tongue. And now he does it even in his sleep. He cannot speak to me yet, and so I decide, here on the river, that I will speak to him. In this way maybe his tongue will loosen some. Maybe some of the poison that courses through him might be released in this way. Words are all I have left now.[62]

It is Xavier who becomes the teacher of Elijah, who appears to have lost his skills and traditional training in the course of his residential school upbringing. Consequently, Xavier remains secluded from the other (Canadian) soldiers and keeps this difference very much alive throughout the novel:

> We've been over here in this place that some call Flanders and others call Belgium for three weeks now. I felt stupid and small when Elijah had explained to me that Belgium is a country, like Canada, and Flanders is just one small part of it, like Mushkegowuk. I'm still uncomfortable with the language of the wemistikoshiw. It is spoken through the nose and hurts my mouth to try and mimic the silly sound of it. I opt to stay quiet most of the time, listening carefully to decipher the words, always listening for the joke or insult made against me. The others think that I'm something less than them, but just give me the chance to show them what I am made of when it is time to kill.[63]

Xavier thus positions himself in antagonism to his fellow soldiers, and, gradually, also against Elijah. He remains an outcast throughout almost the entire narrative.

Besides Xavier, his aunt Niska functions as the second powerful narrative Indigenous voice. She is the bearer of Indigenous customs, habits, and lifestyle. Niska's character appears to be a very self-confident representative of Indigenous past and present. She functions as the connective link between the growing influence of modernity and colonialism on Indigenous life as well as the resilience of traditional ways. Niska is a forceful storytelling agent within *Three Day Road*; it is her firm belief that only telling one's story enables survival—both in personal as well as in collective, cultural terms:

> I steer the canoe into the faster current and let us drift with it, using my paddle only as a rudder. The mist is disappearing now and I can see a long way down the bank, can keep an eye sharp for the movement of animals along the shore. Nephew cries out but then goes silent again. The sound of it, the animal fear at the very bottom of that cry, makes me think something I haven't thought about in a long time. It is the story of my childhood. Now I tell it to you, Xavier, to keep you alive.[64]

Schulze-Engler remarks that "the whole novel is narrated by two homodiegetic narrators . . . , and narrative perspective and control is firmly placed into Indigenous hands."[65] Niska and Xavier share this narrative agency, and, consequently, the novel engages in a dialogue between Indigenous reality in Canada and the intrusion of European modernity.

> After the death of my father, your grandfather, Xavier, our people were directionless. Flakes of snow in swirling wind. Some went back to Moose Factory and never really left it again, became homeguard Indians where they learned to stomach the wemistikoshiw food and ways. You could tell you were approaching Moose Factory on the river by the stink of sewage and refuse piled up onshore. And they all wondered where the diseases came from.[66]

Niska tells powerful stories of resilience in the midst of non-Indigenous dominance; encounters with the "white" people that have left her with even more determination to remain detached from "white" society. Boyden lets Xavier put this inherent paradox in an apt formula:

> I've been walking a well-marked trail that leads from the rivers of my north home across the country they call Canada, the ocean parting before me like that old Bible story that nuns forced upon me as a child, ending right here in this strange place where all the world's trouble explodes.[67]

Niska recounts how she has become the bearer of their kin's heritage by becoming the *windigo* killer—a position that is passed on from one generation to the other. Finally, she rescues Xavier from certain death, retreats with him into the bush, and performs a ritualistic cleansing from the "white" world for Xavier. Her solution is to retreat to the "natural habitat" of the Indigenous population in order to realign with nature and its spirits, and to make peace with the world and Xavier's war experiences.

> In a little while I will have to add more wood to keep the chill away. Nephew breathes calmly. I listen to the sounds of the night animals not so far away. I hear the fox and the marten chasing mice. I hear the whoosh of great wings as an Arctic owl sweeps close by, and after that the almost silent step of a bigger animal, a lynx perhaps, keeping watch with her yellow eyes. I look at the sky, then at the river, the black line of it heading north. By tomorrow we'll be home.[68]

One is struck by the picturesque and idealized description of their return to the bush. Again, *Three Day Road* seemingly positions an almost romantic version of Indigenous existence against the backdrop of the carnage at work in the trenches of Europe and the hostility of non-Indigenous Canada. The solution for those Indigenous people who come in contact with this foreign, alien world and its spirits seems to lie within the possibility of being reconciled with their native origins.

However, upon scrutiny, it becomes obvious that Boyden is by no means an advocate for "self-contained indigenalities."[69] At some point, Niska tells Xavier the story of the Cree family turned *windigo*. A *windigo* is someone who eats human flesh, and there are protectors among the Cree community who are in charge of killing the *windigo*. Niska recounts:

> Micah's wife and the baby turned windigo. The children in camp stopped sleeping, cried in fear, no longer felt their hunger. We'd grown up on stories of the windigo that our parents fed us over the winter fires, of people who eat other people's flesh and grow into wild beasts twenty feet tall whose hunger can be satisfied only by more human flesh and then the hunger turns worse. I listened to the adults of the camp talk nervously among themselves, their voices interrupted by the wife's growls and mad language. They talked about my father's reputation as a windigo killer, of how as a young man he became our hookimaw after killing a family of them who roamed near where we trapped, a family who had once been a part of the caribou clan but had turned one hard winter and begun preying on the camps of unsuspecting Cree. "He must kill windigos once again," the adults whispered to one another. "We are too weak already and Micah's woman's madness can surely spread in these bad times." My father knew this too, and made preparations to act as his own father had taught him.[70]

This passage foreshadows developments that the reader is about to encounter. Consider, for example, how Xavier unconsciously lays the explanatory foundations for the events to come:

> Elijah's reputation [as a sniper] is growing, I know, and Elijah's vanity being fed makes him content and happy. But the real job still lies ahead of us, and if Elijah can get the Hun whose reputation grows like a legend in this place, bigger than Elijah's even, then Elijah's reputation will be secured, and mine will be too, and we will be given a higher rank, and we will make more money and have more freedom. Thompson tells us all of this. While I lie still at night, though, I begin to wonder about this Hun sniper.[71]

Xavier, who considers himself to be a "true" Indian in the midst of strange European men, is forced to watch Elijah excel. He is successful not only in terms of warfare and killing skills but also in regard to making connections with other soldiers. Xavier stays behind while Elijah fully engages in exchanges with his fellow soldiers, and Elijah's ability to bond with others appears to make Xavier a little jealous. After a while, Elijah supposedly turns *windigo* (at least this is the explanation that Xavier provides us with), for Elijah has made it a habit to scalp his victims during battle. In the course of the narrative, Xavier suspects Elijah of eating human flesh as an ultimate sign of victory over their enemies' very bodily existence. Having turned *windigo* is the only proper explanation for Xavier with regard to Elijah's deteriorating state of mind and increasing violence.

Elijah, one might argue, has not been able to cope with the horrors of war, and has thus developed some degree of insanity. This is also an explanation that Xavier offers the reader when he describes Elijah in action:

> Elijah kneels in the tall grass, a young German pinned below him. The German is bleeding but still alive, looks up in shock and fear at Elijah. Just as I approach him from behind, Elijah cuts hard into the soldier's solar plexus with a knife, muttering. I can't make out what he says. The man below him writhes and screams. I watch Elijah as he plunges his knife once again into the man. I can see the horror in the eyes turn to the dullness of death as Elijah's hand moves to his own face. "Elijah," I mutter. Elijah turns to me. Blood is smeared across his cheeks. His eyes are wet with tears.[72]

At this point, Xavier has already made up his mind: in his eyes, Elijah is mad.

> "I'm not crazy," Elijah says. I continue to stare at the horses. "You must listen to me, X. This is war. This is not home. What's mad is them putting us in trenches to begin with. The madness is to tell us to kill and award those of us who do it well. I only wish to survive." "You've gone beyond that," I say.[73]

Xavier, who represents a rather conservative Indian, appears able to evaluate the horrors of war, and he knows what it has done to him. Yet he mistrusts his best friend Elijah who has no problems whatsoever with blending in with the Canadian soldiers. Due to his upbringing in a residential school, Elijah has a very good command of English and is even capable of mimicking accents as he goes along. He can "out-talk even the officers with his nun's English and his quick thinking."[74] The other soldiers are drawn to him, admiring him for his shooting skills, whereas Xavier feels "forced by my poor English to sit back and watch it all happen, to see how he wins them over, while I become more invisible. A brown ghost."[75] Thus conceived, Elijah counters Niska's and Xavier's unambiguity: being introduced as the *weesageechak*, Elijah Whiskeyjack, the trickster and shapeshifter, he transgresses boundaries that Xavier continuously helps to re-erect. While Xavier is concerned and occupied to uphold the strict differentiation between Indigenous and non-Indigenous, Elijah easily surpasses these limitations and oscillates between the poles. When Xavier feels marginalized for not being able to speak English sufficiently—a refusal that he maintains stubbornly—Elijah even mimics accents. When the soldiers begin to admire Elijah for his skills—which are attributed to his "savage" background—Xavier feels like a ghost. This trickster, Elijah, travels between identities and cultures as if it were an easy undertaking. The character of Elijah, for example, ventures way past all possible attempts to label him culturally or historically. He is a mythological trickster figure, the shapeshifting *weesegeechak*, while he is at the same time a hybrid, a crosser of linguistic and cultural boundaries as if they were nonexistent. It remains an aspect of further analysis why exactly the conservative native, Xavier, finally becomes judge, jury, and executioner to Elijah.

One might accordingly argue that Boyden has introduced a figure that is traditionally associated with Indigenous mythology and oral traditions.[76] In his pioneer study, Paul Radin has described the trickster figure as indicative of a rather primitive evolutionary stage of mankind, and the embodiments of this underdevelopment are to be found in native American mythology.[77] One might rightfully claim that *Three Day Road*, with its strong agenda of returning the agency of historical representation to the Indigenous, required another character who is strongly embedded in Indigenous mythology. However, there is another aspect that is pertinent to understanding why Elijah is the way he is. More recent takes on the recurrent phenomenon of the shape-shifter understand him[78] as a rather transcultural phenomenon: the trickster is a prominent and recurrent protagonist, he belongs to all world cultures—and none.[79] He is a "wily"[80] character who has become a literary theme across various genres and cultures.[81] The trickster is a hybrid figure, a character who operates at the margins of a given collective, because he likes to appear in contexts where he can put a finger on hypocrisy and deficiency. Harold Scheub sees him "exist[ing] in a society that espouses traditional values while actually sanctioning dehumanizing modes of behavior."[82] He is also an "agent of chaos," capable of "disrupting existing orders," and is suspected to "impose his own corrupt sense of order" onto the world that surrounds him.[83] His task is to shed light on established values and frameworks, to emphasize the existence of moral and ethical standards in a given society, and he does that by "profan[ing] nearly every central belief and making us question the origins of this belief."[84] Thus conceived, the trickster is the performer of the underlying grid that governs social cohesion and collective formations. The shape-shifter is capable of playing with these general norms and frameworks and consequently is able to transcend them. Pursuing a liminal existence, he is "sometimes fool, sometimes hero, sometimes villain."[85] His actions always convey and construct meaning, although his meaningfulness does not necessarily promptly meet the eye:

> Tricksters are the timeless energy, the eternally liminal, the ordering and the chaotic. They are the alpha and the omega, the ying and the yang, the contradictory, the ambiguous, the unending. They are primordial, now sublime and now debased, neither the one nor the other, but a combination that emerges

in strange, quirky, and unpredictable ways. We see ourselves in the trickster. It is that trickster who is at the heart of the epic, the core of the tale, the soul of the creative myth. Whenever there is chaos and order, the trickster is there.[86]

His mode of representation and expression is usually associated with the comical, with humor, and even the grotesque, but there are also examples where the trickster does not make the spectator laugh.[87] The trickster can oscillate between various identities, masks, and personas and thus break up the framework of definiteness personified by Niska and Xavier.

As such, the trickster shares structural resemblances with another very prominent literary persona. In the previous chapter on the carnivalesque, we already briefly encountered one of the major protagonists of carnival—the fool. While the trickster used to be associated with Indigenous mythology, the fool is traditionally located within the Western tradition of representation and narrative world-making. However, if we take a closer look at the fool and compare his traits, prowess, and (in)abilities with the trickster, one finds a strong resemblance. The fool is supposed to exist in a "in a kind of twilight of the semi-detached," leading a life from the margins.[88] He remains an outcast who places himself "in opposition to dominant discourses of the historical moments in which they occur."[89] This existence at the margins is made possible by his constant search for masks or personas that help him to "depict . . . the absurdity of the human condition."[90] Fools, as well as the trickster, necessarily stand outside the society or collective they comment upon. Tim Prentki directs our attention toward the fact that a fool is never fully attached to a family, friends, or kinship structures or ideologies, because he defies any category or framework that would govern and limit his possibilities of existence.[91] As a boundary crosser by definition, the fool "lures us towards definition only to vanish at the moment when the analyst believes she is approaching an understanding."[92] The fool, in this sense and similarly to the trickster, personifies the "art of survival," and this survival is inextricably linked to and with change.[93] Thus conceived, the fool shares another trait with the trickster: both figures intervene into the construction of commonly held and well-established conventions and truths, for they constantly make us question these beliefs in the first place through their engagement with them. Both challenge authorities and subvert dominance. Prentki claims that the trickster may have been the antecedent of the fool, that there may be "cultural differences in the manifestation of the fool, but the function sounds essentially the same as the fool in the official carnivals of medieval Europe."[94] He further highlights their common features:

> Folly and carnival go hand in glove with the powerful for it is in the act of exerting control over other humans or over our environment that we are most vulnerable to forgetting our natures and becoming prey to antisocial desires

and inhuman aspirations. This is why the fool is subversive, he cannot be revolutionary.[95]

The fool as well as the trickster do not provide us with illusions about our human (co)existence but instead "strip human beings of all their illusions about their natures."[96] Thus conceived, the fool is also universal in his appearance throughout world cultures and can accordingly be perceived as a transcultural literary character.[97]

Elijah, in this sense, shows many traits that are attributed to both trickster and fool. Thus conceived, he is the trickster-fool who on the one hand points a finger at existing boundaries, limitations, and containers, yet playfully moves beyond them. He is neither fully Indian nor Euro-Canadian: Elijah is capable of oscillating between languages, behavior, and frameworks that govern belonging and exclusion. He masters all of them but remains unmastered by them. Boyden's trickster-fool is condemned to lead a marginal existence right in the center of other people's attention. In the course of the war he becomes fully aware of what the circumstances have made of him, and with this clairvoyant assertion he stands alone. Xavier frequently accuses Elijah of perceiving the war as a game for him to play, a spectacle to test his limits and prowess, yet this is exactly what the fool does when being confronted with the absurdity of human existence. Or, more precisely, the trickster-fool appears when there are power imbalances, carnage, and mischief and "speaks the unspeakable":[98]

> The sun is behind Elijah now, and his face is in shadow, light shining brightly about his head. "Do you know what I think?" I say softly. "I think you did more than just kill that young soldier yesterday." I look at Elijah as I say this to see his eyes, but he remains a shadow. "Why do you say that?" he says. He speaks loudly so that I can hear him. When I do not answer, he seems about to walk away, but then looks in my eyes, makes sure that I can see his lips, see what he is saying. "I came to talk to you to offer you help. We have a great future after this war. We will return home as heroes. I will become a great chief. I won't let you or anyone else take that away." He turns and walks away, hands in his pocket. My stomach cramps again and makes me cry out. I lie on my side in the sand, staring out at the river and the late afternoon sun sparkling on it. Niska, what am I to do?[99]

This episode is indicative of the status of their relationship. One is prompted to accept Xavier's view of doubt about the sanity of the war-struck Elijah. The reader is well advised to be cautious about the "truths" that Xavier's narrative provides us with. However, the dialogue above is another example of Elijah's apt knack of anticipation: Xavier will after all be the one who returns home as a war hero, as he will take on the identity of fallen Elijah. In any case, the status of hero is a very limited issue for a native soldier. None of them could have known that Indigenous soldiers would not be eligible for veteran support after the end of the war, and in this vein it is perfectly understandable why Elijah holds the firm view of performing best during their experience of war. Neither of the two Crees will come home and become a great chief—Indigenous communities further deteriorated in Canada as the war progressed. Moreover, this episode underlines the trickster-fool's capacity to shed light on existing moral values and patterns, and as the novel progresses it becomes clear that there is actually nothing to be gained for the Indigenous from their war participation.

At this point, Xavier has already explained Elijah's behavior to himself: to him, Elijah has turned *windigo*. Instead of considering the struggle that Elijah goes through as a shape-shifting negotiator of cultural belonging, Xavier suspects that he has lost his moral compass. The irony at the end of the novel is that Xavier is the one to lose his moral compass, although he is frequently presented as having some moral high ground over the suspected madman Elijah and all other non-Indigenous protagonists. But it is ultimately Xavier who takes on the role of the *hookimaw*, the *windigo* killer, although no one appoints him to perform this role.

Elijah thus embodies a strand of Indigenous identity that points beyond itself, and may as such be counted as a vision of future indigenalities: they will not exist in seclusion anymore, as the end of the novel suggests, but will be prone to influences from other cultures, histories, and mentalities. Joseph Boyden has used World War I theaters, in which soldiers fight for national entities and identities that appear stable and fixed, to construct a vision of a transnational and transcultural space of identity negotiation. Our prime negotiator, Elijah Whiskeyjack, the shape-shifting fool, succeeds in not only transgressing boundaries but also in commenting on Indigenous identity in the light of European dominance. Yet, as one who embodies a version of an Indigenous past (mythology, trickster figure, and *windigo*), present (residential school upbringing, cultural contact, and exchange), and future of Indigenous culture and identity (in oscillation, transformation), he is doomed after all. It is the very scene in which Xavier kills Elijah, the supposed *windigo*, that supports this claim. At first sight, Xavier rationalizes the murder by suspecting Elijah of wanting to take Xavier's life in the first place:

> "We have got to get out of here," I shout. "This bombardment's too heavy." Elijah finally takes his eyes from his scope, looks at me, a sad smile on his bloody face. He says something to me, something I can't make out. *We both can't . . .* he mouths, and then a shell lands close enough to blow and suck a hot wind across us.[100]

The tension is carefully built here: being almost deaf, Xavier is not quite sure what Elijah is saying, and neither is the reader. At this point, it seems impossible that both will survive. Put differently, at this very moment, it is not clear who is going to survive the carnage of the first modern, world-encompassing war and the rivalry of two male friends, the hybrid figure or the conservative Indian:

> *Leave*, he mouths, still smiling, his teeth glinting. Elijah sits up and reaches for me to hug me. When his hands touch me, a cold shock runs the length of my body. I push him back, my wounded arm heavy. Elijah struggles up and reaches to wrap his arms around me again. He's no longer smiling. His mouth is twisted in an angry grimace.[101]

A fight then starts, and the reader is left to figure out whether Elijah actually wants to kill Xavier. "'Are we not best friends, Xavier?' he asks. 'Are we not best friends and great hunters?'"[102] So the struggle continues:

> "Elijah," I whisper, eyes blurring from the tears. "Elijah." Elijah doesn't struggle anymore, just stares up at me. "You have gone mad. There is no coming back from where you've travelled." I press down harder. . . . He tries to whisper words to me but I know that I cannot allow Elijah to speak them. I must finish this. I have become what you are, Niska.[103]

It is not after all a German bomb that kills Elijah but his best friend Xavier. The conservative Indian tasks himself with finishing off the very threat to his existence. First, there is the immediate threat of Elijah killing Xavier. Second, Xavier claims that Elijah has turned *windigo* and that he is thus a threat to the sanity of the Indigenous collective, and the personification of the utmost evil. Third, Elijah's hybrid identity, his ability to playfully oscillate between cultural poles and to master the necessary performances of identity as skillfully as he does, also makes him a threat to "authentic" Indigenous identity. Elijah is the figure who emphasizes the constructed nature of markers of cultural belonging, and their performance becomes a necessary act in order to show their arbitrariness. He is the one who reminds everybody of the growing influence and dominance of "Western" ways on Indigenous cultures and lives. Within the carnivalesque marketplace of identities that Boyden stages for us, Elijah is the trickster-fool who constantly reminds us that unambiguity is the most powerful of all identity constructions—one that is, according to Boyden, not meant to survive.

It is not with the death of Elijah that the novel ends but rather with letting the reader know that Xavier actually stole his best friend's dog-tags, his identity.

> You must get better, Corporal Whiskeyjack, she says to me, her lips moving slowly so that I can understand. You are a good man. You are so brave that they want to give you another medal. Her expression is sad then. Your friend,

Xavier. He is dead. I stare at her mouth. But you tried to save him. Soldiers saw you walk from safety into a bombardment trying to rescue him. They say you were looking for him. That is the most any man could do for his friend.[104]

Xavier neither replies nor corrects the error. He returns home as an amputee and morphine-addict. Elijah's death, the end of a hybrid Indigenous identity, has only opened the floodgates to ambiguous identities. Xavier is not Xavier anymore; he leads an existence somewhere between being Elijah and Xavier, between being a war veteran and a traditional Indian. In this sense, modernity, Western dominance, and the carnage of war have finally left their imprint on the recovering and returning Xavier. The three-day trip into the bushes thus instead becomes a passage into an ambiguous future, one that will overthrow traditional ways of constructing cultural belonging and exclusion. The ostensibly romantic return into the hinterlands consequently marks a point of departure into what is in effect an uncertain future for Niska and Xavier. The last lines of the novel almost sound like a prediction when Niska says, "I lie here and look at the sky, then at the river, the black line of it heading north. By tomorrow we will be home."[105] Home will never look the same.

The Pitfalls of Good Intentions II: Gail Jones's *Sorry*

The notion of home, of belonging and un-belonging, also plays a central role in Gail Jones's historical novel *Sorry*, but with a different identity-political agenda. *Sorry* tells the story of the Keene family, who move from London to the Australian outback. Perdita, "wise beyond her years," retells this story of her family, which occurred prior to her birth and during her childhood.[106] World War II is raging as Stella and Nicholas Keene embark to Australia. The last paragraph of Jones's bestselling novel describes an episode of sleeplessness that their daughter Perdita suffers:

> Afraid of slumber agitation, or ghostly visits, I willed myself to think instead of Stella's snow dream: a field of flakes descending, the slow transformation of the shapes of the world, the slow, inconclusive obliteration. I saw a distant place, all forgetful white, reversing its presences. I saw Mary, and Billy, covered in snowflakes. I saw my mother's bare feet beneath the hem of her nightgown. Everything was losing definition and outline. Everything was disappearing under the gradual snow. Calmed, I looked at the sky and saw only a blank. Soft curtains coming down, a whiteness, a peace.[107]

These closing remarks, voiced by a deeply traumatized girl who has just recently recovered her ability to speak, mark the end to a condensed, highly symbolic novel that engages with the discourse of historical guilt and settler trauma in contemporary Australia. Within these lines quoted above, Jones intertwines the text's major narrative strands—or, more precisely, the narrative strands representing Perdita's multifaceted trauma—into a dreamlike state of the self-consciousness. Perdita finally becomes aware of her connection to and her position within the context of her father's murder and the subsequent events that led to the incarceration and finally the death of the forcibly removed Aboriginal housemaid Mary. It seems as if the weight of guilt, the inability to speak about the violent incident, finally lose their crushing power over Perdita. The protagonists involved in the family drama seem to be at peace with their fate—at least in Perdita's half-sleeping mind.

This passage quintessentially represents the identity-political agenda that Jones's novel pursues: *Sorry* ties in with the discourse of revisionist history writing by raising questions of the nature of settler guilt, seeks to place the burden of working through the legacies of the "Stolen Generations" on settler descendants (on Perdita in the diegetic space), and, out of respect, refrains from appropriating and representing Indigenous perspectives. The novel takes on a plethora of grave issues: it paints a very condensed picture of colonialism, settlement, the practice of forcible removal, the search for an Australian identity, and the challenges of overcoming a profound childhood trauma. The characteristically Australian topos of negotiating a relationship between the empire, British settlers, and a second settler generation is revived again, as William Shakespeare becomes an intermediary in this quest. He is a reference point of cultural superiority in *Sorry* as well as a "safe haven" for struggling Stella. This metonymical Shakespeare, who is dragged along into the outback of Australia, becomes a token of elitist culture and colonial education and is indicative of the struggle to delimit a Euro-Australian identity from British settler (self-)images and identities. In order *not* to place the burden of finding ways to express the Stolen Generations legacies solely on Australia's Indigenous peoples, Jones invents a traumatized settler daughter who finds herself voiceless and speechless.

As a result, *Sorry* suffers under the burden of such "good intentions." It is a novel so concerned with reversing colonial hierarchies by dismantling their hypocrisy that the opposite effect is actually achieved. Jones avoids speaking for Australia's Aboriginals, considering it "the right thing to do," but effectively silences them, precisely because her Aboriginal characters have little to no agency. To recover one's voice and to work through trauma eventually becomes a matter of and a task for settler-Australia, if we take Jones's identity-political allegory and perspective literally. The novel's benevolent intentions to rewrite and critically undermine celebratory notions of settlement and the attempt to make the trauma of the Stolen Generations a settler issue only engender settler navel-gazing. Again, the shape of the Australian community is reduced to Indigenous versus settler (descendants), and, as such, revisionist Australian history writing is similarly reduced to a question of how Australia positions itself in relation to its British heritage.

"I Never Saw a Vessel of Like Sorrow": The Sorry Novel and Settler Guilt

Positioning herself as an author with a clear political agenda, Jones emphasizes that "the word 'sorry' has dense and complicated meanings in Australia." At the moment of publication, Kevin Rudd had not yet delivered his apology. *Sorry* was framed as a literary precursor.[108] As the title of Jones's novel already indicates, *Sorry* is a textual, fictional example pertaining to the fact "that there has arisen, out of the conservative political years prior to the Rudd apology, a peculiarly postcolonial fictional genre." Sue Kossew refers to this genre as the "sorry novel"[109] and further outlines its genealogy:

> The "hijacking" of the meaning of history by conservative politicians as well as historians in the now infamous History Wars in Australia . . . has highlighted the importance of narratives of nationhood. Discussions at a national level about what should and what should not be included in the Australian school history syllabus reflected attitudes at a time in Australian history when the Coalition Government under John Howard was speaking a language that many Australians disagreed with and that clearly excluded Indigenous perspectives on this "whiteout history" or "comfort history" which was being posited so forcefully in opposition to so-called "black armband" history.[110]

These "sorry novels" attest to the fact that the dominant national narrative of Australian settlement, and the prolonged phase of collective silence on Indigenous suffering, also came under *artistic* scrutiny. Such texts set out to fictively "correct" misrepresentations of Australian history and thus pluralize Australia's "single national story" as an act of Indigenous empowerment. In this regard, Jones's novel seeks to form part of these countermovements to an Australian version of "comfort history."[111] Jones states her wish

> to acknowledge that Aboriginal Australians are the traditional custodians of the land about which I write, and that their spiritual and material connection with this land is persistent and precious. This text is written in the hope that further native title grants will be offered in the spirit of reconciliation and in gratitude for all that Indigenous Australians have given to others in their country.[112]

Jones thus positions herself—as an author, a citizen of the Australian country, and an academic[113]—right within the center of the discourses that accompany Australian reconciliation. Jones's mode of choice to comment on apology and reconciliation is historical literary fiction, thus further contributing to the understanding that history is written and disseminated through multiple media and genres. This novel shows how an author, driven by the desire to make a point about contemporary identity politics, politicizes her text to make the past shed a specific light on the present.

Consider how this political agenda is unfolded in the novel. As a trained anthropologist from Britain, Nicholas naturally seeks to study the Aboriginal population of Australia:

> Nicholas had a meeting in Perth with the Chief Protector of the Aborigines, and was told that his field-work projects would be useful in the governance of the natives. Aboriginal people were susceptible to the misguided influence of Reds and Foreigners and likely to be persuaded to sedition by God-bothering missionaries. They needed to be watched, assessed.[114]

This short episode is representative for the narrative's goal to paint a specific image of Nicholas: he is the ironized representative of British high culture and brings "knowledge" and "British superiority" to the country of the savages. In order to avoid any possible doubts about the role of Nicholas as the villain within the narrative, he is depicted not only as a despicable husband and father but also as an (arguably incompetent) anthropologist, a representative of the colonial gaze. The latter is a normative instrument based on misguided racial superiority, a regulatory gaze that is directed toward seemingly inferior peoples. With its agenda to get the message across, the text makes clear that Nicholas's "field studies" are void of methodology and fail to produce any valid insights into the culture of the "savages."

> Nicholas chose Australia for his field work because it appealed to his sense of the insane: what intelligent Englishman would go willingly to Australia? A black continent, certainly, and full of intractable mysteries. Perhaps Nicholas also wished to punish his pale insipid wife, to drag her away from her sisters, to make her more dependent.[115]

From the very beginning, the representative mode that Jones chooses is hyperbolic, clichéd, exaggerated, and carnivalesque. Rigorously implementing the mechanisms of reiteration and reversal, *Sorry* identifies this settler family and their misguidedness as responsible for Indigenous suffering, and this family is allegorized as the "source" of Australia's trauma. Already within the first chapters of the novel, it becomes clear that Jones adamantly seeks to criticize these notions of cultural superiority, and this overzealousness results in a gradual movement toward an involuntary parody.

It comes as no surprise that Stella and Nicholas's marriage was more a matter of inflated expectations and pleasing appearances than of mutual affection:

> On their second meeting she wore her very best hat, a cloche in grey felt adorned by a peacock feather eye, but realized that Nicholas seemed not to notice at all. . . . There would be no endearments or simple sweet gestures, no love notes, or flowers or remarks on her looks. Both were given, by long practice, to attitudes of compromise. Both recomposed into the formal shape that would become a marriage, shrank themselves into the half-lives to which they had been subtending.[116]

Nicholas had met Stella, his future wife, in a tiny café; it occurred to him that she would be capable of being a good wife and mother. However, what she later experiences paints a different picture. Consider for example the depiction of the Keenes' first night in Australia, when Nicholas and Stella fight over the reality of settlement:

> The bed they shared, enclosed against the tropical night and its steam of buzzing life, was sweltering and forlorn. It represented the world made brutal, another entrapment. Stella wept before she performed her wifely duty. Later, sticky with sweat and sexual fluids, aware of the smarting pain that had overtaken her face, she woke in the middle of the night, released herself from the net, and sat alone, on a hard chair, softly reciting sonnets.[117]

The living situation of the newly arrived settler couple in an alien and abhorrent country, as perceived by Stella, amounts to being trapped in an undesirable place, both as a wife and a mother. A tropical night, obviously horrid wifely duties, sticky sexual fluids and sweat allow no room for misinterpreting Stella's unfortunate and undesired situation. One immediately feels reminded of the dictum "Close your eyes and think of England," which a British mother would tell her daughter in preparation for her wifely duties, and of the colonial trope of exotic, alien Australia. Here, *Sorry* almost reads like a dime novel. In this tradition of championing message over nuance, a specific image of the Keene marriage is constructed that is upheld and further developed throughout the novel: the supposedly cultural superior settlers are in fact morally corrupt and utterly incapable of surviving in the outback. The attempt to reverse the notion of settler superiority is closely tied to the Keenes' deteriorating marriage. Stella saw in Nicholas "an escape," yet she was unable to "forgive Nicholas his presumption in dragging her, unconsulted, to the dark other side of the planet."[118] For Nicholas, "marriage had not been what he expected; frustration and regret were always its features."[119] Jones overburdens this image of an imperfect marriage and distorts it into an instance of involuntary reverse carnivalization, presenting a marital bond that is constructed as a cluster of melodrama and clichés. What is meant as an ironic inversion of these discursive remnants of colonialism loses its ambiguity, and therefore its critical edge, because *Sorry* reiterates and reverses in a binary manner. In effect, Jones's agenda to criticize and subvert the narrative of settler superiority by its reversal is well intended, but it appears too transparent. The narrative imbues the reader with character constellations, explanations, and representations that are in combination a burden to the narrative, because it is always one layer, one image, and one turn of the melodramatic screw too many.

Consider in this context the role of William Shakespeare as an intertextual referent. Mother Stella feels trapped in her Australian purgatory, which she seeks shelter from by clinging to Shakespeare. Shakespeare's works are introduced as presenting a remedy to Stella's pain as she finds relief and solace within his sonnets.[120] As the novel progresses, William Shakespeare assumes a double role within the novel. *Sorry* firmly establishes a link between Shakespeare's works, worlds, and words and the developments within the narrative. It thus comes as no surprise to find the link between negotiating the Australian national (post)colonial narrative by creating a nexus with the famous artist. Shakespeare and colonial modernity are deeply interwoven, and to employ fictional versions of him, or parts of his works, has a long tradition within the (post)colonial representational arsenal.[121] Many of his plays negotiate social value systems that arose in relation to colonialism as a global force and the colonial local enterprises, and as such are effectively much more ambiguous than the level of intertextuality that *Sorry* proposes.[122]

Ania Loomba and Martin Orkin state that "both Shakespeare and colonialism have left their imprint on cultures across the globe, . . . due to the nature of their global presence."[123] They are both global players up to the present day. Shakespeare was read as being a key witness to and an expression of an alleged cultural superiority that was built on racism and xenophobia, and this colonialist-serving interpretation is of course no less than an instrumentalization of Shakespeare's corpus to further solidify the colonial mindset.[124] Shakespeare was regarded as the epitome of British high culture, and acts as a vehicle for the dissemination of the latter. Frank Schulze-Engler describes how Shakespeare's works reflect upon and depict "love for the brave new world," as well as the alleged superiority of the colonial master.[125] Shakespeare's renderings of colonial contexts are by no means praises of colonialism, nor do they serve as mere backgrounds to his plays, as Schulze-Engler outlines; instead, they engage critically with this global regulatory force that divided the world into superior and inferior.

In an ironic twist, this Shakespeare—who was not entirely uncritical of the colonial endeavor—very much became the token of elite culture, in particular throughout the nineteenth century.[126] It is very much along these lines that Gail Jones utilizes Shakespeare and his words. Shakespeare's stance on colonialism as represented within his oeuvre is much more complex, and *Sorry* fails to represent this complexity. This utterly stereotypical Keene family brings one of the most powerful tokens of this superiority to the outback, and Jones's Shakespeare is used to create a tension between British superiority and Australian savagery, between the dark country and enlightened, light-bringing culture in order to critically subvert it.

Sorry is hence a case of intertextual engagement that is supposed to serve an identity-political agenda. On the one hand, Shakespeare's works shape the narrative of *Sorry* itself, and the flow of Jones's text is interspersed and at times interrupted by quotes from his famous works. On the other hand, the playwright becomes the token of this very high culture, and his words become "empty vessels" of a long-gone English past that Stella frantically clings to. Jones's Shakespeare seemingly divides the world into good and bad, into superior and inferior:

> [B]y the time she was nine Perdita knew [Hamlet's] most famous lamentations by heart:
>
>> O, that this too too solid flesh would melt
>> Thaw and resolve itself into a dew!
>> Or that the Everlasting had not fix'd
>> His cannon 'gainst self-slaughter! O God! God!
>> How weary, stale, flat and unprofitable,
>> Seem to me the uses of this world!
>> Fie on 't! Ah, fie! 'tis an unweeded garden,
>> That grows to seed; things rank and gross in nature
>> Possess it merely. That it should come to this!
>
> Perdita was not entirely sure what this meant, but liked the animating grizzle, the bad tempered tone. Stella declared that this speech, and others like it, were about the "big questions." She told her daughter that everything one needed to know about life was contained in a volume of Shakespeare; that he was all-wise, incomparable, the encompasser of every human range.[127]

Shakespeare has indeed been regarded as the "encompasser of every human range," but Jones's Shakespeare, however, is an "empty vessel" as a means to intervene into Australian post-settlement identity in the making. The Shakespearean world models in *Sorry* do not suffice, because Jones's Shakespeare can only ironize the very attempt to make him a vehicle to differentiate British settler identity from a second settler generation as represented by Perdita. This specific Shakespeare cannot contest or criticize this alleged cultural advantage, since he is also reduced to this overly simplistic role of being a pawn to Jones's political message.

In this particular family setting, Stella is solely responsible for the cultural education and the transmission of (cultural) values to her daughter. Stella's sanity hinges on the recitation of verses, and her learning them by heart is the only education that young Perdita receives from her parents. Consider, for example, the following scene where Stella teaches her daughter at home:

> The Shakespearean lessons were those Perdita loved best because they were stories. When her mother recited she was at a loss, completely bamboozled by the half-English, half-ornament quality of the verse, the overwrought pomposity of it all, the lavish sentiments. But when Stella first read aloud from Charles Lamb's summaries, the plots became intelligible, and Perdita was entranced how heroic people could be, how many monarchs were mad, how many lovers disguised, how many women were faithless, or exceeding in beauty, how mistaken identity was everywhere and disastrously abroad, how easily stabbings or poisonings or suicides might occur, to shuffle off, Shakespeareanly, one's mortal coil.[128]

This is a textual example of how Jones intertwines intra- and extratextual realities; of how mediated Shakespearean worlds become blueprints of Perdita's environment, and how Perdita tries to make sense of her world through Shakespeare. Yet, upon closer scrutiny, it becomes evident that it is Stella who filters Perdita's reception of Shakespeare, and it is Lamb's summaries that shape Perdita's perception of his works. Shakespeare thus comes to Perdita in a highly mediated form. With this tight link to and with Shakespeare, Jones strives to reverse, to ironize, the idea that the act of settlement resulted in the imperative to elevate the "savages" into a higher standard of existence, and that it was the "achievements" of the settlers, convicts, and emancipists that literally cultivated the country of "savages." Valérie-Anne Belleflamme holds that

> Jones's discursive strategies involve a mapping of the dominant discourse, including inter-discursive Shakespearean references, in order to expose its underlying assumptions, before dismantling these assumptions from the cross-cultural standpoint of both the novel's culturally hybrid protagonist and its readers. It is by first establishing an inter-discursive link with Shakespeare that Jones subsequently and most successfully manages to distance herself from the dominant discourse and to assert her own counter-discourse.[129]

It is in this vein that Perdita "knew this to be false" and that these specific Shakespearean world models, in this context meaning colonial world models, do not suffice as explanatory structures within the Australian outback.[130] In contrast to the stance that Belleflamme takes in the quote above, the distancing from superiorist discourses fails because that is the only strategy the text employs. The fighting-fire-with-fire approach that Jones pursues runs counter to her benevolent identity-political agenda to correct Australia's national narrative, because the internal rifts of this first settler generation overshadow all other discourses relating to settlement and Indigenous mistreatment. What is more, all other perspectives and discourses are relegated to the outskirts of the diegetic universe, if not completely silenced. This representational conundrum is effectively never solved.

Consequently, the involuntary carnivalization of *Sorry*'s non-"whiteout" stance continues. Instead of envisaging a Shakespeare that enables a "writing back" against cultural hierarchies, and instead of standing against the impossibility of the Keene family who actually display their very prominent shortcomings all by themselves, this particular Shakespeare connection that Jones invokes ties in with Shakespeare's use as a token of British identity, while the Australian settler is in search of an identity in the form of independence from, and in contrast to, the British colonial masters.[131] Accordingly, Jones considers it necessary to revive these discourses in order to make a point about contemporary struggles for reconciliation with the Aboriginal people of Australia. In this case, the setting does not reflect the tensions between Aboriginals and Euro-Australian settlers but between settlers and their British predecessors.

This involuntary reverse-carnivalization of Jones's own critical categories and representations has an effect on the representations of Aboriginals, the (post)colonial quintessential Other. Captain Smith, on the passage from Britain to Australia, instructs Nicholas on the country, nature, and character of the "savages" that Nicholas is about to encounter:

> The Aborigine, he said, like all the primitive peoples, had a tendency to expire on contact with a superior race. It was the sad duty of Civilised Man to raise or erase the lesser humans, to enable the March of Progress and the Completion of God's Plan. He confirmed that knowledge of how the black buggers thought would be useful in their management and control.[132]

On the one hand, *Sorry* establishes England as the locus of civilization and high culture, and on the other hand, we meet this dark, undesirable, far-off country. This dichotomy—albeit meant ironically—is reinforced at every possible corner. Here the colonial trope of the "white man's burden" is invoked, but Jones's novel effectively renders working through the Stolen Generations legacy as a "white girl's burden."

Shortly after arriving in Australia, Stella becomes pregnant, but all attempts to terminate the pregnancy fail. Daughter Perdita is born into the midst of a further deteriorating marriage: Nicholas's civilizing mission in Australia amounts to the "sexualizing of the terra incognita," and, along with it, its inhabitants.[133] Her father frequently forces himself on the Aboriginal servants of the neighboring estates, while her mother further retreats into her obsessions with the works of Shakespeare. Perdita is left unwanted and unloved by her parents. She only finds love, a family structure, and security among the "savages," the Aboriginals who happen to be Nicholas's objects of study, proven unfit to comply with Western standards of family and culture:

> Nicholas added that kin would have to be destroyed if Aborigines were to enter the modern world. It made them share everything, he said, so they were always poor and could never accumulate property. It made them think in communal, not individual terms, so that they were always bound to the past, to tribal savagery, not looking forward to the new self that would equip them for twentieth-century Australia. This was one of the chief propositions of his research "hypothesis."[134]

Yet again, we encounter a disproportionate amount of "whiteout" settler perspective. The utter dysfunctionality and misguidedness of the Keenes, however, is not contrasted by self-confident Indigenous protagonists:

> When Nicholas pulled back the yellow curtains he saw in the distance a clump of acadia, and beneath it, in sparse shade, resting in the grove of a dry creek-bed, a family group of about ten or twelve people. They would be the subjects, or rather, the objects of his research. They looked, he thought, rather mundane, not noble savages or extraordinary specimens of humanity. They wore cast-off clothes, mostly filthy and shredded, and had a matted hair and looks of dreary resignation. They roasted a lizard—one he would later know as goanna—in the ashes of a fire, and passed a canvas water bag between them, each taking a swig. He had read of this communalism, but found the sight of it disturbing him—so much bodily correspondence, so much touch and exchange.[135]

Jones reactivates the stereotype of the "noble savage" in order to contest it, but there is just too much effort expended to render them authentically Indigenous and, more importantly, authentically victimized to make it seem credible. As such, natives are grouped together in the outback, looking rather ragged and filthy, and appear to be weary of their own existence. They are rendered as communal beings because the narrative makes them circle the water bag while at the same time preparing an "authentic" Aboriginal meal. These Aboriginals are actually noble because they take selfless care of settler daughter Perdita. The task to reiterate and reverse results once more in the opposite effect: natives in *Sorry* remain both savage and noble.

Since the novel does not allow Indigenous protagonists to counter this simplistic and underdeveloped image, by word or by action, the stereotypical depiction of Aboriginality remains unchallenged. Instead of becoming an empowering statement of Indigenous resilience, the narrative involuntarily parodies the attempt to write against a solely "white" perspective on settlement, forcible relocation, and education. Jones's Aboriginals become archetypical victims and not self-empowered examples of resilience.[136]

Consider another textual example of this involuntary but in effect narcissistic carnivalization of Jones's own political endeavor. Perdita reminisces about her time in the care of a neighboring Aboriginal kin:

> My early childhood was watched over by Sal and Daff, and by Billy Trevor. They called me Deeta. Sal and Daff continued, for several years, to work at the Trevors' house—a big station homestead, just a quarter of a mile up the track—but then Sal, and one month later Daff, disappeared with no warning. I was six, perhaps, when they abandoned me. I cried for days and days, as did Billy beside me, holding one of my hands while he flapped the other, like a broken bird-wing, like a trapped cockatoo.[137]

Sal and Daff are obviously Aboriginal representatives, as is Billy, who is disabled by impaired hearing. Although it is not clear whether Sal and Daff fall victim to forcible relocation to another settler family or homestead, this episode can also be read as fortifying the stereotype of the unreliable, mysteriously disappearing Indigenous who cannot be trusted with serious tasks like caring for a little white girl. The scene continues with Perdita pointing out that

> [a]lthough I was a whitefella, a *kartiya,* Sal or Daff would carry me angled on their bony hips, and take me down to the creek-bed, to sit with their people. I would be passed, like other small children, from body to body, nestling there, cradled in capacious laps, and I would feel the long fingers sift through my hair for lice, and the stroking of my arms, and the tickle of a tease. I was nourished and cared for in ways my parents were incapable of understanding.[138]

A few lines down from the episode where Sal and Daff disappear into thin air, the image is constructed that *even though* Perdita is a white child, the natives are willing to take care of her and treat her with everything that is part of the Aboriginal (emotional and cultural) inventory that Jones allows for in her novel. The Aboriginals in this passage are yet again only depicted in relation to Perdita, through Perdita's first-person narrative, and not as sovereign independent characters with their own voice. Aboriginals are confined to be silent once more. It is clear that Jones seeks to picture the Aboriginals as the locus of love and familial care, but this benevolent intention results in turning this reading upside-down. Aboriginals are shown to be naturally gifted caretakers of young Perdita, graciously enduring their own miserable existence—as for example reflected by the description of their "bony hips" and the image of the "trapped cockatoo"—in order to provide a "home" for Perdita. The search for lice almost reminds one of this specific ritualistic practice as carried out by monkeys and apes. The close association with animals and spirits is even further evoked when Billy is described as follows:

"Spirits ebrywheres," [Daff] said. "Ebrywheres, all roun."

Billy, Billy was different; but the small group in the creekbed fed him and played with him and taught him skills with his hands. The spirit within him was particular and probably unknowable. Only when I was older I realized how much I loved Billy, how faithful and consistent a companion he had been. He was an odd-looking boy—pigeon-chested, with crooked teeth and dappled skin. He had bottle-grey eyes, which he forgot to blink, so that they appeared watery, as if he was on the verge of tears. These features made him look stupid and wise, and old-man Dauwarrngu said that Billy knew things, secret things, like blackfellas, this one Billy-fella.[139]

Again, the text does not provide any comical, ironical, or satirical relief to this simplistic rendering of Aboriginality. Indigenous characters in *Sorry* are reduced to foils on which to project—ironically—Jones's noncomforting and "whiteout" history. Here, the reader is able to see that Jones attempts to make the devastating living situation of Aboriginal communities palpable, but, in the process, the natives in *Sorry* become once again "empty vessels" in service of Jones's political project. They are pawns in her narrative, inserted to counter the inhumanity of the Keene family. These oversimplified (historical and cultural) identities, binary explanatory models, and the overpowering concern with this settler family puts a strain on the political message of *Sorry* that it does not recover from. The negotiation of historical truths and identities, for which the text stands allegorically, becomes a self-serving Euro-Australian perspective and, consequently, leaves the reader with a feeling of profound unease, because the natives are marginalized and silenced once more. While Jones pursues her task of correcting historical representations and commenting on the present, she involuntarily resurrects clichés and consequently carnivalizes her initial noble task to set the record straight.

Empty Vessels: Carnivalizing Settler Trauma

In many ways, Perdita is the main protagonist of this "sorry novel" and the focus of the narrative to which its protagonists gravitate. At times, Perdita is the personal narrator of the story; on other occasions, the narrative voice focuses on a variety of characters, but Perdita forms the center. As the narrative progresses, it becomes clear that it was actually Perdita who stabbed her father to death after having witnessed him raping her close friend Mary. In the aftermath of her deed and the trauma that results from this murder, she loses not only her speech but also her memory. Perdita recovers her memory in therapeutic sessions, and the unfolding recuperation of her life story governs the narratological shape and structure of the novel: it progresses and digresses, jumps between focalizations and contexts, all to resemble the attempt to master a traumatic episode.

Sorry has thus been widely received as a text that engages with trauma in culture.[140] The novel has consequently been identified as a text that links trauma, silence, speechlessness, and recovery with forgetting, remembering, and responsibility.[141] Silence and the inability to speak are widely disseminated literary[142] and, according to Kossew, postcolonial tropes.[143] Indeed, Michele McCrea regards this novel as an utterly "postcolonial project" that seeks to intertwine the trinity of memory politics—"the diversities of the present," "the ghosts of the past," and "the demands of the future"—performatively and productively.[144] In a similar vein, Rosanne Kennedy locates *Sorry* within the realm of trauma literature and attributes a specific discursive power to Jones's text: it "knowingly draws on the discourse of trauma to frame events and responses to them."[145] In other words, *Sorry* seemingly offers the possibility of understanding trauma in Euro-Australian culture, of (re)visiting the narratives that form the layers of trauma within a community, and of emphasizing the significance of opening up a discursive field to excavate what was buried. Trauma and recovery have thus become tropes, and a (literary) engagement with them has been rendered a political undertaking, and a vital part of the genre of the "sorry novel."[146] Rosanne Kennedy further contributes to this understanding:

> In recent years, there have been numerous calls for the field of trauma studies to expand beyond its European and North American origins. It is especially important, as the insights of trauma theory are extended to a wider range of geopolitical sites and conflicts and into resistant fields such as law, that critics attend to the ways in which the discourse of trauma travels, how it is used or resisted in specific national or local contexts, and with what cultural and political effects.[147]

Within these few lines, Kennedy maps out how the engagement with trauma has been highly politicized. Jones primarily engages with a case of individual trauma, that of Perdita most prominently, and her (individual) trauma is in turn reframed as a literary engagement with settler trauma as its collective equivalent. The "history wars" have shown that engaging with politically correct narratives of the settler past has resulted in posing pertinent and painstaking questions about the nature and degree of settler guilt. *Sorry* seemingly makes a case for the existence of settler guilt and the corresponding collective trauma—the inability to face this guilt and to speak about it—and this is Jones's point of entry into the trauma discourse in relation to Australia's processes of reconciliation. Doris Herrero remarks that

> [t]he murder is the center of the story and, as is often the case with traumatic experiences, the story's protagonist and internal narrator will recall it over

and again in disconnected segments that resemble camera flashes or a cinematic montage of visceral images, which she simply cannot remember or put together.[148]

Jones invents a traumatic episode—the murder of Perdita's own, albeit despicable, father—and embeds the incident in a narrative that resembles a trauma.[149] A traumatic event is basically defined as an occurrence that is so forceful in its impact on the individual that the victim is unable to integrate this event into his or her own life story, experience, and "knowledge" of the world.[150] The incident that could not be reconciled with the victim's identity and story of the self "returns to haunt the survivor" and consequently escapes the control of and mastery by the victim.[151] The allegorical trajectory that *Sorry* pursues is to make clear that this trauma haunts settler identity in Australia, for it haunts Perdita. Herrero continues to outline that the event's "pathology cannot be defined by the event itself, nor in terms of a distortion of the event. It consists, rather, in the way in which this event is *not* experienced or received."[152]

Yet this fictionalized case of Euro-Australian trauma circles solely around itself. Consider for example the murder scene, which functions as the reason for and explanation of Perdita's trauma—and most notably not for Mary's:

> When Nicholas falls, the knife is still lodged in his neck—he is being yanked into awareness of *what has happened*, that he is doomed and will die, ignoble and prostrate—Stella is already, certainly, present in the room. She is standing there, yes, she is calmly reciting *Macbeth*. There is no point crazier than this moment, nothing less plausible. Perdita sees how her mother's hair flies upward as if electrified, how she has a stony gaze and a solid intention. Her voice is loud; she is performing on a private stage. [Stella recites Shakespeare.] Blithering Shakespeare. Who would believe that a wife recites while her husband bleeds to death, that she converts into fancy, high-falutin speech at this senseless moment, this wasteful gash? She counterfeits art because blood letting is familiar and known. Blood-lusting Shakespeare. Incarnadine words.[153]

This melodramatic scene continues to shift the focalization from Perdita to Stella and back. Mary, however, is blocked from view. Finally, Perdita—who is the murderer—is allowed to appear as "tear-blinded and overwhelmed," as "if a cloud has blown through her eyes and into her head," "but wants nothing more than to fall into oblivion of fatigue and forgetting."[154] This killing scene with its rather disproportionate featuring of Stella, with Mary who is completely absent from the narrative as an active agent but was the initial reason for the act of murder, becomes the quintessence of Jones's political message: she relocates the trauma discourse and translates it into the settler context, shifting the focus of attention to settler culture away from Indigenous suffering.

Within the Australian reconciliation discourse, however, the notion of trauma is closely associated with the Indigenous populations in general and the victims and survivors of the system of forcible removal in particular. The processes of reconciliation seek to break with the paradigm of being centrally concerned with the role and representation of settlers in Australian history. It was an Australian specificity to emphasize the uniqueness of the Australian historical and cultural trauma in the context of colonialism, and to postulate that the time has come to recognize, to become aware of the profound and lasting traumatization of Indigenous populations. One of the most important tasks of the "politics of regret"—if not *the* task per se—is to enable a voicing-out for the survivors, to provide a stage for them to tell their story and consequently to render Indigenous trauma a collective Australian, thus transcultural, narrative—one that unites rather than divides. Personal stories of trauma thus travel toward the realm of the collective and consequently become collectivized. Reconciliation is framed to help with overcoming silence and the inability to "speak the unspeakable."[155] The unspeakable, in Jones's realm, becomes settler guilt as represented by Perdita—being guilty of murdering her father *and* of letting Mary take the fall for it.

Critics have argued that Perdita is evidently the one who has suffered a major traumatic event, whereas it is utterly clear that Perdita is by far not the only traumatized white protagonist.[156] Stella develops insanity, which is also due to her abhorrent marriage conditions. Nicholas is a World War I veteran, to some extent a war invalid, who was unsuccessful enough in life to become the man he is. As one can see, the notion of trauma is omnipresent and omnipotent within Jones's novel, yet it seems to refrain from affecting other ethnicities. Herrero makes the following comments:

> Significantly, though, it is only Perdita's trauma, and to a lesser extent Stella's, to which the novel testifies and which it explores. Here lies its most bitter irony. The Aboriginal girl is the true victim of the story, as is often the case in novels written by Aboriginal authors, because she takes the blame for Perdita by "confessing" to the crime. In fact, *Sorry* can only be properly problematized and understood by addressing the social and historical contexts of the Stolen Generations and of the trauma caused by the forcible removal of half caste Aboriginal children from their parents. . . . As Perdita's murder of her father is catalyzed by his rape of Mary, and as Mary is the victim of permanent abuse and ill-treatment, she is the one character who should show symptoms of chronic childhood trauma.[157]

It is the character of Mary in particular that surprises the reader. Jones twists the Australian trauma paradigm and transfers it to a settler family setting, where it is unfolding, sought out, cured, and addressed, and leaves the Aboriginals to be marginalized once again and to remain silent. Nicholas is a cruel father figure and a despicable husband in any case, so this family tragedy does not require an Aboriginal character, a forcibly removed housemaid who is raped by Nicholas, in order to render it a devastating family situation. He repeatedly abuses and mistreats Stella as well as his daughter Perdita. However, Herrero somewhat misses the point by claiming that Mary should be the only one suffering from trauma, because Perdita has after all stabbed her father to death, and this most certainly results in trauma. In fact, the narrative frames the murder almost as a good deed, to have stood up for Mary and to have freed the world from Nicholas's tyranny. Perdita consequently remains the true heroine of the story, for she is the one who has intervened and subsequently killed her father, because he was raping Mary, not because he frequently abused Stella, her own mother. As an infant who has witnessed countless troublesome events and much violence, Perdita cannot be held morally accountable for ending the life of her own father. At least this is how the narrative frames it in order to explain why Perdita left Mary incarcerated. She has after all killed for Mary, and Mary in turn takes the fall for it. It is instead the case that a prominent Aboriginal character is not required for the narrative, for the multiple shortcomings of the Keenes may actually stand for themselves. Perdita's trauma in particular, and Euro-Australian settler trauma as its collective equivalent, suffocate Indigenous (and all other) traumas within *Sorry*. The narrative thus remains trapped in a circular movement that inevitably leads back to Euro-Australia, rendering it a self-serving, narcissistic endeavor.

As a result, Mary is a character so underdeveloped that Rosanne Kennedy calls her "anemic," and she has no other function within the narrative than to underline the complete failure of the Keenes as parents and settlers.[158] Although Mary has been raped multiple times by Nicholas and has been sent to a girl's home and to prison subsequently, Jones has her state the following when Perdita visits her:

> "So why did you protect me, Mary?" . . . "Deeta, I chose. I chose to help you, eh? And now I have no choice. No one will believe the word of a bush blackfella. Unless," she added, "they're confessing a crime." Mary paused. She looked away. The clanging sound—something metallic being loaded and shifted—ceased to meet her silence. . . . "But it was me . . ." "Yeah, Deeta, it was you. And you were a child. A *child*, Deeta." "I knew what I was doing."[159]

Mary as a protagonist has nonetheless had to come to life to a certain degree, because the political aim of the novel—to contribute to the questions of the nature of reconciliation and the public apology—requires Aboriginal presence. The presence of Mary (and the other minor characters of Aboriginal descent) is supposed to render it an intervention into the discourses of reconciliation.

One might contend that the relocation of trauma from the context of the forcibly removed to the realm of the settlers is in itself striking and thought-provoking, as some critics have argued, and to herald Jones's text as an act of literary engagement with collective guilt on behalf of the non-Indigenous Australian majority—a move that was long overdue:

> It is my contention that *Sorry* engages in a metatextual discussion of the ethics of reconciliation and cultural contrition. Interestingly enough, Jones claims that *Sorry* has "a political-allegorical aspect—as one would expect, claiming such a title"—but "that it is not centrally concerned with representing the Stolen Generations. As a white Australian, it would be presumptuous to do so and it would risk appropriation of others' painful experience." . . . Jones seems keen to subvert the stereotypical discursive manifestations of the Australian Reconciliation.[160]

Instead of subverting stereotypes, which are the (by)product of discourses of reconciliation—such as the "damaged Native," for example—*Sorry* instead reproduces stereotypes that continue to circulate in the context of the (post)colonial realm (as represented by the failing anthropologist, Shakespeare as the token of the British cultural elite, etc.) and that continue to serve as explanatory structures within postcolonial societies. This result of Jones's narrative strategy of the use of the hyperbolic is actually a reenactment of colonial race relations (inferior/superior) through its employment of dim Aboriginal protagonists and an overemphasis on settler trauma/identity and recovery—in other words, it offers a narcissistic carnivalization of a literary apology. Dolores Herrero ventures in a similar direction, stating that *Sorry* is

> yet another example of a recurrent phenomenon in contemporary Australian literature, namely the desperate attempt to heal the anxieties of (un)belonging that haunt settler culture. These anxieties were reinforced and gathered unprecedented strength with the growing realization among certain white settlers that their existence and well-being, together with the foundation of the nation itself, had come about at the expense of unutterable acts of Aboriginal dispossession and genocide.[161]

Jones wants Perdita to become the representative of a refined, chastened settler generation that has learned its moral lesson through experience and by acknowledging guilt. Valérie-Anne Belleflamme argues that Perdita transports that transcultural position, that Perdita's situation of living between the poles, of oscillating between the different lifestyles and worldviews—as represented by her British parents and her Aboriginal friends—and of being part of the second settler generation renders her a character who transports the transcultural experience.[162] In contrast to Perdita's alleged transculturality, *Sorry* makes reconciliation a question of how settlers position themselves toward

British colonialism, its representatives and histories, and not so much about how this second settler generation posits itself in relation to the Aboriginals. In effect we discover a self-serving narrative of lessons the second settler generation had to learn in order to be able to reconcile. It is the overall problem of this novel that, although it seeks to clarify and excavate settler guilt, it takes the wrong track and makes it about British colonial identity guilt, further shoving aside the possibility of engaging with the relationship between Euro-Australians and Aboriginals. Self-criticism—the initial task that *Sorry* has set for itself—becomes its own version of narcissistic carnivalization, as *Sorry* is unable to break out of the cycle of self-reference and self-referentiality.

In Conclusion: Fearing the Transcultural?

Offering a sense of revised, more nuanced accounts of formative historical narratives, *Sorry* and *Three Day Road* both pursue the task of providing alternative readings of hegemonic collective memories. The "politics of regret" in both countries provided the stage for these two texts to engage with national and (trans)cultural histories. The two authors made it their personal task to contribute artistically to the discourses of reconciliation. The identity politics that *Three Day Road* and *Sorry* pursue are carnivalesque in nature, because they identify, reiterate, and (attempt to) reverse formative national narratives that also have a bearing on contemporary Australia and Canada.

Despite the novel's benevolent intentions, *Sorry* reverse carnivalizes the notion of Indigenous empowerment. In an attempt to avoid culturally appropriating the Indigenous voice, and to confront Australians with their colonial legacies, this novel ultimately silences its Aboriginal characters. Moreover, *Sorry*'s main protagonist Perdita, the settler daughter, is framed as suffering from trauma that requires her to work through it to reclaim her voice. Perdita's story allegorizes Australia's struggle to come to terms with its involvement in the system of forcible removal; to gain independence from Britain is reframed as having caused settler trauma. Jones's novel reengages with this discourse of negotiating what it means to be Australian and depicts the hypocrisy and utter shortcomings of a—in Jones's terms—representative British settler family. However, Jones's ambiguous project—the "sorry novel"—turns into an involuntary, reverse carnivalization of Jones's well-intended political message. Instead of inscribing Indigenous agency into the context of settlement, Jones reinforces received power hierarchies by prioritizing the negotiation of settler guilt over any valid Indigenous perspective, thus producing an entirely whitewashed perspective. This novel is an example of the pitfalls of both overzealousness with regard to "sorry politics" and a notion of empowerment that simply builds on reiteration and reversal.

Three Day Road offers a much more nuanced picture of the struggle to imagine (trans)cultural identities in the context of reconciliation. But Boyden's novel can also be accused of making use of overly simplistic notions of collectives: he juxtaposes a quite homogenous Canadian settler-soldier identity with a similarly compartmentalized idea of Indianness. The heterogeneity of both the broader Canadian society and Indigenous identities remains unrepresented. Notwithstanding their unambiguity, or more precisely because of their unambiguity, such identity containers also play an important role in the context of Canadian "politics of regret," because these processes structurally rely on and reiterate these simplistic notions. However, Boyden inserts the character of Elijah into this neatly mapped field of identities, and he complicates these matters profoundly. Elijah's transculturality, however, is connoted as problematic, because it is aligned with morphine addiction and the invocation of increasing madness on Elijah's part. The text presents the demise of Boyden's trickster-fool to make it look like a mercy killing, and like an act of cleansing indigeneity from cannibalistic hybrids.

The two literary examples discussed here refrain from or fail to produce sustainable, convincing versions of the experience of transculturality.[163] Both Gail Jones and Joseph Boyden struggle to imagine viable transcultural identities. Jones's ambitious project, which sought to critically contribute to the discourse of reconciliation and apology, has involuntarily ended in a persiflage of identities, discourses, and truths, and it renders reconciliation a quest for dissociating a well-meaning settler culture from a hypocritical, cruel British colonialism. This political endeavor in the shape of a novel has been pressured by identity politics to the extent that the author finds it inappropriate to appropriate the Indigenous voice, or any other voice that points beyond its very own cliché. Perdita instead appears like an empty vessel filled with empty lessons on culture and life rather than a self-confident, self-reflexive transcultural identity, crossing borders and shaping new forms of the in-between, the transgressive, the interspatial. *Sorry* can be read as an example of how the crisis of settler identity continuously revolves around itself and renders the process of reconciliation a self-serving endeavor, thus leaving no room to imagine transcultural identities.

It remains debatable whether it was an authorial strategy or artistic creativity going astray that led to Elijah's death in Boyden's *Three Day Road*. He was after all the transcultural trickster-clown who points toward a modern transcultural Canadian identity. Elijah was able to overcome all cultural and ethnic boundaries; still (or because?) Boyden killed him. More precisely, his best friend, the "true" Indian Xavier, the savior of "authentic" indigeneity, ends Elijah's life. This death haunts Xavier, the narrative, and arguably the reader until the very end of the novel. One remains puzzled by the seemingly quite simple message that *Three Day Road* offers: First Nations, go back to the bush, turn your back on modernity and non-Indigenous reality, and all will be well. It is Xavier, the savior, who tasks himself with maintaining an "authentic" Indigenous identity and subsequently kills his friend Elijah. It is Perdita's task to end the existence of a bully, a perpetrator, a representative of cultural-container mentality, while Xavier finishes off trickster Elijah. Perdita kills not only her father but also what he stands for: an allegedly superior culture that imposes itself physically, violently, and literally on its subalterns. Xavier does not simply end the life of a madman, a victim of the circumstances of war, but also the one who can move between cultures.

One might read both novels as calls for action to the non-Indigenous majority of Australia/Canada to face up to their country's troubled past. They can also be seen as statements regarding new forms of (inter)relationships between both parts of Australian/Canadian society. The nature of relationships between Indigenous and non-Indigenous peoples has been further complicated by these two fictional contributions, because the answers that both texts provide in this regard appear rather simplistic. Akin to Boyden, Jones's vision of transcultural identities—as unconvincing as hers might be—also appears rather pessimistic. Viable transcultural identities would point to a possible future of national narratives and identities, but both texts remain at best ambivalent about the foundation and practice of such renewed relations. After all, Perdita is lost, as her name already indicates, and commits patricide, while Xavier strives to "save" a form of cultural essentialism that is a fiction in itself. Consequently, as readers, we are supposed to conclude from *Sorry* and *Three Day Road* that a transcultural identity/character as a token of "new beginnings" and "possible futures" is by default an impossible existence. Both the protagonists who (might) transport this experience—Perdita on the one hand and Elijah on the other—kill or are killed.

With regard to the victim paradigm that the "politics of regret" inadvertently produce, Boyden's and Jones's texts present us with very different and highly ambiguous victims. *Three Day Roads* ends with Elijah's double victimization: first, he is subjugated to colonial cultural reeducation with all its long-lasting effects. Second, he falls victim to his best friend Xavier, a fact that the novel somewhat oddly frames as necessary and a result of war trauma. *Sorry* altogether sidelines Indigenous victimhood, relegates it to a position at the diegetic margins, and wallows in Perdita's multifaceted trauma. Perpetrators in both cases are to a lesser extent represented as structural, abstract forces and more as actual human beings with close ties to the novels' main protagonists. What is more, they are to a certain degree held accountable for their wrongdoings—Nicholas dies at the hands of his daughter, and Xavier must live with the knowledge of having ended the life of his best friend. Xavier loses a leg on the battlefield and with it a sustainable perspective for his and his kin's future.

Notes

1. Joseph Boyden, *Three Day Road* (London: Phoenix, 2005), paratext.
2. See Martin Loeschnigg and Marzena Sokolowska-Paryz, eds., *The Great War in Post-memory Literature and Film* (Berlin: De Gruyter, 2014), for further reading.
3. See Karin Ikas, *Reconstructing National Identity: The Nation Forged in Fire-Myth and Canadian Literature* (Wiesbaden: Peter Lang, 2018).
4. See Hanna Teichler, "Joseph Boyden's *Three Day Road*: Transcultural (Post-)Memory and Identity in Canadian World War I Fiction," in *The Great War in Post-memory Literature and Film*, ed. Martin Loeschnigg and Marzena Sokolowska-Paryz (Berlin: De Gruyter, 2014), 239–53.
5. Summer Block, "Interview with Gail Jones," *January Magazine*, May 2008, retrieved 21 December 2016 from http://januarymagazine.com/profiles/gailjones.html.
6. Eric Andrew-Gee, "The Making of Joseph Boyden," *The Globe and Mail*, 4 August 2017, retrieved 29 November 2020 from https://beta.theglobeandmail.com/arts/books-and-media/joseph-boyden/article35881215/?ref=http://www.theglobeandmail.com&.
7. Andrew-Gee, "Making of Joseph Boyden."
8. Jorge Barrera, "Joseph Boyden's Shape-Shifting Indigenous Identity," APTN, 23 December 2016, retrieved 29 November 2020 from http://aptnnews.ca/2016/12/23/author-joseph-boydens-shape-shifting-indigenous-identity.
9. Eric Andrew-Gee traces Boyden's claims of Indigenous heritage to a legal dispute surrounding the purchase of Sandy Island. In one sworn affidavit, Boyden refers to himself as Métis and presents an ID card as proof. However, the Ontario Métis Aboriginal Association (also known as the Woodland Métis Tribe)—which issued this card—is known for its "lax membership policy that does not require any proof of indigenous ancestry." Andrew-Gee, "Making of Joseph Boyden."
10. Joseph Boyden, "My Name is Joseph Boyden," MacLeans, 2 August 2017, retrieved 29 November 2020 from http://www.macleans.ca/news/canada/my-name-is-joseph-boyden/.
11. Andrew-Gee, "Making of Joseph Boyden."
12. Jane Onyanga-Omara, "Grey Owl: Canada's Great Conservationist and Imposter," BBC News, 19 September 2013, https://www.bbc.com/news/uk-england-sussex-24127514.
13. James Freeman, "From the Archives 1995: Writer Demidenko Revealed to be Helen Darville," *Sydney Morning Herald*, 21 August 2020, retrieved 29 November 2020 from https://www.smh.com.au/culture/books/from-the-archives-1995-writer-demidenko-revealed-to-be-helen-darville-20200813-p55ldc.html.
14. Eva Rask Knudsen, "Aboriginal Affair(s): Reflections on Mudrooroo's Life and Work," *Literature in North Queensland* 39 (2012): 106.
15. See Parul Sehgal, "He Was a Prominent Holocaust Survivor. But His Story Was a Hoax," *New York Times*, 28 August 2018, retrieved 29 November 2020 from https://www.nytimes.com/2018/08/28/books/review-impostor-javier-cercas-enric-marco.html.
16. Stefan Maechler, *The Wilkomirski Affair: A Study in Biographical Truth* (New York: Schocken Books, 2001). See also Blake Eskin, *A Life in Pieces: The Making and Unmaking of Binjamin Wilkomirski* (New York: W. W. Norton, 2002).
17. Fiachra Gibbons and Stephen Moss, "Fragments of a Fraud," *The Guardian*, 15 October 1999, retrieved 29 November 2020 from https://www.theguardian.com/theguardian/1999/oct/15/features11.g24.
18. Gibbons and Moss, "Fragments."
19. Gibbons and Moss, "Fragments."
20. Renata Salecl, "Why One Would Pretend to Be a Victim of the Holocaust," *Other Voices: The (e)journal of Cultural Criticism* 2, no. 1 (2000): retrieved 29 November 2020 from

https://web.archive.org/web/20100902060300/http:/www.othervoices.org/2.1/salecl/wilkomirski.html.
21. Maureen Clark, "Mudrooroo: Crafty Imposter or Rebel with a Cause," *Australian Literary Studies* 21, no. 4 (2004).
22. Robert Jago, "The Boyden Controversy Is Not about Bloodline," *The Walrus*, 10 January 2017, https://thewalrus.ca/the-boyden-controversy-is-not-about-bloodline/.
23. See Darryl Leroux's tweet from 13 April 2019, retrieved 29 November 2020 from https://twitter.com/DarrylLeroux/status/1116873010542252032.
24. Boyden, *Three Day Road*, 85–86.
25. Eric Thompson, "Canadian Fiction of the Great War," in *Canadian Literature* 91, no. 4 (1981): 81–96.
26. Thompson, "Canadian Fiction," 85; Brigitte Glaser, "(Re)Turning to Europe for the Great War: Representations of World War I in Contemporary Anglophone Canadian Fiction," *Zeitschrift für Kanadastudien* 20, no. 2 (2010); and Peregrine Acland, *All Else Is Folly* (Toronto: Dundurn Press, 2014 [1929]).
27. See Martin Kuester, "The English-Canadian Novel from Modernism to Postmodernism," in *History of Literature in Canada: English-Canadian and French-Canadian*, ed. Reingard M. Nischik (Rochester, NY: Camden House, 2008), 310–29; Karin Ikas, "Formative Years: (Dis)ability, War and the Canadian Nation," in *Global Realignments and the Canadian Nation in the Third Millennium*, ed. Karin Ikas (Wiesbaden: Harrassowitz, 2010), 35–44.
28. Kuester, "English-Canadian Novel," 325.
29. See Kuester, "English-Canadian Novel," 325, and Sherrill Grace, "Remembering *The Wars*," in *The Great War in Post-memory Literature and Film*, ed. Martin Loeschnigg and Marzena Sokolowska-Paryz (Berlin: De Gruyter, 2014), 219–38.
30. Glaser, "(Re)Turning to Europe," 64.
31. Michael Rothberg, "Remembering Back: Cultural Memory, Colonial Legacies, and Postcolonial Studies," in *The Oxford Handbook of Postcolonial Studies*, ed. Graham Huggan, (Oxford: Oxford University Press, 2013), 359–79, 376.
32. See, e.g., Gordon Boelling, "'A Part of Our History That so Few Knew About': Native Involvement in Canada's Great War—Joseph Boyden's Three Day Road" in *Inventing Canada/Inventer le Canada*, ed. Klaus D. Ertler and Martin Loeschnigg (Frankfurt am Main: Lang, 2008), 253–68; Glaser, "(Re)Turning to Europe"; and Teichler, "Joseph Boyden's *Three Day Road*."
33. Caroline Rosenthal, "English-Canadian Literary Theory and Literary Criticism," in Nischik, *History of Literature in Canada*, 302.
34. Loeschnigg and Sokolowska-Paryz, "Introduction," 2.
35. Frances Itani, *Deafening* (Toronto: HarperCollins, 2003).
36. Jane Urquhart, *The Underpainter* (London: Penguin Books, 1997).
37. Jane Urquhart, *The Stone Carvers* (London: Bloomsbury, 2001).
38. See also Hanna Teichler, "Re-imagining the Sacred Site: The Vimy Ridge Memorial and Transcultural Canadian Memory of the Great War in Janes Urquhart's The Stone Carvers," in *Disasters of War: Perceptions and Representations from 1914 to the Present*, ed. Steffen Bruendel and Frank Estelmann (Wiesbaden: Wilhelm Fink, 2019), 211–28.
39. Glaser, "(Re)Turning to Europe," 71.
40. James Dempsey, "Aboriginal Soldiers in the First World War," Canadian Government Archive, retrieved 6 June 2016 from www.collectionscanada.gc.ca/aboriginal-heritage/020016-4002-e.html.
41. Dempsey, "Aboriginal Soldiers."
42. Boelling, "Part of Our History," 5.

43. Glaser, "(Re)turning to Europe," 69.
44. Glaser, "(Re)turning to Europe," 72.
45. Boelling, "Part of Our History," 254.
46. Boelling, "Part of Our History," 255.
47. Boelling, "Part of Our History," 255.
48. Boelling, "Part of Our History," 256.
49. Samuel Hynes, "Personal Narratives and Commemoration," in *War and Remembrance in the Twentieth Century*, ed. Jay Winter (Cambridge: Cambridge University Press, 1999), 206, emphasis in the original text.
50. Hynes, "Personal Narratives," 207.
51. Schulze-Engler, "Global History, Indigenous Modernities, Transcultural Memory: World War I and II in Native Canadian, Aboriginal Australian, and Māori Fiction," in *Comparative Indigenous Studies*, ed. Mita Banerjee (Tübingen: Universitätsverlag Winter, 2016), 403.
52. Boyden, *Three Day Road*, 19.
53. Schulze-Engler, "Global History, Indigenous Modernities," 400.
54. Schulze-Engler, "Global History, Indigenous Modernities," 397.
55. Samuel Hynes, *A War Imagined: The First World War and English Culture* (London: Pimlico, 1990), xi.
56. Niska is surprised to find Xavier instead of Elijah when she arrives at the train to pick up the survivor. She was told that Xavier had died on battlefield and that Elijah was to return from the trenches as an amputee.
57. Schulze-Engler, "Global Histories, Indigenous Modernities," 399–400.
58. Boyden, *Three Day Road*, 213.
59. Boyden, *Three Day Road*, 213.
60. Boyden, *Three Day Road*, 212.
61. Boyden, *Three Day Road*, 215–16.
62. Boyden, *Three Day Road*, 100.
63. Boyden, *Three Day Road*, 14, emphasis in the original text.
64. Boyden, *Three Day Road*, 39.
65. Schulze-Engler, "Global History, Indigenous Modernity," 402.
66. Boyden, *Three Day Road*, 100, emphasis in the original text.
67. Boyden, *Three Day Road*, 25.
68. Boyden, *Three Day Road*, 432.
69. Schulze-Engler, "Global History, Indigenous Modernities," 418.
70. Boyden, *Three Day Road*, 49–50.
71. Boyden, *Three Day Road*, 134.
72. Boyden, *Three Day Road*, 395–96.
73. Boyden, *Three Day Road*, 397.
74. Boyden, *Three Day Road*, 73.
75. Boyden, *Three Day Road*, 73.
76. See Harold Scheub, *Trickster and Hero* (Madison: University of Wisconsin Press, 2012), and William J. Hynes and William G. Doty, eds., *Mythical Trickster Figures: Contours, Contexts, and Criticisms* (Tuscaloosa: University of Alabama Press, 1993).
77. Paul Radin, *The Trickster: A Study in American Indian Mythology* (New York: Schocken, 1988).
78. The trickster is not necessarily male; there are several female examples. However, since Boyden's trickster Elijah is male, I will continue to use male pronouns.
79. See, for example, Harold Bloom, ed., *The Trickster* (New York: Infobase Publishing, 2010), xv.
80. Bloom, *Trickster*, xv.

81. For further reading on the literary representations of the trickster in Western literature (e.g., in Melville, Kafka, Twain), see Bloom, *Trickster*.
82. Scheub, *Trickster and Hero*, 6.
83. Scheub, *Trickster and Hero*, 6.
84. William J. Hynes and William G. Doty, "Introducing the Fascinating and Complex Trickster Figure," in *Mythical Trickster Figures: Contours, Contexts, and Criticisms*, ed. William J. Hynes and William G. Doty (Tuscaloosa: University of Alabama Press, 1993), 2.
85. Scheub, *Trickster and Hero*, 11.
86. Scheub, *Trickster and Hero*, 12.
87. See Hynes and Doty, *Mythical Trickster Figures*.
88. Tim Prentki, *The Fool in European Theatre: Stages of Folly*, 1st ed. (Basingstoke: Palgrave Macmillan, 2012), 2.
89. Prentki, *Fool in European Theatre*, 2.
90. Prentki, *Fool in European Theatre*, 2.
91. Prentki, *Fool in European Theatre*, 3.
92. Prentki, *Fool in European Theatre*, 3.
93. Prentki, *Fool in European Theatre*, 3.
94. Prentki, *Fool in European Theatre*, 5.
95. Prentki, *Fool in European Theatre*, 10.
96. Prentki, *Fool in European Theatre*, 185.
97. See, e.g., Vicky K. Janik, ed., *Fools and Jesters in Literature, Art, and History: A Bibliographical Sourcebook* (Westport, CT: Greenwood Press, 1998), and Prentki, *Fool in European Theatre*; and Ralph Lerner, *Playing the Fool: Subversive Laughter in Troubled Times* (Chicago: University of Chicago Press, 2009).
98. Lerner, *Playing the Fool*, 2.
99. Boyden, *Three Day Road*, 398.
100. Boyden, *Three Day Road*, 416, emphasis in the original.
101. Boyden, *Three Day Road*, 417, emphasis in the original.
102. Boyden, *Three Day Road*, 417.
103. Boyden, *Three Day Road*, 418.
104. Boyden, *Three Day Road*, 424, emphasis in the original.
105. Boyden, *Three Day Road*, 432.
106. Catherine Schwerin, "Speaking the Unspeakable—Manifestations of Silence in Gail Jones' *Sorry*," *Bulletin of the Transilvania University of Brasov* 2, no. 51 (2009): 38.
107. Jones, *Sorry*, 214.
108. Jones, *Sorry*, "Acknowledgments."
109. Sue Kossew, "Saying Sorry: The Politics of Apology and Reconciliation in Recent Australian Fiction," in *Locating Postcolonial Narrative Genres*, ed. Walter Goebel and Sakia Schabio (New York: Routledge, 2013), 172.
110. Kossew, "Saying Sorry," 172.
111. Sue Kossew also analyses the novels of Kate Grenville in her essay and incorporates Grenville's work in the body of "sorry novels." Grenville pursues a similar strategy as Jones: particularly in her novel *The Secret River*, Grenville engages with a settler family who tries to make their living in the penal colony that Australia was at that time. Yet, she dedicates her text to "the Aboriginal people of Australia: past, present and future." This novel has also been assessed critically and was at times harshly contested for its rather apologetic tone with regard to mass killings of Aboriginals. However, both "sorry novels" task themselves with rectifying the settler narrative. Kate Grenville, *The Secret River* (Edinburgh: Canongate, 2005), paratext.

112. Jones, *Sorry*, 217.
113. Gail Jones is a teacher at the University of Western Australia and has won several prestigious awards.
114. Jones, *Sorry*, 11.
115. Jones, *Sorry*, 11.
116. Jones, *Sorry*, 6.
117. Jones, *Sorry*, 16.
118. Jones, *Sorry*, 9.
119. Jones, *Sorry*, 11.
120. See also Valérie-Anne Belleflamme, "'Shakespeare Was Wrong': Counter-discursive Intertextuality in Gail Jones's Sorry," *Journal of Postcolonial Writing* 51, no. 6 (2015): 661–71.
121. See in particular Ania Loomba and Martin Orkin, eds., *Postcolonial Shakespeares* (New York: Routledge, 1998), and Thomas Cartelli, *Repositioning Shakespeare: National Formations, Postcolonial Appropriations* (London: Taylor & Francis, 2013).
122. See Frank Schulze-Engler, "Englischsprachige Literaturen," in *Handbuch Postkolonialismus und Literatur*, ed. Dieter Göttsche, Axel Dunker, and Gabriele Dürbeck (Stuttgart: Metzler, 2017), 343–54.
123. Ania Loomba and Martin Orkin, "Introduction" in Loomba and Orkin, *Postcolonial Shakespeares*, 1.
124. Schulze-Engler, "Englischsprachige Literaturen."
125. See Schulze-Engler, "Englischsprachige Literaturen."
126. See Schulze-Engler, "Englischsprachige Literaturen."
127. Jones, *Sorry*, 36, emphasis in the original text.
128. Jones, *Sorry*, 36–37.
129. Belleflamme, "Shakespeare Was Wrong," 663–64.
130. Jones, *Sorry*, 37.
131. The identity template of the Australian bushman was posited against the imperial masters. See, for example, the introduction to the value of the bush and its human representative for Australian national identity that the government homepage provides. The Government of Australia, retrieved 11 April 2017 from http://www.australia.gov.au/about-australia/australian-story/austn-bush. A quintessential literary representation of this Australian settler identity is most certainly Henry Lawson's short story "The Drover's Wife," which can be regarded as the founding narrative of Euro-Australianness. See, e.g., Liesel Hermes, "Henry Lawson's 'The Drover's Wife' and the Australian Short Story," in *Global Fragments: (Dis)Orientation in the New World Order*, ed. Anke Bartels and Dirk Wiemann (Amsterdam: Rodopi, 2007), 301–12; and Christine Vandamme, "'The Drover's Wife': Celebrating or Demystifying Bush Mythology," in *Commonwealth Essays and Studies* 38, no. 2 (Spring 2016): 73–82. This influential short story takes up the identity template of the Australian bushman and reframes it with a female protagonist. It is still very indicative of the strife to differentiate Australian settler identity from British colonial high culture. Henry Lawson, "The Drover's Wife," in *The Drover's Wife and Other Stories*, ed. Murray Bail (St. Lucia: University of Queensland, 1984). For further reading on the bushman myth, see Russel Braddock Ward, *The Australian Legend* (Melbourne: Oxford University Press, 1978).
132. Jones, *Sorry*, 12.
133. Anne McClintock, *Imperial Leather: Race, Gender and Sexuality in the Colonial Contest* (London: Routledge, 1995), 7.
134. McClintock, *Imperial Leather*, 71.
135. Jones, *Sorry*, 19.

136. For further reading on the archetypical victim in (post)colonial discourses, see Robert Young, *Colonial Desire: Hybridity in Theory, Culture and Race* (London: Routledge, 2006).
137. Jones, *Sorry*, 32.
138. Jones, *Sorry*, 32, emphasis in the original text.
139. Jones, *Sorry*, 32.
140. For further reading on cultural trauma and (postcolonial) literature, see, e.g., Stef Craps, *Postcolonial Witnessing: Trauma out of Bounds* (London: Palgrave Macmillan, 2015).
141. Michele McCrea, "Collisions of Authority: Nonunitary Narration and Textual Authority in Gail Jones' Sorry," in *Encounters: Refereed Conference Papers of the 17th annual AAWP Conference*, Flinders University, Adelaide 2012, retrieved 3 October 2014 from http://d3n8a8pro7vhmx.cloudfront.net/theaawp/pages/87/attachments/original/1385085229/McCrea.pdf?1385085229.
142. See, e.g., Walter Goebel and Sakia Schabio, eds., *Locating Postcolonial Genres* (New York: Routledge, 2013); Kossew, "Saying Sorry"; Dolores Herrero, "The Australian Apology and Postcolonial Defamiliarization: Gail Jones' Sorry," *Journal of Postcolonial Writing* 47, no. 3 (July 2011): 283–95; and Schwerin, "Speaking the Unspeakable," 34–41.
143. Kossew, "Saying Sorry," 175.
144. McCrea, "Collisions of Authority," 1–2.
145. Kennedy, "Australian Trials," 334.
146. Naomi Oreb, "Mirroring, Depth, and Inversion: Holding Gail Jones' *Black Mirror* against contemporary Australia," *Sydney Studies in English* 25 (2009); and Kennedy, "Australian Trials."
147. Kennedy, "Australian Trials," 333.
148. Herrero, "Australian Apology," 283.
149. Herrero, "Australian Apology," 284.
150. See, in particular, Cathy Caruth, ed., *Trauma: Explorations in Memory* (Baltimore: John Hopkins University Press, 1995), and Herrero, "Australian Apology."
151. Herrero, "Australian Apology," 284.
152. Jones, *Sorry*, 284, emphasis in the original.
153. Jones, *Sorry*, 284, 124–25.
154. Jones, *Sorry*, 284, 125.
155. Schwerin, "Speaking the Unspeakable."
156. See Herrero, "Australian Apology"; Kennedy, "Australian Trials of Trauma"; and Schwerin, "Speaking the Unspeakable."
157. Herrero, "Australian Apology," 285–86.
158. Kennedy, "Australian Trials," 346.
159. Jones, *Sorry*, 203–4.
160. Valérie-Anne Belleflamme, "Saying the Unsayable: Imagining Reconciliation in Gail Jones' Sorry," *English Text Construction* 8, no. 2 (2015): 161–62.
161. Herrero, "Australian Apology," 286.
162. Belleflamme, "Saying the Unsayable," 161–62.
163. Landsberg, *Prosthetic Memories*, 11.

Chapter 4

"Double Visions"

Intimate Enemies and Magic Figures in Kim Scott's *Benang* and Tomson Highway's *Kiss of the Fur Queen*

In his apology speech, former Canadian prime minister Stephen Harper draws on the policies and effects of forcible removal and cultural reeducation:

> Two primary objectives of the residential school system were to remove and isolate children from the influence of their homes, families, traditions and cultures, and to assimilate them into the dominant culture. These objectives were based on the assumption Aboriginal cultures and spiritual beliefs were inferior and unequal. Indeed, some sought, as it was infamously said, to "kill the Indian in the child." Today, we recognize that this policy of assimilation was wrong, has caused great harm, and has no place in our country.[1]

Here Harper invokes a well-known trope with regard to the Canadian Indian residential school legacy: the ill-advised impetus to "elevate" the natives to a more advanced cultural status represents the mindset that enabled the execution of forcible removal in the first place. Yet, as Harper asserts, such attitudes belong to the past and are as such an expression of times when these ideas were viable. Harper further acknowledges that

> [t]he government now recognizes that the consequences of the Indian residential school policy were profoundly negative and that this policy has had a lasting and damaging impact on Aboriginal culture, heritage and language.[2]

In contrast to the well-chosen and neatly arranged words that Prime Minister Harper uses, words that were meant to sooth rather than to irritate, Kim

Scott's *Benang* confronts readers with an unsettling degree of both verbal and physical violence:

> "We'll all have to make our way in this world," Grandad said, "on your own. I want to give you an even chance. You will never get that with your father."
> Grandfather—Ernest Salomon Scat—told me that my father had agreed it was for the best. At first, adjusting to the new circumstances, I had an unfortunate run of bed-wetting, but once cured of that—with an ingenious system my grandfather designed whereby an electric shock was administered to my penis each time the sheets became wet—I was off to the very best of boarding schools.[3]

Harley, Scott's half-caste protagonist and breeding-out project of his own grandfather, Ernest Salomon Scat, endures this violence and sense of continuous displacement within his very own, white family. As the novel progresses, Harley, as the victim, turns the tables on his grandfather, who is the closest agent of the colonial system in Harley's life, and turns power hierarchies upside down. Scott's main protagonist effectively carnivalizes, and thus unsettles, the position of the victim.

Offering a different take on the relation between victim and perpetrator, Tomson Highway's novel *Kiss of the Fur Queen* frames the "damaging impact" on the Indigenous population as follows:

> The rotund Jimmy Roger Buck broke into a back-alley jig. "It's alive, it's alive, it's alive-alive-oh!" The stench was so hideous it was a while before either could squat down for a closer look. Her ragged skirt hiked almost to her hips, the woman lay beside a toppled garbage can whose multicoloured spew included a rat's frozen corpse. An object by her head caught Jeremiah's eye. Metal. Empty. Lysol.
> "All right, up and at 'em." Jimmy Roger Buck shook the heap with a heavy mitted hand. No response. "Come on, girl," Jeremiah pleaded, "you're gonna freeze to death out here." The woman was ageless, her face a ground-beef patty, holes for eyes. . . .
> The team had to grunt for a good minute before the bulk achieved enough verticality to be dragged down the alley to the old van. "Winnipeg Indian Friendship Centre, Street Patrol," it said on the side. Jeremiah had always thought the sign should include, "See a passed-out Indian? Call us first."[4]

What appears to be the reproduction of a cliché—the drunk Indian in the gutters of a street, unable to take care of herself or to lead a "virtuous life"—actually resonates within the discourse of reconciliation. Victimhood as a permanent status is quite easily evoked and has become a powerful identity template within the context of reconciliation. Australian and Canadian "politics of regret," as I have argued, are both complicit in evoking a specific image of the broken, drug-abusive, and marginalized Native.[5] The processes of reconciliation seek to pay tribute to this "damaged Indigenous," but inadvertently petrify it.

This identity template of the victim is taken up by Highway's *Kiss of the Fur Queen* and Scott's *Benang: From the Heart* and dealt with in explorative ways.[6] The idea that belonging to the "wrong," "inferior" culture makes one sick, disabled, or damaged is a strong remnant of colonial (discursive) dominance. As such, both novels are examples of how the artistic, creative exploration and carnivalization of the "damaged Indigenous" becomes a powerful counternarrative to the reconciliation discourse. Furthermore, *Benang* and *Fur Queen* ask pertinent questions about the medium of the written text and the genre (historical) novel as tools to artistically intervene in Australian and Canadian memory politics.

Education, Elevation, and a Lightweight: Kim Scott's *Benang*

Set mostly at the beginning of the twentieth century and stretching well into the 1950s, *Benang* presents its take on notions of more contemporary Indigenous and non-Indigenous identities in the light of the effects of forcible removal and cultural reeducation. Scott's novel sets out to find a language to express the suffering of its protagonists and to make sense of a people's unclaimed past. Told from the viewpoint of first-person narrator Harley, a journey to retrieve individual and collective histories and identities unfolds. He introduces himself to the reader within the very first lines of the text

> [a]s the first-born-successfully-white-man-in-the-family-line I awoke to a terrible pressure, particularly upon my nose and forehead, and thought I was blind. In fact, the truth was there was nothing to see, except—right in front of my eyes—a whiteness which was surface only, with no depth, with little variation.[7]

He is his grandfather's assimilation project: Ernest Salomon Scat has tasked himself to pursue the endeavor to rigorously breed out Harley's Aboriginality. Ern's grandson, of particularly fair skin due to various instances of interracial (mostly forced) coupling in his family line, is supposed to be the "first white man born"—not only in terms of his skin color, but, more importantly, because of his reeducation in a Western image. Half-castes and Aboriginal children with skin as white as possible were the ones who were primarily introduced into the system of forcible removal, and Harley is, within *Benang*, the main fictional representative of victims of this assimilation policy. Ern undertakes his breeding project by severing Harley from his Aboriginal heritage and (his)stories and by punishing every behavior that is deemed unworthy of his "white" identity. This educational program involves indoctrination and physical pain, and thus undertakes a concerted attack on Harley's mind and body. Bodily appearance (fair skin as a marker of being "whiter" than others) and mental state (through cultural reeducation) were supposed to be aligned within these reeducated children to make them worthy members of Australian non-Indigenous society. They were to be "elevate[d] . . . to our own plane," as chief protector of the Aboriginals and mastermind of the system of forcible removal, Auber Octavius Neville, so poignantly enunciates.[8]

One day, this specific plane comes crashing down, as Harley finds Ern's study with all the important documents, family trees, and "scientific" inquiries related to the subject of rendering him the "first white man born":

> I turned away from the old man and in a sort of controlled tantrum—oh, no doubt it was childish—I plucked papers from drawers, threw them, let them fall. I made books fly, index cards panic and flee. Occasionally, rising and falling in all that flurry, I paused to read from a book which had passages underlined on almost every page. There was a couple of family trees inscribed on the flyleaf. Trees? Rather, they were sharply ruled diagrams. My name finished each one. On another page, there was a third, a fourth. All leading to me.[9]

Upon this discovery, Harley immediately starts destroying all documents. On this occasion, Ern suffers a stroke that initially deprives him of his speech and mobility, and Harley begins to turn the tables on his grandfather. In this manner, Scott's novel fundamentally reverses the victim-perpetrator relationship: Ern is now silenced, and Harley attains power. Arguably this setting can be considered a rearrangement of power relations in a binary manner. Yet *Benang* also breaks open this reversed relationship, and even strengthens the notion of empowering Indigenous identities, because Harley decides against revenge and punishment. Harley instead takes Ern with him on his journey to explore, experience, and recover his Indigenous heritage.

In the course of the narrative, we make the acquaintance of several members of Harley's family, their fates, stories, and their strategies of resilience. The abstract and schematic family tree dissolves into personal stories, into individual and collective identities. As the novel unfolds, the reader bears witness to varying degrees of oppression and regulation imposed on the Indigenous peoples.

Benang is thus about the hardship of finding a relationship to a former perpetrator, to one's own grandfather as the agent and enforcer of the system of forcible removal, about how difficult it is to understand, forgive, and move on from the attempted destruction of an identity that was still in the making. It is the unsettling yet powerful character and identity template of the "damaged Indigenous" that Harley makes available for us. Scott's and Harley's project of discovering and exploring a family's past calls into question how the individual reader and a heterogeneous readership understand the category of history itself, and how individual renderings of collective histories interfere with what the reader might know about such histories.

Harley has thus far felt sick, as being physically impeded—an explanation he provides to himself and the reader in order to make sense of his position in between the cultural poles. Neither does he fully belong to Ern's white circle nor does he yet have a notion of his Aboriginal heritage. As a means to represent this in-between-ness, *Benang* endows Harley with a special capacity: he can float, and his weightlessness makes him frequently lose contact with the ground and at risk of drifting away. Indeed he often "[floats] through the house"[10] and assures the reader that his special capacity is

> not purely mindless, this floating on the breeze. It required a certain concentration, and I chose it not just for the fun, but also because I wanted to view those islands resting in the sea, and to get that aerial perspective. I couldn't have said why. The wind ruffled my hair as I rode its currents toward the islands.[11]

Harley, in this sense, is an allegorical "lightweight," unsure of his place of belonging and story-of-the-self to pin him down, and, in this sense, he also an unreliable narrator.[12] It appears as if he is condemned to a passive state, as if he is not in command of his special, magic gift, and nobody else within the story-world seems to see him float. His overarching impression of being an object that is dealt with as someone else pleases fundamentally changes as soon as he turns the tables on his violent grandfather:

> Yes, my grandfather was a shrewd man. A rat-cunning mind, dear reader, mark my words. (And here I must interrupt myself to record my grandfather's response to having such words read to him. His mouth went tighter, his nose and cheeks began to twitch. At the time I was encouraged by such behavior.)[13]

Now it is his grandfather who is not in the best of health and who has to relinquish his position of power. Ern, temporarily restricted to a wheelchair, is dragged along by Harley as he rediscovers his ancestry and becomes a victim to a fair amount of cruelty on Harley's part. Due to his disability, Ern is forced to listen and witness as Harley's Aboriginal history and identity unfolds and thrives. This is precisely the moment when Scott's narrative carnivalizes the inferior position and identity template of the "damaged Native," freeing the victim from being confined to passivity and suffering. As an apt allegorical representation of Australia's struggle to come to terms with its (post)colonial history, this novel carnivalizes colonial (discursive) hierarchies in the process. The novel ends with a quintessential statement and realization as Harley makes peace with his status of the in-between, the juxtaposed:[14]

> Speaking from the heart, I tell you that I am part of a much older story, one of a perpetual billowing from the sea, with its rhythm of return, return, and

remain. Even now we gather, on chilly evenings, sometimes only a few of us, sometimes more. We gather our strength in this way. From the heart of all of us. Pale, burnt and shrivelled, I hover in the campfire smoke and sing as best as I can. I am not alone.

I acknowledge that there are many stories here, in the ashes below my feet—even my grandfather's. . . .

We are still here, Benang.[15]

Benang is particularly skillful in intertwining History and histories, of blurring boundaries of genre, as it engages with metafictional and metahistorical questions of making, of writing, of discovering history and identities, oftentimes pitted hard against the backdrop of narratives of colonialism and victimhood. They are still here, because Kim Scott writes them into being, writes them into resilience.

"Little Histories" and Grand Narratives: *Benang* as Memory Politics

In an interview, Kim Scott reflects on the process of conceiving and writing *Benang*:

> On the one hand, I explore and create narratives in English, and let the work find its way according to largely aesthetic, "literary" considerations. On the other, I try to revitalise my ancestral language by bringing together archival linguistic knowledge and descendants of the linguistics' informants in ways that, by spreading in ever-widening, concentric circles, attempt to help a contemporary Noongar community (as the Aboriginal and Torres Strait Islander Arts Board puts it) "claim control and enhance" our heritage.
>
> I became aware of how my formal education's stories interfered with what I was trying to say. As that novel begins, so did the writing of it, but more so with a sensibility akin to that of frontier stories, of pioneer stories, of an individual consciousness seeing Aboriginal people as the "other."[16]

In accordance with this statement, *Benang* is frequently read as a case of metahistory.[17] For instance, Nadine Attewell remarks that "*Benang* invites readers to have an idea of what it feels like to do Aboriginal intellectual and genealogical history."[18] As such the text is deemed to be a "genealogical project" in the form of a novel:[19]

> *Benang* is a hybrid history that gathers together the quiet voices and little histories of Nyoongar people to contest and protest against colonial ideology. In so doing, Scott writes a counter-history that demands that Indigenous people be listened to and that a new future be forged that respects and enables differ-

ence. Scott's appropriation and annexation of colonial records into his textual topography exposes their genocidal and racist agenda. His speech is concealed behind and within the plurality of this multi-voiced text.[20]

Scott sets out to retrace his own family history and to produce a fictional recuperation of Nyongaar (hi)stories as a result. He seeks a proper mode, language, and form of expressing this retrieval and re-narrating of his cultural heritage and remembrance, and takes individual stories as his starting point.

Paul Ricoeur asks why the engagement with those closest to us—family and kin—is a powerful way to construct a sense of historical consciousness:

> Does there not exist an intermediate level of reference between the poles of individual memory and collective memory, where concrete exchanges operate between the living memory of individual persons and the public memory of communities to which we belong? This is the level of our close relations, to whom we have the right to attribute a memory of a distinct kind. These close relations, these people who count for us and for whom we count, are situated along a range of varying distances in the relation between self and others.[21]

Benang is full of "varying distances"—not only regarding the intrafamilial relations within the complicated structure of Harley's family but also in terms of the relation between individual and collective historical consciousness. *Benang* shows that, through the institution of family, histories and identities are reciprocally conditioned and exist in dependence on one another. Scott's text displays how these categories are inevitably interwoven, that there is no national, cultural and collective historical inventory that is to be conceived in independence from individual experiences, and these categories cannot be disentangled. Ricoeur stresses "[v]arying distances but also variation in the active and passive modes of the interplay of distantiation and closeness that makes proximity a dynamic relationship ceaselessly in motion: drawing near, feeling close."[22]

This oscillation between closeness and alienation is represented in the form of the narrative. The recovery of Harley's family history unfolds in ellipses and circles, in dead ends and streams of consciousness. The narrative structure follows more of an associative pattern than a linear causal composition and thus imitates the processes of remembering and storytelling (as an oral tradition). Chapter lengths, for example, vary to a great degree. At times, they are merely a page long, others appear seemingly "out of nowhere" with regard to the overarching narrative composition. The timeline bounces back and forth, and it is virtually impossible to connect narrative and narrated time, or to give an account of their duration. Thus it is hardly a surprise that we only find out about Harley's mother on page 398:

In my early drifting, especially when I was still finding my place, I often wondered about my mother. My biological mother. It was one of the reasons I went to visit my Aunty Ellen. There were many Aunty Ellens, and how was I to know which might she be? . . . But I know of the mother, if not who or where she is now. My mother. Confusingly—but this is reality for you, how will it not fit the neatness a story requires—her name was Ellen. She was another of Ern's domestics. . . . Ellen. Her voice was soft, and—who knows?—perhaps it was she Mr Neville had in mind when he wrote; the young half-blood maiden is a pleasant, placid, complacent person as a rule, while the quadroon girl is often strikingly attractive with her ofttimes auburn hair, rosy freckled colouring, and good figure, or maybe blue eyes and fair hair . . .

I suppose it was hard to keep a particular person in mind after all those women, all those boys, all those years.[23]

Scott's novel is thus a case of retracing family and cultural history, of family and cultural history in the making, in ceaseless motion. Scott addresses the boundaries between facts and fiction, between historical accuracy and historical fictions.[24] Scott's text is as much a case of metahistory as it bears the marks of and plays with metafictional qualities. Uncertainty and the quest for some kind of "knowledge" about Harley's family are represented in the arrangement of the narrative, and as such form and function align. Harley is conscious of these associative processes that enable him to

pluck Ernest Salomon Scat from my memories of his insecure dotage, and plant him with his arm inserted in the filing system, up to the elbow in the documents of the very respectable Auber Neville's office. My grandfather, so recently arrived from his own country, had come to his distant relation Mr. A O Neville, the Chief Protector of Aborigines, no less, and—until recently—chief of a department representing the odd combination of the North-west *and* Aborigines *and* Fisheries.[25]

This episode is indicative of the strategy of interweaving individual and collective accounts that *Benang* employs. Harley's personal quest—the retrieval of family history—blends into and merges with the powerful narratives of colonial dominance and racism on the one hand and resilience and survival on the other. *Benang* interweaves several levels, or, more precisely, several realities, as Harley discovers his stories. Harley's own quest thus becomes part of a vast array of quests, of violent pasts and undetermined presents. The reader bears witness to the reclaiming of an allegorically Australian colonial archive in Ern's study, to the destruction of the despicable breeding project as documented, filed, and rendered into diagrams. One of the papers reads as follows:

Breeding up. In the third or fourth generation no sign of native origin is apparent. The repetition of the boarding school process and careful breeding

> . . . after two or three generations the advance should be so great that families should be living like the rest of the community.²⁶

Scott transgresses the threshold between facts and fiction and carnivalizes these notions. By inserting A. O. Neville, the chief protector of Aboriginal affairs, into the narrative, he allows Neville, as the representative, the personification of the system of cultural removal, to be present in the novel and have his say. Most of the documents that Scott inserted into the narrative of *Benang*—such as the one quoted below—either are direct abstracts from the book that the historical figure of Auber Octavius Neville actually published or are represented accordingly.²⁷ This fictive Neville becomes a structural device within the text. His words appear as prologues to chapters, are interspersed in the course of a chapter, or are referenced by other protagonists. As a consequence, Neville and his doctrines do not remain abstract or distant; he—and by extension, the system of forcible removal—become tangible:

> Our policy is to send them out into the white community, and if the girl comes back pregnant our rule is to keep her for two years. The child is then taken away from the mother and sometimes never sees her again. Thus these children grow up as whites, knowing nothing of their environment. At the expiration of the period of two years the mother goes back into service. So that it really doesn't matter if she has half a dozen children. (A O Neville)²⁸

Neville's name is often represented as A O Neville—the missing punctuation after each capital letter prompts thoughts of Alpha and Omega as the quintessential beginning and end of mankind. Neville, in this case, is the Alpha and Omega for Indigenous peoples in general, and for Harley in particular. The scene quoted above continues with Harley recapitulating how Ern "liked to hug all the maids, to help them pat the pillows and turn the blankets. Every so often, Ern took a maid to the railway station and changed her for another one."²⁹ The doctrine of "breeding out" is put into practice by Ern, and the text invigorates these theorems, performing them for the readership.³⁰

As a historical novel conscious of its mechanisms, *Benang* sets up a direct link between the rules and the practice of forcible removal and cultural reeducation, and between the norms of the genre and its creative exploration. Harley as the homodiegetic and arguably unreliable narrator invites us to follow him on his journey to rediscover his ancestral narratives and engages in a very lively relationship with the outer-textual world. Harley is very conscious of his role through the story as the guide, the intermediary between the reader and the diegetic world. He frequently addresses the reader directly and thus seeks to establish a bond by reflecting on his lack of skills to produce a coherent account: "But once again I digress. The mind of a child. No sticking power. Some atavistic fault, I hear someone say, in the character of the narrator."[31] This narrator is thus not solely the agent of the narrative but is aware of his Janus-faced position of mediating truth and fabrication, reality and fiction, Aboriginality and non-Aboriginality for us, yet he is at the same time part of the imagined and the imaginary. In this way, Harley carnivalizes the subject position of the narrator by making it one to begin with. He does not simply serve as a technical necessity within the structure of the novel but recuperates his own subject position.

Consider in this context how Harley and his family are frequently confronted with the power of the written word—as represented by letters to the chief protector of Aboriginals and by the documents in Ern's study. As such, the novel juxtaposes the written word with the spoken as a mode of reconnecting with and reconstructing Aboriginal history. The narrative

> foreground[s] the story *Benang* tells about Aboriginal literacy, legible not just in Harley's own struggles with writing, but in references to the letter-writing campaigns inaugurated by his ancestors Sandy One Mason and Fanny; to Jack and his sister Kathleen's appetite for the written word, stoked by school; to Jack's cousin Will Coolman's love of westerns; and to the early date at which Harley's Nyoongar family learned to read and write. To thus attend to Aboriginal habits of reading and writing is not to deny writing's centrality to colonial governance projects.[32]

Harley's narrator-subject position is located somewhere in between the written and the spoken word. The materiality of colonial dominance is represented by the documentation of Ern's breeding project and other texts that are interwoven into the narrative, while the dynamics of storytelling, of retelling stories of past and present selves, is associated with the spoken word. In the colonial context, however, the written word is of particular regulatory force:

> Rather than a didactic resistance to the dominant language and its stories, Scott's wordplay and use of archival material expose language and history's susceptibility to manipulation, thereby undermining the hierarchical authority of the written word and its linguistic colonialism. The written word, far from being definitive, is portrayed as having an ambiguous and slippery nature, serving the whims, needs and prejudices of those who control it.[33]

Benang foregrounds a consciousness about the process of writing, and writes about writing. It comments on how the written word was a powerful colonial tool, yet *Benang* reclaims the written word as well as the spoken for its own purposes of doing Aboriginal history. The text draws on the old dichotomy between colonial literacy and Aboriginal orality (or illiteracy), and, with a *coup de main*, carnivalizes this dogmatic dichotomy: *Benang* blurs the boundaries between the written and the spoken because the novel's stylistic rendering, its wording and plotting, blurs the line between literacy and orality. More precisely, it renders this distinction obsolete. *Benang* makes a case for realizing that the written is included in the spoken, as well as the spoken lives in the written. I argue that to emphasize this reiterated binarism, as many critics have done, is to block from view the more fruitful, novel strategies that Scott employs to make his political case. The analysis of Scott's novel would fall short of an important aspect to this strategy of "writing about writing" if it stopped at this binary system of orality and literacy: *Benang* not only claims the written word for Aboriginal peoples but it also emphasizes that writing is no longer a practice for exerting colonial dominance. Harley thus reclaims the written word as a transcultural power, a tool that belongs to anyone, and no one:

> It was still [Ern's] story, his language, his notes and rough drafts, his clear diagrams and slippery fractions which had uplifted and diminished me.
> I wanted more.
> I dare say he was all the time thinking, When and how will I appear in this history? Hoping. Worrying.
> Oh, I promised I would get to him.
> I did not continue the readings [of Ern's documents].
> It may have been a desire to transform myself, or even self-hatred, which suggested I slash and cut words into my own skin. But I soon turned to my grandfather's flesh. I wanted to mark him, to show my resentment at how his words had shaped me.[34]

Now Harley returns the favor of altering bodily appearances by the use of words, and he does so in a Kafkaesque manner. Consider how the power of the "colonial word" falls victim to parody here: words on paper have dominated Aboriginal lives, have regulated almost every aspect of Indigenous existence. Appearance and character were described and prescribed, documented and archived. When Harley writes words *on* his grandfather, words lose their connection with their medium—paper—and are displaced to where they mattered the most in the colonial context: the body. Within this short scene, Scott produces a carnivalization of the written word itself, when it becomes translated onto human skin, even white skin, which is sacrosanct in the colonial logic that *Benang* captures so magnificently. At the same time, it carnivalizes the powerful notion of the "savage" who has the right mindset to carve words onto a living person—associations with scalping as well as narratives and paintings on animal skin may be triggered. It is the body of an agent of forcible cultural reeducation that experiences the power of the prescriptive word. One is easily tempted to dismiss this scene as an outburst of inappropriate violence and cruelty on Harley's part, yet this is the key moment when the colonial historical discursive heritage becomes transcultural. The scene marks the instance when the written word is disconnected from being a colonial tool of dominance and is reframed as a transcultural device. Overall, *Benang* carnivalizes the dominance and importance of the dichotomy between the written and the spoken word and highlights the empowering potential of claiming the English language by emphasizing that there are more important issues to contemplate than this postcolonial discourse.

The question hence arises if it is at all productive to dwell on whether *Benang* is a classical historical novel:

> In relation to conventional stylistic rendering, standard plotting, and illusionistic consistency of realist voice, as may be found in the classic historical novel (and its cousinly genres the Bildungsroman and the Künstlerroman), the genre conventions deployed by contemporary postcolonial novels are often shown as periodically unstable and discontinuous, variously subject to narrative displacement, parodic intervention, distortion and inversion. These artistic "deformations" gainfully deconstruct the generic "purity" of the historical novel on its way to becoming a postcolonial novel. One key form of parodic intervention is historiographic metafiction.[35]

In an attempt to flesh out *Benang*'s metafictional achievements, Frances Johnson—like many other postcolonial scholars—resorts to the connection between the (historical) novel and Europe, between the most dominant literary genre of modernity and its impact on the colonial subject:

> The production of literary parody via applied metafictional techniques enables a dissident laughter to be directed towards the coloniser and colonial history. In the first instance, the hieratic, realist illusion of the historical colonial novel as with the overarching colonial "story" is destabilised. Such techniques therefore enable the new story to challenge the habitual ways in which power relations between coloniser and colonised subject are read.[36]

If we follow Johnson here, a novel like *Benang* opens up a site to newly negotiate the concept of the historical novel in light of more inclusive history writing. This is arguably a rather trivial understanding of genre and its regulatory impacts, and Scott's novel consequently moves beyond this dichotomy, carnivalizing the importance of genre and form in Australian postcolonial literatures. It is one of the most prominent claims of postcolonial scholarship that the genre of the novel has been appropriated by Indigenous writers, that the most formative of all colonial genres has been used by the formerly oppressed to write back, and so counter colonial narratives, and in doing so subvert the genre's cultural importance. It is my claim that *Benang* moves beyond these questions. Polemically speaking, Scott shows that there is no such thing as an ideologically postcolonial novel. Instead he points toward the idea that the novel is by no means a fixed and fully defined entity of world-making. It has to be more broadly considered, and in particular not necessarily always in relation to the European novel. To play with the form of the novel is to carnivalize the importance of form as a regulatory and culturally coded means of world-making. *Benang* thus asks the question whether the form governs the content, and answers it by establishing a reciprocal, nonhierarchical relationship between form and function.

Carnivalizing Cultural Coding

This claim is strengthened by a specific representative mode that Kim Scott uses.[37] *Benang* is a prominent case of an author using the effects and impact of the literary aesthetic known as magic realism. As we have already seen, Scott employs Harley's special capacity of floating to represent the feeling of un-belonging. His ability to float or inability to stay connected to the earth, to exist in discordance with the rules of gravity, is the thematic thread that contributes to structuring the text on the one hand and serving as a poignant image for Harley's continuous sense of un-belonging on the other. Scott helps introduce Harley by evoking a peculiar image, as Harley realizes that his "face was pressed hard against a ceiling."[38] A few lines before, Scott presents Harley as under the impression that he is (color)blind, as he is having trouble seeing anything that is not plainly white: "In fact, the truth was there was nothing to see, except—right in front of my eyes—a whiteness which was surface only, with no depth, and very little variation." It was in fact the ceiling that Harley had floated against. We then encounter Harley floating about on several occasions throughout the novel, and the image forcefully reappears right at the very end, just as Harley has indeed retrieved one important aspect of his life story, his Aboriginal origin story and family history:

> Uncle Jack said to me, "To start with, what you are is Nyongaar." Sandy One was no white man. Just as I am no white man, despite the look of me and the sudden silence—the temporary laughter and disbelief—of distant nephews nieces cousins grannies when they saw me come gliding in above the fire. I hover in the campfire smoke, and hum with resonance of that place. Those nameless women from my past invited friends and relations to come to visit, see me perform.[39]

Magic realism, according to Barbara Klonowska, can be broadly defined as introducing the "art of illusion" to literary representation.[40] This definition relates back to an understanding that the connection between (a possible) reality and its representation is grounded in reason, in scientific probability and intelligibility. An artist who uses the mode of representation referred to as magic realism introduces another dimension to the supposedly realistic representational inventory characteristic for the European historical novel. Such a magic realist text leaves behind the realm of the scientifically possible or proven and ventures into the spheres of the magic, the mystic, the unintelligible, and the impossible. This insertion of something strange, and uncanny, into the narrative may come in the form of characters who display magic traits or special capacities, or it might unfold through the occurrence of strange events or seemingly unfathomable incidents. The two categories—the real and the magic—stand, at first sight, in utter contrast. Magic realism thus appears to be a "strange oxymoron," seeking to combine the Western traditions of realistic disclosure and "possible" explanations with the uncanny, the unknown forces beyond a rational attitude toward worlds and world-making.[41]

To understand magic realism as oxymoronic requires a specific notion of the real and the magic. The real, in this context, alludes to a category that is unambiguous by default. It reflects something "non-imaginary, pragmatic, down-to-earth," and it is our "20th-century pragmatic attitude" that allows for such a definition of the real.[42] Critics hold that the very concept of magic realism amounts to "an expression of eurocentrism and exotisation of non-European (in particular indigenous) subjects and cultures," since its basic conceptual understanding seemingly relies on reopening the dichotomy between the possible (Western) and impossible (non-Western) of representation.[43] But this stance ignores the postmodern position of acknowledging that the real is a fiction in itself, embedded in a sign system that requires a retrospective connection to what a given collective perceives and denotes as real. The real is as much a matter of convention and regulation as it is imagined. The concept magic realism itself, according to Kolonowska, is "inherently ambiguous, split between trickery and faith."[44] This inherent ambiguity stems from the tension between what we "know" and what we are able to believe, and as such it counters the understanding that an artist strives to test the "good faith" that a reader has in a text and its strategies of world-making.

Barbara Klonowska speaks of two different strands of magic realism, or, more precisely, two different interpretations of the nature of this specific mode of representation:

> Its first sense denotes an art of illusion, presenting it as conjuring, using tricks and sleight of hand, and thus can be related to the first definition . . . in which "magic" signifies an unusual perspective, or even deception introduced by an artist into the otherwise perfectly normal reality. Another meaning of the word "magic" defines it as secret forces controlling events and people with the help of spirits, magic formulas and rituals, and finds its reflection in the other understanding of "magic realism": that of mystery and witchcraft existing without contradictions together with the everyday and mundane.[45]

Magic realism can be found in a variety of literary fields and is employed by a range of different authors, but it is also profoundly connected with works gathered under the designation of postcolonial literature.[46] Magic realism is a representational strategy that abundantly makes clear that there are aspects of (human) existence completely foreign to those unfamiliar with a specific, in her case Latin American, culture, and that magic realism enables a coming to literary life of these cultural differences and negotiations of (cultural) identities.[47] Interestingly, Klonowska refers to a singular Latin American culture in this instance. Liliana Sikorska and Agnieszka Rzepa emphasize that artists who employ magic realism seek to convey experiences of clashing cultures, of cultural contact, of cultural differences.[48] Somewhat polemically they even speak of an act of "cultural appropriation" committed by literary critics who coined the concept in the first place.[49] With regard to Latin America magic realism, Klonowska argues similarly that "[t]o primitive cultures, then, magic was not merely a part of reality: it was the reality as such and the dichotomy of the realms did not exist."[50] Magic realism is consequently oftentimes associated with belonging to the representational repertoire of Indigenous cultures, an assessment that closely associates the unreal(istic), the superstitious, the uncanny with non-Western cultures.

A mode of world-making such as magic realism is thus not only a literary device but also an identity-political tool, opening up a seeming dichotomy between the magic and the real, between primitive and nonprimitive cultures and their respective modes of world-making. It also engages in dialogue with the notion of the carnivalesque that this study employs. Sikorska and Rzepa relate magic realism to an increasing investment of artists and authors in processes of cultural transformations and exchange. Both authors suggest that magic realism is more fruitfully used as a means to describe subversive social forces, to display "empowerment of marginalized subjects" through specific modes of representation.[51] Jeanne Delbaere-Garant holds that authors use these "crazy disguises" that characterize magic realism to reflect the status of the in-between that many (post)colonial peoples consider themselves existing in.[52] She further emphasizes "that Canadian identity can no longer be constructed from a double nor for that matter from a multicultural viewpoint decided by the hegemonic centre, but by the creation of a number of hybridized third spaces of ever-changing white, aboriginal and ethnic formations."[53]

In more general terms, magic realism is a symptom, an expression of processes of (forcible) cultural exchange, transformation, and a reaction to these processes at the same time. In that sense, magic realism "explicitly address[es] the specific and troubled context of native and non-native interactions," but it also offers an outlook onto possible futures and imagined relations between the two seemingly antagonistic cultural poles. Magic realism, thus conceived, powerfully contests cultural container schemata. It is precisely the moments of encounter, of mutual transformation and associations, of traveling cultures, memories, and meanings that magic realism seeks to lend expression to. It forms a bridge between worlds, and is a concept that is easily relatable to the notion of the carnivalesque with its temporary, oftentimes humorous reversals of social hierarchies and dominant identities. Magic realism points toward "third space" dynamics, at various cultural sign systems that engage in contact, in exchange with others and each other.[54]

It is quite evident why Harley, the representative of a transcultural existence *par* force and *par* retrieval of his ancestors' histories, has this magic capacity. The victim Harley has this special gift, and it gradually becomes clear that the reader encounters a very specific kind of victim in *Benang*. One of the key narratives produced by "sorry politics," that of Indigenous suffering on an individual and a collective level, can be easily reframed and (mis)interpreted as centering the narrative of the "damaged Indigenous."

Harley, the victim of forcible cultural reeducation, is both a trickster-fool and a magician. The realm of magic or the supernatural has limitless resources when it comes to representing experiences that divert from what we would perceive as "normal," or standard. Since Harley is the main narrative force in *Benang*, the reader is after all not sure whether his floating is just a product of Harley's vivid imagination or if he is the only one who sees himself detached from the ground. He is thus clearly an unreliable narrator, and so it is not so much a question whether Harley's floating is (scientifically) possible at all but rather an issue of whether he, and by extension we as readers, consider it credible in the overarching narrative composition. It has to be convincing within the possible world that *Benang* writes into being. Harley, who is forced to oscillate between the cultural poles, translates this feeling of being caught between the chairs into his capacity to detach himself from the earth, as he becomes the very representative of unambiguity and belonging. In Harley's world, the categories of the real(istic) and the (super)natural are ironically intertwined: Ern is the representative of a rational, scientific tradition of perceiving the world, yet his breeding project is surreal to the extent that *Benang* even questions this distinction. His Aboriginal ancestry and their stories are more closely associated with the surreal, the mystic, but this Aboriginal world that Harley gradually discovers makes more sense to him than any scientifically credited theory on race to which he has been subjected. Harley frames this interconnectedness of victim and perpetrator from which there is no escape in a scene that follows the discovery and destruction of Ern's study, the moment within the narrative when power hierarchies are reversed. His grandfather's abilities are still impeded by the stroke he suffered, and Harley forces himself frequently not to "succumb to the temptation to let him fall":[55]

Despite the power and strength I felt at such times, I nevertheless felt impoverished, weakened, reduced. It appeared that the little family history my grandfather had bequeathed me had disappeared. It seemed an inexorable process, this one of we becoming I. This reduction of a rich and variously shared place to one fragile, impoverished consciousness.[56]

Harley is in power and control now, and even has superpowers, whereas Ern is forced to sit, listen, and watch. Before Harley discovers Ern's study and his own status as a breeding project, he feels sick and considers himself an embarrassment to look at: "I know I make people uncomfortable, and embarrass even those who come to hear me sing."[57] He is a stranger to himself, caught in an existence of shifting patterns and truths, between insides and outsides that do not want to align properly:

> Hovering before a mirror, I saw a stranger. It was hard to focus, but this much was clear; he was thin, and wore some napkin around his loins. Dark blue veins ran beneath his creamy skin, and his nipples and lips were sharply defined.
> The image shifted, and changed shapes as I have seen clouds do around granite peaks above the sea. But it was terrible to see these shapes, the selves I took.
> I stood motionless against a setting sun; posture perfect, brow noble, features fine.
> I saw myself slumped, grinning, furrow-browed, with a bottle in my hand.[58]

Harley, at this point, is a fabrication, a construction, an invention conjured up by his grandfather, and is "full of self-pity."[59] The fact that Ern raises Harley in a European image makes his grandson feel that something is not quite right with him: "I saw how I shimmered, just like the aliens do on the television, and although a variety of images were shown, they were all of a kind."[60] Cultural (un)belonging is thus represented as a state of constant alienation, even being associated with a state of physical illness and, with his ability to float, a disability of failing to stay attached.

However, the time comes for Harley to turn the tables on those who made him into this being, who seemingly condemned him to the subject position of the undetermined, the unfulfilled, and the unreal. The feeling of alienation, of sickness, is translated into a sense of being supernatural, and of being specifically powerful. Scott prepares this shift of power relations magnificently: "I was still ill. It is difficult to appreciate the way a cultural and spiritual uplift can affect one. And then he had his first stroke."[61] The metaphor of disease is used here to mark the effects of forcible cultural reeducation, and now Ern, the agent and enforcer of this system, becomes seriously ill. Upon finding Harley destroying his study along with its dearly held contents, Ern suffers a stroke:

> My grandfather was still in the doorway, now on his knees. One hand clutched his chest, while the other waved feebly at me. I remembered a similar scene, but this time did not flee from him but picked my way among the sprawling books, softly slowly stepped through rustling papers, so sharp-edged and so pale.
>   Uplift a despised race.
>   "Well, old man, fuck me white."
>   I helped him to his feet.[62]

Consider how Scott skillfully interweaves many layers of meaning in this short passage. We encounter the image of flying, floating again, as Aboriginals are supposed to be uplifted. Yet, it is Harley who is uplifted permanently and who displays a special capacity. Allegorically speaking, Euro-Australia crumbles to its knees in the light of the discovery of a self-confident Indigenous agency. It bends in sight of the discovery of the hypocrisy of its scientific approach to national politics. It is struck by the metaphoric lightning as it loses the power of its own archive and history. The "despised race" has been "uplifted" to the extent that it frees itself from the "care" of the agents of forcible reeducation, and from the questions of cultural essentialism. There is no need to flee from the oppressor, because Harley realizes that, in this literally historical instant, things have changed fundamentally, and that he is now in power. Uplift and downfall exist in pairs, and they can be temporarily reversed and, in short, carnivalized.

Harley and the reader both bear witness to the "destabilizing process of not being able to recognize oneself in the other."[63] Ern wants to shape Harley into an image of himself and his fellow culture-men, and this fact renders Harley unrecognizable in his own eyes. He is the stranger, the alien, that not even he himself can see properly. Thus conceived, Scott puts Harley into the vulnerable position of the victim, of the identity in formation, in the making, but by other hands than his own.[64] "Harley is himself a fiction, and Ern is his creator."[65] In a Frankensteinesque manner, Harley turns against his creator, as Erns falls ill:

> The old man's speech came slow and croaking. He told me nothing new, and there was no comfort in any of it.
>   He snarled at me, his jokes shaking. *A most dangerous age.* I had spent months looking after him, and no sooner had he regained some fluency to his speech than he uttered those words, trying to manipulate me once again, grabbing at power whichever way he could.[66]

This is a complete reversal of subject positions. Up to this point, Harley was the product, the creation, the victim of Ern. Now, Ern is in need of help and support, for is he unable to maintain himself. The silence and the fact of not knowing where he actually came from made Harley powerless, voiceless, and without a self-consciousness that he could rely on. This has a strong resonance within the processes of reconciliation where the retrieval of a cultural history and the possibility to speak out about abuse and suffering is so central. Upon the discovery of Ern's study, the tables turn, and "there was the grandfather to take care of now."[67]

With this narrative twist, Scott destabilizes the colonial hierarchy profoundly, but with a nod toward indigeneity and magic. Those who have regulated the Indigenous mind and body lose control over their very own bodily functions, while Harley displays superhuman capacities. This is of course a strong message that Scott sends in relation to Australian memory politics. Scott's victims are by no means powerless; they are in fact very powerful, for they are able not only to find themselves, literally, but also to confine the former oppressor to a position where he is forced to listen. In a sense, the colonial agent becomes the object of colonial logic:

> Once I would have insisted this little story represent nothing other than its grumpy, unhappy narrator. This fuck-me-white and first one born. This drifting lightweight who so wanted to be his grandfather's failure. This (let me do away with all vanity) faceless, empty-scrotumed, limp-dicked first man born.[68]

More importantly, Scott's text fundamentally challenges and transforms the notion of the victim and the perpetually damaged Indigenous. Scott's victim, however, does not seek retribution in a physical sense, after Harley has overcome the desire to hurt his grandfather as he has hurt him. When he realizes that he has to take care of Ern now, "and—having found his grandfather's life's work—and seeing that it seemed incomplete, and seeing, moreover, how it so directly led to the grandson himself—the aforementioned boy [Harley] wanted to help."[69] This is also a very skillful interweaving of colonial discourses and their transformation in light of the Australian "politics of regret." The notion of benevolence, of wanting to help the natives to be transformed into an existence that was "fit" for modernity, was at the heart of the colonial logic and exerted through the processes of cultural reeducation. Now it is Harley's turn to "help" the one in need, to not abandon his grandfather in light of his structural helplessness and silence:

> I decided it was better for Ernest to walk, and so I sat in the wheelchair and pushed the wheels at just the right speed to keep him stumbling along behind me. Weighed down by the wheelchair, I could relax and not have to concentrate on remaining earthbound. I often arrived home with an exhausted Ern on my lap which, given the nature of our earlier relationship, both amused and repelled me.[70]

Again, this is another textual example in which Scott—through Harley—makes clear that the histories and lives of the Euro-Australians and Indigenous are inextricably interwoven. There is none without the other. This time, Ern and Harley's relationship is characterized through reversed roles, because Ern is the disabled, the impeded now, while Harley discovers his autonomy, but always in relation to what Ern has turned him into. The former victim is self-conscious and powerful to the extent that Harley takes over the control of Ern's financial affairs. Harley is—after Ern's stroke—capable of finding and retrieving several aspects of his identity, and that also includes his connection to Ern and the colonial system.

Lisa Slater argues that

> [t]he world is beyond our comprehension, yet we are reliant upon it and those who dwell in it for our subjectivity. Ethics is reliant on self-exposure—an openness to the other. Despite the pain of the impossibility of knowing, as Andrew Gibson suggests, "it is also the seed of the most extraordinary and unexpected regenerations and renewals." . . . In the performative utterance of addressing one's unknowable interlocutor, a gap is opened in one's identity, in which the self is reconfigured.[71]

Scott's carnivalization of victimhood—as represented by Harley's transformation—and the reconfiguration of discursive dominance in a postcolonial Australia—as embodied by Ern's demise—is the most striking intervention into the discourses of reconciliation. *Benang* offers an outlook onto how to rearrange the relations between the dominant and the still marginalized. Harley as the purveyor of transcultural existence is as powerful an agent of being composed of different identities that he can overthrow his own subject position as a victim. He is not totally free from being the creation of someone else, of someone else's system, but he is able to reconfigure this victim position in light of the dwindling power of Ern.

Owning the Space In-Between: Hedonist Victims and Transculturalized Perpetrators in Tomson Highway's *Kiss of the Fur Queen*

In her essay on the dynamics of literary representation in the context of Canadian reconciliation, Sophie McCall comments on the importance of and emphasis on healing in the context of reconciliation:

> *Healing*, like *reconciliation*, presents its own conceptual complexities, particularly in colonial contexts, since the notion implies that it is up to the Indigenous people to restore themselves to health in spite of contending with the

ongoing effects of assimilative and genocidal policies in Canada. Prevailing notions of healing, stemming from a Western psychoanalytical conceptual framework, emphasize the *victim's* responsibility in pursuing therapy, overlooking the pathology of the perpetrator and bracketing larger historical contexts of colonialism and the intergenerational transmission of trauma.[72]

Highway's first and only novel, *Kiss of the Fur Queen*, features a substantial amount of damaged Indians; victims of forcible removal and, above all, cultural reeducation.[73] *Fur Queen* directly relates to the Canadian "politics of regret" by showcasing Indigenous peoples attempting to "heal (themselves)" and deal with what McCall refers to as "ongoing effects of assimilative and genocidal policies in Canada." One of the novel's main protagonists, Gabriel Okimasis, is not only unable to follow reconciliation's directive to heal after becoming a victim of colonial reeducation and violence but eventually turns fatally ill. He finally succumbs to AIDS—a disease that is closely associated with (Western) modernity—which he in all probability caught while leading what can be termed a rather hedonistic lifestyle. Jeremiah and Gabriel are the central victims of colonial forces: the two brothers attend an Indian residential school where they are sexually abused by the priests who run it. This damage impacts their life profoundly and leads to the gradual loss of their First Nations' cultural identity.

Fur Queen paints a condensed picture of the agents and effects of cultural reeducation in the context of colonialism and offers a specific take on struggles to make sense of contemporary Indigenous identities, and of the rhetoric of political reconciliation put into practice. As the coming-of-age-novel unfolds, the two brothers embark on different ways to find their place in life and make sense of the two cultural backgrounds they were forced to set into relation. Gabriel becomes a professional dancer, traveling the world as a popular ballet star. At times, however, Gabriel secures his livelihood as a male prostitute. The text leaves the impression that Gabriel is never quite able to form a "good relationship" to others. Jeremiah develops an ambiguous love for classical music, but his initial passion for the piano fades away, and he becomes a social worker for Indigenous peoples. After ten years of absence, he rediscovers the piano and begins to write his own "Indian opera." As the two brothers lose the connection with their homelands, they exploit the space of the city for themselves. On their journey through life, the two protagonists mediate several different stages of victimhood and ongoing victimization—either through their own experiences or by portraying the suffering of others. Throughout the entire text, the reader does not encounter any Indigenous protagonist who seems to have coped with the so-called residential school experience.

Carol Ann Howells observes that Highway's novel "offers a devastating critique of white racism and can barely conceal its rage at the violence perpetrated against Aboriginals by whites."[74] Hence, while this novel can be accused of displaying an obvious undercurrent of continuous victimization of First Nations, it is remarkably powerful in terms of exploring radically transformed, transcultural identities, and the representation of such, in light of physical and emotional abuse, dispossession, and seeming rootlessness.[75] Despite a very prominent focus on victimhood, *Fur Queen* deals in a very specific and interesting way with the figure of the perpetrator. What is more, *Fur Queen* laments the loss of an "authentic" First Nations cultural identity, sending its protagonists into devastating circles of (self-)harm and (self-)pity, but the text also enables its reader to bear witness to modern, pragmatically transcultural identities in the making, and this also includes a repositioning of the perpetrator. Highway's text embeds rape by Catholic priests in First Nations mythology in order to integrate the character of the perpetrator in a transcultural sign system that *Fur Queen* evokes.[76] Highway, in a sense, transculturalizes the figure of the perpetrator—through framing the abusive Catholic priest as *Weetigo*—while the mystic Trickster–Fur Queen instead becomes an item of popular transculture rather than a signifier of "authentic" indigeneity.

In this sense, Highway's novel transforms and broadens the representational repertoire and carnivalizes the idea that the trickster belongs to a specific culture: the Fur Queen who is the guardian of Jeremiah and Gabriel as well as the representative, topos, and token strongly associated with Indigenous culture instead bears testimony to a representational inventory that is transcultural and no longer definitely culturally coded. The trajectory that this characteristically mythical figure undertakes—her image, stemming from a "real" kiss and its photography, turns her into a trickster figure who bears traces of a variety of cross-cultural influences—calling notions of cultural appropriation and authenticity into question. Realist narrative conventions are dominant in the novel, yet this narrative mode is interrupted by incidental portions of magic. Highway's novel also further carnivalizes the notion of an authentic (non-)Indigenous identity and both cultural inventories, shedding light on the wide-reaching transformations that, in the end, both cultures (had to) face.

In what Howells calls a "double vision," *Fur Queen* also creates a narrative space that allows for both the identification of systems of "Western" as well as Indigenous representation, intertwining them thoroughly.[77] Highway's complex cultural interplay carnivalizes the sacrosanctity of religion and myth (both Indigenous and non-Indigenous), emphasizing that the performance of underlying normative frameworks shows not only their cultural constructed-ness but also their transformative power: once it becomes possible to destabilize cultural, religious, and mythological sacrosanctity, they become a connective rather than divisive element in the struggle for contemporary

Canadian identities. Humor becomes the vehicle used not only to frame traumatic events but also to show that Gabriel and Jeremiah cope with the cards that colonial reeducation has dealt them. It is in this vein that Highway's novel demystifies the political rhetoric of reconciliation, for he plays with categories and discourses that continue to shape both the assumptions about First Nations and the expectations raised by Canadian reconciliation discourses.[78] The text thus offers an outlook into the configuration of "reconciled" identities: as one can already see, *Fur Queen* presents a wide range of cultural entanglements, ever stressing the inevitable transculturality of subject positions in light of (post)colonialism. The text is at its best when it outlines and explores its humorous, oftentimes highly pragmatic approach to transcultural identities in light of the rapid deterioration of "authentic" indigeneity.

A Fur Queen Carnivalizes Cultural Representation

Highway is a prominent Indigenous voice in the Canadian context. He is well-known for his plays and dramaturgical adaptions of First Nations' cultures, histories, languages, and identities. On his homepage, Highway's origin and cultural background are captured as follows:

> Tomson Highway was born in a snow bank on the Manitoba/Nunavut border to a family of nomadic caribou hunters. He had the great privilege of growing up in two languages, neither of which was French or English; they were Cree, his mother tongue, and Dene, the language of the neighbouring "nation," a people with whom they roamed and hunted.[79]

He is a "gay Rock Cree playwright from Northern Manitoba" and inhabits the space at the crossroads of various cultural influences.[80] As a public intellectual, Highway is highly invested in issues of promoting Native art and is the official cofounder of the Committee to Re-Establish the Trickster. Allen J. Ryan outlines his life and career as follows:

> In 1986 Highway, along with a small group of fellow Native writers, founded the Committee to Re-Establish the Trickster. Based in Toronto, Ontario, it sought to "consolidate and gain recognition for Native contributions to Canadian writing—to reclaim the Native voice in literature." . . . That same year, Highway became artistic director of Native Earth Performing Arts, an enterprise dedicated to staging new works by Native playwrights. It is no coincidence that a company devoted to reclaiming the Native voice would be equally committed to reaffirming the relevance of the Trickster. They are, in fact, one and the same project. And who better to spearhead such a project than Highway? As fellow playwright Tina Mason says, "I think . . . Weesakayjak takes

on different identities throughout the centuries. I seriously believe he inhabits Tomson Highway's body right now."[81]

Highway's works are known for the insertion of characters of First Nations mythology into an artistic oeuvre that employs the English language and classical literary genres such as drama and, regarding the work at hand, the novel. He is a representative of "syncretic techniques such as intertextuality, a blending of Native and Western imagery, and the crossing of several genres and artistic traditions," yet he does so in favor of strengthening Indigenous presence and recognition in Canadian literature—or so it may seem.[82] In *Fur Queen*, he specifically engages with the trickster and shape-shifter *Weesegeechak*, as well as with the personification of the utmost evil, the flesh-feeding *Weetigo*—both of which we have already made the acquaintance of through Joseph Boyden's *Three Day Road*. Ryan's comment above is indicative of a certain discourse in Canadian literary studies and analysis, whereby to reaffirm, to resurrect a decidedly Native cultural identity unfolds in connection with and through mythological characters, and such "Aboriginal literary nationalism even advocates a tribal-specific criticism."[83] Aesthetical and representational choices are translated into identity-political means of expression. Put differently, in this framing the trickster and its evil counterpart "belong" to the Natives and their (artistic) representatives, and ought to be critically treated in their specifically national or cultural context. Sophie McCall frames this movement to reauthenticate Indigenous representation in connection to reconciliation discourses as follows:

> In Indigenous literary studies, the fissures in approaches to reconciliation stem from and echo other, overlapping tensions between critics who argue for Indigenous nationalist positions, emphasizing the need for deeper engagement with tribal traditions of storytelling, governance, and cultural practice versus those who draw on postcolonial theories that focus on issues such as cultural hybridity, liminality, and white-settler complexes of guilt and complicity.[84]

At first sight, Highway appears to position himself on the side of those who claim and support—as McCall puts it—an Indigenous nationalism, arguing for regaining ownership of culturally coded representations of indigeneity. To resurrect the trickster (and other mythological characters who by default belong to First Nations' representative repertoire) can be perceived as a symptom of such container-thinking. *Fur Queen* has, in a similar vein, been identified as a text that explores the experience of cultural marginality,[85] the traumatic legacies of colonialism in Canada,[86] and a literary testimony to the resistance and resilience of Canada's First Nations.[87] As Katja Sarkowsky points out, "[I]ssues of mythology, language, sexuality, sexual violence, and the rewriting of colonial scripts dominate the critical literature on *Kiss [of the*

Fur Queen]; also, critics all point to the importance of cultural mixture in Highway's works and in his novel in particular."[88] The general thrust of interpreting *Fur Queen* rests on the tension between the cultures and their fruitful "mixture." Yet, it is my contention that Highway's text moves beyond this still lingering cultural essentialism, for it shows in an exemplary manner how processes of cultural transformation have effected strategies of representation. Highway temporarily reverses these gridlocked representational systems.

In a semiautobiographical approach, Highway allows for parallels between his own experience and that of his brother René.[89] René was, just like *Fur Queen*'s protagonist Gabriel, a professional dancer, a victim of the colonial system and abuse, and openly gay. Eventually, he died of AIDS, and although the name of the disease is not spelled out in *Fur Queen*, it is safe to assume that Gabriel also falls victim to AIDS.[90] Tomson and his brother René both attended residential schools and were subjected to colonial reeducation. Highway fictionalizes his own family (hi)story, consequently transgressing the threshold between experience and fiction, and emphasizes the inevitable interrelatedness of individual and collective memory, the public and the private sphere in the context of reconciliation: the two brothers Jeremiah and Gabriel Okimasis—initially named Champion and Ooneemeetoo by their parents and renamed by Catholic priests—are brought to the fictional Birch Lake Indian Residential School in Northern Manitoba because their parents, Mariesis and Abraham Okimasis, have to obey the law. The text comes across as a "memoir," progressing in a mostly linear fashion.[91] While migrating from their hunting grounds back to the reserve during a family trip, Mariesis and Abraham stop to take a break. In the vicinity of "a largish island in the middle of the lake, that, some say, had once been fished by 'someone named Weesageechak,'" both parents come to a realization:

> "Come December," said Mariesis with an undercurrent of sadness, "Champion will be seven years old." Like all lovers of long standing, they could reach each other's thoughts. "Seven years," replied Abraham, casting a sweeping glance over the thawing lake before them. "That's a good time. Myself, when I was seven, I bagged my first moose." Abraham loved teasing his wife; he had been fourteen when the legendary event had taken place, and she well knew it. A breeze from the south ruffled a strand of her long, black hair. Her heart was too heavy; the hunter's joke had missed the mark. "He will be leaving us soon. Champion. Does he have to go to that school in the south?" The question fell upon the hunter's chest like a cold hand. . . . "What Father Bouchard wants, I guess," he finally admitted, wishing dearly that he had some say in the matter. "But couldn't he wait two years? Until Gabriel can go with him? That school is so far away." "*Sooni-eye-gimow's* orders, Father Bouchard says. It is the law."[92]

Highway's extradiegetic narrator skillfully intertwines the two cultural realities in this scene. On the one hand, we encounter the two parents who seem to hold on to a certain native identity. Abraham reminisces about his first rite of passage, the bagging of a moose. For the younger generation, however, the moment of inauguration into adulthood is marked by leaving the reserve and attending a residential school in the care of Catholic missionaries. This scene is central to understanding many developments within the novel; the brothers' time in the care of Catholic missionaries becomes zero hour for the narrative. While Abraham's moose killing marks the affirmation of First Nations' customs and culture, the transference of the Indigenous youth to a residential school means the exact opposite: it is the designated aim of these schools to eradicate indigeneity and to render First Nations' descendants "fit" for a Western modernity, secluded from bushes, rivers, and hunting. Yet the traditional First Nations' way of life that Abraham both stands for and refers to has already been dramatically altered by settler presence and colonialism. Furthermore, as the reader learns through the course of the novel, "Indian" skills such as hunting and sled-racing are no longer a means of sustaining both the livelihood of Indigenous families and their cultural inventory. They have, in a sense, become empty representatives of a formerly independent, self-aware culture and cultural identity. Through this reading, this seemingly unambiguous scene at the lake unveils itself as an instance when the narrative plays with and consciously reverses cultural coded-ness.

Although it seems as if Mariesis and Abraham communicate in English, they are never in full command of the "colonizer's tongue." Their dialogue has been rendered in English, yet within the novel's story-world, the two speak Cree. The figure of the narrator mediates these two language-worlds without the reader being aware. The printed word on the page diverts from the meaning it invokes. This English, although it is rendered in English words, actually is not English, but Cree in disguise. The institution of the narrator, or, more precisely, the narrative perspective, underlines the programmatic ambiguity central to this novel. The narrator seems to look upon the events and stories unfolding, offering at times humorous, at times ironic commentaries and explanations. It gradually becomes clear that this narrator is itself caught between the cultural poles; it attempts to negotiate these powerful forces and, ultimately, transculturalizes these categories. With a resemblance to the troublesome and stony path through the two brothers' lives, this narrator oscillates between at times obtrusive omniscience and close focalization, continuously shifting the pace and amount of commentary and thus rendering the narrative voice difficult to pinpoint, to get a hold of, or grasp as the guide through the story. Its ambiguity speaks to the problem of representing and narrating truths in a context of constantly shifting cultural and historical identities. The relationship between language, representation, and the power of mediation through the institution of the narrator is not only clearly identified as problematical by Highway but also further complicated by *Fur Queen*.

Another pivotal event within the narrative, the dogsled race that Abraham Okimasis wins, has also moved far away from First Nations tradition and culture and has become more of a popular, even touristic event. On occasion of the 1951 Millington Cup World Championship Dog Derby at the Trapper's Festival in Oopaskooyak, Manitoba, Abraham has set himself the task to win this event.[93] The focalized narrator explains what is going through Abraham's head as he races along:

> He had sworn to his dear wife, Mariesis Okimasis, on pain of separation and divorce, unthinkable for a Roman Catholic in the year of our Lord 1951, that he would win the world championship just for her: the silver cup, that holy chalice was to be his twenty-first-anniversary gift to her. With these thoughts racing through his fevered mind, Abaraham Okimasis edged past musher number 54—Jean-Baptiste Ducharme of Cranberry Portage. Still not good enough.[94]

Already at this early stage of the narrative, the reader encounters Highway's specific perspective on the world—one that meets the tides of life with a smile—as well as the full force of Canadian transculturality. Abraham, a Roman Catholic Indian who pursues a trophy from a commercial event, outruns a French Canadian citizen of whom we will not learn more than that he exists. It is not even a simple trophy: it is a "holy chalice." The narrative perspective once again leaves it open to interpretation whether Abraham actually thinks of the trophy in Christian terms or if it is the sly, mocking narrative voice that describes it that way. However, a little later, Abraham even starts to call for divine intervention:

> "Please, please, God in heaven, let me win this race," a voice inside the caribou hunter's body whispered," and I will thank you with every deed, every touch, every breath for the rest of my long life, for hallowed be thy name. . . ." The prayer strung itself, word by word, like a rosary, pulling him along, bead by bead by bead, "Thy kingdom come, thy will be done on Earth. . . ."[95]

It is clear how skillful Highway is here in unsettling the reader, their expectations in terms of cultural belonging, in this passage. While marking Abraham as Indigenous—for he is, after all, still a caribou hunter—Highway lets him cite the Lord's Prayer, a well-known religious performance. At this very early stage of the narrative, Highway manages to temporarily and skillfully reverse markers of cultural belonging (being a caribou hunter, the Lord's Prayer, or the reference to the rosary), opening them up for further use as his novel progresses. To carnivalize established categories and sacrosanct institutions, both within the novel and as a suggestion to look beyond it, is programmatic in *Fur Queen* as we can see, for example, in how Highway frames the boys' residential school experience:

> "Hail Mary, full of grace, the Lord is with Thee; blessed art Thou amongst women and blessed is the fruit of thy womb, Jesus," recited Brother Stumbo in a sleep-inducing monotone as he paced down one aisle and up another, his large black rosary beads swinging from both hands. Identically attired in pale blue flannel pyjamas, thirty-seven newly bald Cree boys knelt beside their little beds in the junior boys' dormitory. "Hello merry, mutter of cod, play for ussinees, now anat tee ower of ower beth, aw, men." Gabriel rattled off the non-sensical syllables as nimbly as he could, pretending he knew what they meant. But, his knees hurting from the cold, hard linoleum, he couldn't help but wonder why the prayer included the Cree word "*ussinees.*" What need did this mutter of cod have of a pebble?[96]

Although one is tempted to laugh, this episode foreshadows the terrible events to come. Yet, and as one can gather from the above quote, Highway's narrative is able to almost add zest, a certain productive dynamic, to the violence that is unfolding, for it is the author's stylistic and identity-political choice to make the reader laugh. As such, humor as a means of representation is able to open up traumatic narratives, temporarily free them from their traumatic burden on the narrative, and "[promote] a healing experience."[97] According to Rubelise da Cunha, "ludic play" as represented by the humoristic undercurrent is a strategy of survival, both in terms of developing a stance of ironic distancing and of approaching serious matters in an unorthodox manner to be able to say the unsayable, to represent the unrepresentable.[98] The notion of the carnivalesque, as envisaged by Bakhtin, understands the element of laughter as quintessential in order to temporarily reverse existing social hierarchies and truths.[99] In Bakthin's terms, the originality, hence authenticity, of the lower classes can be given proper expression by lending voice and face to folk humor, folk laughter.[100] Carnival, in this vein, offers a completely different, nonofficial, extra-ecclesiastical, and extrapolitical aspect of the world and, more importantly, of human relations.[101] Consequently the carnivalesque is not only a specific mode of literary representation and world-making but also an identity-political tool in the repertoire of artists.

Highway, known for his capacity of "comic troping of serious themes," inserts humor into the narrative, because he, in alliance with Bakhtin's carnivalesque, seeks to degrade and debase the higher, the powerful, and the dominant.[102] The emphasis on humor reverses the solemnity and self-ascribed gravity of the higher classes, and the heaviness of pain and suffering. Highway thus introduces a representational double bind: in the scene quoted above, the onomatopoeic representation of the Lord's Prayer desanctifies and demystifies the power of religious rituals and performances. Religion, or, more precisely, a voluntary distortion of religious ethics and truths, has after all led to the systems of cultural reeducation. Moreover, carnival's indispensable trait is, according to Bakhtin, ambivalence.[103] Humor and the grotesque as means of expressing the carnivalesque within and of societies, "consecrate" inequality, ambivalence, and hybridity.[104] Highway not only bridges the cultural gap between the Lord's Prayer and "newly bald Cree boys" through provoking a laugh at the peculiar pronunciation, but he also emphasizes religion's very performative aspect by debunking its most famous formula. Edgars Ošiņš offers this explanation:

> Challenging forcefully imposed Christianity as the hard core of the colonial power discourse becomes a legitimate prime target for Native writers who deconstruct and parody the biblical script, religious dogmas, and church rituals. The Native narrative strategies aim at scrambling and erasing the biblical code to release and empower submerged aboriginal religious creeds.[105]

Religion's sacrosanctity on the one hand and its self-serving, hypocritical representatives on the other are reversed by one sleight of the representational hand. Yet, and in opposition to Ošiņš's stance, Highway demonstrates that a mode of world-making such as the carnivalesque does not belong to a specific culture and that the use of such means of literary representation can be very productively opened up toward expressing the transcultural. *Fur Queen* is thus an example of how such categories elude cultural ownership and pave ways for (further) understanding the transcultural.

The temporal reversal of truths and categories continues and is programmatic to this novel. Our caribou hunter finally manages to win the derby. On this occasion, Abraham receives a congratulatory kiss from a "White Beauty Pageant Fur Queen."[106] This kiss is captured on a photo that will, in a sense, develop a life of its own through the course of the novel:

> When the queen turned for one fleeting second to smile at the screaming throngs below, Abraham looked down at his hands. There lay the large silver bowl, the Millington Cup, . . . and in the bowl, a cheque in the amount of one thousand dollars. He had won. . . . Abraham pulled his stunned gaze from the silver bowl to the Fur Queen's brilliant smile, where it became imprisoned once again. And then the Fur Queen's lips began descending. Down they came, fluttering, like a leaf from an autumn birch, until they came to rest on Abraham's left cheek. There. After what seemed like years to Abraham Okimasis, she removed her lips from his cheek, expelling a jet of ice-cold vapour that mushroomed into a cloud. Her lips, her eyes, gold and silver beads of her tiara sparkled one last time and then were swallowed by the billowing mist. The

next thing Abraham knew, or so he would relate to his youngest sons years later, the goddess floated up to a sky fast fading from pink-and-purple dusk to the great blackness of night, then become one with the northern sky, became a shifting, nebulous pulsation, the seven stars of the Great Bear ornamenting her crown.[107]

The "real" woman, a token and symptom of popular culture and capitalism, transcends her own earthly existence and floats away into the sky, a nature that is strongly marked as an Indigenous space. This is precisely the instance when *Fur Queen* broadens its representational inventory toward the uncanny, the magic, and becomes a text characterized by magic realism. As we have already established in the previous chapter on Kim Scott's *Benang*, magic realism is seemingly oxymoronic, for it inserts the magic into an otherwise completely realist textual composition and setup. Realism is supposedly a Western representational strategy, while the realm of the "magic" is oftentimes closely associated with Indigenous storytelling and cultural representation.

It is precisely the combination of these two narrative modes that relieves storytelling from being unambiguously culturally coded. Magic realism is a token and a symptom of transcultural representation and world-making and has, in a similar manner as the carnivalesque, become a vehicle of representing the transcultural experience. This Fur Queen becomes the queen of both cultures, or, more precisely, the leader of a Canadian transculture. This ambiguous trickster figure accompanies Jeremiah and Gabriel's journey through the cultures, and oftentimes almost clairvoyantly forebodes the development that both brothers are going through: the formation of a transcultural identity. The Fur Queen's kiss marks the point when representational boundaries undoubtedly blur: The beautiful young woman, winner of this beauty pageant, is presented as a "real" character in the story-world that *Fur Queen* unfolds, described with means that the realist convention allows for, yet she is transformed into a magic apparition. On the one hand, she is rendered a token of Abraham's success, as represented by the photograph of the kiss, and on the other hand, she merges into a transcultural figurine in the word sense: the image on the photograph leaves the frame behind, coalesces with the native mythological figure of the *Weesageechak*, the trickster/shape-shifter, yet maintains strong markers of being of popular-cultural descent as a beauty pageant winner. This move carnivalizes representational unambiguity, for it temporarily reverses possible certainties of belonging and understanding: the Fur Queen never completely severs herself from being a representative of Western popular culture, while at the same time she grounds herself firmly in the overarching trickster narrative. The kiss marks the point of departure for transcending cultural and representational boundaries. Hence, this trickster does not fully belong to the Indigenous representational arsenal, nor can this

Fur Queen be fully grasped through adhering to the realistic and reason-based mindset through which realism comes into being. Highway's Fur Queen and the manifold shapes she takes on as the novel progresses become an internal structuring device, the beginning, middle, and end to and of Gabriel and Jeremiah's story. The photo of the Fur Queen's kiss follows Gabriel and Jeremiah on their journey through the Indian residential school they are forced to attend. She watches them as they suffer sexual abuse and rape at the hands of Catholic priests, but she fails to watch over the two brothers. In the end, she stands beside the bed in which Gabriel succumbs to AIDS.

Until Gabriel's untimely death, the novel follows its two protagonists on their journey of becoming artists. This novel, which structurally resembles a sonata, displays markers of being a *Künstlerroman*, something regarded as a quintessentially European narrative genre.[108] The narrative encompasses thirty-six years, roughly stretching from 1951 to 1987. These thirty-six years are, however, of less importance as a specific time span, but are instead indicative of how destructive the influence of settler culture on Indigenous lifestyles had already been. As it has already been noted, both brothers develop an affection for the "fine arts," or, more precisely, what is commonly perceived as Western expressions of high culture—ballet and classical music. *Fur Queen* is structured into six parts, which in turn refer to a classical symphonic structure. Each part is given a title that represents "movements in classical music"[109]: *Allegro man non troppo*, for example, covers the pre–residential school period in the Indian reserve of Eemanapiteepitat, the place where both brothers were born and brought up. Eemanapiteepitat is also less of a locus of traditional Indian ways but rather a conglomerate of victims of colonial dominance and forcible relocation. The brothers' time in the residential school—which impacts their lives profoundly—is referred to, for example, by the title *Andante cantabile*.[110] Sarah Krotz sees a parallel between this specific way of structuring the text and developments within it:

> The "Allegro ma non troppo" pulsates through the wind-whipped landscape of the Trapper's Festival dogsled race, the births of Champion/Jeremiah and Ooneemeetoo/Gabriel, and the seasonal caribou-hunting expeditions that give shape to their world. ... Felt behind the rhythms and cadences of everyday life in the Northern Manitoba community of Eemanapiteepitat, the "Allegro" unifies the lively realm of sound and song in which the brothers spend the first years of their childhood. The tempo instructions that follow ... continue this synaesthetic effect.[111]

In a countermovement to onomatopoeia, Highway translates experiences, time frames, and episodes in his protagonists' story of the self into classical music patterns. Thus, Highway undertakes more than producing a structuring equivalent to frame synesthetics. Classical music and its expression in the form of the novel can be regarded as an overemphasis on the colonizer's culture and its worthiness in terms of "high culture," as Krotz and others purport.[112] Classical music and ballet can be seen as tokens of the still dominant settler culture.

Yet the stories of Gabriel and Jeremiah cannot but elude the tight framework of a symphony. Their lives and identities pursue paths that cannot be grasped by such a dogmatic organizational pattern. It is my contention that Highway intends to deceive the reader with this specific structuring device: instead of producing clarity, predictability, and stability, Gabriel's and Jeremiah's identities defy all attempts at mastering them, of being subject to preformed patterns and *tempi*. Instead of evoking the decidedness of the structure of a symphony, Gabriel's and Jeremiah's life stories evoke dissonances, (im)possibilities, and ambiguities—something that can hardly be accommodated in a classical symphony. Once again, Highway skillfully plays with the readers' and critics' preformed expectations, in particular with regard to whom the realm of classical music actually "belongs" to, and that it amounts to an act of cultural appropriation of classical music on the part of the native writer. In a similar move to inserting the trickster into the narrative as a means to counter cultural belonging, both within the novel and beyond, Highway opens up classical music—traditionally a token of European cultural dominance—toward the transcultural. It is in this vein that both protagonists never seem to truly come to terms with their artwork and occasionally struggle with their passion for what can be perceived as "high culture." Yet again, this is just another representational thread that Highway weaves into the narrative, inevitably relocating one's understanding of cultural belonging. Cultural inventories on both ends become transcultural commodities and enable the development of transcultural identities.

A Cree Dorian Gray and a Catholic *Weetigo*

While this emphasis on transculturality on many levels within *Fur Queen* is its most powerful critical angle, this text is still complicit in further reinforcing the image of the "damaged Indian."[113] As we have already seen, the very structure of Australia's and Canada's processes of reconciliation runs the risk of producing a monodimensional rendering of indigeneity. By featuring and centering the plurifold stories of violence and abuse, *Fur Queen* allows a master narrative of the "damaged Native" to unfold.[114] Indigenous resilience is reduced to a narrative that "pathologizes" the Indigenous by rendering them in constant need of state interference and support.[115] Moreover, the "issue of the forced removal of children is framed specifically and characteristically as an Indigenous experience."[116] With regard to the depiction of victimhood and suffering under the colonial yoke, Matthias Merkl remarks that *"Kiss of the Fur Queen* is one of the most disturbing and touching literary requiems."[117] This assessment is a rather understandable reaction to the utter violence and despair narrated in Highway's novel. The text does indeed mourn losses, but in an almost compulsive manner it revolves around victimhood and victimization. Surprisingly, there is not a single character to be found in *Fur Queen* who does not see themselves in a devastating situation, hardly able to cope with the effects of cultural reeducation. Highway comments on his very own struggle with his personal pain, and Suzanne Methot provides the explanatory framework:

> Aboriginal people believe that unacknowledged pain leads to an imbalance among mind, body, and spirit that is manifested in sickness. In Highway's case, the pain was insistent and the sickness serious. "I didn't have a choice," Highway says, "I *had* to write this book. It came screaming out because this story needed desperately to be told. Writing hit me hard in terms of my health. So I went to a medicine man, who helped me defeat the monster. We lanced the boil and cured the illness," he says.[118]

Methot's comment frames Indigenous suffering as a pain that can be remedied in a specific cultural context alone. The understanding that suppressed pain leads to physical illness also harks back to a psychoanalytical context; the representation of trauma in literature is decidedly not an angle that this study pursues. However, it is the specificity of Aboriginal suffering invoked in the context of Canadian reconciliation that echoes in these lines. *Fur Queen*, more or less unconsciously and in contrast to Highway's comment above, bears witness to a different kind of engagement with this historical legacy of victimhood: this suffering and making sense of systematic violence is and cannot be a monocultural endeavor, and his text bears witness to its structural transculturality.

Fur Queen's programmatic temporary reversal of cultural categories and strategies of representation arrives at its most productive, most prominent epiphany once the analysis turns toward the victims and perpetrators depicted in *Fur Queen*. The fate of the two brothers and the developments that their life stories undertake are, unsurprisingly, closely related. As Coral Ann Howells aptly remarks, Gabriel and Jeremiah stand for a "twinning of experience" and a "twinning of protagonists" that makes the doubling of experience even possible:[119]

> [A] postcolonial Native identity is beset with ambivalence, so it is not surprising to find that this novel is structured on binary patterns, filled as it is with doubles and split selves, mirror images, parallels and contrasts.... This "twinning" of the protagonists signals that double vision which is the novel's most

remarkable feature as it moves continually between the two worlds, exploring the destabilizing effects of the warring impact of white and Native cultures on the brothers' life.[120]

This rather enthusiastic identification of doubling on all levels is exaggerated to a great extent, but it is the obvious interrelation of the two brothers that builds the basis for important developments within the novel: in order to understand the centrality of victimhood to Highway's novel, it is vital to consider the rendition of rape in more detail. Note how the focalization moves from Gabriel to Jeremiah in this passage:

> When Gabriel opened his eyes, ever so slightly, the face of the principal loomed inches from his own. The man was wheezing, his breath emitting, at regular intervals, spouts of hot air that made Gabriel think of raw meat hung to age but forgotten. The priest's arm held him gently by his right, his right arm buried under Gabriel's bedspread, under his blanket, under his sheet, under his pyjama bottoms. And the hand was jumping up, reaching for him, pulling him back down. . . . Gradually, Father Lafleur bent, closer and closer, until the crucifix that dangled from his neck came to rest on Gabriel's face. The subtly throbbing motion of the priest's upper body made the naked Jesus Christ—the sliver of silver light, this fleshly son of God so achingly beautiful—rub his body against the child's lips, over and over and over again. Gabriel had no strength left. The pleasure in his centre welled so deep that he was about to open his mouth and swallow the whole living flesh—in his half-dream state, this man nailed to the cross was a living, breathing man, tasting like Gabriel's most favourite food, warm honey—when he heard the shuffle of approaching feet. . . . Jeremiah had awakened with a start from a dream of playing concerts to vast herds of caribou. Why, he didn't know, but he thought he might have heard a whimper from Gabriel. Once his eyelids adjusted to the darkness, he decided to check on him, perhaps giving him just one kiss. . . . But Gabriel was not alone. A dark, hulking figure hovered over him, like a crow. Visible only in silhouette, for all Jeremiah knew it might have been a bear devouring a honey-comb, or the Weetigo feasting on human flesh. . . . When the beast reared its head, it came face to face, not four feet away, with that of Jeremiah Okimasis. The whites of the beast's eyes grew large, blinked once. Jeremiah stared. It *was* him. Again.[121]

Jeremiah, as we later learn, was also raped by Father Lafleur, but has locked away his memories so deeply that they at some point forcefully return to haunt him. Here the connection between the two brothers is perceivable as the said "double vision." To recap these events, Gabriel and Jeremiah both entered the residential school system at a very young age. Jeremiah is the first one to leave home, with Gabriel following him some time later, accompanied by the famous photograph of the Fur Queen's kiss. It, or, more precisely, she is supposed to guard the two children; they kiss the Fur Queen good night. Eventually Father Lafleur takes advantage of the boys and starts sexually abusing them. Jeremiah, as we later learn, had managed to suppress his memory of his own sexual abuse, but the reader bears witness to these returning memories. Jeremiah and Gabriel are busy composing an "Indian opera," and while they read the following commentary on the premiere, Jeremiah remembers:

> "'Respected Cree dancer-choreographer Gabriel Okimasis,'" read Amanda, "'doing his first turns as actor and director, is surely the most beautiful man who ever walked the earth.' Blah, blah . . . wait a minute. Here. 'But the cannibal spirit shedding his costume at death, revealing a priest's cassock, confuses the viewer. The image comes from nowhere.'" "What's she talking about?" Jeremiah growled. "You didn't ask loud enough, Jeremiah," said Gabriel. "Didn't say what loud enough?" Jeremiah tried to ask again. But, finally, his memory opened the padlocked doors.[122]

Gabriel with his great beauty is once again the point of departure. From there, the text moves toward a break in the convention of sublime beauty that appears to have irritated the author of the comment above. Set in a pre-reconciliation era, the brother's artistic performance in reflection of Gabriel's abuse by Father Lafleur unsettles this particular viewer, but it also unsettles Jeremiah. Up to this point, the reader remains uncertain whether it was only Gabriel who suffered under the priest's "care." *Fur Queen* becomes palimpsestic at this moment: a glimpse from the extradiegetic world—the comment—is incorporated into the present of Gabriel and, more importantly, Jeremiah, and triggers the latter's painful process of remembering his own abuse. The recovery of memory unfolds in a nonlinear, associative, and uncontrollable manner, and Highway's novel lends this process its aesthetic expression: the next episode almost resembles a stream of consciousness, but without its distinct narratological markers as being delivered by one single character. It is instead a programmatic outpouring, a stream of consciousness that is interwoven with other perspectives. This passage is worthy of quoting at length, as it further outlines Highway's strategy of transculturalizing notions not only of identity but also of suffering and abuse:

> "Silent night," sang a crystalline soprano. To Champion Okimasis, it was the earth serenading him. "Holy night . . ." Beyond the aria, he could hear the endless stands of spruce groaning within their shrouds of snow, the air so clean it sparkled: silver, then rose, then mauve. Four-year-old Champion knelt at the front of his father's dogsled. He hung on to the canvas siding with one hand, and, with the other, waved a miniature whip, chiming "*Mush*, Tiger-Tiger, *mush, mush!*" . . . Behind him, his father brandished his moose-hide-whip—"*Mush*, Tiger!"—below, his mother, her back against the *kareewalatic*.

Inside her goose-down sleep robe, Gabriel lay suckling at her breast. Jeremiah laughed. What's this? A face? Yes, in the forest and larger, blotting out the trotting dogs. Champion closed his eyes, hoping it would go away. . . . Gradually, against the old man's mouth, an artic fox appeared. The pretty white creature wore a sequined gown of white satin, gloves to her elbows, white wings wirring. And she was singing, not to anybody but to him, the little Cree accordion player: "Holy infant so tender and mild." Such pouty red lips. "Jeremiah," said God the Father from behind the singing lady fox, "Jeremiah, get out of bed." Thunder? In December? "Come with me." The fox—maggeesees—was gone. Sleepily, Champion-Jeremiah slid out of bed. By the light of the moon full to bursting, the now eight-year-old floated down an aisle lined with small white beds, cradles filled with sleeping brown children. Out a door, and up and down corridors, the long black robe swaying like a curtain, smelling of cigar smoke, incense, sacramental wine. By the puffy armchair of pitch-black leather, Father Roland Lafleur, oblate of Mary Immaculate, unbuttoned his cassock, unzipped his trousers. So white, thought Champion-Jeremiah, so big. Black and white hair all around the base, like . . . a mushroom on a cushion of reindeer moss. Now he remembers the holy man inside him, the lining of his rectum being torn, the pumping and pumping and pumping, cigar breath billowing somewhere above his cold shaved head.[123]

Tomson Highway hammers it home: at first, Jeremiah is not Jeremiah, but Champion, and this is a reference to pre-abuse time and identity. As the scene unfolds, Champion becomes Champion-Jeremiah, and finally, after the fact, he will never be Champion again and will always be Jeremiah. He has been permanently marked by Highway's rendition of Canadian Christianity. Sexual references prepare what is going to happen to the little boy, and are spread throughout this short passage. It is by no means a "holy night" that Jeremiah has to endure. Spruces are "groaning," the moon is about to burst. Death seems imminent through the reference to white shrouds of snow. It is, however, not a true death, but rather the end to Jeremiah's, or, more precisely Champion's innocence, as further emphasized by "crystalline soprano" and her aria. An almost romantic depiction of Jeremiah's early childhood and his brother being nursed by his mother—both strongly marked as Indigenous— blends into the face and command of Father Lafleur, telling the boy to come with him. The Fur Queen announces her presence; she also oscillates between being an object of sexuality and of being the conveyor of painful truths. These "pouty red lips" could belong to both: Jeremiah who is about to be raped, or the iridescent Fur Queen in all her ambiguity. In any case, she fails to protect Jeremiah, and so Father Lafleur becomes one with God Almighty in the eyes of the remembering Jeremiah. This textual example is all about sounds and images: the rhythmic patterning of Highway's narrative voice when it refers to "endless strands of spruce groaning within their shrouds of snow" or "blotting out the trotting dogs." Images blend into one another, sounds mingle and create a synesthetic pattern of representing rape. Strategic repetitions and alliterations complete the stylistic inventory in order to delineate the return of traumatic, suppressed memories.

In an obvious paralleling to Jeremiah's recalling of his first rape, Gabriel's experience and its rendition bear resemblances: it is nighttime, and dreamlike states befall both protagonists. In the second line, an allusion to flesh—more precisely, rotten flesh—is evoked in connection with the actions of Father Lafleur. The air is hot, while Jeremiah's remembering tells us about the coldness of winter. Jesus Christ, dangling in Gabriel's face as he is trying to make sense of what is happening to him, is suddenly fleshly. This Jesus Christ, however, is of a worldly beauty; the narrative establishes a parallel to Gabriel's perceived extraordinary beauty. In Gabriel's mind, which is caught between pleasure and disgust, this Jesus, akin to the Fur Queen, develops a life of its own: outrightly blasphemous, Highway evokes a merging of Jesus Christ dangling from the cross and into Gabriel's face with the priest's penis, ejaculating "warm honey" into the mouth of the young boy. The rules of culturally coded representation are bent and blur, political or cultural correctness do not play any role. Jeremiah becomes the witness to Gabriel's sexual abuse, and the focalization moves over to Jeremiah as soon as Gabriel—and, by extension, the reader—have made sense of Gabriel's half-dreaming mind. With a beautiful representational *coup de main*, Highway positions the character of Gabriel in close proximity to a well-known literary figure who is leading an extraordinary life for an eternity. Gabriel, in a sense, becomes a transcultural Dorian Gray: he is strikingly beautiful, though somehow it is a larger-than-life beauty that is rather unsettling because of its constant reiteration. His striking outer appearance oftentimes serves as an explanation of why people in general, and men in particular, are drawn to Gabriel. One is tempted to read this as Highway lamenting his brother, while at the same time criticizing him, contesting his choices, and mourning his ultimate loss. Gabriel leads a life that enjoys art for art's sake, and life for life's sake, and tries to shape his life in delimitation against victimhood as the overarching identity template. Jeremiah considers himself to be responsible to keep his brother in check: "When are you gonna get serious about your life?" Gabriel shed duplicity, evasion, untruth with his parka on the tired old sofa. "You don't want me to dance. . . . You don't want me to make friends. What am I supposed to do?"[124] This scene is representative of how the narrative perspective, the focalization, appears to move from protagonist to protagonist, offering insights into states of mind, thoughts, and feelings yet actually blocking from view that it is mostly Jeremiah who appears to look at Gabriel. To some extent, then, the two brothers stand for Howells's "double vision," and the narrative is structured to juxtapose the two brothers, frequently in opposition. Yet, it is Jeremiah who envies Gabriel, is worried for him, criticizes him, but at the end of the day Gabriel makes an apt observation with regard to Jeremiah's life: "'And you?' Gabriel grabbed the wrist and flung it to the side with such force that Jeremiah reeled. 'You'd rather diddle with a piano than diddle with yourself. You're dead, Jeremiah. At least my body is still alive.'"[125]

To a certain degree, Gabriel becomes the foil onto which Jeremiah projects his own misery, because Gabriel, through the way he leads his life, is able to problematize the category of the victim. More precisely, he carnivalizes the notion of a passive, constantly suffering victim, an image that is well evoked by Highway's text itself:

> "Who is this . . . Gregory Newman?" "What are you? The FBI? Mariesis Okimasis? Father Lafleur?" Gabriel was all of seventeen, for God's sake, barely past childhood—cradle snatcher! "Mom and Dad told me to look after you," Jeremiah lied. "You try too hard. At everything. You and those lily-white fingers. That is what you want, isn't it? To become a whiteman." Jeremiah's hand hit Gabriel so hard his cheek, for a moment, turned pale. "What were you doing with . . . that guy . . . last night?" "Nothing. . . ." "You . . . had your tongue shoved down his throat, for God's sa—" "So what? It's not your tongue."[126]

Gabriel leaves the state of victimhood behind without completely ceasing to be a victim. However, it is the perspective of the narrator that constantly draws us back into seeing him as such. Jeremiah as the most prominent focalizing point is complicit in revictimizing Gabriel constantly. In this vein, Howells also detects a certain tension between the two brothers. This tension often results in "deadly conflicts," in particular with regard to Gabriel's utterly hedonistic lifestyle.[127] The scene above is representative of the different developments that the life stories of the two brothers undertake. Gabriel is openly gay and engages in a variety of questionable yet passionate relationships in the course of the novel. Gabriel leads, in a sense, an antagonistic lifestyle to Jeremiah. His life as a professional dancer allows him to travel the world to some degree. Gabriel has fought for a notion of freedom from the yoke of victimhood, and that is to make one's own choices, whether or not they are always wise. At times, Gabriel does indeed become a male prostitute; his story-of-the-self is not without ruptures, fissures, and dead ends. Gabriel, however, allows us to see beyond the cloak of victimhood, for he, within the tight frame that his traumatic childhood allows for, has set out to master his own story, his own life.

It is the tension between the two different coping mechanisms that governs the dynamics between the two brothers. Gabriel is utterly aware of his effect on men, and when the "bronze Cree angel" enters a bar, heads turn, which makes him feel how "a hundred eyes enveloped Gabriel [Okimasis]."[128] He is comfortable with this situation, but "[h]alf of [him] had an urge to run, to Barry Sexton's party and Jeremiah, the other half to dive in and wallow shamelessly."[129] This scene ends with Gabriel engaging in a kind of sexual orgy. Here, we once again encounter a Dorian Gray–esque situation: "Everywhere he looked, naked limb met naked limb met naked limb, an unceasing domino effect of human flesh, smell, fluid. Whisky, beer, wine swirled, splashed like blood, smoke from marijuana rose like incense."[130] Everything is there in abundance, but the potions that comprise hedonism always carry a sense of lingering danger, of decay, of death, with them. The word "incense" prepares the narrative transition toward sexual abuse, and Gabriel's remembrance of being raped by Father Lafleur:

> The body of the caribou hunter's son was eaten, tongues writhing serpent-like around his own, breath mingling with his, his orifices punctured and repunctured, as with nails. And through it all, somewhere in the farthest reaches of his senses, the silver cross oozed in and out, in and out, the naked body pressing on his lips, positioning itself for entry. Until, upon the buds that lined his tongue, warm honey flowed like river water over granite.[131]

Again, it is the narrative perspective, this time with a rather unclear focalization, that invokes a connection between sex and being consumed by an evil spirit. Gabriel tests his limits, explores the city and its nightlife, and is indeed oftentimes reminded of the abuse he suffered. Notwithstanding his troubled past, it is the strong influence that this narrative perspective exerts on the reader that drags Gabriel's test drive of himself, his limits, and the limits of heteronormativity toward the forbidden, the impossible, the inappropriate.

The kiss that Jeremiah wanted to bestow on his brother to wish him goodnight, right before Lafleur enters the scene, sets another obvious parallel to the title-giving kiss of the Fur Queen that Abraham received. It was, in a sense, the kiss that signaled that modernity had not spared the Indigenous populations. Now, this kiss that never made it onto Gabriel's skin marks the end of all Indigenous innocence and, in a way, ushers in the beginning of a (post)colonial modernity for our two brothers. This modernity is inevitably characterized through ambiguity, through the loss of the alleged authentic and the decline of their "true" First Nations heritage. This kiss is, in addition, indicative of the coming of a supernatural, magic force. Initially, it is the Fur Queen's kiss that initializes her transculturation. Within the passage above, the kiss that never happened introduces an opposing force to the goodness and slyness of the trickster: the *Weetigo*. The purveyor of utmost evil and moral decay in First Nations mythology represents Father Lafleur. Father Lafleur is not a father figure, nor does he have the permission to deflower the two boys (and, presumably, many others). He simply feeds on human flesh, an apt representation of a raping Catholic priest.

Sophie McCall points out that "[o]n the surface, . . . Highway . . . represent[s] the figure of the Weetigo in a negative light as a manifestation of the linked force of colonial institutions such as the residential school."[132] The *Weetigo* not only traditionally represents quintessential evil but also signals the intrusion of a disruptive force into an Indigenous community.[133] Not only does Hanne Birk understand this remarkable use of the *Weetigo* character as an actualization, as an act of translating the mythical figure into the Canadian contemporary, but she also holds that the *Weetigo* is among the most prominent representational means to mark cultural (re)enactment.[134] Furthermore, Birk perceives the *Weetigo* as a carrier of cultural memory. In this case, it can be seen as the aesthetic embodiment of cultural destruction. Yet this reading falls short of understanding another mechanism at work in Highway's text: in the context of and through the discourses of reconciliation, the perpetrator has been marked as white, European, and to some extent Christian. The structure of the systems of forced cultural reeducation allowed for sexual predators to have their way. In a traditional sense, the *Weetigo* is marked as native, as belonging to the representational inventory that may resurrect and emphasize First Nations culture.[135] What Highway actually does is to transculturalize the figure of the perpetrator—both by representational means, as we have already seen, and by the very act of explaining Lafleur's transgressions, which he committed as a representative of the Catholic church—through the framework of the *Weetigo*. As we have already seen in Boyden's *Three Day Road*, the *Weetigo* frequently serves as the "explanatory matrix"[136] for all kinds of (immoral) wrongdoings.[137] It thus comes as no surprise that young Jeremiah, who has just left the care of his family, makes sense of what he sees by resorting to his culturally coded heritage. McCall ventures as far as to state that Gabriel actually embraces his "inner Weetigo" while himself performing "Weetigo-like sexual practices."[138]

However, the Lafleur-*Weetigo* is clearly a grotesque figure. It is described as a "dark, hulking figure" that "hovered" over its victim, resembling "a bear devouring a honey-comb."[139] This apparition is characterized through "smacking of lips, mastication."[140] This "beast" has teeth and claws, and large intimidating eyes.[141] The *Weetigo* is a fitting image for describing and representing a raping priest. Sophie McCall argues that the very act of dressing up the perpetrator in First Nations' garments makes visible the limits of representing the unrepresentable.[142] I argue that the exact opposite is the case: Highway has found a way to stress the profound entanglement of histories, memories, identities, and representations in the context of Canadian reconciliation, and there is little use to insist on or look for cultural unambiguity. Moreover, the grotesque is another part of the representational inventory of the carnivalesque: the physical, the bodily appearance, and the very functions of the body traditionally "belong" to the lower classes. An expression or exploration of the bodily is set in antagonism to the seemingly dis(em)bodied realm of the higher classes, and specifically, in this case, the religious caste and its supposed chastity.

In this vein, the *Weetigo* in *Fur Queen* resonates within the realm of the carnivalesque and is easily imaginable as the purveyor of evil, decay, and ultimate death. Highway's text moves beyond the connotation of Indigenous representational "authenticity" and notions of cultural belonging, and the novel opens up the mythological figure to other, more productive readings. The grotesque description of Father Lafleur and its denomination as *Weetigo* disallow grasping the perpetrator only in "Western" terms of world-making. The raping Catholic priest exists in the in-between of Indigenous and non-Indigenous descriptions, traits, and interpretations. As such he is a carnivalesque figure in the literal sense, temporarily revoking representational regimes in order to transculturalize them. It is Highway who plays with the expectations and explanations of readers and critics when he, with one representational twist, bridges the seeming gap between cultural representations by rendering them obsolete. Father Lafleur as the *Weetigo* stands neither for an essentialized Euro-Canadianness nor for the same in Indigenous terms. To transculturalize the perpetrator, to temporarily reverse and relocate one's sense of whose culture the perpetrator actually belongs to is programmatic for Highway's novel. In what can be perceived as an outlook on reconciled identities or, more precisely, on an idea of how a sense of reconciliation can come into being in the Canadian context, Highway detaches both victim and perpetrator from their allocated place in the logic of cultural belonging. It may be seen as a glimpse into a future that Highway imagines: only the realization of the radically transcultural configuration of victim and perpetrator and the attempt to structurally overcome binary models of Canadian identity can bring about a sense of reconciliation with colonial history.

This idea is carried forward toward the end of the novel. The death of Gabriel, however, is not the end of Gabriel, or the end of one's struggle for identity:

> "Who do you think met Dad? On . . . the other side?" Gabriel's soft voice drifted through the white walled room. "Jesus? Or Weesageechak?" Reclined on pillows, the hunter's youngest son gazed at the portrait of the Fur Queen kissing his father, the hand that held the photo connected by tubes to plastic-bagged fluids. Jeremiah stood at the window, scowling at the evening traffic seven floors below. "The Trickster, of course," Gabriel finally answered himself, "Weesageechak for sure. The clown who bridges humanity and God—a God who laughs, a God who's here, not for guilt, not for suffering, but for a good time. Except, this time, the Trickster representing God as a woman, a goddess in fur. Like this picture. I've always thought that, ever since we were little kids. I mean, if Native languages have no gender, then why should we? And why, for that matter, should God?"[143]

What might be discarded as the ramblings of a man facing death is rather emblematic in *Fur Queen*. With the full force of narrative world-making, this text breaks down boundaries that have been carefully erected for centuries, and have been used as the foundation of colonial dominance. The idea or possibility of transcending our earthly existence into a life after death is closely connected with the never-ceasing quest of finding one's (cultural) identity. At the time of his death, Gabriel has, through this statement, realized that he has already transcended the question of being native or non-native—he exists in the middle ground, in the sphere beyond unambiguity. The focalized narrator Jeremiah reconnects Gabriel with his ancient cultural traditions of hunting, but the reader has already become aware of the now "inauthentic" status of hunting in modern Canada. It was after all a sled race for money, on which occasion a beauty-pageant-winning young woman transformed into the infamous Fur Queen and follows the two brothers throughout their journey in life. Finally, the trickster figure is relieved of her monocultural association and becomes the connective element between this world and the other, only to arrive at the conclusion that boundaries are there to be overcome, to be contested and crossed. *Fur Queen*'s protagonists, in particular the victim Gabriel and perpetrator Father Lafleur, are representative of the fact that traumatic narratives and memories are mobile and affect various parts of Canadian society. With these movements across cultural borders, narrative representation also loses its unambiguity. The perpetrator—rendered in the shape of the *Weetigo*—leaves behind its European connotation and becomes a transcultural, albeit negative, character. The victim—Gabriel in particular—is not a representative of indigeneity anymore, neither of a resilient example nor of an utterly destroyed figure. It is in this vein that *Fur Queen* is not a requiem, as Merkl perceives it; it is, more importantly, an exploration of radically modern identities. To some extent this novel provides us with its own vision of reconciliation, and this notion is grounded upon the fact that both cultures are not only represented while reworking colonial legacies but are actually intertwined and interconnected.

In Conclusion: Carnivalizing Victim-Perpetrator Paradigms

Kim Scott's *Benang* and Tomson Highway's *Kiss of the Fur Queen* are multifaceted explorations of victim-perpetrator relations and their representations. Australia's and Canada's "politics of regret" effectively sidelined these dynamics and turned perpetrators into abstract historical forces. These novels deal with the effects that forcible cultural "reeducation" had on individuals and collectives at the time of their being practiced, but they also shed light on the aftermath, on Indigenous modernities.

Benang is a complex text that renders the act of pushing boundaries as programmatic. This novel is considered as generically historical, but the complex entanglements of written history and colonial archives, of oral history and playful explorations of Indigenous (hi)stories, carry forward the carnivalesque agenda. The reader watches Harley, the product of his grandfather's outbreeding experiment, oust his elder from his position of power. Scott thus poignantly allegorizes Australia's struggle of coming to terms with the legacy of the Stolen Generations: Ern suffers a stroke precisely at the moment when he realizes that Harley has discovered his project. This discovery ultimately changes Ern's colonial record and position of power, as well as, by extension, Australia's. Harley's grandfather is subsequently represented as disabled, as having lost his speech, and this can also be read as an identity-political statement in relation to the change in power relations in the context of Australia's "politics of regret." However, *Benang* moves well beyond a playing out of revenge and torture, because Harley brings Ern along as he discovers his Indigenous heritage. In so doing, this novel imagines victim-perpetrator relations that leave behind the binary deadlock of reversal and revenge. It shows these narratives as ultimately intertwined, and forming an equal part of Australia's national narrative.

Moreover, *Benang* productively complicates cultural relations and notions of cultural belonging. In this manner, Scott's text engages with one of the most powerful fictions of reconciliation that Australian and Canadian "sorry politics" produce: a binary representation of Indigenous and non-Indigenous groups. Harley's initial sense of cultural un-belonging is translated into a powerful image of floating. The fact that Harley might be an unreliable narrative voice further underlines the constructed nature of cultural belonging and highlights how subjective, dependent on performance, and prone to exploration identity formations are. To regard this text as an example of magic realism, as critics have argued, runs the risk of effectively reiterating this cultures-as-containers logic that informs magic realism's oxymoronic identity. Scott's version of victim-perpetrator relations emphasizes that such entanglements are leftovers from the systems of cultural reeducation, but that they also offer the possibility of new beginnings and mutual exchange. In *Benang*, the rifts and frictions of victim-perpetrator relations become the very resources for imagining radically different identity formations.

Tomson Highway's *Kiss of the Fur Queen* also engages with imaging and representing victim-perpetrator relations, but it paints a more pessimistic picture. It retraces how Jeremiah and Gabriel realize how deeply the colonial mission has cut into the fabric of Indigenous communities, leaving alcoholism and disease in its wake. Indigenous modernities are characterized by perpetuated victimhood, and only death seems to promise relief from this status. Perpetrators go unpunished. Thus, *Fur Queen* can be read as a commentary on

Canada's struggle for reconciliation. Highway's text places a similar emphasis on the figure of the victim as the official "politics of regret." Yet, *Fur Queen* is particularly powerful when it comes to imagining the perpetrator figure. To recode the perpetrator as a transcultural figure and to frame the boys' guardian angel as a wily and cunning commentator on radically transformed transcultural identities carnivalizes notions of cultural containments that are the product of "sorry politics." *Fur Queen* uses carnivalesque aesthetics—the grotesque rendering of Father Lafleur, the humorous trickster-fool nature of the Fur Queen—to further its identity-political agenda and to emphasize transcultural dynamics in the context of Canadian reconciliation. Highway's text is also considered to be a magic-realist novel, and in a similar manner to Kim Scott's *Benang*, *Fur Queen* dismantles the essentializing character of such stylistic ascriptions. The carnivalesque agenda manifests itself in reiteration and reversal but, more importantly, also in imagining, testing, deceiving, questioning, and performing selves, others, and the in-between. The carnivalesque, both as identity politics and aesthetics, carries and produces transcultural identities and histories, rendering these formations that move across boundaries a possible Canadian national narrative.

In summary, both examples discussed in this chapter shed light on the importance of imagining and reintegrating the perpetrator figure into the national narratives of Australia and Canada. They show how this figure was part of what forcibly removed children had to consider "home." Both novels attest to the fact of making sense of the systems of cultural reeducation and how they affected notions of family, individual and collective identities, and cultural belonging. In this context, *Benang* and *Fur Queen* reiterate and reverse in a carnivalesque manner, and they imagine protagonists who cut across cultural boundaries, power hierarchies, representational traditions, and subject positions. The carnivalesque becomes both an attitude and an aesthetics for venturing into and intervening in Australian and Canadian processes of reconciliation.

Notes

1. Government of Canada. "Indian Residential School Statement of Apology—Prime Minister Stephen Harper." N.d. Retrieved 15 May 2015 from http://www.aadnc-aandc.gc.ca/eng/1100100015677/1100100015680.
2. Harper, "Statement of Apology."
3. Kim Scott, *Benang: From the Heart* (Sydney: Freemantle Press, 1999), 16–17.
4. Tomson Highway, *Kiss of the Fur Queen* (Norman: University of Oklahoma Press, 1998) 220–21.

5. See also chapter 2 of this study.
6. The titles of the two novels will subsequently be abbreviated to *Benang* and *Fur Queen*.
7. Scott, *Benang*, 11.
8. Scott, *Benang*, 11.
9. Scott, *Benang*, 27.
10. Scott, *Benang*, 159.
11. Scott, *Benang*, 163–64.
12. For further reading, see, for example, Ansgar Nuenning and Carola Surkamp, *Unreliable Narration: Studie zur Theorie und Praxis unglaubwürdigen Erzählens in der englischsprachigen Erzählliteratur* (Trier: Wissenschaftl Verlag Trier, 2013).
13. Scott, *Benang*, 43-44.
14. The idea of juxtaposition rather than opposition relates back to Chadwick Allen, *Trans-Indigenous: Methodologies for Global Native Literary Studies* (Minneapolis: University of Minnesota Press, 2012).
15. Scott, *Benang*, 495.
16. Quoted in Natalie Quinlivan, "Kim Scott's Writing and the Wirlomin Noongar Language and Stories Project," *Journal of the Association for the Study of Australian Literature* 14, no. 3 (2014): 2.
17. See, e.g., Quinlivan, "Kim Scott's Writing"; Nadine Attewell, "Reading Closely: Writing (and) Family History in Kim Scott's *Benang*," *Postcolonial Text* 7, no. 3 (2012): 1–25; Frances Johnson, "Dissident Laughter: Historiographic Metafiction as Parodic Intervention in *Benang* and *That Deadman Dance*," in "Art as Parodic Practice," ed. Marion May Campbell, Dominique Hecq, Jondi Keane, and Antonia Pont, special issue, *TEXT* 33 (October 2015): 1–18, retrieved 17 May 2018 from http://www.textjournal.com.au/speciss/issue33/content.html; and Lisa Slater, "Kim Scott's *Benang*: An Ethics of Uncertainty," *Journal of the Association for the Study of Australian Literature* 4 (2005): 147–58.
18. Attewell, "Reading Closely," 1.
19. Attewell, "Reading Closely," 2.
20. Lisa Slater, "*Benang*, This 'Most Local of Histories': Annexing Colonial Records into a World without End," *Journal of Commonwealth Literature* 41, no. 1 (2006): 52.
21. Paul Ricoeur, *History, Memory, Forgetting* (Chicago: University of Chicago Press, 2004), 131.
22. Ricoeur, *History*, 131.
23. Scott, *Benang*, 398–99, emphasis in the original.
24. See Quinlivan, "Kim Scott's Writing"; Attewell, "Reading Closely"; Johnson, "Dissident Laughter"; and Slater, "An Ethics of Uncertainty."
25. Scott, *Benang*, 37, emphasis in the original.
26. Scott, *Benang*, 26, emphasis in the original.
27. See "Acknowledgments" in Scott, *Benang*, 497.
28. Scott, *Benang*, 157.
29. Scott, *Benang*, 158.
30. In the acknowledgments, Scott provides a list, indicating that the "words attributed to A O Neville" are actually taken from Neville's own publications and are not a result of Scott's imagination. See Scott, *Benang*, 497–500.
31. Scott, *Benang*, 459.
32. Attewell, "Reading Closely," 2.
33. Quinlivan, "Finding a Place," 3.
34. Scott, *Benang*, 37.
35. Scott, *Benang*, 3.
36. Johnson, "Dissident Laughter," 3.

37. The title is a reference to the title of the essay by Lisa Slater, "Making Strange Men: Resistance and Reconciliation in Kim Scott's *Benang*," in *Resistance and Reconciliation: Writing in the Commonwealth*, ed. Bruce Bennett et al. (Canberra: Association for Commonwealth Literature and Communication, 2003), 358–70.
38. Scott, *Benang*, 11.
39. Scott, *Benang*, 494.
40. Barbara Klonowska, *Contaminations: Magic Realism in Contemporary British Fiction* (Lublin: Marie Curie-Sklodowska University Press, 2006), 12. For further reading on magic realism and the sphere of postcolonial literature, see Jean-Pierre Durix, *Mimesis, Genres, and Post-colonial Discourse: Deconstructing Magic Realism* (Basingstoke: Palgrave Macmillan, 2000). For further reading on the connection of Holocaust literature and magic realism, see Jenni Adams, *Magic Realism in Holocaust Literature: Troping the Traumatic Real* (Basingstoke: Palgrave Macmillan, 2011).
41. Jeanne Delbaere-Garant, "Towards a 'Third Space': Magic Realisms in English Canadian Literature," in *Eyes Deep with Unfathomable Histories: The Poetics and Politics of Magic Realism Today and in the Past*, ed. Liliana Sikorska and Agnieszka Rzepa (Frankfurt am Main: Peter Lang, 2012), 12-29,17.
42. Delbaere-Garant, "Towards," 14.
43. Liliana Sikorska and Agnieszka Rzepa, "Editorial," in *Eyes Deep with Unfathomable Histories: The Poetics and Politics of Magic Realism Today and in the Past*, ed. Liliana Sikorska and Agnieszka Rzepa (Frankfurt am Main: Peter Lang, 2012), 8.
44. Sikorska and Rzepa, "Editorial," 12.
45. Klonowska further traces the origins of magic realism back to the Latin American literary sphere in general, and to the works of Luis Borges in particular. Klonowska, *Contaminations*, 12.
46. Two of the most prominent representatives in the Anglophone literary sphere are Salman Rushdie and Toni Morrison. Jorge Luis Borges and Gabriel García Márquez are prominent for their use of magic realism in Hispanophone contexts, and Borges is frequently heralded as the founding father of this specific mode of literary representation.
47. Klonowska, *Contaminations*, 9–10.
48. The authors also hold that magic realism is a decidedly Canadian mode of literary representation, and that it forms a vital part in the Canadian nation-building process. Sikorska and Rzepa, "Editorial," 8.
49. Sikorska and Rzepa, "Editorial," 9.
50. Klonowska, *Contaminations*, 13.
51. Sikorska and Rzepa, "Editorial," 11.
52. Delbaere-Garant, "Towards," 20.
53. Delbaere-Garant, "Towards," 30.
54. Liliana Sikorska, Agnieszka Rzepa, and Jeanne Delbaere-Garant most prominently draw on Homi Bhabha's concept of "the third space" in their analysis. Sikorska and Rzepa, "Editorial," 8.
55. Scott, *Benang*, 31.
56. Scott, *Benang*, 31.
57. Scott, *Benang*, 1.
58. Scott, *Benang*, 32.
59. Scott, *Benang*, 20.
60. Scott, *Benang*, 159.
61. Scott, *Benang*, 22.
62. Scott, *Benang*, emphasis in the original.
63. Slater, "Ethics of Uncertainty," 149.

64. Scott, *Benang*, 150.
65. Scott, *Benang*, 152.
66. Scott, *Benang*, 30. Emphasis in original.
67. Scott, *Benang*, 31.
68. Scott, *Benang*, 31.
69. Scott, *Benang*, 31–32.
70. Scott, *Benang*, 33.
71. Slater, "Ethics of Uncertainty," 149.
72. Sophie McCall, "Intimate Enemies: Weetigo, Weesageechak, and the Politics of Reconciliation in Tomson Highway's *Kiss of the Fur Queen* and Joseph Boyden's *Three Day Road*," *SAIL* 25, no. 3 (Fall 2013): 57–80, emphasis in the original.
73. The title of Highway's novel will be abbreviated to *Fur Queen*.
74. Howells, "Tomson Highway," 89.
75. See Silvie Vranckx, "The Ambivalence of Cultural Syncreticity in Highway's *Kiss of the Fur Queen* and Van Camp's *The Lesser Blessed*," in *Old Margins and New Centers: The European Literary Heritage in an Age of Globalization*, ed. Marc Maufort and Caroline De Wagter (Brussels: Peter Lang, 2011), 291–306; and Lindsey Smith, "'With These Magic Weapons, Make a New World': Indigenous Centered Urbanism in Tomson Highway's *Kiss of the Fur Queen*," *Canadian Journal of Native Studies* 29, nos. 1–2 (2009): 143–64.
76. See McCall, "Intimate Enemies."
77. Howells, "Tomson Highway," 84.
78. See McCall, "Intimate Enemies," and Rubelise da Cunha, "The Trickster Wink: Storytelling and Resistance in Tomson Highway's *Kiss of the Fur Queen*," *Ilha do Destero: A Journal of English Language, Literatures in English and Cultural Studies* 56 (January–July 2009): 93–118.
79. Retrieved 2 May 2017 from http://www.tomsonhighway.com.
80. Vranckx, "Ambivalence," 292.
81. Allan J. Ryan, *The Trickster Shift: Humor and Irony in Contemporary Native Art* (Vancouver: UBC Press, 1999), 4, footnote.
82. Vranckx, "Ambivalence," 293.
83. Vranckx, "Ambivalence," 291; see also McCall, "Intimate Enemies."
84. McCall, "Intimate Enemies," 57.
85. See Vranckx, "Ambivalence"; Smith, "With These Magic Weapons."
86. See, e.g., Sarah Wylie Krotz, "Productive Dissonance: Classical Music in Tomson Highway's *Kiss of the Fur Queen*," *Studies in Canadian Literature* 34, no. 1 (2009): retrieved 17 May 2018 from https://journals.lib.unb.ca/index.php/SCL/article/view/12386/13260; Andrew Buzny, "Kissing Fabulose Queens: The Fabulous Realism of Tomson Highway's *Kiss of the Fur Queen*," *Postcolonial Text* 6, no. 3 (2011): 1–18; and Hanne Birk, *AlterNative Memories: Kulturspezifische Inszenierungen von Erinnerungen in zeitgenössischen Romanen indigener Autor/innen Australiens, Kanadas und Aotearoas/Neuseelands* (Trier: Wissenschaftlicher Verlag Trier, 2008).
87. See e.g. Sarah Henzi, "Resistance and Transformation: Negotiating Political Rhetorics in First Nations Literatures," *Australasian Canadian Studies* 27, nos. 1–2 (2009): 117–28; and da Cunha, "Trickster Wink."
88. Katja Sarkowsky, *AlterNative Spaces: Constructions of Space in Native American and First Nations' Literatures* (Heidelberg: Winter, 2007), 126.
89. See Buzny, "Kissing Fabulose Queens," and Howells, "Tomson Highway."
90. See e.g. Shoshannah Ganz, "Canadian Literary Representations of HIV/AIDS" in *HIV in World Cultures: Three Decades of Representations*, ed. Gustavo Subero (London: Taylor and Francis, 2013), 1–12.

91. Howells, "Tomson Highway," 86.
92. Highway, *Fur Queen*, 39–40, emphasis in the original.
93. Highway, *Fur Queen*, 5.
94. Highway, *Fur Queen*, 4.
95. Highway, *Fur Queen*, 5.
96. Highway, *Fur Queen*, 5, emphasis in the original text.
97. Highway, *Fur Queen*, 94, see also Henzi, "Resistance and Transformation."
98. da Cunha, "Trickster Wink," 94.
99. See Mikhail M. Bakhtin, *Rabelais and His World* (Bloomington: Indiana University Press, 1984).
100. Bakhtin, *Rabelais*, 4.
101. Bakhtin, *Rabelais*, 6.
102. da Cunha, "Trickster Wink," 93.
103. Bakhtin, *Rabelais*, 20.
104. Bakhtin, *Rabelais*, 10.
105. Edgars Ošiņš, "Multicultural Canada: Two First Nations Voices" in *American Multiculturalism and Ethnic Survival*, ed. Sabina Matter-Seibel, Renate von Bardeleben, Klaus H. Schmidt (Frankfurt am Main: Peter Lang Verlag, 2012), 227.
106. da Cunha, "Trickster Wink," 100.
107. Highway, *Fur Queen*, 11–12.
108. Howells draws parallels between *Fur Queen* and James Joyce's *A Portrait of the Artist as a Young Man*.
109. da Cunha, "Trickster Wink," 99.
110. The other four parts are titled *Alegretto grazioso*, *Molto agitato*, *Adagio espressivo*, and *Presto con fuoco*.
111. Krotz, "Productive Dissonance," 6.
112. See also Sherrill E. Grace, *Canada and the Idea of the North* (Montreal: McGill-Queen's University Press, 2001).
113. McCall, "Intimate Enemies," 68.
114. See Ronald Niezen, *Truth and Indignation: Canada's Truth and Reconciliation Commission on Indian Residential Schools* (Toronto: University of Toronto Press, 2013).
115. Matt James, "A Carnival of Truth? Knowledge, Ignorance and the Canadian Truth and Reconciliation Commission," *International Journal of Transitional Justice* 6, no. 2 (2012): 182–204.
116. Denise Cuthbert and Marian Quartly, "Forced Child Removal and the Politics of National Apologies in Australia," *American Indian Quarterly* 37, no. 1 (Winter/Spring 2013): 185.
117. Matthias Merkl, "'Surviving the Residential School': Negotiating Cultural Re-education in Tomson Highway's *Kiss of the Fur Queen*," in *Literature on the Move: Cultural Migration in Contemporary Literature*, ed. Michael Heinze (Trier: WVT, 2010), 67–78. Emphasis in the original.
118. Suzanne Methot cites Highway, quoted in Merkl, "Surviving the Residential School," 69, footnote.
119. Howells, "Tomson Highway," 85.
120. Howells, "Tomson Highway," 85.
121. Highway, *Fur Queen*, 77–79. Emphasis in the original.
122. Highway, *Fur Queen*, 285.
123. Highway, *Fur Queen*, 285–87, emphasis in the original.
124. Highway, *Fur Queen*, 206–7.
125. Highway, *Fur Queen*, 207.

126. Highway, *Fur Queen*, 207.
127. Howells, "Tomson Highway," 86.
128. Highway, *Fur Queen*, 166.
129. Highway, *Fur Queen*, 167.
130. Highway, *Fur Queen*, 168.
131. Highway, *Fur Queen*, 169.
132. McCall, "Intimate Enemies," 63.
133. McCall, "Intimate Enemies," 65.
134. Birk, *AlterNative Memories*, 390.
135. Hanne Birk correctly remarks that to speak of *a* trickster figure is a bit simplistic, since this character belongs to a range of First Nations cultures in the Canadian north, and is by no means of specifically Cree origin. Birk, *AlterNative Memories*, 389–94.
136. McCall, "Intimate Enemies," 64.
137. In *Three Day Road*, an Indigenous family is deemed *Weetigo* after they eat human flesh in order not to starve in a particularly cold winter. The surviving members of this family turn insane, and, according to the inner logic of this myth, need to be killed by the *Weetigo* killer.
138. McCall, "Intimate Enemies," 67.
139. Highway, *Fur Queen*, 79.
140. Highway, *Fur Queen*, 79.
141. Highway, *Fur Queen*, 79.
142. McCall, "Intimate Enemies," 63–64.
143. Highway, *Fur Queen*, 298.

Chapter 5

FROM VICTIMOLOGY TO EMPOWERMENT?

Zacharias Kunuk's *Atanarjuat* and Baz Luhrmann's *Australia*

Australian and Canadian "politics of regret" are centrally concerned with attaining a sense of justice through revising national narratives by centering on the stories of victims. Reconciliation opens up national narratives toward realizing that the processes and structures of colonizing the Indigenous populations continued alongside Canada's and Australia's rise to economic and social power in independence of Britain. Through reconciliation, negotiations of national and (trans)cultural identities unfold against the backdrop of acknowledging on a collective level that, while Canada and Australia prospered, both countries' Indigenous peoples suffered and were almost eradicated.

Within the next pages, two filmic examples that engage with the subject positions of Indigenous peoples in the overarching, and conceivably reconfigured, national narrative will be analyzed. Inuit director Zacharias Kunuk created a filmic epos that resurrects and dwells in Inuit history; *Atanarjuat: The Fast Runner* (2001) remediates an Inuit oral legend onto the filmic screen.[1] Kunuk's feature film won several prestigious prizes and made its way to the Cannes Film Festival. Baz Luhrmann's blockbuster *Australia* (2008) envisions an Australian national identity and narrative that is reconciled with both Australia's achievements as a settler colony and the difficult historical legacy of the Stolen Generations. As the analysis will show, both films are centrally engaged with empowering its Indigenous protagonists: *Atanarjuat* testifies to an Inuit identity that celebrates its origins, while, at the same time, it is capable of representing transcultural entanglements. It challenges the "colonial gaze," a formative derogatory representational strategy connected with the cultivation of Canada. *Australia* carnivalizes the formative bush myth—usually associated with male Euro-Australian agency—and opens it up to those who were structurally and discursively excluded from this national narrative. Furthermore, *Australia*'s Indigenous protagonists become the primary enablers of Lady Ashley's "Australian dream." The bush and the tundra become spaces of Indigenous empowerment. In this vein, both filmic examples attempt to move beyond the victim paradigm, and both imagine Indigenous protagonists and identities that transcend cultural boundaries. However, while *Atanarjuat* successfully carnivalizes notions of cultural authenticity and compartments, *Australia* struggles under the narrative and aesthetic simplicity of Luhrmann's enforced reconciliation: his attempt to bring together and reconcile various narratives and legacies of Australia's versatile (post)colonial history results in reinforcing stereotypes and eventually leaves its Indigenous protagonists bereft of agency.

Carnivalizing Authenticity: Zacharias Kunuk's *Atanarjuat*

In 2001, a special feature film literally claimed the international stage, and its director, Inuit filmmaker Zacharias Kunuk commented on its scope as follows:

> We show how our ancestors dressed, how they handled their dog teams, how they argued and laughed and went through hard times—how they confronted evil and fought back. They *had* to get along, to work things out no matter what. This is the story we are passing on to others, just like it was passed on to us.[2]

Atanarjuat won several prestigious awards, including the Golden Camera at Cannes, the Toronto-City Award for Best Canadian Feature Film, and the Winner Special Jury Prize and the Prix du Public of the Montreal Film Festival.[3] Zacharias Kunuk's feature film remediates the famous myth of the Fast Runner from the oral realm onto the filmic screen.[4] The story of Atanarjuat has been handed down from generation to generation for centuries. The film tells the story of young Atanarjuat, the "fast runner," son of influential Tulimaq and brother of Amaqjuaq, the "strong one." After being betrayed by Sauri, Tulimaq's rival, an act prompted by an evil shaman, Tulimaq and his family are forced to the margins of the community. As the years pass, both sons grow up to become the community's most successful hunters. Furthermore, Atanarjuat wins the heart of the beautiful Atuat, who was initially promised to Oki, Sauri's son. As one can imagine, this love triangle causes dismay within the camp. Oki tries to murder the two brothers in their sleep, but Atanarjuat is able to escape, and flees naked over the ice. A spiritual intervention facilitates his miraculous survival, and he is nourished back to health by an old couple who live on the outskirts of the community. "After an inner struggle to reclaim his spiritual path," as the Isuma TV synopsis puts it, the hero returns to the camp as a renewed man, willing and able to restore peace and harmony to the disrupted community.

Reviewers have praised Kunuk's work for "fill[ing] the screen with stunning images bathed in pink blue Northern light, and performances of beautiful spontaneity," while others highlight—note the framing!—that "the performances, all by Inuit, have a simple power that strikes us straight between the eyes, as fast and true as an arrow."[5] *Atanarjuat*, undoubtedly, is an Inuit community project. It was written, produced, directed, and edited by Inuit, and the actors were cast from the Inuit community. This feature film is centrally concerned with resurrecting an Inuit cultural identity that has been lost due to the processes of colonialism and cultural reeducation. It reiterates a long-gone past and to a great extent emphasizes a perspective on "authentic indigeneity" that is newly reconfigured. Recalling Landsberg's notion of prosthetic memory, *Atanarjuat* provides a connective thread to Inuit cultural memories, because it enables the experience of a cultural identity that seems lost to colonialism and modernity. *Atanarjuat* can literally be *seen* as a document of resilience and resistance, of survival and cultural resurrection on behalf of the Inuit peoples.[6]

As one can gather from the review above, stereotypical understandings and romanticized notions of what is Inuit culture are close at hand. There is, however, a powerful ambiguity to this movie, and this equivocation works in two directions: Kunuk's film undermines the colonial gaze while at the same time subverting its counterpart—the ethnographic gaze that literally looks for authentic indigeneity. The colonial gaze is broadly understood as a derogatory instrument for constructing an inferior colonial other, and the images they produce continue to circulate in popular culture.[7] The ethnographic gaze, in contrast, can also be understood as a result of a "native turn" in (Canadian) politics, and it is ethically much more appealing. The ethnographic gaze is accompanied by the expectation of "true indigeneity," the promise of watching the—in this case—Inuit "as they really were." Critical evaluation and analysis of native art is oftentimes stuck in and with the self-proclaimed imperative to make sense of Indigenous artworks of reminiscence and with reference to culturally specific contexts and meanings. Lastly, it is also a marketing strategy that might increase the publicity of *Atanarjuat* once it has found a label as an "authentic" take on indigeneity.

These discourses, perspectives, and scopic regimes are complexly intertwined within and through Kunuk's feature film, and they cross, supersede, and enable each other simultaneously.[8] I argue that this inner complexity renders *Atanarjuat* a witness to transculturality. This feature film does not remain confined to or is merely concerned with excavating what is Indigenous (and what is not); it instead destabilizes remnants of the colonial logic, worldviews, and perceptions by temporarily reversing them. The very specific use of the filmic medium makes itself complicit in carnivalizing preformed notions of essentialized cultural and historical identities: *Atanarjuat* plays with a Western audience's expectations and viewing habits. It is a complex media text, and an analysis that seeks to categorize this feature film in a unilateral framework of interpretation runs the risk of missing this complex layering of meaning. In other words, with a powerful balancing of intertextual references, delicate ironic comments on cultural difference, and a distinct sense that certain plots, certain characters and developments are recognizable beyond cultural boundaries. This film does not simply bear witness to constructing authenticity but carnivalizes the expectation of cultural essentialism. *Atanarjuat* testifies to transculturality.

The Canadian Gaze: Moving Images as Agents of Empire and Multicultural Canada

Atanarjuat's complexity and intricacy is owed to a multifaceted engagement with other media texts, formative narrative categories, and viewing habits. This feature film consciously engages with the Canadian history of the moving image and the discourses it evokes and shapes, responds to them, and, simultaneously, opens up a different chapter in the metaphorical history book on Canadian film.

Film was used as an agent of empire-building and participated in introducing the settler state Canada to a public audience.[9] Under colonial rule, film was used to construct Canada as an imaginary homeland outside of England, waiting to be cultivated and civilized by the superior forces of British colonialism. The Indigenous populations were framed as inferior, childlike, as subhuman because of their perceived closeness to nature. The colonial mission was to civilize and cultivate nature. After the end of British colonialism, Canada was able to gain gradual independence from Britain in the aftermath of World War I. Colonization by the British forces was driven back, yet the process of inner colonization continued. The Indigenous populations were still regarded as inferior to a newly emergent (Euro-)Canadian civil society. It is in this tradition that—in today's terms—blatantly racist documentaries like Robert Flaherty's *Nanook of the North* (1922) became famous and were widely received.[10]

Documentary was the genre of preference for these early colony-building enterprises,[11] as documentaries enabled the formation of an imaginary framework that established a perspective on colonial Canada and a specific image of

Canada as a colony. Viewers thus encountered renderings of a vast, beautiful, untamed natural resource. To immigrate to Canada was then framed as a contribution to furthering the empire and bringing British culture into the world:

> Both the CPR [Canadian Pacific Railway Company of Colonization and Development] and the Canadian government realized the potential of film to act as an agent for the settlement of the West. Many more films were produced to create a desire for emigration to Canada, but a very specific emigration revolving around the matter of whiteness and the furthering of the British Empire. At this time, Canadian nation-building occurred within the British Empire, and was tantamount to empire-building.[12]

The representation of Canada within documentaries such as, for example, *Harnessing the Virgin Prairie* by James S. Freer (1898) contributed to fostering a common understanding of what needed to be done in Canada: not only was the country supposedly in need of concerted cultivating efforts, and the power to do so rested with white, male British emigrants, but, simultaneously, categories arose along which colonial hierarchies were determined and arranged.

Some aspects and specific qualities of the filmic medium and the spatial arrangement in cinemas made moving images an ideal partner for constructing these colonial hierarchies. Martin Jay observes that the modern era is characterized by an emphasis on the visual:

> The modern era, it is often alleged, has been dominated by the sense of sight in a way that set it apart from its premodern predecessors and possibly its postmodern successor. Beginning with the Renaissance and the scientific revolution, modernity has normally been considered resolutely ocular centric.[13]

Thomas Elsaesser and Malte Hagener describe the emphasis on the visible and visuality as follows:[14]

> We also call [the cinematic experience] a double movement: from the disembodied but observing eye, to the privileged but implicated gaze (and ear); from the presence of image as seen, felt and touched, to the sense organs that become active participants of filmic reality; from the sensory and perceptual surface of film that requires the neurological brain, to the unconscious that registers deep ambivalences in the logic of the narrative, where rational choice or rational agency theories see merely an alternating succession of action and reaction. At the limit, film and spectator are like parasite and host, each occupying the other and being in turn occupied, to the point where there is only one reality that *un*folds as it *en*folds, and vice versa.[15]

As this statement suggests, the cinematic experience works with different aspects of how we perceive and explain the world, as well as represent it. The cinematic or filmic realm is a site that on the one hand lives on a certain relationship of distance and proximity, both to the actual screen and what is shown, and on the other hand enables a constant renegotiation of this relationship.[16] To watch moving images onscreen implies a "passage from one world into another," and this is a reciprocal movement. The cinematic arrangement gives the impression that the world unfolding on the screen is complete and self-contained. Yet the spectator looks at a culturally and historically coded world unfolding on the screen; one that is framed, cut, and edited to evoke a certain understanding of the filmic narrative, and that avoids breaking with the illusion that "reality" is brought to the screen.

Hence, the power and danger of film, as Elsaesser and Hagener elaborate, lies within its potential to reduce people to objects that are subjected to the viewer's curiosity on the one hand and to our judgment on the other.[17] Narrative strategies and aesthetics of representation on the part of the film do not encounter a blank page in the shape of a spectator; the cues of decoding and interpretation meet "mental preconstructions" and preexisting frameworks of perception.[18] The spectator looks at the images provided by the filmic narrative and scans for (familiar) social markers, making sense of the patterns of meaning they evoke. Hence, the viewer unconsciously identifies and makes sense of codes and clues provided by the filmic narrative and rendering.[19] Thus, the filmic medium foregrounds the power of the visual—the eye as the creator and simultaneous discloser of the cinematic universe, images as representations, camera perspectives as narrator, etc. World models collide, and worldviews mingle.

> [T]he scopic regime of modernity may best be understood as a contested terrain, rather than a harmoniously integrated complex of visual theories and practices. It may, in fact, be characterized by a differentiation of visual subcultures, whose separation has allowed us to understand the multiple implications of sight in ways that are now only beginning to be appreciated.[20]

One of the most formative scopic regimes of modernity is the colonial gaze, a visual petrification of native identity as inferior, uncanny, superfluous. This understanding of the power of film stands in the tradition of Michel Foucault and Judith Butler, emphasizing that gender roles, social status, and norms of behavior are constructed and reinforced by the instrument of the look. Christian Metz distinguishes between primary (that of the spectator with the perspective of the camera) and secondary identification (that of the spectator with the [look of] characters).[21] Once the spectator identifies with the perspective of the camera, it becomes increasingly difficult to understand the filmic universe as constructed and the view of the spectator as manipulated. Secondary identification leads to a complete conflation of the look of the camera, which is, in a sense, the narrator in film, and the look of the spectator *on* the issues unfolding on the screen. It leads to a breakdown of distance. The narrative constructed on the screen may confirm and solidify certain worldviews and formative categories that the viewer brings along to the cinematic experience. Belief systems—such as the categorical inferiority and subhumanity of Indigenous peoples—can easily be solidified and amplified. To realize that, for example, a documentary is also a fictional construct governed by a certain ideology is a difficult process, and to decipher ideologies and political agendas behind filmic narratives is not an easy endeavor due to the nature of moving images on screen. The more "realistic" the appearance of issues on the screen, the more complex the process of detachment to dismantle fictionality.

In this sense, the spectator of such "nation-building" documentaries was guided through a succession of "realistic" images that were arranged to foster a specific idea of Canada as a colony—in dire need of intervention and cultivation—and of the settler as a superior force that would tame nature and create a sense of Canada as part of the Empire. As a consequence, the Indigenous inhabitants were categorized as being part of nature and would hence be cultivated along with it.[22] Their existence presented a threat to British hegemony when it came to producing a certain image of the Canadian settler state. The destruction of Indigenous culture was not only a precondition to colonization, as Christopher E. Gittings argues, it was also necessary to obtain total control of the *image* of Canada that was produced: winning mastery over nature meant attaining mastery over the Indigenous population, and controlling representations of civilizing nature and population resulted in substantiating colonization.[23] Hence, film was a "social art" that had an impact on public consciousness and self-perception, representing a notion of Britishness that functioned as the foil against which all other forms of existence and identity were judged.[24]

> In the interests of creating a racially, culturally homogenous, unitary idea of nation, images of a white Anglo-Saxon or Anglo-Protestant Canada are circulated at home, and more importantly in Britain, to solicit an immigration that might reflect this fictive ethnicity of the nation projected on to the movie screen and the national psyche.[25]

Canadianness[26] was, at that time, framed as entirely dependent on Britishness: not only were the settlers of British origin, but settlement in Canada, becoming Canadian in this particular sense, meant to translate (alleged) cultural superiority to another geographical location. Notions of a Canadian identity that existed independently from Britishness were ground down or transferred into a different context. The medium of film, through the genre documentary, further enabled a construction of the imperial subject and object, helping to categorize the "new world" along notions such as colonizer and colonized, inferior and superior. At this stage of identity formation, the colonial object, Indigenous people, had already been constructed as the inevitable Other. Canadian national cinema in this early stage was concerned with representing and spreading a white, male, immigrant discourse that framed indigeneity as the Other against which white superiority was clearly visible. Paradoxically, Canadian national consciousness was evoked through narratives and renderings of Britishness on the screen, which laid out "Canadianness" to future Canadians.

The end of British colonialism did not mark the end of colonial hierarchies, evoked and continued through moving images projected onto a screen. In fact, the project of attaining a sense of Canadianness became even more important. Inner-Canadian colonialism continued after independence from Great Britain, and the role of natives was in the perception of them as part of nature, and thus as a counterpart to civilization. It is in this climate that Robert Flaherty, an American from Michigan, directed his infamous documentary on Inuit life and customs, *Nanook of the North* (1922).[27] Flaherty was hired by the Canadian Pacific Railway to explore the area of Hudson Bay, and he frequently returned to shoot his documentary. A reviewer for *The Guardian* tells the story of *Nanook*'s genesis as follows:

> Flaherty was a pioneer of the documentary, and one of those whose work sparked many of the continuing arguments about truth and falsehood within the genre. His style is often patronized as naïve and schematic. . . . The filming of an Eskimo community took place over almost two years on the eastern shore of Hudson Bay, and Flaherty's goal was complete authenticity. . . . Nanook and his family were real, but the film is not a straightforward recording of their everyday life: they amiably enacted some of it for Flaherty's cameras. But so honest and instinctive was their playing that it was undoubtedly truth of a sort. . . . [The documentary] hints at that old cliche [*sic*] about the noble savage being pushed towards civilization that will destroy him. But it does that with a rare feeling for a timeless landscape and a way of life that had remained unchanged for centuries.[28]

This remarkably nonreflective stance on *Nanook* blocks from view the fact that this documentary was not only heavily scripted by Flaherty himself—he wanted to evoke a specific idea of the Inuit—but also complicit in cementing the stereotype of the general inferiority of natives through its wide reception. Nanook, whose name was actually Allakariallak and who was considered an outstanding huntsman within his community, is at times depicted as a childlike explorer of his own environment, and Flaherty's camera bears witness to Inuit everyday life as if the Inuit themselves are actually trying to make sense of it. In one scene, the camera rests on Nanook while he has his first encounter with a gramophone—one that does not do any good to the image of nobility but clearly foregrounds the idea of savagery and childishness. Kerstin Knopf holds that *Nanook*, along with Flaherty's two other films he produced with a similar stance on indigeneity,

> are clearly manifestations of colonialist politics: exploration of foreign, exotic worlds, mapping these "other" worlds in film discourse, and objectifying them in films that combine an anthropological desire for knowledge with an interpretation that harks back to preconceived eurocentric notions of these worlds. . . . Abandoned customs are reintroduced and signs of Western influences are banished.[29]

Flaherty's film amounts to nothing less than a "colonialist ethnographic source":[30]

> The barbarity of Flaherty's *Nanook* . . . is wrapped in a paternalistic veneer that . . . has for far too long been taken at face value as authentic compassion. In fact, the film has served rather to project "fantasies of the master race" (to borrow Ward Churchill's provocative book title) on the perceived blank of the white Arctic . . .[31]

As one can see from the review quoted above that is as recent as the year 2000, this powerful imagery of performatively "feasting on" how Inuit culture "really is", and displaying a misplaced sense of empathy, is still formative and disseminated. Notwithstanding its racist thrust, *Nanook* is a representative of the general mindset, the general stance on indigeneity that was common at the beginning of the twentieth century in Canada.[32] As such, it is a representative of the colonial gaze. The discourse that the review above relates to, namely the firm belief that native populations have been forced to encounter modernity and technology, and that this encounter evidently unfolded against the very nature, the very capabilities of the natives, remains an integral part of the general image of the native in contemporary Canada.

The National Film Board (NFB), which was founded in 1939, continued to uphold the practice of constructing Canadian national identity, and it was mandated to describe "Canada to Canadians and other nations."[33] According to the NFB's first commissioner, John Grierson, producing documentaries was the key to fostering such a sense of national identity.[34] Documentaries, in his view, conveyed a certain "realistic" stance of the "actual conditions" that determined Canadian life and existence, even more so when the "iron grip" of Britishness had mostly been withdrawn. The National Film Board was concerned with displaying the "virtues of a free society" and sought to galvanize national identity, and, gradually, over the course of its existence, it began to broaden the scope of Canadian identity from monolithic, narrow representations of Euro-Canadianness toward marginalized groups and cultural minorities.[35] The idea of film as a "matter of public duty" persisted, and the narrative mode grounded on a stance of realism remained a distinguishing feature of NFB-funded productions.[36] During the 1960s, the NFB's scope was broadened toward feature films, a strategy that resulted in the establishment of the Canadian Film Development Corporation in 1967, which was restructured into Telefilm Canada in 1984. All the aforementioned commissions are in charge of developing funding (loans, subsidy, tax deductions) in order to enable the production of and the investment in Canadian film projects.[37] In the spirit of prospering discourses on human rights in the early 2000s, Indigenous activism, lobbyism claiming rights for marginalized, and the increasing awareness of an intrinsically multicultural society were successful in broadening the scope of representing "Canadianness" toward, and granting funding for, films on minorities, ethnicities, and cultures that form part of the contemporary Canadian community.[38] It thus comes as no surprise that the National Film Board was coproducing *Atanarjuat* through its Aboriginal Filmmaking Program.[39]

Atanarjuat: The Fast Runner—First Nations within the Nation and Beyond

The search for nations within the nation, and the shift toward more inclusive Canadian feature film history, has most certainly become more prominent through Zacharias Kunuk's project, the feature film *Atanarjuat*. This special film ties in with and relates back to many of the discourses raised in the previous chapter: it is part of what can be termed Canadian cinema and is a result of the shift toward a more inclusive representation of Canadian national identity. It was partly funded by the NFB, and contributes to a broader acknowledgment of the diversity of the Canadian film industry. This film was received by an international audience, and therefore, in a sense, it continues the tradition of explaining Canadianness to Canadians and others. The Inuit are part of Canada, and at least since the release of Kunuk's film, they have inscribed themselves to Canadian national cinema discourses:

> The three-hour feature film *Atanarjuat* is one of the most celebrated Canadian films of the past few years. It is the first Inuit dramatic film made in Inuktitut to receive nationwide and international attention. The film was screened at various film festivals and program theaters in the world and won six Genie Awards including Best Picture, and *Caméra d'Or* for Best First Feature at the Cannes Film Festival in 2001.[40]

Atanarjuat is a community project; an endeavor to bring together Inuit people to reiterate and resurrect aspects of their cultural identity through "electronic storytelling."[41] *Atanarjuat*'s structural ambiguity is already represented in the difficulty of allocating a label and designating a genre to it: the popular film database IMDb lists it as a drama and speaks of a "telling of an Inuit legend."[42] Amazon ranks it under romance and drama and refers the interested viewer to other Indigenous film projects.[43] Netflix sees it as "Action & Adventure,"[44] and Wikipedia, regarding it as a "Canadian epic film," even provides its title in Inuktitut syllabics.[45] Others list *Atanarjuat* as an Arthouse and Fourth World Cinema, stressing its seemingly culture-specific rendering and community-project character.[46] Reviewers praise its unique capacity to be "a complete revelation and reinvention of cinematic form," "a landmark in its own right," and hold that a "[t]housand year old tale of festering evil on the frozen tundra should find a warm welcome worldwide."[47]

The legend of Atanarjuat, the fast runner, is a central myth in Inuit oral tradition, and it has set off to travel the world.[48] Set in the vast lands of the Canadian tundra, the story begins when a mysterious shaman disrupts the harmony of Atanarjuat's community. His presence sows the seeds of envy, rivalry, and treachery, and leads to the death of the chief. The coming-of-age story of Atanarjuat, known as the Fast Runner, forms the center of the narrative. He falls for Atuat, but she is promised to the new chief's son, Oki. A battle for Atuat ensues; Atanarjuat emerges as the victor and wins the bride's hand, much to the dismay of rival Oki. In an act of revenge, Oki and his companions try to assassinate Atanarjuat and his brother as they sleep. Atanarjuat is forced to flee across the icy tundra and is eventually taken in by an elderly couple. After being nursed back to health, Atanarjuat returns to his community to mend the rifts and restore harmony.

The narrative of this feature film is a result of collecting different versions of that myth circulating within the Inuit community. Kunuk and his team arranged and layered these renditions, producing an amalgamation that serves as the narrative backbone of the feature film. *Atanarjuat* is also a community project on many levels: the story of the Fast Runner was conveyed to Kunuk and his scriptwriter, Paul Apak Angilirq, in their childhood.[49] Prior to shooting the film, they consulted elders and other members of the Inuit community as well as ethnographical records of Inuit songs from the early stages of colonialism in order to forge their version of the legend. The feature film is a "fleshed-out and filled-in interpretation" of the myth of the Fast Runner, an aspect that will be discussed in more detail in a later section.[50]

There is no "official" or "true" version of the legend, but only different versions circulating within the Inuit context.[51] The basis of the narrative is Inuit songs, a mode through which the oral inventory of Inuit culture is constructed, framed, and disseminated.[52] These songs are not to be understood as "independent lyric poems"; they are "embedded in complex narrative frames in which the storytellers say where, when, and from whom they first heard the story, the reasons for retelling it, and what the formative role of the listener is."[53] Within the filmic universe of *Atanarjuat*, narrative time and narrated time almost seem to conflate and thus create a sense of orality, of a song performed to others in real time.[54] The film is recorded entirely in Inuktitut, the language of the Inuit: Paul Apak Angilirq arranged several sources, both written and performed orally, and produced a screenplay in English and in Inuktitut syllabary.[55] For a non-Indigenous audience, subtitles are provided to enable access to *Atanarjuat*. The occasional deployment of a handheld camera and the abstinence from using any artificial light sources create a naturalistic atmosphere, further contributing to conveying the impression that the spectator witnesses "authentic" indigeneity unfold, that the viewer watches a rendering of an—arguably long gone—Inuit past and culture.[56] The Isuma TV production team describes *Atanarjuat*'s genesis as follows on their webpage:

> Igloolik is a community of 1200 people located on a small island in the north Baffin region of the Canadian Arctic with archeological evidence of 4000 years of continuous habitation. Throughout these millennia, with no written language, untold numbers of nomadic Inuit renewed their culture and traditional knowledge for every generation entirely through storytelling. *Atanarjuat* is part of this continuous stream of oral history carried forward into the new millennium through a marriage of Inuit storytelling skills and new technology. Atanarjuat is Canada's first feature-length fiction film written, produced, directed, and acted by Inuit. An exciting action thriller set in ancient Igloolik, the film unfolds as a life-threatening struggle between powerful natural and supernatural characters. Atanarjuat gives international audiences a more authentic view of Inuit culture and oral tradition than ever before, from the inside and through Inuit eyes. For countless generations, Igloolik elders have kept the legend of Atanarjuat alive to teach young Inuit the danger of setting personal desire above the needs of the group. The tale of making the film is itself made up of many stories . . .[57]

In this vein, *Atanarjuat* blends in with this "continuous stream of oral history" and is identified as continuing this practice with "updated technology." The plot is set in an atemporal realm in Northern Canada. One can only develop a sense of timing on the basis of the aging processes of the main characters and the seasons as they change.[58] The narrative does not place any specific emphasis on a particular time frame or point in time. Igloolik, "the place of houses," is where the community stays during the long artic winters.[59] The protagonists seem to revolve around and return to this centripetal location. The film takes its time displaying the Arctic in her breadth and beauty. "Powerful landscape images" are evoked by "[e]xtremely long shots [that] reveal the vastness and beauty of the arctic landscape."[60] *Atanarjuat* reinscribes its narrative onto a landscape that is laden with meaning. The emphasis on (re)presenting the Artic relates back to some of the most formative discourses of Canadian colonialism. On the one hand, the Arctic is a vast space that needed to be cultivated by the arriving settlers. It is also the habitat of the Inuit that needed to be civilized alongside this vast and beautiful example of nature. The tundra also served as the resource for the fur trade and a means of sustenance for European settlers. In the process of gaining independence from Great Britain, the Canadian tundra became the metaphorical "blank page" on which the newly arisen Canadian nation inscribed its own identity.[61] On the other hand, *Atanarjuat*'s redundant lingering on the Arctic vastness also bears a reference to the North American discourse associated with the desert—this national narrative holds that the American settler endured hardship and an existence at the margins of civilization and yet managed to enable the prosperity of the United States of America as history moved along. A similar connection with the land, in this case with the outback, is also a prominent venue of identity negotiation in Australia. Processes of gaining independence from England were oftentimes closely associated with the necessity to master the sheer vastness of the colonial land. Consequently, the tundra is the quintessential Canadian desert, or outback, a palimpsestic realm that used to reconfigure various stages of Canadian identity. *Atanarjuat* engages with these discourses and firmly places Inuit identity into and onto this palimpsestic space that is transcultural by default.

These plurifold interdiscursive references relating to the Arctic are only one example of the plethora of instances when *Atanarjuat* moves beyond the plainly obvious and attaches a second and third layer of meaning to representation, in particular with regard to such interdiscursive references to transculturality. Through the prominence of the tundra in *Atanarjuat*, the film emphasizes the interconnectedness of (post)colonial histories that reach beyond national and cultural boundaries.

As part of this complex negotiation process of (Canadian) identities, *Atanarjuat* reengages with and comments on one of the most formative images of native identity in general and Inuitness in particular. As such, *Atanarjuat* engages in an intertextual relationship[62] with Flaherty's *Nanook of the North*, not only carnivalizing the image of the childish, inferior native who was pushed into modernity against better judgment of their capabilities but also reversing colonial hierarchies that still linger in the present. As stated, Flaherty's scripted documentary was widely received and very influential in terms of establishing the colonial gaze, a gaze that is both derogatory and patriarchal. Indeed, at some point Nanook returns from a hunting trip, and he has miraculously "managed" to squeeze several members of his family as well as puppies into the belly of his kayak. Once the kayak arrives on shore, to the great amusement of the viewer he "produces" all his companions as they climb out of the vessel. The arrival on shore not only becomes a parody of the kayak as a means of transportation but also barely avoids being a slapstick interlude. A merry tune accompanies this scene, adding a certain zealous lightheartedness to a deeply racist rendering. The effect that is produced by this scene is ridicule and degradation of what is rendered Inuit identity.

Atanarjuat, conscious of this infamous representation of indigeneity, subtly takes up this scene: Atanarjuat also returns from a hunting trip, his wife Atuat awaiting his arrival by the shore. She is in the late stages of her pregnancy.[63] Atanarjuat is obviously moved by her waiting for him, and almost jumps out of the kayak. He goes on his knees and kisses and hugs Atuat's enormous belly. This specific rendering of homecoming paints a different picture entirely. While Nanook is the object of the camera's relentless gaze that subjects him to scrutiny, curiosity, and ridicule, Atuat and her future child are the center of attention. The camera perspective makes her stand tall and self-assured, waiting for her husband to return. *Atanarjuat* anticipates and praises the future of native Canada, as represented by the unborn child, while Nanook has been allocated the role of being unable to cope with what the future "has in store" for non-European Canadians—modernity. He is the "primitive," the "curiosity," a representative of the "resourcefulness" and "gentleness" of the Inuit, who arguably were "whiter" than other colonized peoples, thus occupying a higher position in the colonial system.[64] In *Nanook*, all people getting off the canoe seem to belong to the same group within the colonial logic, that of subhumans and things, and they are subjected to the spectator's curiosity and judgment. The "documentary" fosters the idea that this particular behavior is typical for the Inuit, and feeds the "Western public's fascination" with them.[65] Atanarjuat, who is by no means a flawless hero or ideal father figure before his coming-of-age through a somewhat forced learning phase, is represented as proud, independent, and self-assertive. He is a subject of his own making. *Atanarjuat* turns against this reductionist perspective that *Nanook* was complicit in rendering paradigmatically for Inuit identity and centers and emphasizes the humanity, the resilience, and the pride of Atuat and Atanarjuat. This scene—like the entire film—notably also holds Atuat in particular, and the woman and wife in general, in high esteem. This feature film comments on gender roles: the female characters in *Atanarjuat* are in no way dependent or mute, they appear as self-determined (Atuat choosing Atanarjuat over Uqi, although she was initially promised to the latter[66]), witty (the film evokes the impression that Puja's mother sees through Puja and Uqi's revenge plan from the very beginning[67]), and powerful (Panikpak, Kumaglak's wife and also a shaman, rids the community of the evil spirits in the end[68]). They are the ones who are capable of maintaining a connection with the ancestors and the realm of the mystic. When men falter and lose sight of what is framed as the "right way," the female characters remain determined, strong, and manage to survive.

Thus conceived, *Atanarjuat* "films back" to this patriarchal and misguided yet influential stance on Inuitness that *Nanook* helped create. What is more, it also carnivalizes the derogatory gaze as a perspective on native Canada: despite the strong markers of Inuitness that the protagonists, scenography, and equipment display, this return scene seems to accentuate and enunciate a common humanity, a common Canadianness. The citing of *Nanook* is not so much about literally correcting the misguided idea that Inuit are, in their own peculiar way, "resourceful" people and can "manage" their kayak trips with high efficiency. This intertextuality is instead about invigorating Inuit humanness and "visual sovereignty."[69] Part of this is achieved in how *Atanarjuat* takes its time to embark on a careful and patient depiction of its protagonists: shots are slow-paced studies of faces, movements, clothing—markers of Inuit identity and symbols of Inuit culture, as a Western audience might expect, are (re)presented. This aspect of slow and patient displaying of individuals and the body contributes to establishing specific aesthetics that characterize *Atanarjuat*. The film transforms objects into subjects, both with regard to political ideologies and the pitfalls of the medium of film. *Atanarjuat*'s protagonists are not objects that can be submitted to the desire of the colonial gaze but subjects who confront the spectator with one's own perspectives on what makes one human. Arguably, this film displays a double agenda. On the one hand it seeks to revive an understanding of Canada's "contemporary ancestors," and on the other hand it destabilizes the cultural-container logic that comes with it.[70] This is the carnivalesque gesture per se: the citation of a norm while at the same time reversing it.

Atanarjuat uses the "new technology" that supposedly sits well with "Inuit storytelling skills."[71] Yet *Atanarjuat* is more than a remediation of an oral legend. It is a reiteration of cultural inventory and identity as well as a process for once more creating a common narrative to Inuit communities. With its wide-reaching echo, *Atanarjuat* has made Inuit identity and its representation available to a potentially worldwide audience. Experiences of Inuitness that they "remember only by means of stories, images, behaviors among which they grew up" suddenly become memories in their "own right" to a larger audience.[72] (Post)memory and prosthetic memory are "affective forces" that can unite as well as divide audiences and collectives. The "post" in Hirsch's term *Postmemory* thus does not refer to a "belatedness" in processes of remembering, but it attempts to shed light on how memory endeavors to suture narratives of rupture of continuity and cohesion:[73]

> Postmemorial work . . . strives to *reactivate* and *reembody* more distant social/national and archival/cultural memorial structures by reinvesting them with resonant individual and familial forms of mediation and aesthetic expression.[74]

Postmemory and its representations tend to resort to "familiar and unexamined cultural images," and are thus prone to revive "authenticity" as a normative category. Authenticity is an example of such unexamined representations and identities. Virginia Richter elaborately outlines the problematic aspects of the concept, in particular with regard to (self-)representations of marginalized communities,[75] and argues that the idea of a particular agency with a somewhat more "truthful" access to cultural reality and its representations than others is profoundly misguided:

> The problem of authenticity is even more evident in the context of post-colonial literature and of writings concerned with the Holocaust. In such cases, congruence either between a writer's life and his or her subject-matter is demanded, or between the subject-matter and the real experiences of the groups represented. In other words, equivalence between the signifiers of the fictional text and the real-life referents is presupposed.[76]

Authenticity is still a formative category that governs aesthetics and ethics, particular in the context of Australian and Canadian reconciliation processes. When called upon, authenticity both enunciates and presupposes a generally valid coding and decoding of the symbolic order: there is a "right" and "truthful" way to represent, and then there is another.[77] As such, it oscillates between the demands and expectations of the audience, turning authenticity into a cultural commodity and into the "correct" representation of a group by author, director, and, ultimately, viewer. Richter explains:

> Identity positions cannot be simply dismissed, since they are bearers of phantasmatic investments: . . . It is the precise failure of representation—the structural impossibility of authenticity—that opens up the way to a discursive rearticulation of the political signifier. It is *because* we live in an era of globalization, migration, and displacement, not in spite of it, *that* stories about identity which are always also stories about its loss, continue to be told and read. But in the process, these identities are constantly reformulated.[78]

In line with this argument, it appears to be astonishingly difficult to critically receive *Atanarjuat* in (seeming!) independence of colonialism and European presence, and without resorting to Western narrative schemata and formative stories:

> No machines, no electric or telephone lines, nothing—and where no European person, name, or word exists; indeed, every one of the characters in the film is Inuit, and the dialogue is entirely in Inuktitut, the language of the Inuit. *Atanarjuat* in this regard could well be criticized for indulging the fantasy that Europe had never invaded the North.[79]

This emphasis on Inuit authenticity on the part of critics and viewers produces strange effects, resulting in a division of the audience into insiders and outsiders. In his essay on audience and reception of *Atanarjuat*, Arnold Krupat distinguishes between three types of spectators. The first encompasses a tight-knit community of viewers with native, even Inuit, backgrounds who are capable of understanding the world presented on the screen.[80] The second group of spectators is composed of people who are able to see "with a native eye," who are willing and capable of "moving their epistemological center" toward an attempt to decipher culturally coded narratives that are not "their own."[81] Interestingly enough, Krupat includes academics in this second group of spectators, assuming that they are capable of this shift or perspective by profession. The third group of viewers is, however, absolutely unwilling and incapable of appropriating another perspective on the world but their own, hence the members of this group make sense of the filmic narrative unfolding by "translating the film into familiar categories."[82] According to Krupat, most of the spectators belong to the third group. Krupat seeks to explain this result by claiming that the film represents "an Inuit sense of the way the world always was and still is," and that this world is somewhat inaccessible to non-Inuit viewers.[83] Again, this assertion misses the point: as the director Zacharias Kunuk has stressed several times, this film revives a cultural inventory that is long gone and is at risk of being lost to contemporary Inuit communities. There is hardly anyone with "special knowledge" still alive, yet there is a specific urge to resurrect and store "real" indigeneity for those who may not "know":

> In our postmodern culture, the authentic is inaccessible; it can be viewed only as a lost referent—in short, authenticity has been thoroughly deconstructed and discarded as the product of an impossible nostalgia for "pure origins."[84]

The concept of authenticity forms part of processes of identity construction, specifically in times when there arises a need to (re)focus on what is supposedly essential within a culture or community. Indigeneity has become a strong memory politics referent and identity label within the Canadian society, although its nature, essence, and status remain a constant site of negotiation. Identity labels "must miss the density and complexity of lived experience" and are caught between "appellation and individual experience," and thus are prone to be carnivalized.[85] As a mnemonic text, *Atanarjuat* calls upon an image of traditional Inuit lifestyle and, in the process, produces a version of how members of the contemporary Inuit community explain and represent their heritage. This is an instance where *Atanarjuat* carnivalizes (mass-)mediated images of Inuitness and Canada, and both, on the side of production and reception.

Consider, for example, the task that Michael Evans assigns to the representation of shamanism within *Atanarjuat*. Although shamanism did not play a role in most of the traditional versions of the legend of the Fast Runner, the film introduces another aspect of Inuit culture to its audience: the existence and importance of spiritual powers.[86] Within the diegetic world, the reason for the initial disruption of the community is the introduction of the utmost evil, the devil-like shaman Tuurngarjuaq. The evil shaman had come to the community to engage popular Kumaglak in a spiritual battle. Sauri, Kumaglak's son, had himself collaborated with this evil spirit, which henceforth disrupted the community. After the death of his father, Sauri becomes the new community leader. In the wake of this new era under Sauri, Tulimaq and his family are excluded from the community. It is this disruption of the collective order that lays the groundwork for all subsequent conflicts that unfold. This first spiritual intervention results in a battle between good and evil, creating a parallel between the conflicts that humans face and the quarrels that reach beyond our world. Shamanism, and the belief system associated with it, has supposedly almost entirely vanished from the cultural agenda of contemporary Inuit communities.[87] Nowadays, shamanism has lost its prominence as a result of the spread of Christianity in the Artic, which today is the most prevalent religion or belief system. Yet supernatural powers and occurrences still serve as markers for indigeneity, and the realm of the magic "belongs" to the representational and (ir)rational reservoir of—in this context—Inuit people:

> This understanding of shamanism [as being something to deny nowadays] adds an interesting note to the characters in the movie. Typically, shamanistic powers were considered neutral; they were not good or evil in themselves but could be used for good or evil purposes. . . . By representing Tuurngarjuaq as pure evil—and Atanarjuat, Qulitalik, and others as full members of the good side—the film moves away from the human realm shown by the interactions of camp life and closer to the kind of Olympian struggles seen in many Greek tragedies.[88]

Atanarjuat wants to represent a "truthful" insight into Inuit ways of life, seemingly undisturbed by colonial intrusion, for the non-Indigenous and the Indigenous world to see: authenticity is reinvigorated through the introduction of shamanism, an "authentic" token of Inuitness. Yet this reading falls short of another perspective that *Atanarjuat* provides its audience with, and this perspective hinges not so much on the reintroduction of shamanism as an (identity-)political statement but on the equation of colonial forces and the disruption of Atanarjuat's community with an evil spirit. Again, this film cites a cultural signifier for native authenticity—shamanism—and reconfigures the associations that come with it, in particular on the part of a Western viewership. In a carnivalesque move, shamanism suddenly becomes an allegorical expression of colonial intrusion, as Shari Huhndorf outlines:

> As a story about a community ravaged by outside influences, the film functions as a colonial allegory as well as a narrative about identity reconstruction in

the wake of this catastrophe. The evil that descends on the community in the opening scenes and results in a change in leadership provides a stark parallel with colonial policies that similarly disrupted social relations and traditional practices.[89]

Thus conceived, *Atanarjuat* carnivalizes the expectation of cultural essentialism and its representations. This film is ambiguous and complex, because it precisely does not follow one specific agenda. On the one hand, it relishes its own Inuitness and praises the "visual sovereignty" that it posits against the colonial gaze and its contemporary remnants.[90] *Atanarjuat* thus can be labeled as auto-ethnography, but it also carnivalizes the expectation of a definite label, either as a political statement against colonialism or a somewhat epic stance on Inuitness yet undisturbed by colonial impact. Like a trickster figure, this film is a shape-shifter: it transgresses boundaries while erecting new ones and slips from one's grasp whenever one tries to pin it down. With this inherent ambiguity, the film has, to a significant degree, moved away from Kunuk's initial aim of representing Inuit culture as it "always was."

The task of locating *Atanarjuat* and making sense of it in a specific cultural and historical tradition could eventually be addressed by showing that a somewhat universal quality can be attributed to Atanarjuat's story. Kerstin Knopf contends that this film "could have happened anywhere and anytime in the world, and could be part of other world mythologies."[91] She continues her argument by emphasizing that there is a lot of "love and hate, sex and rivalry, pride and resentment that is not unique to Inuit cultures."[92] In addition, one can find "much humor in the film, many bodily jokes, references to sex life in songs and conversations."[93] Knopf concludes that "[t]his universality, coupled with the autonomous presentation of Inuit culture from an inside perspective, works toward demystifying and de-exoticizing the material filmed."[94] Here the viewer encounters traditional elements of carnival and the carnivalesque—emphasis on the bodily, the sexual, and the hedonistic. This carnivalesque, however, is an expression of transculturality rather than one that relates back to Western histories of representation. *Atanarjuat* is a witness to transcultural encounters precisely because one can see how it cuts across notions of cultural belonging that are connected with representational regimes.

For example, the murder scene and its skillful blending of representational clues toward a media text is not, as Knopf would have it, universal, but instead bears testimony to transculturality. As soon as summer arrives, the families split up in order to hunt, gather, and prepare for the winter. Atanarjuat is sent to hunt caribous when, on his way, he encounters the summer residence of Sauri's family, who "cordially" invite him to take a rest.[95] On this occasion, Atanarjuat connects with Puja, Sauri's sly daughter. She is sent to accompany him on his hunting trip, since Atuat has to remain home due to her pregnancy. During this trip, Puja and Atanarjuat begin a love affair, and Puja becomes Atanarjuat's second wife—much to the dismay of Atanarjuat's brother and his wife. In what follows, Puja betrays Atanarjuat with his brother and comes up with a revenge plan with her brother Uqi. While Atanarjuat and his brother are sleeping, Uqi and his two sidekicks attempt to murder Atanarjuat, but instead kill his brother.[96] With the help of spiritual intervention in the shape of his grandfather's ghost, Atanarjuat manages to escape and is forced to flee over the icy tundra, barefoot and without any clothes.[97] Qulitalik, also a shaman, finds Atanarjuat and gives him shelter and spiritual tokens to fight the evil spirits.[98] During Atanarjuat's absence—he is presumed dead—Uqi expels Atuat and her little son, Kumaglaq, from the community and stabs his own father, Sauri, to death in order to become the new community leader.

Atanarjuat is forced to undergo a time of healing, learning, and reorientation before finally returning to take his rightful place as the community leader—and *Atanarjuat* bears witness to its protagonist's coming-of-age process. Atanarjuat is by no means a knight in shining armor. He does not starts off intending to be the devoted, morally sure, natural leader of this community. He is by no means a flawless hero, endowed with virtues, an unshakable moral compass, and a sense of just leadership. Atanarjuat has flaws, makes questionable decisions, and engages in (love) quarrels. We also encounter the figure of the antihero, Uqi. Driven by ignoble motives such as revenge, mastery, and pride, he is posited as the radically alternative draft to Atanarjuat. Uqi remains entangled in his viciousness, whereas the hero passes through a process of learning and development. In the end, Atanarjuat does not enact revenge and does not kill his enemies, the ones who killed his brother and plotted revenge, but shows mercy to his opponents in order to restore peace within Igloolik. In the aftermath, the evil spirits are expelled along with Uqi, his companions, and treacherous sister Puja in a mystic ceremony. The community's peaceful cohesion is then restored.

This hero-antihero configuration as well as the coming-of-age or rite-of-passage elements of the plot can easily be understood as Western strategies of storytelling and representation. Margaret Atwood attributed Homerian qualities to this narrative, thus setting up a discursive link to one of the most formative texts (and poets) of Western culture. Such an understanding of the configuration of *Atanarjuat*'s plot structure and character settings misses how *Atanarjuat* effectively transculturizes these paradigms of storytelling. Lucas Bessire holds that *Atanarjuat* (and Kunuk's other filmic productions)

> are revealed as open bicultural systems in which Indigenous agendas can actively be expressed. This multicultural fluency . . . enables the success of films

such as *Atanarjuat* by accommodating dominant society's signifying practices, yet at the same time seeking to undermine and change the very nature of the primitivism that informs them.[99]

This feature film seemingly employs Western narrative strategies to further Indigenous agendas. This is, however, not where *Atanarjuat* stops with its resignifying practices. It, in a sense, carnivalizes the assumption of monoculturally coded strategies of world-making, because it opens them up toward the transcultural. *Atanarjuat* bears witness to precisely how signifying structures cut across cultural boundaries, and eventually moves beyond them. The film thus emphasizes the inherent transculturality of Canadian society, in the sense that identities and stories are interrelated and intertwined.

This can be regarded as a comment on Canadian "sorry politics" and transcultural identities in the context of reconciliation in Canada, and thus reaches beyond the diegetic universe that the film provides. Offering mercy and leniency to the culprits while expelling them from the community marks a turn in power relations: after a time of suffering, self-empowered Inuit identities move beyond the stage of incessant and reiterated victimhood, and the "spirit of the past" needs to be driven out of the Canadian community. The act of expelling the culprits offers a signal that it is time for Canada to move beyond the dichotomy of settler-perpetrator and Indigenous-victim configurations and makes a demand for mapping out common ground rather than identifying divisive forces.

From Multicultural Australia to Enforced Reconciliation: Baz Luhrmann's *Australia*

Baz Luhrmann's filmic epos *Australia*[100] was released in 2008, and it is the third most successful movie in Australia in terms of revenue.[101] The release of *Australia* coincided with the discourses of reconciliation having once again gained momentum in the Australian public sphere. The *Bringing Them Home Report* had already been published a decade earlier, but the continuous lobbying for Indigenous causes, decisive court decisions, and Kevin Rudd's election campaign—spearheaded by the promise of an apology to the Stolen Generations, which was actually delivered in 2008—enabled reconciliation to become visible once more. The political and social climate in Australia was thus favorable to reconciliation discourses and of the reevaluation of Australian (post)colonial history. Director Baz Luhrmann described how his movie engaged with these discourses and reflected them:

> I started the project with six months of researching general Australian history. I was looking for the canvas to play out a story, so really the film could have

been set at any point—at one stage I was looking at the First Fleet [the eleven ships that set sail from Britain in 1787 to set up the first colony in New South Wales]—but there were a few specific issues I wanted to explore. One was our relationship with England, the parent country, and why, when Australians have self-confidence in so many areas, do we not have the confidence for self-governance? Another was to do with Australia's indigenous population.[102]

Australia is a cinematic exploration of Australian historical narratives and aims to grasp a reconciled Australian national identity. The film engages with these identity politics, with how Australia—in Luhrmann's terms—has come to realize itself. *Australia* is framed as a national epos: it covers historical ground that ranges from British imperialism to the world wars, from the Stolen Generations to *Australia*'s own version of reconciliation. This gesture of reiterating Australia's national history follows a double trajectory: it unfolds from a contemporary point of view and stages an act of remembering Australia's ambiguous past. *Australia* tasks itself with reconciling many facets of Australian history—which are oftentimes highly controversial—within one film and strives to reconcile Australian national identity with the difficult legacy of enforced cultural reeducation of its Aboriginal peoples. Luhrmann's filmic epos looks back on Australian history from a standpoint that has witnessed the inquiry into the forcible removal of Aboriginal children and the publication of the *Bringing Them Home Report*:

> By choosing to set the film between the two world wars, I was able to bind the historical romance to what really is the greatest scar in the history of this country: the Stolen Generation. It was a miracle to be making the film with so many Aboriginals and members of the Stolen Generation in the film and working on it with us. Just as we finished filming, the Prime Minister [Kevin Rudd] came out and delivered the long-awaited and much-needed apology to the Stolen Generation, which has put us on a road of change.[103]

The movie features Lady Sarah Ashley, played by Nicole Kidman, an English aristocrat who moves to Australia to ensure the survival of the cattle farm Faraway Downs. Her husband, who was the owner of the cattle farm, has just been murdered. Although Lady Ashley initially seems repulsed by this foreign country and its odd inhabitants—the silent and unapproachable Drover, played by Hugh Jackman, is among the first Australians she meets—she later not only develops a fondness for both country and people, including half-caste Aboriginal Nullah, but also transforms into a female Drover: fearless and unladylike, she accompanies the Drover, his Aboriginal mate, and Nullah on a highly dangerous cattle drive across the Australian outback. It is Nullah who—with the help of an Aboriginal elder called King George—eventually ensures the success of the cattle drive. The tides of Australian history separate the protagonists as the movie unfolds, yet in the end the Drover and Lady

Ashley marry, and Nullah becomes their adopted son. The movie concludes with Nullah leaving his new family to go on his Walkabout, an Aboriginal tradition that marks the passing from boyhood into adulthood, after which he will likely return to his new parents.

Australia seeks to bring the story of multicultural Australia onto the cinematic screen, and all three protagonists together can be read as allegories of Australian national identity. All three national narratives are interwoven within this family, and, as such, Australia is to be reconciled with its controversial history. This Australian history is negotiated within and through the outback, and *Australia* harks back to the specific role that the outback plays in the process of discerning Australia from Britain. It is the mythical space (and place) where British settlers become Australians. Within this national narrative, the outback becomes the Other to imperial culture. Luhrmann's *Australia* both takes up the national narrative and destabilizes it: Lady Ashley grows into a female Drover and thus enables a move beyond the paradigm of the male rural worker who is the central representative of this bush myth. Nullah, the half-caste with his deep, mythic understanding of and connection to the outback, also uses the outback as a space of empowerment, because he becomes the enabling force behind the cattle drive that secures the existence of Faraway Downs.

Australia thus deconstructs the formative national image of an outback that is male and white and reorients it toward historically marginalized voices. The film pursues alternative myth-making, because traditionally both the Aboriginals and women were written out of Australia's pioneer story, but they are central within the diegetic world of *Australia*, both to the story itself—it is Nullah's voiceover that narrates this Australian epos for most of the time—and the survival of Faraway Downs. It is my contention that *Australia*'s aesthetics are influenced by the carnivalesque, parody, and (slapstick) comedy, and that its favorite gesture is exaggeration, the hyperbolic. What is more, the movie also establishes an intertextual and aesthetic connection to *The Wizard of Oz*, a film that can be read as an allegory of the settler's discovery and disclosure of a mythical land, as well as a testament to female self-empowerment. Moreover, *The Wizard of Oz* is read as an ironic, carnivalesque engagement with pertinent social, political, and economic discourses in America around 1860. In a similar vein, Luhrmann's carnivalesque pretends to be apolitical in its aesthetics, yet it is deeply identity-political in its meaning. It evokes the idea that *Australia* is an equally powerful carnivalesque comment on political climates and discourses. However, its rather simplistic take on Australian reconciliation, one that rests on a segmentary, happy-go-lucky multiculturalism, hinders from unfolding any truly subversive potential: *Australia* strives to counter Australia's difficult historical legacies with a song and a smile, but it places a sugary coating on national narratives and formative myths and so is devoid of the ironic aptness of *The Wizard of Oz*. Luhrmann's movie seems to have found the perfect recipe to smooth over the tensions and inequalities that national myths bring with them, and Luhrmann's agenda to include, even center, indigeneity in his Australian epos leads to the movie giving consent on behalf of the Aboriginals to be part of this national narrative. *Australia*, consequently, is not the voice of, but a voice for the Aboriginals.

Moreover, *Australia*'s rendering of indigeneity might even fortify a specific stereotypical image of the Aboriginal, namely the noble savage. Although Luhrmann's movie tries to pit itself against stereotypes, it recreates and to some extent even strengthens them. *Australia* is an example of how the carnivalesque as an aesthetic choice and an identity-political tool can fail to destabilize preformed notions of indigeneity. It remains, in a sense, carnivalesque only on the surface, and lacks the subtle and subversive potential of *The Wizard of Oz*. The filmic rendering—*Australia*'s bright and gay colors, its parodic elements, its rather schematic characters—supports the impression of a self-contained universe, a filmic world that forms an optimistic whole where all falls into place in the end. It is, after all, a somewhat odd take on the prospects of reconciliation if all turmoil over history is solved by framing an Englishwoman turned Mother Australia who welcomes and adopts Australia's stolen child, thus reestablishing colonial power hierarchies. I label Luhrmann's vision of reconciliation, as represented in *Australia*, as enforced reconciliation. The imperative to arrive at a sense of closure, of reconcilability in relation to Australia's history, takes its toll on *Australia*: the narrative and its aesthetics falter under the heavy framework of Luhrmann's enforced reconciliation[104] and thus, in the end, (re)produce the opposite to its benevolent political agenda.

In "a Land Far, Far Away": Australian National History and the Land of Oz

Discourses of nation and identity have not lost their appeal in the Australian public sphere, yet it is still a difficult task to "produce a positive image of Australia," as Adi Wimmer observes.[105] Australia still maintains an ambiguous relationship to its imperial mother Great Britain, and the inclusion and negotiation of this "Anglo-Celtic" heritage in Australian national narratives is still a matter of contestation. Wimmer remarks that "the British [were] enviously perceived as calm and self-assured about their identity," while in Australia, identities and certainties were in flux after World War I.[106] In resonance with the processes of reconciliation and the apology by Prime Minister Kevin Rudd, a discursive adjustment of the image of the Australian nation unfolded, and two national narratives came into conflict. On the one hand,

Australia takes pride in having become a culturally and economically established community, especially with regard to its "inauspicious origins" as a penal colony.[107] Yet the systems of cultural reeducation are a blemish on this celebratory image of Australian history. Marcia Langton, professor of Australian Indigenous studies, is quoted in *The Guardian* with the following praise of *Australia* and its agenda: it has supposedly "given Australians a new past" and "a myth of national origin that is disturbing, thrilling, heartbreaking, hilarious, and touching."[108] *Australia* engages with the discourse of distancing (from imperial dominance) and approximation (the task of finding a distinct Australian identity) and precisely addresses these issues. Furthermore, the legacy of the Stolen Generations is interwoven into *Australia*'s historical fabric and thus identified as central to Australian national identity.

The scope of national narratives addressed in *Australia* corresponds with Luhrmann's aspirations to create an Australian epos.[109] Epic texts establish a relationship with national history, as they draw on historical events and reframe, retell, and reevaluate them. An epos engages with stories that are of central importance to the self-understanding of a community and bestows them with a universal quality. Traditionally, the epos is also associated with the fine arts, with a certain generic sublimity. But because of its transgenerational and oftentimes cross-cultural circulation, an epos can be understood as a transcultural narrative strategy and the effective form for imagining a people's history.

Australia weaves an epic national reconciliation cloth out of these formative and quite opposing narratives: the notion of heroic settler achievements, Britain's alleged cultural superiority, and the Stolen Generations narrative. The filmic techniques of *Australia* further support this logic of intertwining master narratives by establishing a chapter structure. Episodes are consolidated into substructures of the plot by a clear demarcation of beginning and end, with such subsections introduced by a bird's-eye camera perspective that slowly descends on the action unfolding. Once the "chapter" is about to end, the camera zooms out, concluding the respective scene with a panoramic view of the landscape. As a consequence, the landscape acquires a special function within the narrative framework of *Australia*. It is used as a structuring device, allowing the outback to become the point of reference that frames these chapters. In addition, the outback develops its own discursive function within Luhrmann's feature film and thus reinforces the importance of this formative landscape for Australian national identity. The vast landscape, epic in itself, becomes the canvas on which Luhrmann projects his national epos of reconciliation.

Within his seminal study *The Australian Legend* (1958), historian Russel Ward established the bush myth as the central element for negotiating an Australian identity distinct from but also, and interestingly enough, connected to

British identity.[110] In the process of distinguishing Australia's national identity from Great Britain's, the outback became the primary space of projection. At the heart of the bush myth was the question of who actually inhabits and cultivates the land, and out of this proprietary scheme an identity was born, with the bush myth establishing a noble bushman who is virtuous, practical, resilient, and determined.[111] "Like American pioneers, bushmen entered and conquered the alien landscape. They tamed the hostile environment, made it human, and thus performed a central civilizing, nation-building function."[112] Accordingly, the outback was promoted as being distinctly, characteristically Australian, and its physique captured the uniqueness of Australia. It was both mythicized and idealized, while along with it, the bush and its hero, the bushman, became "real Australians."[113] According to this logic, the Australian rural worker is often pitted against the decay and decadence of either the Australian city or British imperial culture and its corruption.[114] Inevitably, "membership" in this "Australian club" was rather exclusive: falling outside this definition of Australianness were women, Indigenous peoples, other ethnic minorities, and town-or-city people.[115] In this sense, the bush myth and the drover as its representative are deeply racialized and misogynist images of Australian national identity.

However, within *Australia*, this strange country is not referred to as "the land far, far away," as the name of Lady Ashley's cattle farm Faraway Downs might suggest; it is England that is invoked as the alien place far, far away from Australian civilization.[116] This is the first instance where one witnesses a carnivalesque reversal of existing discursive hierarchies. The audience's first encounter with Lady Sarah Ashley is accompanied by Nullah's voiceover that introduces her as the "strangest woman" who is not from this country, Australia, but from a "country far, far away"—England.[117] This is clearly a reference to the realm of fairy tales, further sustained by repetitive references to "storytelling" as the prime human ability.[118] In this spirit, *Australia* does not shy away from contesting the seminal national narrative of the bushman and the outback by addressing Australia's structural racism.

For example, the question of whom *Australia* sends into the outback on the hazardous cattle drive is revealing. At one point in the narrative, the survival of the cattle farm can only be secured if the cattle are sold in Darwin. This means that fifteen hundred animals have to be guided through the Australian outback. In the aftermath of Fletcher's demise,[119] the farm is short- and malstaffed for such a perilous undertaking and in dire need of capable people to lead the drive. Nullah hurries to fetch the Drover, whose second appearance in the movie clearly frames him as a reproduction of the Australian legend outlined above: on horseback, he rushes to the farm to assess the situation, and to eventually remedy it. The Drover is portrayed as the noble but slightly savage hero, the enabler that the lost English aristocrat Lady Ashley has been waiting for.[120] The Drover's reentry sets up a connection to another frontier-existence-related genre, the Western. Panoramic shots and camera angles that frame the Drover from a slightly upwardly tilted angle make him appear larger than life and properly hero-esque, and connect him with the landscape that he is literally performing on. Cuts and fast transitions create suspense that culminates in Lady Ashley convincing the Drover that the drive can actually be managed by the "impossible seven": Lady Ashley, Nullah, and the Drover; an Aboriginal woman, Magarri; Drover's Aboriginal friend; the Chinese cook; and the chronically drunken farm accountant, Kipling Flynn, embark on this perilous journey. In this manner, *Australia* breaks open the male, misogynist, racist discourse of the bush myth and transforms it into a testimony to multicultural Australia.

Moreover, in the tradition of revisionist history writing, this national narrative is broadened and politically corrected. All subjects that have been not only marginalized within the bush myth but also structurally excluded from Australian identity are literally reinscribed into the narrative and onto the formative landscape. The Australian outback indeed becomes a place where "dreams do come true," as the song "Somewhere over the Rainbow" famously suggests.[121] This special group of drovers—all shunned by the formative bush myth—symbolizes an act of carnivalesque reversal within *Australia*, for it writes and imagines marginalized groups right onto the canvas where Australianness is seemingly already precluded—the Australian outback. The question of who populates the mystic land and who is able to get by on and with it is a prominently addressed issue in *Australia*, and the social hierarchies that are constructed through the bush myth are temporarily reversed. Australia's blatant racism toward its Aboriginal peoples, its anti-British and anti-aristocratic attitude, and the marginalization of other ethnicities (like the Chinese) are projected onto the canvas of the outback and temporarily overridden. In the process, *Australia* inscribes the marginalized into the mainstream national discourse. The seven drovers (six after Kipling's death) represent the cultural compartments that represent multicultural Australia, and thus become important parts of an imagined, reconciled Australia.

Furthermore, Nullah plays a significant role in this setting, for he, along with his grandfather King George, becomes the primary enabler of the dangerous endeavor of the cattle drive. Fletcher and his villains wreak havoc on the group because they scare the fifteen hundred animals into a stampede.[122] By setting fires, they force the rampaging cattle toward a cliff and certain destruction. Nullah manages to get in front of the stampede, standing close to the edge of the cliff. He is forced to watch how Kipling Flynn is trampled to death under the hooves of the herd yet is able to unleash his magic onto the animals. The film frames his magic intervention as a mixture of song and incantation, summoning and spell. He gesticulates, hums, sings, and augurs the stampeding cattle until they mysteriously come to their senses and stop right at the edge of the cliff. With this heroic act, the Aboriginal child not only saves the cattle herd, the driving party, and by extension also Faraway Downs, he also becomes the main facilitator of the "Australian Dream" that Lady Ashley dares to harbor. Although this dream is still a "white" one, *Australia* changes the paradigms of this story.

In the Loving Embrace of "Missus Boss": Sugary Reconciliation and the Australian Family

However, there is another aspect to Baz Luhrmann's filmic exploration of Australian national identity that falls short of this empowering narrative quality. *Australia* structures its characters in a rather simplistic manner, and throughout the movie they remain emblematic instead of well developed. Their position in the overarching reconciliation narrative that *Australia* seeks to provide is of more importance than their elaboration. Instead of mediating those cultural differences and finding novel ways of articulating and conceptualizing identities that cut across well-established thresholds, *Australia* instead reiterates and reinforces stereotypes. These characters remain compartmentalized in terms of their cultural identities as they represent conventional notions of cultural belonging, and they cannot be read as trailblazing foreshadowings of post-reconciliation Australia.

A case in point is how the scene described above ends.[123] Nullah, who has just saved the entire endeavor by calming the cattle, loses consciousness following this enormous task and falls into Lady Ashley's arms, who assures Nullah that he is safe with her. The Drover rushes to their side and remains with the two long enough for the viewer to capture the representation of a "holy family." The impression of a nuclear family is evoked by a camera angle that is tilted slightly upward, rendering the people in the frame larger than life and evoking the idea that there is something special about this family. The Drover fades out into the background of the arrangement in order to cede all the narrative and visual space to Nullah and Lady Ashley. Odette Kelada points out that this scene establishes an intertextual link with Charles Chauvel's famous melodramatic film *Jedda* (1955).[124] Coincidentally, that movie was the first Australian film not only to be shot in color but also to feature two Aboriginals as leading actors. In *Jedda*, the eponymous Aboriginal girl becomes an orphan and is adopted by the family of the station boss, the McCanns. Sarah, the wife, seeks to assimilate her into white Australian society and raise her in a European image. All traditional Aboriginal ways are forbidden from Jedda, but as she grows older she meets Marbuck, an Aboriginal man from the bush, and they fall in love. The filmic narrative suggests that Marbuck abducts her from the McCann's home. However, Marbuck's tribe further impedes the growing love between the two, as she is deemed unworthy of him because of her light skin color. In the end the two commit suicide as Marbuck jumps off a cliff with Jedda in his arms.

In *Australia* the cliff scene is cited, as Nullah is on the verge of falling off the cliff, yet, contrary to *Jedda*, which suggests the impossibility of assimilation of the "savages" and also precludes a return to the Aboriginal community, Nullah is saved by white Lady Sarah Ashley. Kelada offers the following remarks:

> The cinematic juxtaposition could be read as suggesting that rather than symbolically falling between that rather than symbolically falling between the abyss of assimilation politics and what was conceived as "traditional" tribal Indigeneity, a brighter post-apology future can be imagined now for "Jedda"/indigenous peoples. Luhrmann's homage to Jedda revives and rescues the ghost of this Aboriginal child figure by performing a retrieval from the cliff face and salvation in the familial arms of Lady Ashley and Drover. This fits neatly with a fantasy epic for Australia past and present.[125]

What was meant as a nod to *Jedda* and its heritage ultimately becomes part of an odd revival of colonial power hierarchy and discourse in *Australia*, as it attempts to carnivalize *Jedda*'s stance on the impossibility of Aboriginal assimilation. Instead of temporarily reversing the assimilation paradigm with a clever citation and rearrangement of *Jedda*'s final scene and subsequent death of its eponymous character, *Australia* produces the opposite effect: Lady Ashley sweeps in and fills the space of his Aboriginal mother, and the scene consequently does not reframe Jedda's suicide as Nullah's self-empowerment.

Although Nullah saves the cattle and becomes, in a sense, larger than life through this deed, *Australia*'s arrangement of the cliff scene centralizes Lady Ashley's motherdom and her prowess as a child-saver. In so doing, the moment of Aboriginal empowerment is distorted into an emphasis of the dependence of Australia's Indigenous populations on the white settlers. Lady Ashley once again becomes the point of reference:

> It is important to note that this white mother is a *good* mother. She effectively rescued the "Jedda"-like figure from the fatal descent off the cliff and *clasps* the child to her, with Drover appearing in time to construct a familial embrace. This white mother is one who questions the authorities when they parrot "bad" ideas of the period claiming that Aboriginal mothers did not care for her children. . . . Lady Ashley's protest provides contrast with such "bad" colonialists and presents her as a progressive *good* white person, identifiable and likable/consumable for a contemporary audience. Underlying this, . . . the movie still plays out how the bond between Aboriginal mother and child can be severed with disturbing ease.[126]

Kelada refers to a peculiar binary opposition that *Australia* constructs. On the one hand, the viewer encounters a very progressive female protagonist, Lady Ashley. Her character seems to be far ahead of her contemporaries, both in terms of the way she perceives herself and the attitude she holds toward other socially and/or ethnically marginalized people. She fights against male dominance and refuses to be reduced to her status as a woman—which would restrict her to the domestic sphere and limit her influence on her own development.

In this sense, she is a modern Dorothy who has come to an unknown land to make it accessible to her. Liz Conor refers to *Australia*'s "reference-saturation" in this context and remarks that the "entrenched cultural habit of referencing reality through the 'image bank' . . . of modernity" is one major narrative strategy of Luhrmann's movie.[127] One of the most visible cases is the connection to the American musical fantasy film *The Wizard of Oz* (1939).[128] Despite the proclivity to interpret *The Wizard of Oz* as a filmic adaption of a children's book,[129] some scholars describe its strong subversive and carnivalesque qualities. Henry M. Littlefield's groundbreaking essay was the first to read it as an identity-political statement on the United States at the turn of the century:

> Baum's most thoughtful devotees see in it only a warm, cleverly written fairy tale. Yet the original Oz book conceals an unsuspected depth, and . . . Baum's immortal American fantasy encompasses more than hitherto believed. For Baum created a children's story with a symbolic allegory implicit within its story line and characterization.[130]

Quentin P. Taylor recounts that this new reading was a revelation to many:

> Baum's charming tale concealed a clever allegory on the Populist movement, the agrarian revolt that swept across the [American] Midwest in the 1890's. In an ingenuous act of imaginative scholarship, Henry M. Littlefield linked the characters and the story line of the Oz tale to the political landscape of the Mauve decade. The discovery was little less than astonishing: Baum's children's story was in fact a full-blown "parable of populism," "a vibrant and ironic portrait" of America on the eve of the new century. . . . Baum all but admitted that his writing contained a veiled subtext, confessing his desire to pen stories that would "bear the stamp of our times and depict the progressive fairies of the day."[131]

Australia sets up a strong intertextual relationship with Baum's *The Wizard of Oz* and its filmic adaptation. It is the silhouette of Faraway Downs that emerges through the mist as the viewer is introduced to the story, and it is the invocation of a "land far, far away" that sets the tone for this intertextuality.[132] This land, Oz, will be healed by the mysterious woman from "far, far away."[133]

As the heroine, both powerful and empowering, *The Wizard of Oz* can also be read in terms of its comments on female (self-)empowerment.[134] Lady Ashley sings "Somewhere over the Rainbow" to console Nullah after the unexpected and tragic death of his mother Daisy, reiterating the trope of the land where dreams will come true.[135]

In contrast to *The Wizard of Oz*, Luhrmann's *Australia* does not display the critical finesse of Baum's original text and filmic adaptation. The carnivalesque gesture of *The Wizard of Oz* is well dosed enough to remain a subtle but effective narrative strategy:

> The allegory always remains in a minor key, subordinated to the major theme and readily abandoned whenever it threatens to distort the appeal of the fantasy. But through it, in the form of a subtle parable, Baum delineated a Midwesterner's vibrant and ironic portrait of this country as it entered the twentieth century.[136]

Australia is astonishingly straightforward in transporting rather simplistic solutions and characters, precisely because the carnivalesque aesthetics, the emphasis on comic relief and parodic exaggeration, are *not* subordinated to *Australia*'s identity-political message. Luhrmann's movie seeks to make a very important, pro-Indigenous point about Australian history, and strives to incorporate the major rifts in that history into one perfect whole. This endeavor results in oversimplifications that eventually reverse Luhrmann's benevolent intentions and identity-political message.

Consider, for example, the rendition of Lady Ashley's counterpart, the Aboriginal mother. Daisy, Nullah's mother, is silenced and marginalized by the overarching narrative of *Australia*. While it is true that female Aboriginals held the weakest position in the hierarchy of the marginalized, Daisy as a character appears solely as the facilitator of Lady Ashley's motherhood "by accident." Daisy only has a few words to say before she accidentally drowns in a water tank. In an act of revenge, the recently fired Fletcher tells the authorities about Nullah's existence on Faraway Downs.[137] A police car appears, and an officer approaches Lady Ashley in order to inquire about the existence of a "half-caste fella." The scene is introduced by one of the formative panoramic shots that descend on the actual action unfolding, and it pauses on an Aboriginal tracker who is shown to be complicit in the child-removal endeavor.[138] A cry of "Run, Nullah, run!" interrupts a rather picturesque scene where Lady Ashley is shown in her first attempts at driving cattle. The rise of Lady Ashley is contrasted with the fall of Daisy. In order to escape the policemen, Daisy and Nullah hide in the giant water tank. As the officers appear, one of them starts the pumping mechanism to wash his face—which is clearly marked by *Australia* as a deliberate act based on the assumption that someone could have hidden in the tank. Two narrative strands are interwoven through a parallel montage: the water level rises as Lady Ashley tries to appease the officers and convince them to leave the premises. At some point, Daisy is unable to stay above water anymore, as she appears unable to swim. Although Drover and the others rush to help her as soon as the police drive away, Daisy drowns in the tank, and Nullah survives.[139] Daisy's death is the prerequisite and enabler of *Australia*'s narrative of reconciliation. Only through her disappearance as a mother figure can Lady Ashley take her place and commence her quest to save the country, as Nullah predicted in his introductory remarks.[140]

While Daisy's death is powerfully performed and depicts a grand maternal bond, it is contradicted by Nullah's quick recovery from grief after such a terrible climax. The scene with Lady Ashley [singing "Somewhere over the Rainbow"] that follows his mother's death plays out the notion of disposable emotional bonds between an indigenous mother and a child. . . . The soothing nature of singing and bonding may have worked as a healing scene. However, what is anomalous is that as Nullah is coaxed from his tears and looks up at Lady Ashley in wonder, he becomes strangely invested in the white woman's goal: the objective of transporting her cattle for sale.[141]

Although Lady Ashley later insists that she "is not good with children," the Drover settles the matter by pointing out that a child needs a mother.[142] Lady Ashley replaces Daisy, while Drover will, in the long run, replace Fletcher as Nullah's absent and evil father.[143] As both, Kelada and Connor aptly remark, other Aboriginal and (female) family members are out of the question as surrogate mothers. On the contrary, although we know that Drover was married to an Aboriginal woman, *Australia* lets him utter the inappropriate remark that Aboriginal women are very easy to get along with, and the suggestive potential of this remark is supported by a shot of his groin, to which Drover actually points while making this comment. This scene is an example of *Australia*'s overplayed carnivalesque aesthetics that risk evoking the opposite of its benevolent intentions. In reference to bodily pleasures as a characteristic feature and amusement of the lower classes, Luhrmann's film establishes another connection with the carnivalesque. However, with this scene, the position of female Aboriginals as the farthest away from the center is strengthened rather than contested, and the colonial assumption that Aboriginals are unfit to take care of children is bizarrely taken up again. As Conor notes, *Australia*

> conveniently expunges the kinship network into which Nullah and his ongoing care and education would have ordinarily been inextricably woven. This is clumsily masked by the exception of King George, who himself references the "King Billy" type. He is a "magic man," asserting his right to educate Nullah, who tells Lady Ashley that Nullah too is "magic." King George's claim on Nullah centres on his responsibilities as an elder to initiate the boy, but his status as accused murderer leaves his claim and authority as grandfather and educator unsubstantiated until he is exonerated.[144]

As Nullah falls into her arms by the cliff, Lady Ashley seals her maternal bond with the exclamation: "You're safe with me."[145] From Daisy's death onward, Nullah becomes the facilitator of Lady Ashley's endeavor rather than a distinct individual, and assumes his place in Luhrmann's national allegory. In this sense, Conor speaks of a "domesticated form of Aboriginality."[146] The Aboriginals in *Australia* are drafted to serve a certain purpose in the narrative. Although Nullah introduces himself as a person that belongs to no one, that he is situated between the cultural poles, he becomes common property to and of Luhrmann's reconciliation narrative.

Australia starts off quite promisingly when Nullah's magic capacities are gradually revealed. The connection to the supernatural is strongly evoked when Nullah "senses" and accompanies the death of Lord Ashley. Humming and gesticulating, Nullah waves Lady Ashley toward her dead husband's body that is laid out in the living room.[147] This impression is amplified by Nullah and Lady Ashley's first actual encounter: Nullah has just told the viewer that the country will be saved by this "strange woman," and that he will sing her to him.[148] The camera blends over to Lady Ashley's room at night, and a strange but not frightening voice, female but also childlike, is heard humming and singing a soothing melody. Lady Ashley, however, appears to be frightened by this supernatural apparition. This rather uncanny mood is supported by waving curtains, both preparing the audience for and making them anticipate a ghost. At some point the mystery dissolves into relief, because Nullah physically enters the scene.

At the beginning, the character is mildly irritating, but turns out to be very loveable. The entire uncanny mood is cleared by the bathos of comic relief, and Nullah is returned to the realm of mere humans when he cracks a joke about "wrongside business," a reference to sexual encounters.[149] Nullah tells the sad story of his origins—Fletcher frequently raped his mother Daisy, and she became pregnant with him—yet the film turns it into a joke, and Nullah into a "blackfella" fool. The idea of "wrongside business" reappears when Drover kisses Lady Ashley for the first time and Nullah catches them, inquiring as to whether they would now also engage in such business.[150] It is Nullah's role to disrupt the (melo)dramatic with the wits of a child.

In contrast to characters to be found in other works discussed here, Nullah does not become the powerful and irritating transcultural fool who raises awareness, who disturbs, who contests, and who creates anarchy within existing representational orders. On the contrary, Nullah is represented as a young wizard in Oz, transcending the boundaries between nature and culture. These are ultimately colonial tropes and racially biased representations. King George—*the* Wizard of Oz—and Nullah are both framed as exotic.[151] It is the fantasy that the colonizers had of Aboriginality that manifests itself in the conception of *Australia*'s Aboriginal characters. Conor argues that Nullah is even closely associated with the piccaninny child, a racist and derogatory caricature that was, for example, found in art, on tableware, and on household items. She describes how this figure

> recurred within the twentieth-century mania for mass-produced home decoration objects with an "Australian flavour," which was often achieved through Aboriginal art motifs, or through the romanticized depiction of Aboriginal peoples (Haskins 2000). The "piccaninny" took its place among a plethora of Indigenous motifs emanating from technical colleges from 1890 to 1910 to "add historical and regional authenticity" . . . and to Australianize design. From the 1910s to the 1960s the "piccaninny" became a common household ornament through the enormously popular ceramics of Brownie Downing . . . the Martin Boyd Pottery company, the children's books of Elizabeth Durack and Jane Ada Fletcher (Morris 1993), the watercolours and fabric designs of Peg Malty . . . and the nature writings and photography of Charles Barrett and Axel Poignant. Yet the popularity of the "piccaninny" peaks as the policy of assimilation, which rested on child removals, intensified across each of the states, as Aboriginal children became the principal target for colonial states' governance of Indigenous populations. The "piccaninny" came to embody an "Aboriginality of childhood" . . . that through their removal came to inscribe a white Australian future.[152]

Nullah, the lovable, sweet little boy who is almost always in a good mood and relieves many scenes of their gravity and melodrama through comic relief, comes close to alluding to the piccaninny child. Although Nullah tells most of *Australia*'s story—he provides frequent voiceover—he also becomes an object that settler Australia desires.[153] The "trans-colonially and transnationally" circulated piccaninny child is once more subjected to "a distinctly British acquisitive impulse over the colonized, racialized child," and *Australia* translates this impulse into giving consent for the Aboriginals to be part of Luhrmann's reconciliation epos.[154]

It is in this vein that Nullah remains on the sidelines when Lady Ashley becomes transformed into the Drover's wife, and thus becomes Australian. *Australia* thus establishes another intertextual connection to a seminal bush myth text—Henry Lawson's *The Drover's Wife* (1892). Although Lawson's short story centers on and represents the perspective of a literal drover's wife, it is regarded as a key narrative of the bush myth.[155] Although its main protagonist is female, it perpetuates the male paradigms characterizing this national narrative. There are two key scenes to Lady Ashley's transformation into the drover's wife. The cattle drive party returns to their camp after Nullah has successfully bewitched the herd, but they find their camp in shambles.[156] Fletcher and his villains have destroyed all the belongings that Lady Ashley brought on the trip. This is precisely the moment when the English aristocrat finally becomes a female version of a Drover:[157] she regrets that she has brought "all those things" (commodities, luxury items, clothing) to the outback, as they now seem ridiculously out of place to her. Simultaneously, the Drover discloses that he was married to an Aboriginal woman who died of tuberculosis because the doctors refused to treat Aboriginals.[158] Lady Ashley confesses that she is unable to have children. Nullah, however, remains absent from this scene, and only plays "Somewhere over the Rainbow" on Kipling's harmonica, marking the completion of Lady Ashley's transition and the fulfillment of King George's prophecy—this woman has come to save this land.

The most powerful representation of Lady Ashley's transformation and her acceptance into the fold is the second bar scene.[159] The first bar scene had established Australia's structural racism. The bar is usually a central place in any Western as it is oftentimes the center of the dwelling and the place where the community meets. Within this first bar scene, Drover was marked as marginalized in society and unwelcome, with the Aboriginal Magarri altogether excluded from the bar. Moreover, women were also initially denied entrance. These tropes are taken up again in the second bar scene, which follows the successful cattle drive. As heroine, Lady Ashley is welcomed into the fold of rural Australia(n men), because she has proven herself to be a "true Australian" bush woman. Her joining of the Australian club is marked by her "deserv[ing] a drink like any man." This Australian club eventually opens its doors and broadens the frame of who, according to *Australia*, belongs to multicultural Australia. In the third bar scene, Australia's structural racism is finally overcome, because Magarri is allowed to enter the bar and have a drink in the company of his friends and others. The Aboriginal man, thus conceived, is also incorporated into Luhrmann's national narrative.

Notwithstanding Magarri's introduction into the national fabric, Luhrmann's vision of reconciliation consequently culminates in the quintessential Australian "holy family" with its central mother figure. It does not foreground and imagine an independent notion of indigeneity; instead, *Australia* is satisfied with assimilating the Aboriginals into the Australian national narrative. They are an integral part, but they do not have or receive structural agency that reaches beyond stereotypical uncanny traits. In this sense, *Australia* incorporates indigeneity into the movie's notion of reconciliation in a well-intended but ultimately forced manner, thus presupposing their "consent" to have reconciliation enforced on Indigenous notions of history, identity, and futurity.

In Conclusion: Carnivalizing the Nation Space

Zacharias Kunuk's *Atanarjuat* and Baz Luhrmann's *Australia* (re)present filmic versions of national identities and are considered epic feature films. The national epos has become the genre of choice to explore and remake national imaginaries and (trans)cultural identities. *Atanarjuat* and *Australia* outline the quest for a sense of an "origin story" that can be positively reframed. Nation and nationhood are allegorized into rites of passage that the movies' main protagonists have to undergo in order to find their rightful place and role in the overarching national narratives. Intertextual references as comments on the layeredness and performativity of histories and identities are in both cases part of the aesthetic and identity-political inventory. The Australian outback and the Canadian tundra are identified as the primary spaces where national and (trans)cultural identities are negotiated. *Atanarjuat* and *Australia* are both centrally concerned with emphasizing that Indigenous (hi)stories form an integral part of Australia's and Canada's respective national identities.

However, these films pursue radically different agendas. *Atanarjuat* imagines an Inuit origin story that purportedly exists without any non-Indigenous presence, markers, or protagonists. It has been received as an authentic representation of Inuit identity prior to colonialism, and this stance runs alongside the notion that, due to colonialism, a resurrection of an untethered Inuit identity becomes necessary in the first place. This conundrum is very poignantly solved by Kunuk's feature film, for instead of displaying a sense of inwardness, of directing the filmic gaze onto an imagined Inuit authenticity, this movie breaks open the notion of authenticity and carnivalizes it. Using an array of intertextual references to Flaherty's *Nanook*, *Atanarjuat* shows how conscious it is of the "image bank of modernity," which, through the (Australian and) Canadian "politics of regret," is ironically *still* complicit in constructing a specific and derogatory image of Inuit/Indigenous identity. *Atanarjuat* does not indigenize the epos or simply remediate an oral legend onto the filmic screen, but it, in a carnivalesque manner, plays with these categories. In fact, this ironic inversion of authenticity becomes the most empowering aspect of Kunuk's feature film and thus moves well beyond the reproduction of victimhood and the polarized rhetoric of "us and them" that are the effect of "sorry politics."

Baz Luhrmann's filmic epos sets out to imagine a national narrative, a national epos that "corrects" many of Australia's historical errors. It tasks itself with empowering Australia's Indigenous peoples and reversing power relations by representing Indigenous peoples as powerful in many regards. *Australia* is particularly productive when it addresses Australia's prominent racism and translates it onto a popular culture–cinematic screen. Moreover, *Australia* effectively counters colonial hierarchies in that outback. Most importantly, Nullah (and his grandfather) become the enabling force(s) of this cattle drive, and the movie thus suggests a reading that, without Aboriginal intervention, Lady Ashley's "Australian Dream" would have never come true.

Australia, however, is arguably the most pertinent example of the paradox of carnival. For while the movie longs to be empowering to Indigenous peoples and aspires to include their histories in a national narrative as an act of justice and respect, it produces the opposite effect. In a similar manner to the pitfalls that the "politics of regret" bring with them, Aboriginal Australians are simply incorporated into the national framework, and the legacy of forcible removal is reconciled with Australian history by the allegorical act of Lady Ashley adopting Nullah. The lost children, in this vein, are repatriated and returned to the national fold, and reconciliation is enforced on Australia's Indigenous peoples. In the process, good intentions and well-meaning political agendas undergo a reverse-carnivalization.

Notes

1. Baz Luhrmann, dir., *Australia* (20th Century Fox, 2008); and Zacharias Kunuk, dir., *Atanarjuat: The Fast Runner* (Isuma, 2001). The title *Atanarjuat: The Fast Runner* will be abbreviated to *Atanarjuat*.
2. See Isuma TV, "English Press Kit on *Atanarjuat*," retrieved 30 June 2017 from http://www.isuma.tv/sites/default/files/attachments/Atan_presskit.pdf, 4, emphasis in the original.
3. Isuma TV, "English Press Kit," 1.
4. For further reading, see in particular Astrid Erll and Ann Rigney, eds., *Mediation, Remediation, and the Dynamics of Cultural Memory* (Berlin: De Gruyter, 2012).
5. See Isuma TV, "English Press Kit."
6. Shari Huhndorf, "'Atanarjuat, The Fast Runner': Culture, History and Politics," *American Anthropologist* 105, no. 4 (2003): 822–26; Michael Robert Evans, *The Fast Runner: Filming the Legend of Atanarjuat* (Lincoln: University of Nebraska Press, 2010); and Sophie McCall, "'I Can Only Sing This Song to Someone Who Understands It': Community Filmmaking and the Politics of Partial Translation in 'Atanarjuat, the Fast Runner,'" *Essays on Canadian Writing* 83 (Fall 2004): 19–46.
7. On the use of the colonial gaze, see Jeanne van Eeden, "The Colonial Gaze: Imperialism, Myths and South African Popular Culture," *Design Issues* 20, no. 2 (2004): 18–33; and Tobias Doering, "Turning the Colonial Gaze: Re-visions of Terror in Dabydeen's Turner," *Third Text* 11, no. 28 (1997): 3–14.
8. The concept of scopic regimes relates back to Christian Metz, *The Imaginary Signifier: Psychoanalysis and the Cinema* (Bloomington: University of Indiana Press, 1982).
9. See Christopher E. Gittings, *Canadian National Cinema: Ideology, Difference and Representation* (London: Routledge, 2002); Jim Leach, *Film in Canada* (Oxford: Oxford University Press, 2011); and George Melnyk, *One Hundred Years of Canadian Cinema* (Toronto: University of Toronto Press, 2004).
10. Robert J. Flaherty, dir., *Nanook of the North* (Les Frères Revillon, 1922), title in the following abbreviated to *Nanook*.
11. See Gittings, *Canadian National Cinema*; Leach, *Film in Canada*; and Melnyk, *One Hundred Years*.

12. Melnyk, *One Hundred Years*, 8.
13. Martin Jay, "Scopic Regimes of Modernity," in *Vision and Visuality*, ed. Hal Foster (Seattle: Bay Press, 1988), 3.
14. As Elsaesser and Hagener suggest, there is a plethora of ways to approach film narratology. In their outstanding work, they introduce different schools of film narratology and their historical development. For the present analysis, the institution of the eye and the capacities associated with site are of importance and are hence foregrounded. Thomas Elsaesser and Malte Hagener, *Film Theory: An Introduction through the Senses* (New York: Routledge, 2010).
15. Elsaesser and Hagener, *Film Theory*, 11, emphasis in original.
16. Elsaesser and Hagener draw on the formalist or constructivist school of thought associated with Béla Balázs and Rudolf Arnheim.
17. Elsaesser and Hagener, *Film Theory*, 94.
18. Elsaesser and Hagener, *Film Theory*, 37.
19. See in particular Laura Mulvey, *Fetishism and Curiosity: Cinema and the Mind's Eye* (Basingstoke: Palgrave Macmillan, 2013).
20. Mulvey, *Fetishism*, 3
21. See Metz, *Signifier*. See also Elsaesser and Hagener, *Film Theory*, 89–90.
22. Gittings, *Canadian National Cinema*, 9.
23. Gittings, *Canadian National Cinema*, 9–11.
24. Melnyk, *One Hundred Years*, 12.
25. Gittings, *Canadian National Cinema*, 9.
26. For obvious reasons, the analytical focus rests on Anglo-Canada.
27. Flaherty, *Nanook of the North*.
28. Derek Malcolm, "Robert Flaherty, Nanook of the North," *The Guardian*, 13 April 2000, retrieved 25 July 2017 from www.theguardian.com/film/2000/apr/13/1.
29. Kerstin Knopf, "Atanarjuat—Fast Running and Electronic Storytelling in the Arctic," in *Transcultural English Studies: Theories, Fictions, Realities*, ed. Frank Schulze-Engler and Sissy Helff (New York: Rodopi, 2009), 211.
30. Tom Crosbie, "Critical Historiography in 'Atanarjuat the Fast Runner and Ten Canoes,'" "Comparative Approaches to Indigenous Literary Studies," special issue, *Journal of New Zealand Literature* 24, no. 2 (2007): 137.
31. Crosbie, "Critical Historiography," 138.
32. See Crosbie, "Critical Historiography."
33. Leach, *Film in Canada*, 17. For a detailed historical analysis of the National Film Board of Canada, see, for example, Gary S. Evans, *In the National Interest: A Chronicle of the National Film Board of Canada from 1949 to 1989* (Toronto: University of Toronto Press, 1991).
34. See Leach, *Film in Canada*, 18.
35. Evans, *In the National Interest*, xi.
36. Evans, *In the National Interest*, 4.
37. Gittings, *Canadian National Cinema*, 77.
38. The relationship between Canadian identity and film is still prevalent, and has been translated into a negotiation of identity against the backdrop of an overly powerful American film market. Films that are subsumed under the label "Canadian national cinema" still encounter difficulties finding a national audience: the dominance of Hollywood movies and productions is seen as an obstacle to a commercially successful Canadian cinema. According to Canada's "status as a part of Hollywood's domestic . . . market," Canadian cinema is entirely "invisible." Notwithstanding this "invisibility," the relationship between (the search for) Canadian identity and (the search for) Canadian film has experi-

enced a shift from representing Canadianness monoculturally, monolithically, toward the task of finding other "nations" within the nation. Gittings, *Canadian National Cinema*, 78.
39. Isuma TV, "Filmmaking Inuit Style", retrieved 24 July 2017 from https://www.isuma.tv/atanarjuat/filmmaking-inuit-style.
40. Isuma TV, Isuma TV, "Filmmaking Inuit Style", n.p.
41. See Knopf, "Atanarjuat."
42. See IMDB, retrieved 24 July 2017 from http://www.imdb.com/title/tt0285441/.
43. See Amazon, retrieved 24 July 2017 from https://www.amazon.com/Fast-Runner-Atanarjuat-Natar-Ungalaaq/dp/B00006RG78/ref=sr_1_1?ie=UTF8&qid=1500976986&sr=8-1&keywords=atanarjuat.
44. See Netflix, retrieved 24 July 2017 from https://www.netflix.com/title/60022984.
45. See Wikipedia, retrieved 24 July 2017 from https://en.wikipedia.org/wiki/Atanarjuat:_The_Fast_Runner.
46. See, e.g., The Canadian Encyclopedia, retrieved 24 July 2017 from http://www.thecanadianencyclopedia.ca/en/article/atanarjuat-the-fast-runner/.
47. See Isuma TV, "Reviews," retrieved 24 July 2017 from https://www.isuma.tv/atanarjuat/reviews.
48. See Huhndorf, "Atanarjuat"; Evans, *Fast Runner*; and McCall, "Community Filmmaking."
49. See Arnold Krupat, "Atanarjuat, The Fast Runner and Its Audiences," *Critical Inquiry* 33, no. 3 (2007): 612.
50. See Evans, *Fast Runner*, 63.
51. Evans, *Fast Runner*, 63.
52. Evans, *Fast Runner*, 21–23.
53. Evans, *Fast Runner*, 21.
54. See also Knopf, "Atanarjuat—Fast Running and Electronic Storytelling in the Arctic." In *Transcultural English Studies: Theories, Fictions, Realities*, edited by Frank Schulze-Engler and Sissy Helff (New York: Rodopi), 201–20.
55. This Inuktitut syllabary was invented by Wesleyan missionary James Evans around 1840. For further reading, see, for example, Louis-Jacques Dorais, *The Language of the Inuit: Syntax, Semantics, and Society in the Arctic* (Montreal: McGill-Queens University Press, 2010).
56. Eduardo Fichera, "Running Barefoot across the Arctic Ice: Zacharias Kunuk's *Atanarjuat* and the Challenging of Colonial Representations" *Ethnoscripts*, 15, no. 1 (2013): 108.
57. Isuma TV, "Filmmaking Inuit Style" retrieved 24 July 2017 from https://www.isuma.tv/atanarjuat.
58. McCall, "Community Filmmaking," 22.
59. Krupat, "Atanarjuat," 611.
60. Krupat, "Atanarjuat," 611.
61. See McCall, "Community Filmmaking."
62. See also, for example, Fichera, "Running Barefoot"; Huhndorf, "Atanarjuat"; Michelle H. Raheja, "Reading Nanook's Smile: Visual Sovereignty, Indigenous Revisions of Ethnography, and Atanarjuat, The Fast Runner," *American Quarterly* 59, no. 4 (December 2007): 1159–85; and Knopf, "Electronic Storytelling."
63. *Atanarjuat*, 00:45:20–00:49:00.
64. Lucas Bessire, "Talking Back to Primitivism: Divided Audiences, Collective Desires," *American Anthropologist* 105, no. 4 (December 2003): 833.
65. Bessire, "Talking Back," 833.
66. *Atanarjuat*, 00:45:00.
67. See *Atanarjuat*, e.g. 00:48:00–00:50:00.

68. *Atanarjuat*, 02:35:30–02:44:00.
69. Bessire, "Talking Back," 834.
70. Bessire, "Talking Back," 834.
71. Isuma TV, "Filmmaking Inuit Style."
72. Marianne Hirsch, *The Generation of Postmemory: Writing and Visual Culture after the Holocaust* (New York: Columbia University Press, 2012), 106.
73. Hirsch, *Postmemory*, 106.
74. Hirsch, *Postmemory*, 111, emphasis in the original.
75. Virginia Richter, "Authenticity: Why We Still Need It Although It Does Not Exist," in *Transcultural English Studies: Theories, Fictions, Realities*, ed. Frank Schulze-Engler and Sissy Helff (New York: Rodopi, 2009), 59–74.
76. Richter, "Authenticity," 61
77. Richter, "Authenticity," 60.
78. Richter, "Authenticity," 69, emphasis in the original.
79. Krupat, "Atanarjuat," 611.
80. Krupat, "Atanarjuat," 607.
81. Krupat, "Atanarjuat," 608.
82. Krupat, "Atanarjuat," 609.
83. Krupat, "Atanarjuat," 611.
84. Krupat, "Atanarjuat," 60.
85. Krupat, "Atanarjuat," 67.
86. See Evans, *Fast Runner*.
87. Evans, *Fast Runner*, 28.
88. Evans, *Fast Runner*, 30–31.
89. Huhndorf, "Atanarjuat," 824.
90. Raheja, "Reading Nanook's Smile," 1160.
91. Knopf, "Electronic Storytelling," 216.
92. Knopf, "Electronic Storytelling," 216.
93. Knopf, "Electronic Storytelling," 216.
94. Knopf, "Electronic Storytelling," 216.
95. *Atanarjuat*, 00:50:00–01:04:38.
96. *Atanarjuat*, 01:20:00–01:31:40.
97. *Atanarjuat*, 01:33:00–01:41:40.
98. *Atanarjuat*, 01:41:40–01:45:40.
99. Lucas Bessire, "Talking Back," 833.
100. Baz Luhrmann, "How We Made the Epic of OZ," *The Guardian*, 2 November 2008, retrieved 12 November 2017 from https://www.theguardian.com/film/2008/nov/02/baz-luhrmann-nicole-kidman-australia.
101. *Australia* earned a revenue of $211 million; its economic success is only surpassed by public cinema milestones such as *Crocodile Dundee* (1986), directed by Peter Fairman, and *Mad Max: Fury Road* (2015), directed by George Miller.
102. Luhrmann, "How We Made."
103. Luhrmann, "How We Made."
104. See Theodor W. Adorno, *Noten zur Literatur*, ed. Rolf Thiedemann (Frankfurt am Main; Suhrkamp, 1991).
105. Adi Wimmer, *Australian Film: Cultures, Identities, Texts* (Trier: Wissenschaftlicher Verlag Trier, 2007), 4.
106. Wimmer, *Australian Film*, 1.
107. Wimmer, *Australian Film*, 3.

108. Marcia Langton, quoted by Germaine Greer, "Once Upon a Time in a Land Far, Far Away," *The Guardian*, 16 December 2008, retrieved 14 November 2017 from https://www.theguardian.com/film/2008/dec/16/baz-luhrmann-australia.
109. Roger Ebert, for example, praises *Australia*'s "lush epic beauty," Odette Kelada qualifies it as an "epic film," and Laleen Jayamanne analyzes it as a "preposterous national epic." Roger Ebert, "Australia: A Film Review," 25 November 2008, retrieved 5 January 2018 from https://www.rogerebert.com/reviews/australia; Odette Kelada, "Love Is a Battlefield: 'Maternal' Emotions and White Catharsis in Baz Luhrmann's Post-Apology 'Australia,'" *Studies in Australasian Cinema* 8, nos. 2–3 (2014): 83–95; and Laleene Jayamanne, "The Drover's Wives and Camp Couture: Baz Luhrmann's Preposterous National Epic," *Studies in Australasian Cinema* 4, no. 2 (2010): 131–43. See also Luhrmann, "How We Made."
110. Russel Braddock Ward, *The Australian Legend* (Melbourne: Oxford University Press, 1966).
111. See also Graeme Davison, "Rethinking the Australian Legend," *Australian Historical Studies* 43, no. 3 (2012): 429–51.
112. Davison, "Rethinking," 31.
113. Davison, "Rethinking," 30.
114. Davison, "Rethinking"
115. See also Liz Conor, "A 'Nation so Ill-Begotten': Racialized Childhood and Conceptions of National Belonging in Xavier Herbert's Poor Fellow My Country and Baz Luhrmann's Australia." *Studies in Australasian Cinema* 4, no. 2 (2010): 97–113; Kelada, "Love Is a Battlefield"; and Jayamanne, "Drover's Wives."
116. Nullah introduces himself and the history of Aboriginal dispossession in the beginning of the movie, and the plot is basically unfolded within the first 00:12:20.
117. *Australia*, 0:04:43.
118. Nullah and King George are able to sing "magic songs" in reference to Aboriginal storytelling practices, and Lady Ashley consoles Nullah after the death of his mother with the famous song "Somewhere over the Rainbow." This aspect will be discussed in more detail as the chapter unfolds.
119. Farm manager Neill Fletcher was fired by Lady Ashley, because he repeatedly misbehaved toward the Aboriginal staff on Faraway Down in general and Nullah in particular. Fletcher's behavior worsened after Nullah uncovered Fletcher's treachery. *Australia*, 00:30:00–00:35:42.
120. *Australia*, 00:35:42–00:41:20.
121. Lady Ashley sings "Somewhere over the Rainbow" for Nullah in an attempt to console him after the tragic death of his mother Daisy. *Australia*, 00:48:30–00:52:24.
122. *Australia*, 1:00:00–1:07:29.
123. *Australia*, 1:00:00–1:07:29.
124. Charles Chauvel, dir., *Jedda* (Columbia Pictures and Umbrella Entertainment, 1955). See also Kelada, "Love Is a Battlefield."
125. Kelada, "Love Is a Battlefield," 86–87.
126. Kelada, "Love Is a Battlefield," 88, emphasis in original.
127. Conor, "Nation so Ill-Begotten," 97.
128. Victor Fleming, Noel Langley, Florence Ryerson, and Edgar Allen Woolf, dirs., *The Wizard of Oz* (Metro-Goldwyn-Mayer, 1939).
129. Author L. Frank Baum introduces his famous book as a story that was "written solely to pleasure children of today." See Quentin P. Taylor, "Money and Politics in the Land of Oz," *Independent Review* 9, no. 3 (Winter 2005): 413.

130. Henry M. Littlefield, "The Wizard of Oz: Parable of Populism," *American Quarterly* 16, no. 1 (Spring 1964): 50.
131. Taylor, "Money and Politics," 414.
132. *Australia*, 00:19:45.
133. *Australia*, 00:23:00.
134. See, e.g., Littlefield, "Wizard of Oz," and Taylor, "Money and Politics."
135. *Australia*, 00:41:45–00:48:30.
136. Littlefield, "Wizard of Oz," 50.
137. *Australia*, 00:41:45.
138. *Australia*, 00:43:33.
139. *Australia*, 00:46:44.
140. *Australia*, 00:01:30.
141. Kelada, "Love Is a Battlefield," 89–90.
142. *Australia*, 00:48:20.
143. See also Conor, "Nation so Ill-Begotten," 163.
144. Conor, "Nation so Ill-Begotten," 104.
145. See Kelada, "Love Is a Battlefield," and Conor, "Nation so Ill-Begotten." *Australia*, 01:05:20.
146. Conor, "Nation so Ill-Begotten," 104.
147. *Australia*, 00:19:00–00:20:25.
148. *Australia*, 00:23:00.
149. *Australia*, 00:25:40.
150. *Australia*, 01:12:50.
151. See Edward Said, *Orientalism* (London: Routledge, 1978).
152. Conor, "Nation so Ill-Begotten," 99. Conor further outlines how the "term 'piccaninny' migrated from Britain and the United States via seamen and sealers in the early decades of settlement" and how "the use of Aboriginal motifs in settler art was first encouraged by the Australian artist Margaret Preston in a series of four articles in Art and Australia between 1925 and 1941. She urged that Aboriginal art should become the foundation and inspiration of a modern, national Australian art. Preston's art . . ., is construed from an 'alliance between art, anthropology, modernism and nationalism.'" Conor also describes how a Darwin woman refers to Nullah as a piccaninny in *Australia*.
153. See Conor, "Nation so Ill-Begotten," 104.
154. Conor, "Nation so Ill-Begotten," 104.
155. See, for example, Christine Vandamme, "'The Drover's Wife': Celebrating or Demystifying Bush Mythology?" *Commonwealth Essays and Studies* 38, no. 2 (2016): 73–81; and Liesel Hermes, "Henry Lawson's 'The Drover's Wife' in the Australian Short Story," in *Global Fragments: (Dis)Orientation in the New World Order*, edited by Anke Bartels and Dirk Wiemann (Amsterdam: Rodopi, 2007), 301–12.
156. *Australia*, 1:07:30–1:14:58.
157. *Australia*, 1:07:30.
158. *Australia*, 1:12:50.
159. *Australia*, 1:24:26–1:25:27.

Conclusion

Fictions of Reconciliation

In the introduction to the coedited volume *The Social Work of Narrative*, Gareth Griffiths argues that the

> huge and increasing discrimination of the many people displaced by war and other forms of social violence for which the wealthy countries of the so-called west [*sic*] have to take much responsibility is clearly going to be a major focus in future work on the subject of how human rights are actually practiced. How these issues are recorded and how the stories of those people are told will be a major force in the future public discourse on human rights.[1]

The pertinence of finding strategies to address human rights violations remains a characteristic feature of different historical and identity-political contexts across the world. Although the systems of forcible removal and cultural re-education belong to a (not so distant) past, their impact on national identities and historical inventories remains unbroken, as this study has shown. The Australian and Canadian versions of reconciliation discussed in this work indicate the increasing visibility of Indigenous histories and (post)colonial legacies. This specific framework of reworking the past has "traveled" from South Africa to Australia and Canada and their contexts of state-sanctioned "politics of regret." This trajectory cuts across different Indigenous cultures and simultaneously attests to a demand for trans-Indigenous approaches to identity politics.[2] Although certainly not unproblematic in nature and performance, reconciliation and "sorry politics," as this analysis has outlined, do stand for a general shift in power hierarchies within the global community of marginalized (Indigenous) peoples. In relation to Griffiths's question of how human rights are actually practiced, reconciliation processes and performances of redress provide space for renegotiating national identities, but they also bring to light the difficulties, frictions, inconsistencies, and even injustices that accompany these processes.

"Sorry politics" in the shape of public apologies and inquiries enable the temporary reversal of existing social hierarchies and discursive power structures. They operate with the rhetoric of empowerment of the (formerly) oppressed; commissions facilitate a voicing-out of traumatic experiences in order to move to center stage oftentimes silenced or unperceived Indigenous voices. The public apologies in Australia, and particularly in Canada, paid respect to the resilience and pride of both countries' Indigenous populations.

Nevertheless, the carnivalesque holds its own paradoxes, as this analysis has underlined: When carnival is over, societies return to a status quo ante. Fundamental and tangible social change cannot be brought about by "politics of regret" alone. Moreover, these performative identity politics enable the state to reinvent itself as an agent of reconciliation and ultimately use struggles in coming to terms with traumatic histories to legitimate the status quo. In this way, Indigenous peoples are subsequently incorporated into the national framework and integrated into national narratives. The "politics of regret" are thus prone to slip into and eventually reproduce notions of cultural containment, schematic identities, and even stereotypes. Despite benevolent intentions and righteous identity-political agendas, the work of the truth commissions in both countries has run the risk of reiterating the Indigenous-as-victim template. The rhetoric of empowerment hence often results in performances of victimhood. To describe the identity-political performances of public apologies and truth commissions from a position that is indifferent to transcultural entanglements reduces the carnivalesque to the mechanisms of reiteration and (binary) reversal. "Sorry politics" produce seemingly empowering images and narratives that run against the national identity grain, yet they frame the process of center-staging Indigenous suffering as "the right thing to do," as a righteous and ultimately just act of rectifying history. The subversive nature of the carnivalesque, however, is confined to the backseat.

Since Australian and Canadian reconciliation is structurally rooted in an us-versus-them paradigm, these "politics of regret" fail to represent social and cultural realities. Gareth Griffiths emphasizes that the "cultural imaginary forms the unacknowledged ground upon which both oppressor and oppressed construct their social and legal being."[3] The narrative renderings and performative reiterations of traumatic histories are a vital part of processes of coming to terms with the past. Admittedly, literary fiction and cultural imaginations cannot remedy social imbalances and ultimately make the world a better place. But to engage with violations, with individual and collective traumata, can be seen as a social process as well as a social force in its own right. Fiction can shed light on (trans)cultural realities, historical entanglements, and imagined futures with its own formal and aesthetic inventory, and from its own perspective. Reconciliation's inner tensions and contradictions can become the subject of imaginative, playful and unpredictable explorations of identities and hierarchies that run against reconciliation's "official grain." While one can thus subscribe to Griffiths's emphasis on the importance of cultural productions in identity-political contexts, Griffiths's statement should warn us that undercomplex binary identity schemata, which are characteristic of official reconciliation discourses in Canada and Australia, can also be found in some of the fictional examples discussed here.

Akin to the "politics of regret," simplistic representations of cultures and identities occur when too much emphasis is placed on "political correctness" and ethical imperatives. A productive engagement with historical legacies that involve oppression and cultural eradication cannot but address what Griffiths calls "the change inherent in diversity [that] has to be embraced if humanity is to survive."[4] It is the explorative and imaginary nature of fiction that allows us to look beyond political constraints and "red tapes" in identity politics, because

> [s]tory, image, song and written or spoken memories all act to construct the cultural imaginary from which we derive our own identity and through which we seek, however inadequately, to perceive that of others, recognizing the ways in which they differ from us and the ways in which we share their concerns and needs.[5]

Cultural productions form part of the larger processes of reconciliation in Australia and Canada that predate the "politics of regret" with the two public apologies and the commissions to rework the systems of cultural reeducation. These processes are carried and governed by political climates, activist engagements, court decisions, and grassroots movements, to name just a few of the key agents of reconciliation. They range from national "sorry days" as instances of institutionalized collective remembrance and local initiatives relating to education and healthcare of the respective Indigenous populations to the creation of national archives as resources for a "reconciled future" and changed school curricula and university programs in Indigenous studies. These processes form a concerted but *longue durée* attack on well-established social hierarchies, and they impact national and (trans)cultural identities in the long term. As this study has shown, these processes constitute a much broader framework with ultimately noncontainable trajectories, outcomes, and identity discourses. The carnivalesque as a research perspective contingent on a binary logic reaches its limits here. The notion of reiteration and reversal if taken at face value is too schematic to fully account for the multiple, at times concerted, at times confrontational processes of reconciliation.

As such, it runs the risk of losing its edge if it is deprived of its exploratory and subversive potential so powerfully highlighted by Bakhtin, albeit in a very different context almost a century ago.

In the context of literary fiction and feature films, the carnivalesque becomes the reflection of an identity-political attitude as well as an aesthetics. The writers and directors discussed in this analysis all take a stance on "sorry politics" as well as on ongoing reconciliation processes. In a more or less straightforward manner, the artists voice their positions as publicly visible figures. As such, this analysis helps bring to light the familiar rhetoric of empowering the Indigenous, of storytelling as a form of justice, and the impetus to explore (post)colonial legacies in the national narratives of Canada and Australia. The artist's voice and the identity politics represented in their works aim to leave their mark on reconciliation processes. These authors and filmmakers are driven by the understanding that cultural productions can actually contribute to and leave a mark on identity politics, because they are able to amplify, subvert, or invest in identities and histories that are inaccessible to the political sphere.

Yet, as I have shown, the paradox of the carnivalesque—to be empowering but at the same time limiting as a result of an overemphasis on political, representational correctness—is also visible in the fictional texts discussed here. The structure of this work, the juxtaposition of texts that produce productive and nonschematic identities and histories through carnivalesque inventories and strategies and texts that resort to more simplistic categories, is representative of the fallacy embedded in the carnivalesque, as it can easily become an amplifier for stereotypes and overly simplistic "lessons of history" that are culturally reproduced. In a similar vein to the carnivalesque moment within "sorry politics," an overemphasis on benevolent intentions and identity-political agendas in connection with the paradigms of empowerment, voicing-out, and writing back to Indigenous mistreatment results in texts that struggle under the pressure of having to be politically "correct" and hypersensitive to different notions of indigeneity and the Indigenous voice. In these instances, the carnivalesque is deprived of its cutting edge and its potential to explore and enable aesthetic transgressions.

Canadian author Joseph Boyden and Australian writer Gail Jones both pursued the self-set task to fictionally intervene in "sorry politics." Both artists set out to "correct," to reimagine formative national myths in their respective contexts. *Three Day Road* and *Sorry* pursue these agendas by carnivalizing well-nurtured historical "truths." Boyden, a highly visible and now utterly controversial protagonist in the context of who is to represent indigeneity, emblematically stands for the self-set task to artistically intervene in the discourses of reconciliation, and also the dangers that come with it. *Three Day Road* posits seemingly "authentic Indians" (Xavier, Niska) against "authentic settler descendant Canadians" in an attempt to indigenize the formative Canadian national narrative of World War I participation. This text features the most interesting trickster-fool character, Elijah, who oscillates between the cultural poles but is doomed to be killed by his best friend Xavier, who represents Boyden's notion of authentic indigeneity. Elijah, the carnivalesque protagonist, by contrast is a transcultural figure. He is pitted against at times highly stereotypical renderings of Indigenous and non-Indigenous identities: *Three Day Road* particularly explores notions of Indianness that are hardly viable. The carnivalesque once again displays its paradoxical nature: although it is empowering in terms of introducing the Indigenous to formative national narratives, simplistic identity portfolios are the result, and the complex, subversive, ultimately carnivalesque, and transcultural trickster-fool is doomed to die. *Three Day Road*'s version of reconciliation imagines an Indigenous retreat to the bush as the future of indigeneity.

Gail Jones wanted to produce a literary apology to Australia's Aboriginal population and attempted to refrain from appropriating the Indigenous voice within her historical novel. Yet, this well-intended strategy results in silencing Indigenous characters entirely be reducing them to pawns in a symbolic match between Australian and British identity. Driven by its benevolent identity political agenda, *Sorry* loses itself in reiterating ultimately colonial tropes that are powerful remnants of the quest to construct a sense of Australianness: Aboriginal protagonists are rendered voiceless victims of superior forces, while the question of settler guilt is resolved in settler daughter Perdita. The silenced Aboriginal servant girl goes to prison and sacrifices herself. Perdita becomes the person upon whom reconciliation hinges: *Sorry* bears witness to how she copes with her childhood trauma and recuperates her voice, and renders this narrative an allegory of Australian identity in the context of reconciliation. Moreover, William Shakespeare and his works as intertextual references are used to infer a notion of alleged cultural superiority related to settler identity, which requires transformation into Australianness. Perdita becomes Australian once she addresses her trauma and reconciles with her own personal guilt. Gail Jones's novel renders reconciliation an important part of Australian identity, but in the end it is a self-serving endeavor. Contrary to its benevolent identity-political intentions, *Sorry* reproduces ultimately colonial national narratives, and the initial agenda to reverse them results in simplistic "lessons of colonial history." In this manner, *Sorry* reverse-carnivalizes its potential to intervene in Australian identity-politics.

Tomson Highway's engagement with the discourses surrounding the systems of forcible cultural reeducation paints a more complex picture. He is also a very public figure in the context of pro-Indigenous activism and the promotion of Indigenous art. In *Kiss of the Fur Queen*, Highway intertwines autobiographical aspects with literary fiction, thus centering on family dynamics in the context of suffering, abuse, and the loss of culture. In alignment with the victim paradigm that the "politics of regret" are complicit in reiterating, Highway's novel strangely remains confined to victimizing its protagonists continuously. Gabriel and Jeremiah are stuck in an incessant repetition of suffering, marginalization, loss, and victimhood that only death promises relief from. Yet, Highway's text is particularly powerful in terms of exploring how his protagonists Gabriel and Jeremiah make sense not only of their notion of belonging but also of their traumas through an ultimately transcultural and carnivalesque representational inventory. The perpetrator, whose voice remains curiously absent within the framework of "sorry politics," is represented as a traditionally Indigenous evil character, the *Weetigo*. In fact, the perpetrator is a catholic priest turned *Weetigo*, and this representational strategy points toward transcultural identities and aesthetics that can be described and brought to life with the inventory of the carnivalesque. Moreover, *Kiss of the Fur Queen* features the Fur Queen, a trickster figure who transgresses all notions of cultural containment and becomes the two brothers' guardian angel. The carnivalesque unfolds its full critical and explorative potential precisely through these noncanonical identities and characters and sheds light on the ultimately transcultural entanglements that colonialism and globalization have generated in Canada.

Kim Scott's novel *Benang* with its floating protagonist is particularly powerful in terms of exploring the victim-perpetrator relations. Harley is framed as being constantly detached from the solid grounds of cultural belonging. This text represents the two sides of the colonial coin: *Benang* retraces what it means to be a victim as well as a perpetrator and imagines what a complete reversal of power hierarchies could look like. Harley turns the tables on Ern, rendering him speechless, voiceless, and helpless. This text does not remain confined to the gesture of reversal, but Harley rather invites Ern to come along as Harley discovers his Indigenous heritage. In this manner, *Benang* emphasizes the highly subjective and explorative nature of cultural belonging. *Benang*'s vision of reconciliation imagines inclusion and mutual exchange as paramount to the quest. As the story progresses, doubts as to the fidelity of the narrative voice arise, rendering Harley an unreliable narrator. With this narrative strategy, *Benang* throws the historical novel back on itself, questioning canonical notions of historical knowledge and remembering, rendering it experiential and experimental.

Zacharias Kunuk's feature film *Atanarjuat* ventures into a similar strategic direction when it pretends to imagine Inuit identities and histories in absence of any non-Indigenous or colonial presence. Upon closer observation, this filmic epos plays with cultural entanglements in terms of storytelling, specifically through intertextual connections. *Atanarjuat* thus appears culturally conditioned on the one hand—it is an Inuit oral legend that is shown on the screen, and it deals with conflicts in an Inuit collective. The language is inaccessible to any non-Inuit, and the arctic landscape becomes the space on which Inuit identities and histories are projected. On the other hand, this epic feature film is ultimately conscious of the "colonial gaze," and "films back" to it. It plays with the expectations and conventions of Hollywood cinema, employing epic timing, long shots, handheld cameras, etc. In effect, *Atanarjuat* breaks open a seemingly authentic rendering of Inuit cultural history and carnivalizes the truthfulness of authenticity. The epos becomes both indigenized and modernized through its remediation on the cinematic screen. Moreover, it potentially transports Indigenous histories beyond the Canadian national borders. The aesthetic and formal transgressions that *Atanarjuat* displays are detached from simplistic identities and narratives.

Baz Luhrmann's filmic epos *Australia* is also impacted by its director's personal stance on Australian history. His intervention into the discourses of reconciliation sets out to reconcile settler achievements in Australia with the legacy of the Stolen Generations. This movie is exemplary of the tension embedded in the carnivalesque: with an array of intertextual references, *Australia* strives to open up Australia's formative national narrative, the myth of the bushman as the founding figure and chief representative of a specific notion of Australianness, toward other identities. Nullah, the representative of the Stolen Generations, is particularly powerful, because he is the narrator for most of the movie. Moreover, he saves the cattle drive, and hence enables Lady Ashley's transition into a female drover. *Australia* also addresses and contests the structural racism that is characteristic of the eponymous country. Yet, and in a similar manner to Jones's *Sorry*, Luhrmann's film solves the conundrum accompanying transcultural encounters and reconciliation discourses by imaging a white "Mother Australia" as the culmination point of Australia's struggles, as well as their remedy. Lady Ashley as the born English aristocrat who transforms into a female drover, thus embracing her true Australianness, becomes the solution to and Luhrmann's version of reconciliation: Australia adopts its stolen children. As a result, the promising trickster-fool character of Nullah gradually is rendered a pawn in *Australia*'s identity-political agenda. This movie is indicative of how well-meaning identity-political intentions on the part of its creator result in their involuntary reverse-carnivalization. This dynamic leads to this surprisingly shallow conclusion, and to a disturbing aftertaste that the movie leaves behind.

In the context of cultural productions, the carnivalesque has become a vehicle to transport the text's own notions of reconciliation, or fictions of reconciliation, which mostly embrace difference but also highlight commonalities. As an aesthetic category, it has challenged unambiguity, but it also poses questions as to the viability of radically transcultural identities. Such a carnivalesque text or figure runs against reconciliation's official grain and strives to highlight inconsistencies, frictions and fractions, tensions as well as (im)possibilities, and imaginaries that characterize the struggle to come to terms with the past. The ambiguous nature of the carnivalesque puts an emphasis on subversive aesthetics and not on correction, intervention, and rectification. Joseph Boyden's trickster-fool Elijah is such an example where a carnivalesque aesthetics becomes the enabler of imaging noncanonical identities.

In summary, the carnivalesque has proven to be a relevant and pertinent lens to approach the ways in which Canadian and Australian social relations and transcultural identities are negotiated. It has enabled a description in this work of the reemergence of schematic identities that are a product of "sorry politics." In addition, to reconnect the carnivalesque to its conceptual origins—which lie in cultural productions and fictional narratives—has proven to be vital to work out its subversive and critical potential. This transcultural aspect has frequently gotten lost or even been belittled in the performances of reconciliation. An analysis of fictional engagements with reconciliation contexts through the multiple frameworks that the carnivalesque provides has shown how pertinent cultural productions and artistic imaginations are to contemporary identity politics. Literary and filmic world-making provide venues to negotiate national and (trans)cultural identities without the constraints of a discursive regime of political correctness. Cultural productions are seismographs, amplifiers, clairvoyants, or prophets of doom, and as such, they enrich critical insights into the mechanisms of reconciliation and shed light on identities unfolding. Gareth Griffiths's claim that it will be of interest to academia to study how human rights are actually done, and practiced, resonates within this study, as it hopes to have shown that values, identities, and histories are negotiated in many different arenas, and with and through various agents. An analysis of the practices and performances of human rights that is indifferent to fiction and cultural imaginaries fails to capture its nuances and trajectories.

Notes

1. Gareth Griffiths, "Introduction," in *The Social Work of Narrative*, ed. Gareth Griffiths and Peter Mead (Stuttgart: ibidem, 2018), 4.
2. See Chadwick Allen, *Trans-Indigenous: Methodologies for Global Native Literary Studies* (Minneapolis: University of Minnesota Press, 2012), and chapter 2 of this book.
3. Griffiths, "Introduction," 5.
4. Griffiths, "Introduction," 9.
5. Griffiths, "Introduction," 9.

Bibliography

Aboriginal and Torres Strait Islander Healing Foundation. "Bringing Them Home 20 Years On: An Action Plan for Healing," 2017. Retrieved 20 October 2020 from https://healingfoundation.org.au/app/uploads/2017/05/Bringing-Them-Home-20-years-on-FINAL-SCREEN-1.pdf.
Acland, Peregrine. *All Else Is Folly*. Toronto: Dundurn Press, 2014 [1929].
Adams, Jenni. *Magic Realism in Holocaust Literature: Troping the Traumatic Real*. Basingstoke: Palgrave Macmillan, 2011.
Adichie, Chimamanda Ngozi. "The Danger of a Single Story." TEDGlobal, 2009. Retrieved 5 February 2018 from https://www.ted.com/talks/chimamanda_adichie_the_danger_of_a_single_story.
Adorno, Theodor W., and Rolf Tiedemann, eds. "Noten zur Literatur. 1." *Suhrkamp-Taschenbuch Wissenschaft* 355 (2002).
Ahrens, Rüdiger, and Karin Ikas, eds. *Violence and Transgression in World Minority Literatures*. Heidelberg: Winter, 2005.
Alexander, Cynthia J. "Wiring the Nation! Including First Nations? Aboriginal Canadians and Federal e-Government Initiatives." *Journal of Canadian Studies* 35, no. 4 (2001): 277–97.
Ali, Suki. *Mixed-Race, Post-Race: Gender, New Ethnicities, and Cultural Practices*. New York: Berg, 2003.
Alia, Valerie. *New Media Nation: Indigenous Peoples and Global Communication*. New York: Berghahn Books, 2010.
Alia, Valerie, and Simone Bull. *Media and Ethnic Minorities*. Edinburgh: Edinburgh University Oress, 2005.
Allain, Paul, and Jen Harvie. *The Routledge Companion to Theatre and Performance*. 2nd ed. Hoboken, NJ: Taylor and Francis, 2014.
Allan, Alfred. "The South African Truth and Reconciliation Commission as a Therapeutic Tool." *Behavioral Sciences & the Law* 18, no. 4 (2000): 459–77.
———. "Truth and Reconciliation: A Psycholegal Perspective." *Ethnicity & Health* 5 (2000). Retrieved 25 March 2018 http://www.ingentaconnect.com/content/routledg/ceth/2000/00000005/F0020003/art00002.

Allen, Chadwick. *Trans-Indigenous: Methodologies for Global Native Literary Studies*. Minneapolis: University of Minnesota Press, 2012.
Allen, Jonathan. "Balancing Justice and Social Unity: Political Theory and the Idea of a Truth and Reconciliation Commission." *University of Toronto Law Journal* 49, no. 3 (Summer 1999). http://www.jstor.org/stable/826002.
Amid, Jonathan, and Leon De Kock. "The Crime Novel in Post-Apartheid South Africa: A Preliminary Investigation." *Scrutiny2* 19, no. 1 (2 January 2014): 52–68. https://doi.org/10.1080/18125441.2014.906232.
Amstutz, Mark R. *The Healing of Nations: The Promise and Limits of Political Forgiveness*. Lanham, MD: Rowman & Littlefield, 2005.
Anderson, Benedict R. O.'G. *Imagined Communities: Reflections on the Origin and Spread of Nationalism*. Rev. ed. New York: Verso, 2016.
Anderson, Willow J. "'Indian Drum in the House': A Critical Discourse Analysis of an Apology for Canadian Residential Schools and the Public's Response," *International Communication Gazette* 74, no. 6 (2012): 571–85.
Andrew-Gee, Eric. "The Making of Joseph Boyden." *The Globe and Mail*, 4 August 2017. Retrieved 29 November 2020 from https://beta.theglobeandmail.com/arts/books-and-media/joseph-boyden/article35881215/?ref=http://www.theglobeandmail.com&.
Andrews, Molly. *Shaping History: Narratives of Political Change*. New York: Cambridge University Press, 2007.
Antor, Heinz. "Die Vermittlung interkultureller Kompetenz an der Universität: Das Beispiel Kanada." In *Interkulturelle Kompetenz: Konzepte und Praxis des Unterrichts*, edited by Wolfgang Gehring, Klaus Stierstorfer, and Laurenz Volkmann, 143–64. Tübingen: Narr, 2002.
———, ed. *Inter- und transkulturelle Studien: Theoretische Grundlagen und interdisziplinäre Praxis*. Heidelberg: Winter, 2006.
———, ed. *Refractions of Germany in Canadian Literature and Culture*. Berlin: De Gruyter, 2003.
Appiah, Kwame Anthony. *The Lies that Bind: Creed, Country, Colour, Class*. London: Profile Books, 2016.
Armitage, Andrew. *Comparing the Policy of Aboriginal Assimilation: Australia, Canada, and New Zealand*. Vancouver: UBC Press, 1995.
Armitage, David. *The Ideological Origins of the British Empire*. Cambridge: Cambridge University Press, 2000.
Arnold, Sabine, ed. *Politische Inszenierungen im 20. Jahrhundert: Zur Sinnlichkeit der Macht*. Wien: Böhlau, 1998.
Arnold, Sabine, Christian Fuhrmeister, and Dietmar Schiller. "Hüllen und Masken der Politik." In *Politische Inszenierungen im 20. Jahrhundert: Zur Sinnlichkeit der Macht*, edited by Sabine Arnold, 7–25. Wien: Böhlau, 1998.
Arnsfeld, Andreas. *Medien—Politik—Gesellschaft: Aspekte ihrer Wechselwirkungen unter dem Stichwort Politainment*. Marburg: Tectum, 2005.
Arthur, Jay. "Representing the Stolen Generations in the National Museum of Australia." *Coolabah* 3 (2009): 1–11.
Ashcroft, Bill, Gareth Griffiths, and Helen Tiffin. *The Empire Writes Back: Theory and Practice in Post-colonial Literatures*. London: Routledge, 2002.
Ashkanasy, Neal M., Edwin Trevor-Roberts, and Louise Earnshaw. "The Anglo Cluster: Legacy of the British Empire." *Journal of World Business* 37, no. 1 (2002). Retrieved April 20 2019 http://www.sciencedirect.com/science/article/pii/S1090951601000724.
Askew, Kelly, and Richard R. Wilk, eds. *The Anthropology of Media: A Reader*. Victoria: Blackwell Publishing, 2002.

Asmal, Kader. "Truth, Reconciliation and Justice: The South African Experience in Perspective." *Modern Law Review* 63, no. 1 (2000). http://onlinelibrary.wiley.com/doi/10.1111/1468-2230.00248/abstract. (April 27, 2019).

Assmann, Aleida. *Der lange Schatten der Vergangenheit: Erinnerungskultur und Geschichtspolitik*. München: Beck, 2006.

———. *Erinnerungsräume: Formen und Wandlungen des kulturellen Gedächtnisses*. 3rd ed. München: Beck, 2006.

———. "Formen des Vergessens." *Historische Geisteswissenschaften: Frankfurter Vorträge* 9 (2016).

———. *Geschichte im Gedächtnis: Von der individuellen Erfahrung zur öffentlichen Inszenierung*. München: C. H. Beck, 2007.

———. "How History Takes Place." In *Memory, History and Colonialism: Engaging with Pierre Nora in Colonial and Postcolonial Contexts*, edited by Andreas Gestrich, 151–67. London: German Historical Institute, 2009.

———, ed. "Medien des Gedächtnisses." Special issue, *Deutsche Vierteljahrsschrift für Literaturwissenschaft und Geistesgeschichte* (1998).

Assmann, Aleida, and Sebastian Conrad, eds. *Memory in a Global Age: Discourses, Practices and Trajectories*. Houndsmills: Palgrave Macmillan, 2010.

Assmann, Aleida, and Linda Shortt, eds. *Memory and Political Change*. London: Palgrave Macmillan, 2012.

Assmann, Jan. *Cultural Memory and Early Civilization: Writing, Remembrance, and Political Imagination*. Cambridge: Cambridge University Press, 2011.

———. *Das kulturelle Gedächtnis: Schrift, Erinnerung und politische Identität in frühen Hochkulturen*. München: Beck, 1999.

———. "Globalization, Universalism, and the Erosion of Cultural Memory." In *Memory in a Global Age: Discourses, Practices and Trajectories*, edited by Aleida Assmann and Sebastian Conrad. Houndsmills: Palgrave Macmillan, 2010.

Assmann, Jan, Alessandra Corti, and Elena Esposito. "Soziales Vergessen: Formen und Medien des Gedächtnisses der Gesellschaft." *Orig.-Ausg* 1 (2002).

Attard, Bernard, and Carl Bridge, eds. *Between Empire and Nation: Australia's External Relations from Federation to the Second World War*. Kew: Australian Scholarly Publishing, 2000.

Attwood, Bain. "The Australian Patient: Traumatic Pasts and the Work of History." In *The Geography of Meanings: Psychoanalytic Perspectives on Place, Space, Land, and Dislocation*, edited by Maria Teresa Savio Hook. London: International Psychoanalytical Association, 2007.

———. "The Burden of the Past in the Present." In *Essays on Australian Reconciliation*, edited by Michelle Grattan, 254–59. Melbourne: Bookman Press, 2000.

———. "In the Age of Testimony: The Stolen Generations Narrative, 'Distance,' and Public History." *Public Culture* 20, no. 1 (2008). Retreived 14 March 2019 http://publicculture.org/articles/view/20/1/in-the-age-of-testimony-the-stolen-generations-na.

———. "Learning about the Truth: The Stolen Generations Narrative." In *Telling Stories: Indigenous History and Memory in Australia and New Zealand*, edited by Fiona Magowan and Bain Attwood. Sydney: Allen & Unwin, 2001, 183–212.

———. "Making History, Imagining Aborigines and Australia." In *Prehistory to Politics: John Mulvaney, the Humanities and the Public Intellectual*, edited by Tim Bonyhady, 98–116. Melbourne: Melbourne University Press, 1996.

———. *The Making of the Aborigines*. Sydney: Allen & Unwin, 1989.

———. "The Officers: On the Ground." In *Many Voices: Reflections on Experiences of Indigenous Child Separation*, edited by Doreen Mellor and Anna Haebich. Canberra: National Library of Australia, 2002.

———. "Reconciliation, Assimilation, and the Indigenous Peoples of Australia." *International Political Science Review* 24 (2003): 491–513.

———. *Telling the Truth about Aboriginal History*. Crows Nest: Allen & Unwin, 2005.

Attwood, Bain, and Andrew Markus. *The 1967 Referendum: Race, Power and the Australian Constitution*. 2nd ed. Canberra: Aboriginal Studies Press, 2007.

———. "The Fight for Aboriginal Rights." In *The Australian Century: Political Struggle in the Building of a Nation*, edited by Robert Manne, 264–92. Melbourne: Text Publishing, 1999.

Aufderheide, Patricia. *Documentary Film: A Very Short Introduction*. Oxford: Oxford University Press, 2007.

Augustinus, Aurelius. "Confessions." Edited by Carolyn J.-B. Hammond. *The Loeb Classical Library* 27 (2016).

Auslander, Philip, ed. *Performance: Critical Concepts in Literary and Cultural Studies*. London: Routledge, 2003.

Austin, John L., and James O. Urmson, eds. *How to Do Things with Words*. Cambridge, MA: Harvard University Press, 2009.

Axford, Barrie, and Richard Huggins. *New Media and Politics*. London: Sage, 2001.

Baker, Houston A., Manthia Diawara, and Ruth H. Lindeborg. *Black British Cultural Studies: A Reader*. Chicago: University of Chicago Press, 1996.

Bakhtin, Mikhail M. *Rabelais and His World*. Bloomington: Indiana University Press, 1984.

Banerjee, Mita, ed. "Comparative Indigenous Studies." *American Studies—A Monograph Series* 268 (2016).

Bardeleben, Renate von, Klaus H. Schmidt, and Sabina Matter-Seibel, eds. "Print." *American Multiculturalism and Ethnic Survival* 59 (2012).

Barkan, Elazar. *The Guilt of Nations: Restitution and Negotiating Historical Injustices*. Johns Hopkins Paperbacks. Baltimore: Johns Hopkins University Press, 2001.

Barkan, Elazar, and Alexander Karn, eds. *Taking Wrongs Seriously: Apologies and Reconciliation*. Stanford, CA: Stanford University Press, 2006.

Barker, Chris, and Paul E. Willis. *Cultural Studies: Theory and Practice*. Los Angeles: Sage, 2012.

Barnett, Clive. "'Sing Along with the Common People': Politics, Postcolonialism and Other Figures." *Environment and Planning D: Society and Space* 15, no. 2 (1997). http://oro.open.ac.uk/24196/.

Barrera, Jorge. "Joseph Boyden's Shape-Shifting Indigenous Identity." APTN, 23 December 2016. Retrieved 29 November 2020 from http://aptnnews.ca/2016/12/23/author-joseph-boydens-shape-shifting-indigenous-identity/.

Bartels, Anke, and Dirk Wiemann, eds. *Global Fragments: (Dis)Orientation in the New World Order*. Amsterdam: Rodopi, 2010.

Bassler, Moritz, and New Historicism, eds. *2. aktualisierte Auflage*. Tübingen, Basel: Francke, 2001.

BBC News, "Does Trudeau Apologize Too Much?" 28 March 2019, retrieved 1 December 2020 from https://www.bbc.com/news/world-us-canada-43560817.

Beasley, Edward. *The Victorian Reinvention of Race: New Racisms and the Problem of Grouping in the Human Sciences*. New York: Routledge, 2010.

Belleflamme, Valérie-Anne. "'Shakespeare Was Wrong': Counter-discursive Intertextuality in Gail Jones' Sorry." *Journal of Postcolonial Writing* 51, no. 6 (2015): 661–71.

———. "Saying the Unsayable: Imagining Reconciliation in Gail Jones' *Sorry*," *English Text Construction* 8, no. 2 (2015): 161–62.

Benjamin, Walter. "Über Sprache überhaupt und über die Sprache des Menschen." In *Gesammelte Schriften*, edited by Walter Benjamin, Rolf Tiedemann, and Hermann Schweppenhäuser, 140–57. Frankfurt am Main: Suhrkamp, 1991.

Benjamin, Walter, Rolf Tiedemann, and Hermann Schweppenhäuser, eds. *Gesammelte Schriften*. Frankfurt am Main: Suhrkamp, 1991.
Bennett, Bruce, ed. *Resistance and Reconciliation: Writing in the Commonwealth*. Canberra: ACLALS, 2003.
Bennett, W. Lance. "Global Media and Politics: Transnational Communication Regimes and Civic Cultures." *Annual Review of Political Science* 7 (2004). http://www.annualreviews.org/doi/abs/10.1146/annurev.polisci.7.012003.104804.
Berg, Manfred, and Bernd Schäfer, eds. *Historical Justice in International Perspective: How Societies Are Trying to Right the Wrongs of the Past*. Washington, DC: German Historical Institute; Cambridge University Press, 2009.
Bessire, Lucas. "Talking Back to Primitivism: Divided Audiences, Collective Desires." *American Anthropologist* 105, no. 4 (December 2003): 832–36.
Besterman, Tristram. "Returning a Stolen Generation." *Museum International* 1 (2009): 107–11.
Bhabha, Homi K. "Introduction: Narrating the Nation." In *Nation and Narration*, edited by Homi K. Bhabha, 1–25. London: Routledge, 1990.
———, ed. *Nation and Narration*. London: Routledge, 1990.
———. *The Location of Culture*. London: Routledge, 2004.
———. "The World and the Home." *Social Text* 31 (1992). http://www.jstor.org/stable/i220063.
Bird, Carmel, ed. *The Stolen Children: Their Stories*. Sydney: Random House, 1998.
Birk, Hanne. *AlterNative Memories: Kulturspezifische Inszenierungen von Erinnerung in zeitgenössischen Romanen indigener Autor/inn/en Australiens, Kanadas und Aotearoas/Neuseelands*. Trier: WVT, 2008.
Block, Summer. "Interview with Gail Jones." *January Magazine*, May 2008. Retrieved 21 December 2016 from http://januarymagazine.com/profiles/gailjones.html.
Bloom, Harold, ed. *The Trickster*. New York: Infobase Publishing, 2010.
Boelling, Gordon. "'A Part of Our History That So Few Knew About': Native Involvement in Canada's Great War—Joseph Boyden's Three Day Road." In *Inventing Canada/Inventer Le Canada*, edited by Klaus D. Ertler and Martin Loeschnigg, 253–68. Frankfurt am Main: Lang, 2008.
Boesch, Michael, ed. *Südafrikas Inszenierung der Wahrheit: Die politische Erinnerungskultur nach der Apartheid*. Schwerte: Katholische Akademie Schwerte, 2010.
Bolter, J. David, ed. *Remediation: Understanding New Media*. Cambridge: MIT Press, 2000.
Bombay, Amy, Kimberley Matheson, and Hymie Anisman. "Expectations among Aboriginal Peoples in Canada Regarding the Potential Impacts of a Government Apology." *Political Psychology* 34, no.3 (2013): 443–60.
Bond, Lucy, Stef Craps, and Pieter Vermeulen, eds. *Memory Unbound: Tracing the Dynamics of Memory Studies*. New York: Berghahn, 2017.
Bond, Lucy, and Jessica Rapson, eds. *The Transcultural Turn: Interrogating Memory between and beyond Borders*. Media and Cultural Memory/Medien Und Kulturelle Erinnerung, vol. 15. Boston: De Gruyter, 2014.
Bonyhady, Tim, ed. *Prehistory to Politics: John Mulvaney, the Humanities and the Public Intellectual*. Melbourne: Melbourne University Press, 1996.
Borgards, Roland, ed. *Texte zur Kulturtheorie und Kulturwissenschaft*. Stuttgart: Reclam, 2010.
Bourdieu, Pierre. "Symbolic Power." *Critique of Anthropology* 4, no. 13/14 (1979): 77–85.
Bowe, Heather J., and Kylie Martin. *Communication across Cultures: Mutual Understanding in a Global World*. New York: Cambridge University Press, 2007.
Boyden, Joseph. "My Name Is Joseph Boyden." MacLeans, 2 August 2017, retrieved 29 November 2020 from http://www.macleans.ca/news/canada/my-name-is-joseph-boyden/.

———. *Three Day Road*. London: Penguin, 2005.
Brannigan, John. *New Historicism and Cultural Materialism*. New York: St. Martin's Press, 1998.
Bridge, Carl, and Kent Fedorowich. *The British World: Diaspora, Culture, and Identity*. London: F. Cass, 2003.
Briskman, Linda. *The Black Grapevine: Aboriginal Activism and the Stolen Generations*. Annandale: Federation Press, 2003.
Brito, Alexandra Barahona de, ed. *The Politics of Memory: Transnational Justice in Democratizing Societies*. Oxford: Oxford University Press, 2004.
Brooks, Roy L. "The Age of Apology." In *When Sorry Isn't Enough: The Controversy over Apologies and Reparations for Human Injustice*, edited by Roy L. Brooks. New York: New York University Press, 1999.
———, ed. *When Sorry Isn't Enough: The Controversy over Apologies and Reparations for Human Injustice*. New York: New York University Press, 1999.
Brounéus, Karen. "Analyzing Reconciliation: A Structured Method for Measuring National Reconciliation Initiatives." *Peace and Conflict: Journal of Peace Psychology* 14, no. 3 (2008): 291–313.
Brown, Amy Benson, and Karen Poremski, eds. *Roads to Reconciliation: Conflict and Dialogue in the Twenty-First Century*. Armonk, NY: M. E. Sharpe, 2005.
Brummett, Barry. *The Politics of Style and the Style of Politics*. Lanham, MD: Lexington Books, 2011.
Brunow, Dagmar. "Remediating Transcultural Memory." Berlin: De Gruyter, 2014.
Buckland, Warren, ed. *Film Theory and Contemporary Hollywood Movies*. London: Routledge, 2009.
———. "Introduction." *Film Theory and Contemporary Hollywood Movies*, edited by Warren Buckland. New York: Routledge, 2009.
Bull, Anna Cento, and Hans Lauge Hansen. "On Agonistic Memory." *Memory Studies* 9, no. 4 (2016): 390–404.
Burgess, Jean, Helen Klaebe, and Kelly McWilliam. "Mediatisation and Institutions of Public Memory: Digital Storytelling and the Apology." *Australian Historical Studies* 41 (2010): 149–65.
Burke, Peter. "History as Social Memory." *Memory: History, Culture, and the Mind*, edited by Thomas Butler, 97–113. New York: Blackwell, 1989.
Butler, Judith. *Bodies That Matter: On the Discursive Limits of "Sex."* New York: Routledge, 1993.
Butler, Thomas, ed. "Memory: History, Culture, and the Mind." Wolfson College Lectures, 1989.
Butt, Daniel. *Rectifying International Injustice: Principles of Compensation and Restitution between Nations*. New York: Oxford University Press, 2009.
Buzny, Andrew. "Kissing Fabulose Queens: The Fabulous Realism of Tomson Highway's *Kiss of the Fur Queen*." *Postcolonial Text* 6, no. 3 (2011): 1–18.
Canada, Encyclopedia. "Government Apology to Former Students of Indian Residential Schools." N.d. http://www.thecanadianencyclopedia.ca/en/article/government-apology-to-former-students-of-indian-residential-schools/.
Carey, James W. *Communication as Culture: Essays on Media and Society*. Rev. ed. New York: Routledge, 2009.
Carr, Geoffrey. "Atopoi of the Modern: Revisiting the Place of the Indian Residential School." *English Studies in Canada (ESC)* 35, no. 1 (March 2009): 109–35.
Cartelli, Thomas. *Repositioning Shakespeare: National Formations, Postcolonial Appropriations*. London: Taylor & Francis, 2013.

Caruth, Cathy, ed. *Trauma: Explorations in Memory*. Baltimore: Johns Hopkins University Press, 1995.
Cauvin, Thomas. *Public History: A Textbook of Practice*. New York: Routledge, 2016.
Celermajer, Danielle. "The Apology in Australia: Re-covenanting the National Imaginary." In *Taking Wrongs Seriously: Apologies and Reconciliation*, edited by Elazar Barkan and Alexander Karn, 153–84. Palo Alto, CA: Stanford University Press, 2006.
———. *The Sins of the Nation and the Ritual of Apologies*. New York: Cambridge University Press, 2009.
Chauvel, Charles, dir. *Jedda*. Columbia Pictures and Umbrella Entertainment, 1955.
Chrisjohn, Roland David, Sherri Lynn Young, and Michael Maraun, eds. *The Circle Game: Shadows and Substance in the Indian Residential School Experience in Canada*. Madison: Theytus Books, 2006.
Christie, Kenneth. *The South African Truth Commission*. Basingstoke: Macmillan, 2002.
Claeys, Gregory. "The 'Survival of the Fittest' and the Origins of Social Darwinism." *Journal of the History of Ideas* 61, no. 2 (2000): 223–40.
Clark, Anna. "History in Black and White: A Critical Analysis of the Black Armband Debate." *Journal of Australian Studies* 26, no. 75 (2002): 1–11.
Clark, E. Gillian. *Augustine, the Confessions*. New York: Cambridge University Press, 1993.
Clark, Maureen. "Mudrooroo: Crafty Imposter or Rebel with a Cause." *Australian Literary Studies* 21, no. 4 (2004): n.p.
Clemens, Justin, and Dominic Pettman. "Avoiding the Subject: Media, Culture and the Object." Amsterdam University Press, 2004. http://www.oapen.org/download?type=document&docid=340214.
Coicaud, Jean-Marc, and Jibecke Jönsson. "Elements of a Road Map for a Politics of Apology." In *The Age of Apology: Facing Up to the Past*, edited by Mark Gibney, Rhoda E. Howard-Hassmann, and Jean-Marc Coicaud, 77–95. Philadelphia: University of Pennsylvania Press, 2008.
Cole, Catherine M. *Performing South Africa's Truth Commission: Stages of Transition*. Bloomington: Indiana University Press, 2010.
Collins, Felicity, and Therese Davis, eds. *Australian Cinema after Mabo*. Cambridge: Cambridge University Press, 2004.
Compagnon, Antoine. "Proust's Remembering of Things Past." In *Realms of Memory: Rethinking the French Past*, edited by Pierre Nora and Lawrence D. Kritzman. New York: Columbia University Press, 1996.
Comstock, George A., and Erica Scharrer, eds. *The Psychology of Media and Politics*. Burlington, MA: Elsevier Academic Press, 2005.
Conor, Liz. "A 'Nation so Ill-Begotten': Racialized Childhood and Conceptions of National Belonging in Xavier Herbert's *Poor Fellow My Country* and Baz Luhrmann's *Australia*." *Studies in Australasian Cinema* 4, no. 2 (2010): 97–113.
Conquergood, Dwight D. "Performance of a Moral Act: Ethical Dimensions of the Ethnography of Performance." In *Performance: Critical Concepts in Literary and Cultural Studies*, edited by Ed Philip Auslander, 134–49. London: Routledge, 2003.
Cottle, Drew. "Russel Ward and the Making of the Australian Legend." *Australian Quaterly* 81, no. 3 (2009): 39–40.
Craig, Geoffrey. *The Media, Politics and Public Life*. Crows Nest: Allen & Unwin, 2004.
Crane, Diana, and Kenichi Kawasaki, eds. *Global Culture: Media, Arts, Policy, and Globalization*. London: Routledge, 2002.
Craps, Stef. *Postcolonial Witnessing: Trauma Out of Bounds*. London: Palgrave Macmillan, 2015.

Crocker, David A. "Truth Commissions, Transitional Justice and Civil Society." *Truth versus Justice: The Morality of Truth Commissions*, edited by Dennis Frank Thompson and Robert I. Rotberg, 99–121. Princeton, NJ: Princeton University Press, 2000.

Crosbie, Tom. "Critical Historiography in Atanarjuat—The Fast Runner." "Comparative Approaches to Indigenous Literary Studies," special issue, *Journal of New Zealand Literature* 24, no. 2 (2007): 135–52.

Crotty, Martin, G. W. Rodwell, and John Germov. *A Race for a Place: Eugenics, Darwinism and Social Thought and Practice in Australia*. Callaghan: University of Newcastle, 2000.

Crownshaw, Richard. "Perpetrator Fictions and Transcultural Memory." *Parallax* 17, no. 4 (November 2011): 75–89. https://doi.org/10.1080/13534645.2011.605582.

da Cunha, Rubelise. "The Trickster Wink: Storytelling and Resistance in Tomson Highway's *Kiss of the Fur Queen*." *Ilha Do Desterro: A Journal of English Language, Literatures in English and Cultural Studies* 56 (January–July 2009): 93–118.

Cuthbert, Denise, and Marian Quartly. "Forced Child Removal and the Politics of National Apologies in Australia." *American Indian Quarterly* 37, no. 1 (Winter/Spring 2013): 178–202.

Cuypers, Daniel. ed. *Public Apology between Ritual and Regret: Symbolic Excuses on False Pretenses or True Reconciliation out of Sincere Regret?*. Amsterdam: Rodopi, 2013.

Daase, Christopher. "Addressing Painful Memories: Apologies as a New Practice in International Relations." In *Memory in a Global Age: Discourses, Practices and Trajectories*, edited by Aleida Assmann and Sebastian Conrad. Houndsmills: Palgrave Macmillan, 2010.

Daly, Erin, and Jeremy Sarkin. *Reconciliation in Divided Societies: Finding Common Ground*. Philadelphia: University of Pennsylvania Press, 2007.

Daniels, Roger. *An Age of Apology?* Kingston: Kashtan Press, 2003.

Darwin, John. *The End of the British Empire: The Historical Debate*. Oxford: Blackwell, 1991.

David, Lea. *The Past Can't Heal Us: The Dangers of Mandating Memory in the Name of Human Rights*. Human Rights in History. New York: Cambridge University Press, 2020.

Davison, Graeme. "Rethinking the Australian Legend." *Australian Historical Studies* 43, no. 3 (2012): 429–51.

Delbaere-Garant, Jeanne. "Towards a 'Third Space': Magic Realisms in English Canadian Literature," in *Eyes Deep with Unfathomable Histories: The Poetics and Politics of Magic Realism Today and in the Past*, ed. Liliana Sikorska and Agnieszka Rzepa. Frankfurt am Main: Peter Lang, 2012, 12–29.

Dempsey, James. "Aboriginal Soldiers in the First World War," Canadian Government Archive. Retrieved 6 June 2016 from www.collectionscanada.gc.ca/aboriginal-heritage/020016-4002-e.html.

Dieckmann, Walther, ed. *Politische Sprache, politische Kommunikation: Vorträge, Aufsätze, Entwürfe*. Heidelberg: Winter, 1981.

Divers, John. *Possible Worlds*. Florence: Taylor & Francis, 2014.

Doering, Tobias. "Turning the Colonial Gaze: Re-visions of Terror in Dabydeen's Turner," *Third Text* 11, no. 28 (1997): 3–14.

Dorais, Louis-Jacques. *Inuit uqausiqatigiit: Inuit Languages and Dialects*. Updated ed. Iqaluit, NU: Nunavut Arctic College Media, 2017.

———. *The Language of the Inuit: Syntax, Semantics, and Society in the Arctic*. Montreal: McGill-Queens University Press, 2010.

Dorfman, Ariel. *La Muerte y la Doncella*. Madrid: Ollero & Ramos, 1995.

Dorrell, Mathew. "From Reconciliation to Reconciling: Reading What 'We Now Recognize' in the Government of Canada's 2008 Residential School Apology." *English Studies in Canada* 35, no. 1 (2009): 27–45.

Dow, Coral. "Sorry: The Unfinished Business of the Bringing Them Home Report," 2008. https://www.aph.gov.au/About_Parliament/Parliamentary_Departments/Parliamentary_Library/pubs/BN/0708/BringingThemHomeReport.
Dowell, Kristin. "Indigenous Media Gone Global: Strengthening Indigenous Identity On- and Offscreen at the First Nations/First Features Film Showcase." *American Anthropologist* 108, no. 2 (2006). http://onlinelibrary.wiley.com/doi/10.1525/aa.2006.108.2.376/abstract.
Drechsel, Paul. *Interkulturalität: Grundprobleme der Kulturbegegnung*. Mainz: University of Mainz, 1998.
Druckman, James N., and Donald P. Green, eds. *Cambridge Handbook of Experimental Political Science*. Cambridge: Cambridge University Press, 2011.
Dunnage, Jonathan . "Perpetrator Memory and Memory about Perpetrators," *Memory Studies* 3, no. 2 (2010): 91–94
Durix, Jean-Pierre. *Mimesis, Genres and Post-colonial Discourse: Deconstructing Magic Realism*. Basingstoke: Palgrave Macmillan, 2000.
Eeden, Jeanne van. "The Colonial Gaze: Imperialism, Myths and South African Popular Culture," *Design Issues* 20, no. 2 (2004): 18–33.
Elsaesser, Thomas, and Malte Hagener. *Film Theory: An Introduction through the Senses*. New York: Routledge, 2010.
Enderwitz, Anne. "Ereignis und Wiederholung als Koordinaten von Geschlecht und Gedächtnis." In *Iterationen: Geschlecht im kulturellen Gedächtnis*, edited by Anja Schwarz and Sabine Lucia Müller, 28–48. Göttingen: Wallstein Verlag, 2008.
Episkenew, Jo-Ann. *Taking Back Our Spirits: Indigenous Literature, Public Policy, and Healing*. Winnipeg: University of Manitoba Press, 2009.
Erll, Astrid. "The 'Indian Mutiny' as a Shared Site of Memory: A Media Culture Perspective on Britain and India." In *Memory, History and Colonialism: Engaging with Pierre Nora in Colonial and Postcolonial Contexts*, edited by Ed Andreas Gestrich, 117–51. London: German Historical Institute, 2009.
———. "Travelling Memory." *Parallax* 17 (2011): 4–18.
———. "From 'District 6' to District 9 and Back: The Plurimedial Production of Travelling Schemata," in *Transnational Memory: Circulation, Articulation, Scales*, edited by Chiara DeCesari and Ann Rigney. Berlin: De Gruyter, 2014, 29–50.
———. *Kollektives Gedächtnis und Erinnerungskulturen: Eine Einführung. 3., aktualisierte und erweiterte Auflage*. Stuttgart: J. B. Metzler, 2017.
———. "Travelling Memory in European Film: Towards a Morphology of Mnemonic Relationality." *Image & Narrative* 18, no. 1 (2017): 5–19.
Erll, Astrid, Herbert Grabes, and Ansgar Nünning, eds. *Ethics in Culture: The Dissemination of Values through Literature and Other Media*. Berlin: De Gruyter, 2008.
Erll, Astrid, Marion Gymnich, and Ansgar Nünning. *Literatur, Erinnerung, Identität: Theoriekonzeptionen und Fallstudien*. Trier: Wissenschaftlicher Verlag Trier, 2003.
Erll, Astrid, and Ansgar Nünning. *A Companion to Cultural Memory Studies*. Berlin: De Gruyter, 2010.
———. *Gedächtniskonzepte der Literaturwissenschaft: Theoretische Grundlegung und Anwendungsperspektiven*. Berlin: De Gruyter, 2005.
———, eds. *Medien des kollektiven Gedächtnisses: Konstruktivität, Historizität, Kulturspezifität*. Berlin: De Gruyter, 2004.
Erll, Astrid, Ansgar Nünning, and Sara B. Young, eds. *Cultural Memory Studies*. Berlin: De Gruyter, 2008.
Erll, Astrid, and Ann Rigney, eds. *Mediation, Remediation, and the Dynamics of Cultural Memory*. Berlin: De Gruyter, 2012.

Erll, Astrid, and Stéphanie Wodianka, eds. *Plurimediale Konstellationen*. Berlin: De Gruyter, 2008.

Ertler, Klaus D., and Martin Loeschnigg, eds. "Inventing Canada: Inventer le Canada." *Canadiana* 6 (2008).

Eskin, Blake. *A Life in Pieces: The Making and Unmaking of Binjamin Wilkomirski*. New York: W. W. Norton, 2002.

Esposito, Elena. *Soziales Vergessen: Formen und Medien des Gedächtnisses der Gesellschaft*. Frankfurt am Main: Suhrkamp, 2002.

Evans, Gary. *In the National Interest: A Chronicle of the National Film Board of Canada from 1949 to 1989*. Toronto: University of Toronto Press, 1991.

Evans, Michael Robert. *The Fast Runner: Filming the Legend of Atanarjuat*. Lincoln: University of Nebraska Press, 2010.

Ezra, Elizabeth, and Terry Rowden. *Transnational Cinema: The Film Reader*. London: Routledge, 2006. http://books.google.de/books?hl=de&lr=&id=_y25_wYETb0C&oi=fnd&pg=PA39&dq=film+and+first+nations&ots=lXZklu3NPf&sig=6CVmoFX0EzvCQWawr-sMw7AjJUI#v=onepage&q=film percent20and percent20first percent20nations &f=false.

Fichera, Eduardo. "Running Barefoot across the Arctic Ice: Zacharias Kunuk's *Atanarjuat* and the Challenging of Colonial Representations." *EthnoScripts* 15, No. 1 (2013): 101–11.

Findley, Timothy. *The Wars*. Toronto: Clarke Irwin, 1977.

Fischer-Lichte, Erika. *Ästhetik des Performativen*. 9. Aufl. Frankfurt am Main: Suhrkamp, 2014.

———. "Performance, Inszenierung, Ritual: Zur Klärung kulturwissenschaftlicher Schlüsselbegriffe." In *Geschichtswissenschaften und "performative turn": Ritual, Inszenierung und Performanz vom Mittelalter bis zur Neuzeit*, edited by Ed Jürgen Martschukat. Köln: Böhlau, 2003.

———. *Performativität: Eine Einführung*. Bielefeld: Transcript, 2013.

Flaherty, Robert J., dir. *Nanook of the North*. Les Frères Revillon, 1922.

Flanagan, Thomas. *First Nations? Second Thoughts*. Montreal: McGill-Queen's University Press, 2000.

Fleming, Victor. *The Wizard of Oz*, 1939.

Foster, Hal, ed. "Vision and Visuality." *Discussions in Contemporary Culture*. Seattle: Bay Press, 2009.

Freeman, Mark. *Truth Commissions and Procedural Fairness*. Cambridge: Cambridge University Press, 2006.

Freeman, Michael. "Historical Injustice and Liberal Political Theory." *The Age of Apology: Facing Up to the Past*, edited by Mark Gibney, Rhoda E. Howard-Hassmann, and Jean-Marc Coicaud. Philadelphia: University of Pennsylvania Press, 2008.

Freeman, James. "From the Archives 1995: Writer Demidenko Revealed to Be Helen Darville." *Sydney Morning Herald*, 21 August 2020. Retrieved 29 November 2020 from https://www.smh.com.au/culture/books/from-the-archives-1995-writer-demidenko-revealed-to-be-helen-darville-20200813-p55ldc.html.

Frenette, Yves. "Conscripting Canada's Past." *Canadian Journal of History* 49 (Spring 2014): 49–65.

Fuchs, Elinor. "Presence and Revenge of Writing: Re-thinking Theatre after Derrida." In *Performance: Critical Concepts in Literary and Cultural Studies*, edited by Ed Philip Auslander, 109–18. London: Routledge, 2003.

Fullard, Madeleine, and Nicky Rousseau. "Uncertain Borders: The TRC and the (Un)Making of Public Myths. University of the Western Cape." N.d. http://www.scielo.org.za/pdf/kronos/v34n1/v34n1a09.pdf.

Furniss, Elizabeth. *Victims of Benevolence: The Dark Legacy of the Williams Lake Residential School*. Vancouver: Arsenal Pulp Press, 1995.
Gay, Paul du, and Stuart Hall, eds. *Questions of Cultural Identity*. Los Angeles: Sage, 2011.
Du Toit, André. "The Moral Foundations of the South African TRC: Truth as Acknowledgment and Justice as Recognition." In *Truth versus Justice: The Morality of Truth Commissions*, edited by Dennis Frank Thompson and Robert I. Rotberg. Princeton, NJ: Princeton University Press, 2000.
Gallagher, John, ed. *The Decline, Revival and Fall of the British Empire: The Ford Lectures and Other Essays*. Cambridge: Cambridge University Press, 1982.
Ganz, Shoshannah. "Canadian Literary Representations of HIV/AIDS." In *HIV in World Cultures: Three Decades of Representations*, edited by Gustavo Subero, 1–12. London: Taylor and Francis, 2013.
Garkawe, Sam Boris. "The South African Truth and Reconciliation Commission: A Suitable Model to Enhance the Role and Rights of the Victims of Gross Violations of Human Rights?" *Melbourne University Law Review* 27 (2003): 334–80. http://epubs.scu.edu.au/cgi/viewcontent.cgi?article=1020&context=law_pubs.
Gehring, Wolfgang, Klaus Stierstorfer, and Laurenz Volkmann, eds. *Interkulturelle Kompetenz: Konzepte und Praxis des Unterrichts*. Tübingen: Narr, 2002.
Gestrich, Andreas, ed. *Memory, History and Colonialism: Engaging with Pierre Nora in Colonial and Postcolonial Contexts*. London: German Historical Institute, 2009.
Gibbons, Fiachra, and Stephen Moss. "Fragments of a Fraud." *The Guardian*, 15 October 1999. Retrieved 29 November 2020 from https://www.theguardian.com/theguardian/1999/oct/15/features11.g24.
Gibney, Mark, Rhoda E. Howard-Hassmann, and Jean-Marc Coicaud, eds. *The Age of Apology: Facing Up to the Past*. Philadelphia: University of Pennsylvania Press, 2008.
Gibson, Ross. *South of the West: Postcolonialism and the Narrative Construction of Australia*. Bloomington: Indiana University Press, 1992.
Gifford, Don, and Donald E. Morse, eds. "Zones of Re-membering: Time, Memory, and (Un)Consciousness." *Consciousness, Literature & the Arts* 28 (2011).
Gilfedder, Deirdre. "Testimonial and the Stories from the 'Stolen Generation' in Australia." In *Eye to Eye: Women Practising Development across Cultures*, edited by Susan Perry. London: Zed Books, 2001.
Ginsburg, Faye. "Mediating Culture: Indigenous Media, Ethnographic Film and the Production of Identity." In *The Anthropology of Media: A Reader*, edited by Kelly Askew and Richard R. Wilk. Victoria: Blackwell Publishing, 2002. http://books.google.de/books?hl=de&lr=&id=L2h-pKb2tVAC&oi=fnd&pg=PA210&dq=ginsburg+faye+mediating+culture&ots=BFCudMl_n7&sig=91MDVzCiUOH6gTZaxp-VB1lodP4#v=onepage&q=ginsburg percent20faye percent20mediating percent20culture&f=false.
Girle, Rod. *Possible Worlds*. London: Routledge, 2003.
Gittings, Christopher E. *Canadian National Cinema: Ideology, Difference and Representation*. London: Routledge, 2002.
Glaser, Brigitte. "(Re)Turning to Europe for the Great War." *Zeitschrift für Kanada-Studien* 20, no. 2 (2010): 62–75.
Glaser, Brigitte Johanna. "Cultural Memory in Canada: Revisiting the Battlefields in Reality and Fiction." In *North America, Europe and the Cultural Memory of the First World War*, edited by Martin Löschnigg and Karin Kraus, 79–92. Heidelberg: Winter, 2015.
Goebel, Walter, and Saskia Schabio, eds. *Locating Postcolonial Narrative Genres*. London: Routledge, 2013.
Gobodo-Madikizela, Pumla, ed. *Memory, Narrative, and Forgiveness: Perspectives on the Unfinished Journeys of the Past*. Newcastle upon Tyne: Cambridge Scholars Publishing, 2009.

Göttsche, Dirk. "Cross-Cultural Memoryscapes: Memory of Colonialism and Its Shifting Contexts in Contemporary German Literature." In *The Transcultural Turn: Interrogating Memory between and beyond Borders*, edited by Lucy Bond and Jessica Rapson, Boston: De Gruyter, 2014, 225–46.

Goodman, David, ed. *Multicultural Australia: The Challenges of Change*. Newham: Scribe, 1991.

Gordon, Michael. *Reconciliation: A Journey*. Sydney: UNSW Press, 2001.

Gordon, Neta. "The Artist and the Witness: Jane Urquhart's The Underpainter and The Stone Carvers." In *Studies in Canadian Literature / Études En Littérature Canadienne* 8, no. 2 (2003): 59–73.

Göttsche, Dirk, Axel Dunker, and Gabriele Dürbeck, eds. *Handbuch Postkolonialismus und Literatur*. Stuttgart: Metzler, 2017.

Government of Canada. "Indian Residential School Statement of Apology—Prime Minister Stephen Harper." N.d. Retrieved 15 May 2015 from http://www.aadnc-aandc.gc.ca/eng/1100100015677/1100100015680.

"Government of Canada, Aboriginal Affairs and Northern Development. Are You Eligible?" N.d. https://www.aadnc-aandc.gc.ca/DAM/DAM-INTER-HQ/STAGING/texte-text/br_is_elig_1315710514986_eng.pdf.

Grabes, Herbert. "Cultural Memory and the Literary Canon." *Cultural Memory Studies*, edited by Astrid Erll, Ansgar Nünning, and Sara B. Young. Berlin: De Gruyter, 2008.

Grace, Sherrill. "Remembering the Wars." *The Great War in Post-memory Literature and Film*, edited by Martin Loeschnigg and Marzena Sokolowska-Paryz. Boston: De Gruyter, 2014.

Grace, Sherrill E. *Canada and the Idea of North*. Québec: McGill-Queen's University Press, 2007.

Grant, Agnes. *No End of Grief: Indian Residential Schools in Canada*. Winnipeg: Pemmican Publishing, 1992

Grattan, Michelle, ed. *Essays on Australian Reconciliation*. Melbourne: Bookman Press, 2000.

Green, Robin. "Unsettling Cures: Exploring the Limits of the Indian Residential School System Settlement Agreement." *Canadian Journal of Law and Society* 27, no. 1 (2012): 129–48.

Greer, Germaine. "Once Upon a Time in a Land Far, Far Away." *The Guardian*, 16 December 2008, retrieved 14 November 2017 from https://www.theguardian.com/film/2008/dec/16/baz-luhrmann-australia.

Grenville, Kate. *The Secret River*. Edinburgh: Canongate, 2005.

Grewenig, Adi, ed. *Inszenierte Information: Politik und strategische Kommunikation in den Medien*. Opladen: Westdeutscher Verlag, 1993.

Griffiths, Gareth. "Introduction." In *The Social Work of Narrative: Human Rights and the Cultural Imaginary*, edited by Gareth Griffiths and Philip Mead, 1–13. Stuttgart: Ibidem, 2018.

Griffiths, Gareth, and Philip Mead, eds. "The Social Work of Narrative: Human Rights and the Cultural Imaginary, 2018." *Print: Studies in World Literature*, n.d.

Grunebaum, Heidi. "Talking to Ourselves "among the Innocent Dead": On Reconciliation, Forgiveness and Mourning". *PMLA*, Vol. 117, (2002), 306-310.

———. *Memorializing the Past: Everyday Life in South Africa after the Truth and Reconciliation Commission*. New Brunswick, NJ: Transaction Publishers, 2011.

Gunstone, Andrew. *Unfinished Business: The Australian Formal Reconciliation Process*. North Melbourne: Australian Scholarly Publishing, 2007.

Gunther, Richard, ed. *Democracy and the Media: A Comparative Perspective*. Cambridge: Cambridge University Press, 2000.

Gutman, Yifat, Adam Brown, and Amy Sodaro. *Memory and the Future: Transnational Politics, Ethics and Society*. New York: Palgrave Macmillan, 2014.

Gutmann, Amy, and Dennis Thompson. "The Moral Foundations of Truth Commissions." In *Truth versus Justice: The Morality of Truth Commissions*, edited by Dennis Frank Thompson and Robert I. Rotberg, 23–43. Princeton, NJ: Princeton University Press, 2000.

Gutmann, Amy, and Dennis Frank Thompson. *Why Deliberative Democracy?* Princeton, NJ: Princeton University Press, 2004.

Gword, Matt. "Ask a Prof." The Gateway Online, 2017. https://www.thegatewayonline.ca/2017/01/ask-a-prof-boyden-controversy/.

Haig-Brown, Celia. *Resistance and Renewal: Surviving the Indian Residential School*. Vancouver: Arsenal Pulp Press, 2006.

Halbwachs, Maurice. *Das Gedächtnis und seine sozialen Bedingungen*. Frankfurt am Main: Suhrkamp, 2006.

Halbwachs, Maurice, and Lewis A. Coser, eds. *On Collective Memory*. Chicago: University of Chicago Press, 1992.

Hall, Stuart. *The Fateful Triangle: Race, Ethnicity, Nation*. Cambridge, MA: Harvard University Press, 2017.

———. *The Local and the Global: Globalization and Ethnicity*." *Dangerous Liaisons: Gender, Nation, and Postcolonial Perspectives*. Edited by Ed Anne McClintock. Minneapolis: University of Minnesota Press, 1997.

Hall, Stuart, and Paul Du Gay. *Questions of Cultural Identity*, edited by Stuart Hall and Paul Du Gay. Los Angeles: Sage, 2011.

Hallin, Daniel C., and Paolo Mancini. *Comparing Media Systems*. Cambridge: Cambridge University Press, 2004.

Hallowell, Gerald. *The Oxford Companion to Canadian History*. Ontario: Don Mills, 2004.

Haltof, Marek. "'Gallipoli,' Mateship, and the Construction of Australian National Identity." *Journal of Popular Film and Television* 21, no. 1 1993): 27–36.

Hamber, Brandon. "Transforming Societies after Political Violence: Truth, Reconciliation, and Mental Health." Springer eBooks, 2009. http://www.worldcat.org/oclc/428883107.

Harper, Stephen. "Statement of Apology to Former Students of Indian Residential Schools." Government of Canada, 2008. http://www.aadnc-aandc.gc.ca/eng/1100100015644/1100100015649.

———. "PM Harper Offers Full Apology for the Chinese Head Tax," retrieved 1 December 2020 from http://pm.gc.ca/eng/news/2006/06/22/prime-minister-harper-offers-full-apology-chinese-head-tax.

Havemann, Paul, ed. *Indigenous Peoples' Rights in Australia, Canada and New Zealand*. Repr. South Melbourne: Oxford University Press, 2004.

Hayner, Priscilla B. *Unspeakable Truths: Confronting State Terror and Atrocities*. New York: Routledge, 2000.

———. *Unspeakable Truths: Transitional Justice and the Challenge of Truth Commissions*. New York: Routledge, 2011.

Healey, Justin, ed. *The Stolen Generations*. Rozelle: Spinney Press, 2001.

Hedwig, Tatjana. *Politische Inszenierungen: Politikherstellung durch mediale Politikdarstellung*. Saarbrücken: VDM Verlag Dr. Müller, 2006.

Heinen, Sandra, and Roy Sommer, eds. *Narratology in the Age of Cross-Disciplinary Narrative Research*. Berlin: De Gruyter, 2009.

Heinze, Michael, ed. *Literature on the Move: Cultural Migration in Contemporary Literature*. Trier: WVT Wiss. Verl, 2010.

Henderson, Jennifer, and Pauline Wakeham. "Colonial Reckoning, National Reconciliation? Aboriginal Peoples and the Culture of Redress in Canada." In *English Studies in Canada* 35, no. 1 (2009): 1–26.

———. *Reconciling Canada: Critical Perspectives on the Culture of Redress.* Toronto: University of Toronto Press, 2013.

Henderson, Jennifer and Pauline Wakeham. "Introduction." In *Reconciling Canada: Critical Perspectives on the Culture of Redress,* edited by Jennifer Henderson and Pauline Wakeham, 3–28. Toronto: University of Toronto Press, 2013.

Henderson Youngblood, James Sa'Ke'J. "Incomprehensible Canada." In *Reconciling Canada: Critical Perspectives on the Culture of Redress,* edited by Jennifer Henderson and Pauline Wakeham, 115–27. Toronto: University of Toronto Press, 2013.

Henstra, Sarah. *The Counter-memorial Impulse in Twentieth-Century English Fiction.* Basingstoke: Palgrave Macmillan, 2009.

Henzi, Sarah. "Resistance and Transformation: Negotiating Political Rhetorics in First Nations Literatures." *Australasian Canadian Studies* 27, nos. 1–2 (2009): 117–28.

Hermes, Liesel. "Henry Lawson's 'The Drover's Wife' and the Australian Short Story." In *Global Fragments: (Dis)Orientation in the New World Order,* edited by Anke Bartels and Dirk Wiemann, 301–12. Amsterdam: Rodopi, 2007.

Herrero, Dolores. "The Australian Apology and Postcolonial Defamiliarization: Gail Jones's Sorry." *Journal of Postcolonial Writing,* 1744. http://www.informaworld.com/smpp/content db=all content=a938212944 frm=titlelink.

Hess-Lüttich, Ernest, ed. *Medienkultur—Kulturkonflikt: Massenmedien in der interkulturellen und internationalen Kommunikation.* Wiesbaden: Westdeutscher Verlag, 1991.

Hiatt, L. R. *Arguments about Aborigines: Australia and the Evolution of Social Anthropology.* New York: Cambridge University Press, 1996.

Highway, Tomson. *Kiss of the Fur Queen.* Norman: University of Oklahoma Press, 1998.

Hirsch, Marianne. *The Generation of Postmemory: Writing and Visual Culture after the Holocaust.* New York: Columbia University Press, 2012.

Hirsch, Michal Ben-Josef. "Ideational Change and the Emergence of the International Norm of Truth and Reconciliation Commissions." *European Journal of International Relations* 20, no. 3 (2014): 810–33.

Hobby, Blake, and Harold Bloom, eds. *Bloom's Literary Themes: The Trickster.* New York: Bloom's Literary Criticism, 2010.

Hocking, Barbara Ann, Scott Guy, and Jason Grant Allen. "Three Sorries and You're In? Does the Prime Minister's Statement in the Australian Federal Parliament Presage Federal Constitutional Recognition and Reparations?" *Human Rights Review* 11 (2009). http://www.springerlink.com/content/n15h6ww330q17rp5/.

Hodgson, Geoffrey M. "Social Darwinism in Anglophone Academic Journals: A Contribution to the History of the Term." *Journal of Historical Sociology* 17, no. 4 (2004): 428–63.

Hofmann, Wilhelm, ed. *Die Sichtbarkeit der Macht: Theoretische und empirische Untersuchungen zur visuellen Politik.* Baden-Baden: Nomos. Print, n.d.

Hook, Maria Teresa Savio, ed. *The Geography of Meanings: Psychoanalytic Perspectives on Place, Space, Land, and Dislocation.* London: International Psychoanalytical Association, 2007.

Hooley, Neil. *Narrative Life: Democratic Curriculum and Indigenous Learning.* Dordrecht: Springer, 2009.

Horstkotte, Silke. "Seeing or Speaking: Visual Narratology and Focalization, Literature to Film." Edited by Sandra Heinen and Roy Sommer. *Narratology in the Age of Cross-Disciplinary Narrative Research* 1 (2009).

Howard-Hassmann, Rhoda E., and Mark Gibney. "Introduction: Apologies and the West." *The Age of Apology: Facing Up to the Past,* edited by Mark Gibney, Rhoda E. Howard-Hassmann, and Jean-Marc Coicaud. Philadelphia: University of Pennsylvania Press, 2008.

Howells, Coral Ann. "Tomson Highway: *Kiss of the Fur Queen*." In *Where Are the Voices Coming From? Canadian Culture and the Legacies of History*, edited by Coral Ann Howells, 83–94. Amsterdam: Rodopi, 2004.

———, ed. "Where Are the Voices Coming from? Canadian Culture and the Legacies of History." *Cross Cultures* 73 (2004).

Howson, Peter. "The Stolen Generation's True Believers Take One Step Back." *National Observer* 49 (2001): 61–63.

Hucker, Jacqueline. "'Battle and Burial': Recapturing the Cultural Meaning of Canada's National Memorial on Vimy Ridge." *Public Historian* 31, no. 1 (2009): 89–109.

Hühn, Peter, ed. *Handbook of Narratology*. 2nd ed. Fully revised and expand. 2 vols. Berlin: De Gruyter, 2014.

Huhndorf, Shari. "'Atanarjuat, the Fast Runner': Culture, History, and Politics in Inuit Media." *American Anthropologist* 105, no. 4 (2003): 822–26.

Human Rights and Equal Opportunity Commission of Australia. "Inquiry into the Forcible Removal of Aboriginal and Torres Strait Islander Children," n.d. https://www.humanrights.gov.au/sites/default/files/content/pdf/social_justice/submissions_un_hr_committee/6_stolen_generations.pdf.

Humphrey, Michael. "From Victim to Victimhood: Truth Commissions and Trials as Rituals of Political Transition and Individual Healing." *Australian Journal of Anthropology* 14, no. 2 (2003). http://onlinelibrary.wiley.com/doi/10.1111/j.1835-9310.2003.tb00229.x/abstract.

Hutcheon, Linda. "'Circling the Downspout of Empire': Post-Colonialism and Postmodernism," 1989. https://tspace.library.utoronto.ca/handle/1807/10262.

———. *The Canadian Postmodern: A Study of Contemporary English-Canadian Fiction*. Toronto: Oxford University Press, 1988.

Hynes, Samuel. "Personal Narratives and Commemoration." *War and Remembrance in the Twentieth Century*, edited by J. M. Winter. Cambridge: Cambridge University Press, 1999.

———. A War Imagined: *The First World War and English Culture*. London: *Pimlico*, 1990.

Hynes, William J., and William G. Doty, eds. *Mythical Trickster Figures: Contours, Contexts, and Criticisms*. Tuscaloosa: University of Alabama Press, 1993.

Ikas, Karin. *Reconstructing National Identity. The Nation Forged-Myth and Canadian Literature*. Wiesbaden: Peter Lang, 2018.

———, ed. *Communicating in the Third Space*. London: Routledge, 2008.

———, "Formative Years: (Dis)ability, War and the Canadian Nation," in *Global Realignments and the Canadian Nation in the Third Millennium*, ed. Karin Ikas. Wiesbaden: Harrassowitz, 2010, 35–44.

———, ed. "Global Realignments and the Canadian Nation in the Third Millennium." *Kultur- und sozialwissenschaftliche Studien* 5 (2010).

Itani, Frances. *The Deafening*. Toronto: HarperCollins, 2003.

Jago, Robert. "The Boyden Controversy Is Not about Bloodline." *The Walrus*, 10 January 2017. https://thewalrus.ca/the-boyden-controversy-is-not-about-bloodline/.

James, Matt. "A Carnival of Truth? Knowledge, Ignorance and the Canadian Truth and Reconciliation Commission." *International Journal of Transitional Justice* 6, no. 2 (2012): 182–204.

———. "Uncomfortable Comparisons: The Canadian Truth and Reconciliation Commission in International Context." *Les Ateliers De*, 2010. http://www.creum.umontreal.ca/IMG/pdf_02_James.pdf.

———. "Neoliberal Heritage Redress." In *Reconciling Canada: Critical Perspectives on the Culture of Redress*, edited by Jennifer Henderson and Pauline Wakeham, 31–45. Toronto: Toronto University Press, 2013.

———. "Wrestling with the Past: Apologies, Quasi-Apologies, and Non-Apologies in Canada." In *The Age of Apology: Facing Up to the Past*, edited by Mark Gibney, Rhoda E. Howard-Hassmann, and Jean-Marc Coicaud. Philadelphia: University of Pennsylvania Press, 2008.

Janik, Vicki K., ed. *Fools and Jesters in Literature, Art, and History: A Bibliographical Sourcebook.* Westport, CT: Greenwood Press, 1998.

Jay, Martin. "Scopic Regimes of Modernity." In *Vision and Visuality*, edited by Hal Foster. Seattle: Bay Press, 2009.

Jayamanne, Laleene. "The Drover's Wives and Camp Couture: Baz Luhrmann's Preposterous National Epic." *Studies in Australasian Cinema* 4, no. 2 (2010): 131–43.

Jenkins, Henry. *Convergence Culture: Where Old and New Media Collide*. New York: New York University Press, 2006.

Johae, Antony. "Bakhtinian Carnivalesque in Baz Luhrmann's WILLIAM SHAKESPEARE'S ROMEO+JULIET." *The Explicator* 72, no. 4 (2014): 304–7.

Johnson, Frances. "Dissident Laughter: Historiographic Metafiction as Parodic Intervention in *Benang* and *That Deadman Dance*." In "Art as Parodic Practice," ed. Marion May Campbell, Dominique Hecq, Jondi Keane, and Antonia Pont, special issue, *TEXT* 33 (October 2015): 1–18. Retrieved 17 May 2018 from http://www.textjournal.com.au/speciss/issue33/content.html

Jones, Gail. *Sorry: This Is a Story That Can Only Be Told in a Whisper*. London: Vintage, 2008.

Kalayjian, Ani, and Raymond F. Paloutzian, eds. *Forgiveness and Reconciliation: Psychological Pathways to Conflict Transformation and Peace Building*. New York: Springer-Verlag, 2009.

Kaminer, Debra. "The Truth and Reconciliation Commission in South Africa: Relation to Psychiatric Status and Forgiveness among Survivors of Human Rights Abuses." *British Journal of Psychiatry* 178 (2001). http://bjp.rcpsych.org/content/178/4/373.abstract.

Kansteiner, Wulf. "Finding Meaning in Memory: A Methodological Critique of Collective Memory Studies." *History & Theory* 41 (2002): 179–97.

———. *In Pursuit of German Memory: History, Television, and Politics after Auschwitz*. Athens: Ohio University Press, 2006.

Kaplan, E. Ann. *Trauma Culture: The Politics of Terror and Loss in Media and Literature*. New Brunswick, NJ: Rutgers University Press, 2005.

Kaylor, Brian. *Presidential Campaign Rhetoric in an Age of Confessional Politics*. Lanham, MD: Lexington Books, 2011.

Keating, Paul. "Redfern Speech." N.d. Retrieved 12 February 2018 from https://antar.org.au/sites/default/files/paul_keating_speech_transcript.pdf.

Keenan, Sarah. "Moments of Decolonization: Indigenous Australia in the Here and Now." *Canadian Journal of Law and Society* 29, no. 2 (2014): 163–80.

Kelada, Odette. "Love Is a Battlefield: 'Maternal' Emotions and White Catharsis in Baz Luhrmann's Post-Apology 'Australia,'" *Studies in Australasian Cinema* 8, nos. 2–3 (2014): 83–95.

Keneally, Thomas and Nicholas Jose, eds. *The Literature of Australia: An Anthology*. Sydney: W. W. Norton, 2009.

Kennedy, Rosanne. "Australian Trials of Trauma: The Stolen Generations in Human Rights, Law, and Literature." *Comparative Literature Studies* 48, no. 3 (2011): 333–55.

Kidd, William, and Brian Murdoch, eds. *Memory and Memorials: The Commemorative Century*. Aldershot: Ashgate, 2004.

Kiss, Elizabeth. "Moral Ambitions within and beyond Political Constraints." *Truth versus Justice: The Morality of Truth Commissions*, edited by Dennis Frank Thompson and Robert I. Rotberg, 68–98. Princeton, NJ: Princeton University Press, 2000.

Klonowska, Barbara. *Contaminations: Magic Realism in Contemporary British Fiction*. Lublin: Maria Curie-Skłodowska University Press, 2006.

Knopf, Kerstin. "Atanarjuat—Fast Running and Electronic Storytelling in the Arctic." In *Transcultural English Studies: Theories, Fictions, Realities*, edited by Frank Schulze-Engler and Sissy Helff, 201–20. New York: Rodopi, 2009.

———. "Decolonizing the Lens of Power: Indigenous Films in North America." *Cross/Cultures* 100 (2008).

Kobialka, Michael. "Historical Events and the Historiography of Tourism." In *Performance: Critical Concepts in Literary and Cultural Studies*. Edited by Philip Auslander. London: Routledge, 2003, 213–33.

Koch-Baumgarten, Sigrid, and Katrin Voltmer. *Public Policy and Mass Media: The Interplay of Mass Communication and Political Decision Making*. London: Routledge, 2010.

Korte, Martin, and Nicolas Pethes, eds. *Gedächtnis und Erinnerung: Ein interdisziplinäres Lexikon; Original-Ausg*. Reinbek: Rowohlt, 2001.

Kossew, Sue. "Saying Sorry: The Politics of Apology and Reconciliation in Recent Australian Fiction." In *Locating Postcolonial Narrative Genres*, edited by Walter Goebel and Saskia Schabio. New York: Routledge, 2013.

Krog, Antjie. *Conditional Tense: Memory and Vocabulary after South African Truth and Reconciliation Commission*. Johannesburg: Seagull Books, 2013.

———. *Country of My Skull*. Johannesburg: Random House Struik, 2009.

Krotz, Sarah Wylie. "Productive Dissonance: Classical Music in Tomson Highway's *Kiss of the Fur Queen*." *Studies in Canadian Literature* 34, no. 1 (2009): 182–203.

Krupat, Arnold. "Atanarjuat, the Fast Runner and Its Audiences." *Critical Inquiry* 33, no. 3 (2007): 606–31.

Kuester, Martin. "The English-Canadian Novel from Modernism to Postmodernism." In *History of Literature in Canada: English-Canadian and French-Canadian*, edited by Reingard M. Nischik. London: Camden House, 2008.

Kuhn, Marcus, and Johann N. Schmidt. "Narratology in Film." In *Handbook of Narratology*, edited by Peter Hühn, 2nd ed., fully revised and expanded, 2:384–405. Berlin: De Gruyter, 2014.

Kunuk, Zacharias, dir. *Atanarjuat: The Fast Runner*. Isuma, 2001.

Kymlicka, Will, and Bashir Bashir, eds. *The Politics of Reconciliation in Multicultural Societies*. Repr. Oxford: Oxford University Press, 2009.

LaCapra, Dominick. *History and Memory after Auschwitz*. Ithaca, NY: Cornell University Press, 1998.

Landsberg, Alison. *Engaging the Past: Mass Culture and the Production of Historical Knowledge*. New York: Columbia University Press, 2015.

———. *Prosthetic Memory: The Transformation of American Remembrance in the Age of Mass Culture*. New York: Columbia University Press, 2007.

Langenohl, Andreas, Ralph J. Poole, and Manfred Weinberg, eds. *Transkulturalität: Klassische Texte*. Bielefeld: transcript, 2015.

Lash, Scott, and Jonathan Friedman, eds. *Modernity and Identity*. Repr. Oxford: Blackwell, 1998.

Lawson, Henry. "The Drover's Wife," in *The Drover's Wife and Other Stories*, ed. Murray Bail (St. Lucia: University of Queensland, 1984).

Leach, Jim. *Film in Canada*. Oxford: Oxford University Press, 2011.

Lee, Philip, ed. *Public Memory, Public Media, and the Politics of Justice*. Basingstoke: Palgrave Macmillan, 2012.

Lee, Philip, and Pradip Thomas, eds. *Public Memory, Public Media, and the Politics of Justice*. Basingstoke: Palgrave Macmillan, 2012.

Leighley, Jan E. *Mass Media and Politics: A Social Science Perspective*. Boston: Houghton Mifflin, 2004.

Lerner, Ralph. *Playing the Fool: Subversive Laughter in Troubled Times*. Chicago: University of Chicago Press, 2009.
Levi, Neil. "No Sensible Comparison? The Place of the Holocaust in Australia's History Wars." *History & Memory* 19, no. 1 (2007): 124–56.
Levy, Daniel, and Natan Sznaider. *The Holocaust and Memory in the Global Age*. Philadelphia: Temple University Press, 2006.
Lind, Jennifer M. *Sorry States: Apologies in International Politics*. Ithaca, NY: Cornell University Press, 2010.
Littlefield, Henry M. "The Wizard of Oz: Parable on Populism." *American Quarterly* 16, no. 1 (Spring 1964): 47–58.
Loomba, Ania, and Martin Orkin, eds. *Post-colonial Shakespeares*. New York: Routledge, 1998.
Löschnig, Martin, and Karin Kraus, eds. *North America, Europe and the Cultural Memory of the First World War*. Heidelberg: Winter, 2015.
Loeschnig, Martin, and Marzena Sokolowska-Paryz, eds. "The Great War in Post-Memory Literature and Film." *Media and Cultural Memory / Medien Und Kulturelle Erinnerung* 18 (2014).
Loxley, James. *Performativity*. London: Routledge, 2007.
Luhrmann, Baz. "How We Made the Epic of OZ." *The Guardian*, 2 November 2008, retrieved 12 November 2017 from https://www.theguardian.com/film/2008/nov/02/baz-luhrmann-nicole-kidman-australia.
———, dir. *Australia*. 20th Century Fox, 2008.
Lutz, John Sutton, ed. *Myth and Memory: Stories of Indigenous-European Contact*. Vancouver: University of British Columbia Press, 2007.
MacDonald, David B., and Graham Hudson. "The Genocide Question and Indian Residential Schools in Canada." *Canadian Journal of Political Science*, 45, no. 2 (2012): 427–49.
Macintyre, Stuart, and Anna Clark. *The History Wars*. New updated ed. Carlton: Melbourne University Press, 2004.
MacLachlan, Alice. "The State of 'Sorry': Official Apologies and Their Absence." *Journal of Human Rights* 9, no. 3 (2010). http://yorku.academia.edu/AliceMacLachlan/Papers/294721/The_State_of_Sorry_Official_Apologies_and_Their_Absence.
Maechler, Stefan. *The Wilkomirski Affair: A Study in Biographical Truth*. New York: Schocken Books, 2001.
Mackey, Eva. "The Apologizer's Apology." In *Reconciling Canada: Critical Perspectives on the Culture of Redress*, edited by Jennifer Henderson and Pauline Wakeham, 47–61. Toronto: University of Toronto Press, 2013.
Magowan, Fiona, and Bain Attwood, eds. *Telling Stories: Indigenous History and Memory in Australia and New Zealand*. Sydney: Allen & Unwin, 2001.
Malcolm, Derek. "Robert Flaherty, Nanook of the North," *The Guardian*, 13 April 2000, retrieved 25 July 2017 from www.theguardian.com/film/2000/apr/13/1.
Malreddy, Pavan Kumar, ed. *Reworking Postcolonialism: Globalization, Labour and Rights*. Basingstoke: Palgrave Macmillan, 2015.
Manne, Robert, ed. *The Australian Century: Political Struggle in the Building of a Nation*. Melbourne: Text Publishing, 1999.
———. *Whitewash: On Keith Windschuttle's Fabrication of Aboriginal History*. Melbourne: Schwartz Publishing Pty. Ltd, 2003.
———. "Comment: The History Wars," *The Monthly*, November 2009, retrieved 21 March 2013 from http://www.themonthly.com.au/nation-reviewed-robert-manne-comment-history-wars-2119.
Marchetti, Elena, and Janet Ransley. "Unconscious Racism: Scrutinizing Judicial Reasoning in 'Stolen Generation' Cases." *Social Legal Studies* 14 (2005): 533–52.

Martín-Barbero, Jesús. *Communication, Culture and Hegemony: From the Media to Mediations.* London: Sage, 1993.
Martschukat, Jürgen, ed. *Geschichtswissenschaften und "performative turn": Ritual, Inszenierung und Performanz vom Mittelalter bis zur Neuzeit.* Köln: Böhlau, 2003.
Maufort, Marc, and Caroline de Wagter, eds. *Old Margins and New Centers / Anciennes marges et nouveaux centres: The European Literary Heritage in an Age of Globalization.* New. Brussels: Peter Lang AG Internationaler Verlag der Wissenschaften, 2011.
McCall, Sophie. "'I Can Only Sing This Song to Someone Who Understands It': Community Filmmaking and the Politics of Partial Translation in 'Atanarjuat, the Fast Runner,'" *Essays on Canadian Writing* 83 (Fall 2004): 19–46
———. "Intimate Enemies: Weetigo, Weesageechak, and the Politics of Reconciliation in Tomson Highway's *Kiss of the Fur Queen* and Joseph Boyden's *Three Day Road.*" *Studies in American Indian Literatures* (2013): 57–85.
McChesney, Robert Waterman. *Rich Media, Poor Democracy: Communication Politics in Dubious Times.* Urbana: University of Illinois Press, 1999.
McClintock, Anne, ed. *Dangerous Liaisons: Gender, Nation, and Postcolonial Perspectives.* Minneapolis: University of Minnesota Press, 1997.
———. *Imperial Leather: Race, Gender, and Sexuality in the Colonial Contest.* London: Routledge, 1995.
McCrea, Michelle. "Collisions of Authority: Nonunitary Narration and Textual Authority in Gail Jones' Sorry." In *Encounters: Refereed Conference Papers of the 17th 1 Annual AAWP Conference*, Adelaide, 2012. Retrieved 3 October 2014 from http://d3n8a8pro7vhmx.cloudfront.net/theaawp/pages/87/attachments/original/1385085229/McCrea.pdf?1385085229.
McGonegal, Julie. "The Great Canadian (and Australian) Secret: The Limits of Non-Indigenous Knowledge and Representation." *English Studies in Canada* 35, no. 1 (March 2009): 67–83.
McKenna, Mark. "Different Perspectives on Black Armband History, 1997." Parliament of Australia, 10 November 1997. Retrieved 14 April 2019 from https://www.aph.gov.au/About_Parliament/Parliamentary_Departments/Parliamentary_Library/pubs/rp/RP9798/98RP05.
Mellor, Doreen, and Anna Haebich, eds. *Many Voices: Reflections on Experiences of Indigenous Child Separation.* Canberra: National Library of Australia, 2002.
Melnyk, George. *One Hundred Years of Canadian Cinema.* Toronto: University of Toronto Press, 2004.
Merkl, Matthias. "Surviving the Residential School: Negotiating Cultural Re-education in Tomson Highway's *Kiss of the Fur Queen.*" In *Literature on the Move: Cultural Migration in Contemporary Literature*, edited by Michael Heinze, 67–78. Trier: WVT, 2010.
Metz, Christian. *The Imaginary Signifier: Psychoanalysis and the Cinema.* Bloomington: University of Indiana Press, 1982.
Meyer, Thomas, and Lewis P. Hinchman. *Media Democracy: How the Media Colonize Politics.* Cambridge: Polity Press, 2002.
Miller, J. R. *Shingwauk's Vision: A History of Native Residential Schools.* Toronto: University of Toronto Press, 2011.
Miller, Toby, ed. "A Companion to Film Theory." *Blackwell Companions in Cultural Studies.* Malden, MA: Blackwell, 2007.
Milloy, John S. "A National Crime: The Canadian Government and the Residential School System." *Manitoba Studies in Native History* 11 (2014).
Montrose, Louis Adrian. "Die Renaissance Behaupten: Poetik Und Politik Der Kultur." Edited by Moritz Bassler. Tübingen. *New Historicism* 2 (2001): 67–88.
Morley, David, ed. *Stuart Hall: Critical Dialogues in Cultural Studies.* London: Routledge, 2005.

Moses, Dirk, and Dan Stone. *Colonialism and Genocide*. Hoboken, NJ: Taylor and Francis, 2013.
Mouffe, Chantal. *Agonistics: Thinking the World Politically*. London: Verso, 2013.
Mulvey, Laura. *Fetishism and Curiosity: Cinema and the Mind's Eye*. Basingstoke: Palgrave Macmillan, 2013.
Murphy, Michael "Apology, Recognition, and Reconciliation." *Hum Rights Rev*, 12, 2011, 47–69.
Nagy, Rosemary. "The Truth and Reconciliation Commission of Canada: Genesis and Design." *Canadian Journal of Law and Society* 29, no. 2 (2014) 199–217.
Narogin, Mudrooroo. *Us Mob: History, Culture, Struggle; An Introduction to Indigenous Australia*. Sydney: Angus & Robertson, 1996.
"National Inquiry into the Separation of Aboriginal and Torres Strait Islander Children from Their Families." *Bringing Them Home Report*, 1997. https://www.humanrights.gov.au/sites/default/files/content/pdf/social_justice/bringing_them_home_report.pdf.
Nelson, Thomas E. "Media and Politics." *Cambridge Handbook of Experimental Political Science*, edited by James N. Druckman and Donald P. Green. Cambridge: Cambridge University Press, 2011. http://books.google.de/books?hl=de&lr=&id=ES5PUvvShF8C&oi=fnd&pg=PA201&dq=media+and+politics&ots=WAdFiyMP7X&sig=2gyeAChxi1zXA8UoIsg3608OU0Q#v=onepage&q=media percent20and percent20politics&f=false.
Niezen, Ronald. *Truth and Indignation: Canada's Truth and Reconciliation Commission on Indian Residential Schools*. Toronto: University of Toronto Press, 2013.
Nischik, Reingard M., ed. *History of Literature in Canada: English-Canadian and French-Canadian*. Suffolk: Boydell & Brewer, 2008.
Nobles, Melissa. *The Politics of Official Apologies*. Cambridge: Cambridge University Press, 2008.
Nora, Pierre, and Lawrence D. Kritzman, eds. *Realms of Memory: Rethinking the French Past*. New York: Columbia University Press, 1996.
Nünning, Ansgar, and Birgit Neumann. *Travelling Concepts for the Study of Culture*. Berlin: De Gruyter, 2010.
Nünning, Ansgar, Carola Surkamp, and Bruno Zerweck, eds. *Unreliable Narration: Studien zur Theorie und Praxis unglaubwürdigen Erzählens in der englischsprachigen Erzählliteratur*. Trier: WVT, 2013.
Nünning, Vera, Ansgar Nünning, and Birgit Neumann. *Cultural Ways of Worldmaking: Media and Narratives*. New York: De Gruyter, 2010.
Olick, Jeffrey K. *The Politics of Regret: On Collective Memory and Historical Responsibility*. New York: Routledge, 2007.
Olick, Jeffrey K., Vered Vinitzky-Seroussi, and Daniel Levy, eds. *The Collective Memory Reader*. Oxford: Oxford University Press, 2011.
Onyanga-Omara, Jane. "Grey Owl: Canada's Great Conservationist and Imposter." BBC News, 19 September 2013. Retrieved 9 May 2018 https://www.bbc.com/news/uk-england-sussex-24127514.
Oreb, Naomi. "Mirroring, Depth and Inversion: Holding Gail Jones' *Black Mirror* against Contemporary Australia." *Sydney Studies in English* 35 (2009).
Ošiņš, Edgars. "Multicultural Canada: Two First Nations Voices." In *American Multiculturalism and Ethnic Survival*, edited by Sabina Matter-Seibel, Renate von Bardeleben, Klaus H. Schmidt, Frankfurt am Main: Peter Lang, 2012.
Parodi, Carlos A. "State Apologies under U.S. Hegemony." In *The Age of Apology: Facing Up to the Past*, edited by Mark Gibney, Rhoda E. Howard-Hassmann, and Jean-Marc Coicaud. Philadelphia: University of Pennsylvania Press, 2008.
Patterson, James. "The Politics of Sorry." *AQ—Australian Quarterly*, 2009. http://search.infomit.com.au/documentSummary;dn=160579927917188;res=IELHSS.

Perry, Susan, ed. *Eye to Eye: Women Practising Development across Cultures*. London: Zed Books, 2001.
Peters, Susanne, Klaus Stierstorfer, and Laurenz Volkmann, eds. "Novels." *Teaching Contemporary Literature and Culture* 2 (2008).
Phelps, Teresa Godwin. *Shattered Voices: Language, Violence, and the Work of Truth Commissions*. Philadelphia: University of Pennsylvania Press, 2004.
Philpott, Catherine, Nikola Balvin, David Mellor, and Di Bretherton, "Making Meaning from Collective Apologies: Australia's Apology to Its Indigenous Peoples," *Peace and Conflict: Journal of Peace Psychology* 19, no. 1 (2013): 35.
Platinga, Carl. "Trauma, Pleasure, and Emotion in the Viewing of *Titanic*." In *Film Theory and Contemporary Hollywood Movies*, edited by Warren Buckland. New York: Routledge, 2009.
Posel, Deborah, and Graeme S. Simpson, eds. *Commissioning the Past: Understanding South Africa's Truth and Reconciliation Commission*. Johannesburg: Witwatersrand University Press, 2002.
Power, Samantha. *"A Problem from Hell": America and the Age of Genocide*. London: Zed Books, 2004.
Prentice, Chris. "Reconciliation and Cultural Indifference." In *Resistance and Reconciliation: Writing in the Commonwealth*, edited by Bruce Bennett, 168–86. Canberra: ACLALS, 2003.
Prentki, Tim. *The Fool in European Theatre: Stages of Folly*. Basingstoke: Palgrave Macmillan, 2012.
Quinlivan, Natalie. "Finding a Place in Story: Kim Scott's Writing and the Wirlomin Noongar Language and Stories Project." *Journal of the Association for the Study of Australian Literature* 14, no. 3 (2014): 1–12.
Rabelais, François, and Burton Raffel. *Gargantua and Pantagruel*. Norton paperback. New York: Norton, 1991.
Rabelais, François, and M. A. Screech. *Pantagrueline Prognostication for 1535*. London: ProQuest LLC; Penguin, 2011.
Radin, Paul. *The Trickster: A Study in American Indian Mythology*. New York: Schocken Books, 1988.
Raheja, Michelle H. "Reading Nanook's Smile: Visual Sovereignty, Indigenous Revisions of Ethnography, and Atanarjuat: The Fast Runner." *American Quarterly* 59, no. 4 (December 2007): 1159–85.
Rask Knudsen, Eva. "Aboriginal Affair(s): Reflections on Mudrooroo's Life and Work." *Literature in North Queensland* 39 (2012): 105–17.
Read, Peter. *The Stolen Generations: The Removal of Aboriginal Children in New South Wales 1883 to 1969*. Sydney: Department of Aboriginal Affairs, 2006. http://www.daa.nsw.gov.au/publications/StolenGenerations.pdf.
Regan, Paulette. *Unsettling the Settler Within: Indian Residential Schools, Truth-Telling, and Reconciliation in Canada*. Vancouver: UBC Press, 2010.
Reinelt, Janelle G., and Joseph Roach, eds. *Critical Theory and Performance*. Ann Arbor: University of Michigan, 2007.
Renan, Ernest. "What Is a Nation?" In *Nation and Narration*, edited by Homi K. Bhabha, 8–23. London: Routledge, 1990. http://books.google.com/books?id=1TYOAAAAQAAJ&printsec=frontcover&hl=de&source=gbs_ge_summary_r&cad=0#v=onepage&q&f=false.
Renteln, Alison Dundes. "Apologies: A Cross-Cultural Analysis." In *The Age of Apology: Facing Up to the Past*, edited by Mark Gibney, Rhoda E. Howard-Hassmann, and Jean-Marc Coicaud. Philadelphia: University of Pennsylvania Press, 2008.
Reynaud, Anne-Marie. "Dealing with Difficult Emotions: Anger at the Truth and Reconciliation Commission of Canada". *Anthropologica* 56, no. 2 (2012): 369–82

Reynolds, Henry. *The Other Side of the Frontier: Aboriginal Resistance to the European Invasion of Australia*. London: Penguin Books, 1990.

———. *Why Weren't We Told? A Personal Search for the Truth about Our History*. Sydney: Viking, 1999.

Reynolds, Margaret, ed. *On the Occasion of the National Sorry Day: A Collection of Personal Letters and Extracts from Parliamentary Debates Presented to the Indigenous People of Australia*. Canberra: Senate Printing Unite, 1998.

Richter, Virginia. "Authenticity—Why We Still Need It Although It Does Not Exist." In *Transcultural English Studies: Theories*, edited by Frank Schulze-Engler and Sissy Helff, 59–74. New York: Rodopi, 2009.

———. "Urquhart, Jane, The Stone Carvers." Edited by Susanne Peters, Klaus Stierstorfer, and Laurenz Volkmann. *Novels* 2 (2008): 495–508.

Ricoeur, Paul. *Gedächtnis, Geschichte, Vergessen*. Paderborn: Fink, 2004.

———. Chicago: University of Chicago Press, 2004.

———. *Oneself as Another*. Chicago: University of Chicago Press, 1992.

———. *Time and Narrative*. Vols. 1–3. Chicago: University of Chicago Press, 1984-85.

Ridington, Robert, ed. *When You Sing It Now, Just like New: First Nations Poetics, Voices, and Representations*. Lincoln: University of Nebraska Press, 2006.

Rigney, Ann. "Portable Monuments: Literature, Cultural Memory, and the Case of Jeanie Deans." *Poetics Today* 25, no. 2 (2004): 361–96.

———. "Reconciliation and Remembering: (How) Does It Work?" *Memory Studies* 5, no. 3 (2012): 251–58.

Rigney, Ann, and Chiara Cesari, eds. "Transnational Memory: Circulation, Articulation, Scales." *Media and Cultural Memory* 19 (2014).

Rodwell, Grant. "Curing the Precocious Masturbator: Eugenics and Australian Early Childhood Education." *Journal of Australian Studies* 1 (1998). http://www.questia.com/PM.qst?a=o&d=5001405863.

Roosvall, Anna, and Inka Salovaara-Moring, eds. *Communicating the Nation: National Topographies of Global Media Landscapes*. Göteborg: Nordicom, 2010.

Rosenthal, Caroline. "English-Canadian Literary Theory and Literary Criticism." *History of Literature in Canada: English-Canadian and French-Canadian*, edited by Reingard M. Nischik. Suffolk: Boydell & Brewer, 2008.

Rothberg, Michael. *Multidirectional Memory: Remembering the Holocaust in the Age of Decolonization*. Stanford, CA: Stanford University Press, 2009.

Rothberg, Michael. *The Implicated Subject: Beyond Victims and Perpetrators*. Stanford, Calif: Stanford University Press, 2019.

Rothberg, Michael. "Remembering Back: Cultural Memory, Colonial Legacies, and Postcolonial Studies," in *The Oxford Handbook of Postcolonial Studies*, ed. Graham Huggan. Oxford: Oxford University Press, 2013, 359–79.

Rothfield, Philipa, Cleo Fleming, and Paul A. Komesaroff, eds. *Pathways to Reconciliation: Between Theory and Practice*. Aldershot: Ashgate, 2008.

Rudd, Kevin. "Apology to Australia's Indigenous Peoples." Australian Government, 2008. https://www.australia.gov.au/about-australia/our-country/our-people/apology-to-australias-indigenous-peoples.

Rushdie, Salman. *Imaginary Homelands: Essays and Criticism, 1981–91*. London: Granta Books, 1992.

Rutherford, Jonathan, ed. *Identity: Community, Culture, Difference*. London: Lawrence & Wishart, 1998.

———. "The Third Space: Interview with Homi Bhabha." In *Identity: Community, Culture, Difference*, edited by Jonathan Rutherford, 207–21. London: Lawrence & Wishart, 1998.

Ryan, Allan J. *The Trickster Shift: Humour and Irony in Contemporary Native Art*. Vancouver: UBC Press, 1999.
Ryan, Michael, and Melissa Lenos. *An Introduction to Film Analysis: Technique and Meaning in Narrative Film*. New York: Continuum, 2012.
Said, Edward W. *Orientalism*. London: Penguin Books, 2003.
Salecl, Renata. "Why One Would Pretend to Be a Victim of the Holocaust." *Other Voices: The (e)Journal of Cultural Criticism* 2, no. 1 (2000). Retrieved 29 November 2020 from https://web.archive.org/web/20100902060300/http:/www.othervoices.org/2.1/salecl/wilkomirski.html.
Sarkowsky, Katja. *AlterNative Spaces: Constructions of Space in Native American and First Nations' Literatures*. Heidelberg: Winter, 2007.
Saxer, Ulrich. "Public Relations and Symbolic Politics." *Journal of Public Relations Research* 5, no. 2 (1993): 127–51.
Saxton, Charles A. "Whiteness and Reconciliation." *Australian Psychologist*, 2004. http://onlinelibrary.wiley.com/doi/10.1080/00050060410001660407/abstract.
Schaffer, Kay. "Narrative Lives and Human Rights: Stolen Generation Narratives and the Ethics of Recognition." *Journal of the Association for the Study of Australian Literature*, 2004. http://show20results20www.nationaltreasures.nla.gov.au/openpublish/index.php/jasal/article/viewArticle/31.
Schechner, Richard. *Performance Studies: An Introduction*. London: Routledge, 2002.
———. *Performance Theory*. London: Routledge, 2009.
Scheub, Harold. *Trickster and Hero: Two Characters in the Oral and Written Traditions of the World*. Madison: University of Wisconsin Press, 2012.
Schulze-Engler, Frank. "Englischsprachige Literaturen." In *Handbuch Postkolonialismus und Literatur*, edited by Dirk Göttsche, Axel Dunker, and Gabriele Dürbeck, 343–54. Stuttgart: Metzler, 2017.
———. "Global History, Indigenous Modernities, Transcultural Memory: World War I and II in Native Canadian, Aboriginal Australian, and Māori Fiction." In *Comparative Indigenous Studies*, edited by Mita Banerjee, 383–423. Tübingen: Universitätsverlag Winter, 2016.
———. "Once We Were Internationalists? Postcolonialism, Disenchanted Solidarity and the Right to Belong in a World of Globalized Modernity." In *Reworking Postcolonialism: Globalization, Labour and Rights*, edited by Pavan Kumar Malreddy, 19–35. Basingstoke: Palgrave Macmillan, 2015.
———. "Transcultural Negotiations: Third Spaces in Modern Times." In *Communicating in the Third Space*, edited by Karin Ikas, 149–69. London: Routledge, 2008.
———. "Von 'Inter' zu 'Trans': Gesellschaftliche, kulturelle und literarische Übergänge." In *Inter- und transkulturelle Studien: Theoretische Grundlagen und interdisziplinäre Praxis*, edited by Ed Heinz Antor, 41–55. Heidelberg: Winter, 2006.
Schulze-Engler, Frank, and Sissy Helff, eds. "Transcultural English Studies: Theories, Fictions, Realities." Amsterdam: Rodopi, 2009.
Schwartz, Daniel. "Truth and Reconciliation Commission: By the Numbers." CBC, 2 June 2015. http://www.cbc.ca/news/indigenous/truth-and-reconciliation-commission-by-the-numbers-1.3096185.
Schwarz, Anja, and Sabine Lucia Müller, eds. "Iterationen: Geschlecht im kulturellen Gedächtnis." *Querelles* 13 (2008).
Schwerin, Catherine. "Speaking the Unspeakable—Manifestations of Silence in Gail Jones' *Sorry*." *Bulletin of the Transilvania University of Brasov* 2, no. 51, 2009, 37–40.
Scott, Kim. *Benang: From the Heart*. Sydney: Freemantle Press, 1999.
Searle, John R. *Speech Acts: An Essay in the Philosophy of Language*. Cambridge: Cambridge University Press, 2012.

Sehdev, Robinder Kaur. "Introduction: Residential Schools and Decolonization." *Canadian Journal of Law and Society* 27, no. 1 (2012): 67–73.

Sehgal, Parul. "He Was a Prominent Holocaust Survivor. But His Story Was a Hoax." *New York Times*, 28 August 2018. Retrieved 29 November 2020 from https://www.nytimes.com/2018/08/28/books/review-impostor-javier-cercas-enric-marco.html.

Sen, Amartya. *Identity and Violence: The Illusion of Destiny*. London: Penguin, 2006.

Shanahan, Dennis. "John Howard Revives History Wars in Attack on Labor Curriculum." *The Australian*, 2012. Retrieved 27 May 2021 https://www.theaustralian.com.au/subscribe/news/1/?sourceCode=TAWEB_WRE170_a_GGL&dest=https%3A%2F%2Fwww.theaustralian.com.au%2Fnational-affairs%2Feducation%2Fjohn-howard-revives-history-wars-in-attack-on-labor-curriculum%2Fnews-story%2Fbf937b5efffa28c0cc381e922f8722a2&memtype=anonymous&mode=premium&nk=f859ff3346791b773cfcb95588a28c9f-1622135421&v21suffix=414-b

Shaw, A. G. L. *Convicts and the Colonies: A Study of Penal Transportation from Great Britain and Ireland to Australia and Other Parts of the British Empire*. London: Faber, 1971.

Shea, Dorothy C. *The South African Truth Commission: The Politics of Reconciliation*. Washington, DC: United States Institute of Peace Press, 2000.

Shore, Megan. *Religion and Conflict Resolution: Christianity and South Africa's Truth and Reconciliation Commission*. Burlington: Ashgate, 2009.

Short, Damien. "Reconciliation and the Stolen Generations." In *Essays on Australian Reconciliation*, edited by Michelle Grattan. Melbourne: Bookman Press, 2000.

———. *Reconciliation and Colonial Power: Indigenous Rights in Australia*. Aldershot: Ashgate, 2008.

Sikorska, Liliana, and Agnieszka Rzepa, eds. *Eyes Deep with Unfathomable Histories: The Poetics and Politics of Magic Realism Today and in the Past*. Wiebaden: Peter Lang, 2012.

Simons, Roger I. "Towards a Hopeful Practice of Worrying: The Problematics of Listening and the Educative Responsibilities of Canada's Truth and Reconciliation Commission." In *Reconciling Canada: Critical Perspectives on the Culture of Redress*, edited by Jennifer Henderson and Pauline Wakeham, 129–41. Toronto: University of Toronto Press, 2013.

Singer, Milton. "Search for a Great Tradition in Cultural Performances." In *Performance: Critical Concepts in Literary and Cultural Studies*, edited by Philip Auslander, 57–71. London: Routledge, 2003.

Sitze, Adam. *The Impossible Machine: A Genealogy of South Africa's Truth and Reconciliation Commission*. Ann Arbor: University of Michigan Press, 2013.

Sivan, Emmanuel, and J. M. Winter, eds. *War and Remembrance in the Twentieth Century*. Cambridge: Cambridge University Press, 1999.

Slater, Lisa. "*Benang*, This 'Most Local of Histories': Annexing Colonial Records into a World without End." *Journal of Commonwealth Literature* 41, no. 1 (2006): 51–68.

———. "Kim Scott's *Benang*: An Ethics of Uncertainty." *Journal of the Association for the Study of Australian Literature* 4 (2005): 147–52.

———. "Making Strange Men: Resistance and Reconciliation in Kim Scott's *Benang*." In *Resistance and Reconciliation: Writing in the Commonwealth*, edited by Bruce Bennett, 358–70. Canberra: ACLALS, 2003.

Smith, Lindsey. "'With These Magic Weapons, Make a New World': Indigenous Centered Urbanism in Tomson Highway's *Kiss of the Fur Queen*." *Canadian Journal of Native Studies* 29, nos. 1–2 (2009): 143–46.

Sokolowska-Paryz, Marzena. "Remembering German Canadians in Jane Urquhart's *The Stone Carvers* and Paul Gross's *Passchendaele*: 'Alien Citizens' versus 'the Birth of a Nation.'" In *North America, Europe and the Cultural Memory of the First World War*, edited by Martin Löschnigg and Karin Kraus, 121–32. Heidelberg: Winter, 2015.

Sokolowska-Paryz, Marzena, and Martin Löschnigg. "Introduction: Have You Forgotten Yet . . . ?" In *The Great War in Post-memory Literature and Film*, edited by Martin Löschnigg and Marzena Sokołowska-Paryż. Berlin, Boston: de Gruyter, 2014.

Spence, Louise, and Vinicius Navarro. *Crafting Truth: Documentary Form and Meaning*. New Brunswick, NJ: Rutgers University Press, 2011.

Stanner, W. E. H. *After the Dreaming*. Crows Nest, ABC, 1991.

Stanton, Kim. "Looking Forward, Looking Back: The Canadian Truth and Reconciliation Commission and the Mackenzie Valley Pipeline Inquiry." *Canadian Journal of Law and Society* 27, no. 1 (2012): 81–89.

Starrs, Bruno D. "The Aboriginal Voice and the Left-Leaning 'Australia.'" *Continuum: Journal of Media & Cultural Studies* 26, no. 4 (2012): 625–36.

Strong-Boag, Veronica Jane, ed. *Painting the Maple: Essays on Race, Gender, and the Construction of Canada*. Vancouver: UBC Press, 1998.

Subero, Gustavo, ed. *HIV in World Cultures: Three Decades of Representations*. London: Taylor and Francis, 2016.

Sullivan, Dale, Bruce Maylath, and Russel K. Hirst. *Revisiting the Past through Rhetorics of Memory and Amnesia: Selected Papers from the 50th Meeting of the Linguistic Circle of Manitoba and North Dakota*. Newcastle: Cambridge Scholars, 2011.

Sutton, Peter. "The Politics of Suffering: Indigenous Policy in Australia since the 1970s." *Anthropological Forum* 2 (2001). http://www.mccaugheycentre.unimelb.edu.au/__data/assets/pdf_file/0010/143875/Sutton_2001.pdf.

Swain, Shurlee, and Margot Hillel. *Child, Nation, Race and Empire: Child Rescue Discourse, England, Canada and Australia, 1850–1915*. Manchester: Manchester University Press, 2010.

Tavuchis, Nicholas, ed. *Mea Culpa: A Sociology of Apology and Reconciliation*. Stanford, CA: Stanford University Press, 1991.

Taylor, Charles. *Multiculturalism and the Politics of Recognition*. Princeton, NJ: Princeton University Press, 1994.

Taylor, Charles, and Amy Gutmann, eds. *Multiculturalism: Examining the Politics of Recognition*. Princeton, NJ: Princeton University Press, 1994.

Taylor, Diana. "Transculturating Transculturation." *Performing Arts Journal* 13, no. 2 (May 1991): 90–104.

Taylor, Quentin P. "Money and Politics in the Land of Oz." *Independent Review* 9, no. 3 (Winter 2005): 413–26.

Teichler, Hanna. "Joseph Boyden's *Three Day Road*: Transcultural (Post-)Memory and Identity in Canadian World War I Fiction." *The Great War in Post-memory Literature and Film*. Edited by Martin Löschnigg and Marzena Sokołowska-Paryż, 239–53. Boston: De Gruyter, 2014.

———. "Re-imagining the Sacred Site: The Vimy Ridge Memorial and Transcultural Canadian Memory of the Great War in Janes Urquhart's The Stone Carvers," in *Disasters of War: Perceptions and Representations from 1914 to the Present*, ed. Steffen Bruendel and Frank Estelmann (Wiesbaden: Wilhelm Fink, 2019), 211–28.

Government of Australia. "Apology to the Stolen Generations," n.d. https://www.youtube.com/watch?v=_Dild-xAzJ0.

The Government of Canada. "The Indian Residential School Settlement Agreement." N.d. Retrieved 4 March 2018 from http://www.residentialschoolsettlement.ca/settlement.html.

Thielen-Wilson, Leslie. "Troubling the Path to Decolonization: Indian Residential School Case Law, Genocide, and Settler Illegitimacy." *Canadian Journal of Law and Society* 29, no. 2 (2014): 181–97.

Thomas, Brook. *Civic Myths: A Law-and-Literature Approach to Citizenship*. Chapel Hill: University of North Carolina Press, 2007.

Thompson, Dennis Frank, and Robert I. Rotberg, eds. *Truth versus Justice: The Morality of Truth Commissions*. Princeton, NJ: Princeton University Press, 2000.
Thompson, Eric. "Canadian Fiction of the Great War." *Canadian Literature* 91, no. 4 (1981): 81–96.
Thompson, Graham F. "Approaches of Performance. An Analysis of Terms." In *Performance: Critical Concepts in Literary and Cultural Studies*, edited by Philip Auslander, 138–52. London: Routledge, 2003.
Thompson, Janna. "Apology, Justice, and Respect: A Critical Defense of Political Apology." In *The Age of Apology: Facing Up to the Past*, edited by Mark Gibney, Rhoda E. Howard-Hassmann, and Jean-Marc Coicaud. Philadelphia: University of Pennsylvania Press, 2008.
Trezise, Bryoni. *Performing Feeling in Cultures of Memory*. Basingstoke: Palgrave Macmillan, 2014.
Tridafilopoulos, Tridafilos. *Becoming Multicultural: Immigration and the Politics of Membership in Canada and Germany*. Vancouver: UBC Press, 2013.
Truth and Reconciliation Commission of Canada. *Interim Report*. 10 December 2014. Retrieved 4 March 2018 from http://www.trc.ca/websites/trcinstitution/index.php?p=580.
———. *Honouring the Truth, Reconciling for the Future*. Final report. N.d. Retrieved 4 March 2018 from http://www.trc.ca/websites/trcinstitution/File/2015/Honouring_the_Truth_Reconciling_for_the_Future_July_23_2015.pdf.
———. "Our Mandate." N.d. http://www.trc.ca/websites/trcinstitution/index.php?p=7.
Turner, Victor. "Revelation and Divination in Ndembu Ritual." Ithaca, NY: Cornell University Press, 1975.
Tutu, Desmond. *No Future without Forgiveness*. London: Rider, 1999.
United Nations. "Genocide Convention." N.d. Retrieved 27 May 2021 from https://legal.un.org/avl/ha/cppcg/cppcg.html
———. "Resolution 61/17, International Year of Reconciliation, 2006." Retrieved 5 February 2018 from https://digitallibrary.un.org/record/587002?ln=en.
Urquhart, Jane. *The Stone Carvers*. London: Bloomsbury, 2001.
———. *The Underpainter*. London: Penguin, 1997.
Vandamme, Christine. "'The Drover's Wife': Celebrating or Demystifying Bush Mythology?" *Commonwealth Essays and Studies* 38, no. 2 (2016): 73–81.
Veel, Kristin. *Narrative Negotiations: Information Structures in Literary Fiction*. Göttingen: Vandenhoeck & Ruprecht, 2009.
Veitch, Scott, ed. *Law and the Politics of Reconciliation*. Aldershot: Ashgate, 2007.
Verdeja, Ernesto. *Unchopping a Tree: Reconciliation in the Aftermath of Political Violence*. Philadelphia: Temple University Press, 2009.
Verdoolaege, Annelies. "*Reconciliation Discourse: The Case of the Truth and Reconciliation Commission*. Amsterdam: John Benjamin, 2008.
———, ed. *The South African Truth and Reconciliation Commission and Multicultural Discourse*. London: Routledge, 2008.
Verstraten, Peter. "Between Attraction and Story: Rethinking Narrativity in Cinema." Edited by Sandra Heinen and Roy Sommer. *Narratology in the Age of Cross-Disciplinary Narrative Research* 1 (2009): 154–69.
Villa-Vicencio, Charles. *Walk with Us and Listen: Political Reconciliation in Africa*. Washington, DC: Georgetown University Press, 2009.
Vines, Stephen. "Queen to Say Sorry to the Maori People." *The Independent*, 2 July 1995. Retrieved 1 December 2020 from https://www.independent.co.uk/news/queen-to-say-sorry-to-the-maori-people-1589370.html.
Vranckx, Silvie. "The Ambivalence of Cultural Syncreticity in Highway's *Kiss of the Fur Queen* and Van Kamp's *The Lesser Blessed*." In *Old Margins and New Centers: The European Liter-*

ary Heritage in an Age of Globalization, edited by Marc Maufort and Caroline de Wagter. Wiesbaden Peter Lang, 2011.
Wachanga, D. Ndirangu. *Cultural Identity and New Communication Technologies: Political, Ethnic and Ideological Implications*. Hershey, PA: Information Science Reference, 2011.
Wakeham, Pauline. *Taxidermic Signs: Reconstructing Aboriginality*. Minneapolis: University of Minnesota Press, 2008.
Walsh, Richard. *The Rhetoric of Fictionality: Narrative Theory and the Idea of Fiction*. Columbus: Ohio State University Press, 2007.
———, "The Pragmatics of Narrative Fictionality," in *A Companion to Narrative Theory*, ed. James Phelan and Peter J. Rabinowitz. Malden: Blackwell, 2005.
Ward, Russel Braddock. *The Australian Legend*. Repr. Melbourne: Melbourne University Press, 1993.
Welsch, Wolfgang. "Transkulturalität: Zwischen Globalisierung und Partikularisierung." In *Transkulturalität: Klassische Texte*, edited by Andreas Langenohl, Ralph J. Poole, and Manfred Weinberg. Bielefeld: transcript, 2015.
Wherry, Aaron. "The Commons: The Apology." *Macleans*. 12 June 2008. Retrieved 4 March 2018 from http://www.macleans.ca/uncategorized/the-commons-the-apology/.
Whitlock, Gilian. "In the Second Person: Narrative Transactions in Stolen Generations Testimony." *Biography* 24 (2011): 197–214.
Williams, David. *Imagined Nations: Reflections on Media in Canadian Fiction*. Québec: McGill-Queen's University Press, 2003.
Wimmer, Adi. "Australian Film: Cultures, Identities, Texts." *Focal Point* 7 (2007).
Windschuttle, Keith. *The Fabrication of Aboriginal History: Van Diemen's Land: 1803–1847*. Sydney: Macleay Press, 2004.
Wyndham, Diana. *Eugenics in Australia: Striving for National Fitness*. London: Galton Institute, 2003.
Young, Robert C. *Colonial Desire: Hybridity in Theory, Culture and Race*. London: Routledge, 2006.
———. "Postcolonial Remains." *New Literary History* 43, no. 1 (2012): 19–42.

INDEX

Aboriginals, 5, 17, 18, 31, 35, 73, 111, 118–20, 124, 127, 139, 145, 153, 157, 206–8, 212, 215–19
  Aborigine, 31, 113, 118–19, 143
  Aboriginal, 2, 5, 6, 17, 23, 29–33, 34, 36, 42, 46, 48, 70, 72, 76–79, 89–91, 111–13, 118–21, 124–27, 136, 138, 140–41, 144–46, 148, 150–51, 159, 164, 168, 206–8, 211–13, 215–20, 221, 231
aesthetics, 3, 11–14, 16, 18, 62–63, 68, 82, 141, 148, 159, 166, 170, 175, 179, 186, 190, 199, 200, 207–8, 215–16, 220, 229, 230, 232–34
agency, 4, 11, 17, 28, 44–45, 89, 98, 102, 105, 111, 127, 153, 186, 189, 200, 219
Apartheid, 7, 26–28
amnesty, 7, 10, 27–28, 40
apology, 1, 2, 5, 12, 14–18, 23, 25, 33–34, 38, 47–48, 69, 70–80, 88–89, 112, 125–26, 128, 136, 205–6, 208, 213, 231. *See also* public apology
appropriation, 126, 142, 150, 157, 16
Australia, 2–18, 22–24, 28–35, 37, 40–49, 59, 65–66, 68–82, 88–89, 91, 110–19, 121–27, 129, 137–40, 143, 147, 153–55, 167, 177–79, 185–86, 197, 200, 205–21, 227–34
authenticity, 9–10, 17, 68, 92–93, 157, 163, 176, 186, 188, 192, 199–202, 218, 220

binary, 3, 12, 17, 45, 61, 67, 74, 80, 82, 100, 115, 121, 139, 146, 168, 176, 178, 214, 228, 229

blockbuster, 16, 185
Boyden, Joseph, 16–17, 82, 88–91, 93–100, 102–3, 105, 107–9, 128–29, 159, 175, 230–31, 234

Canada, 1–2, 4–5, 7–18, 22–24, 30, 34–40, 43–49, 59–60, 63, 65–66, 68–70, 72–76, 78–80, 82, 88, 90–94, 96–102, 108, 127, 129, 156, 159, 167, 177, 179, 185–86, 188–89, 191, 193–94, 196, 198–99, 201, 205, 220, 227–30, 232
carnival, 11–12, 14–15, 61–63, 65–66, 69, 78, 106, 163–64, 203, 221, 228
  carnivalesque, 2–3, 10–18, 60, 62, 63–70, 74, 78, 80–82, 89, 106, 109, 113, 127, 150, 151, 163–65, 175–76, 178–79, 199, 202–3, 207–8, 210–11, 214–16, 220, 228–34
  carnivalizing, 1, 14, 17, 80, 121, 127, 137, 140, 144–48, 153, 157–58, 163, 165, 173, 177, 179, 186, 188, 197, 199, 201, 203, 205, 213, 218, 220, 230, 231, 233
  carnivalization, 65, 114, 118, 120, 126–27, 138, 146, 155, 221, 233
  carnival of reconciliation, 12, 78
Chauvel, Charles, 212
citation, 41, 64, 71, 199, 213
  citational 11, 64
clown, 61–62, 128, 176
colonialism, 2, 13, 17, 25, 28, 38, 47, 78, 80, 93, 95, 101, 111, 114, 124, 127–28, 141, 145, 156, 158, 159, 161, 187–88, 192, 195–96, 200, 203, 220, 232

colonial, 2, 4–6, 10, 17, 29–30, 34–40, 44–48, 59–60, 70, 75, 77, 90, 93, 95, 111–18, 126–27, 129, 137–38, 140–43, 145–47, 150, 154–56, 158–60, 164, 166, 168, 174–78, 185–90, 192–93, 197–200, 202–3, 205, 208, 213, 216–18, 220, 227, 230–33
colonial gaze, 17, 113, 185, 187, 190, 193, 197, 199, 203, 233. *See also* postcolonial
commemoration, 96
container, 3, 8, 10–12, 15, 81, 107, 128–29, 151, 159, 178, 199
  compartment, 3, 13, 17, 78, 93–94, 128, 186, 211–12
  compartmentalization, 75
contemporary, 2–4, 12, 16, 25, 41, 59, 70, 81, 97, 111, 113, 118, 126–27, 138, 141, 147, 156, 157, 175, 193–94, 199, 201–3, 206, 213, 234
criminal justice, 3, 7, 27
culture, 10–11, 15, 42, 61–63, 68–69, 71, 75–76, 78, 80–82, 89, 94, 99–100, 105, 107–9, 111, 113, 115–16, 118–19, 122–23, 126, 128–29, 136, 138, 149–51, 153, 157–58, 160–62, 164–67, 169, 175–78, 187, 189–91, 193–96, 199, 201, 203–4, 207, 210, 217, 220, 227, 229, 232
  culturally, 2, 5, 36–37, 68, 81, 105, 117, 127, 148, 157, 159, 165, 172, 175, 190–91, 201, 205, 209, 230, 232
  cultural encounters, 3, 12–13, 203, 233
  See also transcultural identity
  cultural productions, 14, 16, 18, 229–30, 233–34
  essentialism, 9, 68, 129, 153, 160, 188, 203

democracy, 1, 7, 22, 25–26, 28–29, 34, 38, 66, 74
discourse, 3–5, 8–9, 10, 14–17, 23, 27–28, 31–32, 34–35, 37, 41–42, 44, 46–48, 59, 64–65, 69, 81–82, 89, 93–96, 106, 110–12, 117–18, 122–28, 137–38, 147, 154–55, 158–59, 164, 175, 187, 188, 192–94, 196–97, 205, 207, 209, 211, 213, 227, 229–31, 233

discursive, 1–2, 8, 10, 15, 18, 24–25, 27–29, 31, 41, 48, 59–60, 64–65, 67, 82, 114, 117, 122, 126, 138, 140, 146, 155, 186, 197, 200, 204, 208, 209, 210, 228, 234
documentary, 17, 191–92, 197–98

empire, 96, 111, 188–89, 19
  See also imperial
empowerment, 6, 8–10, 18, 28, 39–41, 43, 63, 65, 68, 74, 112, 127, 150, 185–86, 207, 213, 215, 228, 230
  empowering, 3, 11, 23, 27–28, 41, 59–60, 64, 66, 74, 80–81, 119, 139, 147, 185, 212, 215, 220–21, 228, 230–31
enforced reconciliation, 18, 186, 205, 208
entanglements, 3, 14, 27, 42, 66, 68, 81, 89, 158, 178, 185, 228–29, 232
exploration, 11–16, 65, 77, 80–81, 138, 144, 176, 177–78, 193, 206, 212, 229

fiction, 15, 227, 229
fictions of reconciliation, 227
film, 14, 16, 185–86, 188, 193–94
  feature film, 186
First Nations, 1, 5, 36, 44, 71–76, 91, 128, 156–59, 161–62, 174–75, 194
First World War, 99
  See also World War I
Flaherty, Robert J., 221
fool, 12, 16–17, 32, 61–62, 80, 105–9, 128, 151, 179, 217, 231, 233, 234
forcible removal, 6, 9, 14, 29, 33–35, 37–38, 43, 47, 49, 65, 71, 77–78, 82, 111, 124, 127, 136, 138, 139, 144, 156, 206, 221, 227
foster system, 5
framework, 4, 6, 8–10, 12–13, 15, 24, 27–28, 40, 43, 59, 60–61, 63–64, 68, 73, 76, 81–82, 105–7, 156–57, 167–68, 175, 188, 190, 208–9, 221, 227–29, 232, 234

gesture, 1–2, 5, 12, 38, 45, 48, 66, 69–71, 73–74, 77, 80, 98, 114, 199, 206–7, 215, 232
government, 1–2, 5, 7–9, 14, 23–25, 30–31, 34–36, 38–39, 43, 46, 69, 70–75, 77–79, 89, 112, 136, 189

guilt, 6, 17, 25–26, 33, 65, 89, 110–12, 122, 124, 126–27, 159, 176, 231
Harper, Stephen, 1, 5, 12, 23, 70, 71–75, 78, 80, 136
heritage, 16–17, 31–32, 36, 91, 93–94, 99, 102, 112, 136, 138–39, 140–42, 146, 174–75, 178, 201, 208, 213, 232
Highway, Tomson, 16–17, 82, 136–37, 155, 158–59, 171, 177–78, 231
hierarchies, 2–3, 10–13, 16–17, 23, 25, 28, 42, 59–61, 63–65, 68–70, 74, 77–78, 80, 111, 118, 127, 137, 140, 151, 163, 179, 189, 192, 197, 208, 210–11, 220, 227–29, 232
history, 5, 8, 12, 17–18, 23–24, 29, 31–34, 37, 39, 40, 42–44, 45, 47–48, 60, 67–68, 70, 73–74, 76–80, 82, 88–93, 96–100, 111–13, 121–22, 124, 140–43, 145–48, 152–54, 176, 178, 185, 188, 194, 196–97, 205–9, 211, 215, 219, 221, 228, 230, 231, 233
Holocaust, 38, 91–92, 200
homogenous, 68, 75, 128, 191
  homogeneity, 75
  homogenizing 9
human rights, 2, 7, 25–26, 34, 38, 40–41, 69, 80, 194, 227–28, 234
hybrid, 25, 105, 109–10, 117, 128, 141, 150, 159, 164

imperial, 78, 191, 206–10
Indigenous, 1–6, 8–12, 14, 16–18, 23–24, 29–40, 42–49, 59–60, 63, 64–82, 88–91, 93, 94–102, 104–6, 108–13, 118–21, 123–29, 137–39, 141, 144, 146–47, 149–51, 153, 154–59, 161–62, 165–68, 171, 174–78, 185–88, 191–92, 194–96, 202, 204–6, 209–10, 213, 215–16, 218–21, 227–33
  Indigenous peoples, 1–2, 4–5, 9–10, 14, 24, 40, 44–45, 47–48, 65–66, 72, 74, 76–78, 80, 82, 90, 111, 129, 139, 144, 156, 185, 191, 210, 213, 220–21, 227–28
  Indigenous identities, 2, 10, 90–91, 94, 97, 100, 108–10, 128–29, 138–39, 156–57, 220, 231
  Indigeneity, 5, 17, 24, 36, 47–48, 59, 74–75, 90–91, 93–94, 128, 154, 157–59, 161, 167, 177, 187, 192–93, 196, 198, 201–2, 208, 213, 219, 230–31
identity template, 4, 9–10, 12, 28, 45–47, 49, 59, 82, 93, 134, 137–40, 172, 228
imitation, 9, 13, 47, 104, 107
  imitate 142
imposter, 16, 89, 91, 93
  See also mnemonic imposter
inferior, 9–10, 68, 113, 115–16, 126, 136, 138, 140, 187–88, 190–92, 197
inquiry, 6, 23, 34

Jones, Gail, 82, 88, 115, 128, 230, 231

knowledge, 7, 15, 23–24, 31, 37, 40, 44, 74, 93, 95, 98–99, 112–13, 118, 123, 129, 137, 141, 143, 168, 193, 196, 201, 228, 232
Kunuk, Zacharias, 16–17, 185–86, 194, 201, 219, 232

legacy, 5, 22–23, 28, 31, 35, 37, 39, 45, 80, 96, 118, 136, 168, 178, 185, 206, 209, 221, 233
  colonial legacy, 35
Luhrmann, Baz, 16–17, 185, 205, 212, 219–20, 233

marketplace, 11, 15, 61–62, 66–67, 109
memory 4, 5, 7, 9, 13–14, 16, 18, 31, 35, 42, 45, 69–70, 81, 89, 92, 96–97, 99, 121–22, 138, 141–42, 154, 160, 170, 175, 187, 199, 201
  memory politics, 5, 7, 14, 18, 35, 45, 70, 92, 122, 138, 141, 154, 201
minority 9, 34, 67, 75, 81
  minorities, 45, 193–94, 210
mnemonic imposter 16, 89, 91
multicultural, 8, 29, 32, 38, 44–45, 67, 75, 79–80, 150, 188, 194, 204–5, 207, 211, 219
  multiculturality, 80
mythology, 47, 95, 99, 105–6, 108, 157, 159, 174
myth, 61, 81, 88, 96, 98–100, 106, 157, 186, 195, 207–11, 218, 230, 233

national narrative, 6, 7–8, 14–15, 18, 24, 27–29, 31, 38, 40, 42, 44, 59, 60, 63, 74, 76–77, 82, 88–89, 99, 112,

117, 127, 129, 178–79, 185–86, 197, 207–11, 218–21, 228, 230–31, 233
national history, 8, 12, 17, 29, 33, 42, 44, 68, 70, 78, 80, 88, 97, 206, 208, 209
national identity, 6, 7–9, 17, 28–29, 35, 41–44, 48, 72, 75, 79, 81, 96–97, 100, 185, 193–94, 206–7, 209–10, 212, 228
national romantic, 13
norms, 11, 13, 15, 25, 61, 63–66, 71, 105, 144, 190
novel, 14, 16–17, 29, 82, 88–89, 91, 94–102, 108–15, 117–22, 124–25, 127–29, 137–39, 141, 143–49, 156–61, 163–64, 166–70, 173, 176–79, 212, 231–32

oppression, 6, 13, 24, 37–39, 43, 61, 139, 229
Other, 8–10, 12, 23, 61, 75, 80, 95, 100–2, 105, 120, 125, 141, 143, 148–49, 153, 155, 164, 170, 174, 176–77, 189–90, 192, 197, 207, 216
outback, 32, 99, 110–11, 114, 116–17, 119, 197, 206–7, 209–11, 219–20

performance, 2, 5, 9–13, 24, 38, 44–45, 48, 61–65, 68–76, 79, 109, 157, 162, 164, 170, 178, 187, 227–28, 234
  performative 2, 7, 10, 12–13, 25, 43, 64, 68–69, 71, 77–78, 122, 164, 193, 228
perpetrator, 7, 10, 12, 16–17, 26–28, 32, 40, 47, 60, 66, 75–76, 80, 82, 129, 137, 139, 151, 155–57, 168, 175–79, 205, 232
pitfall, 9, 46, 75, 81, 110, 127, 199
politics of regret, 2, 3–4, 7–11, 14, 18, 25, 28–29, 43, 44–45, 47, 49, 63–65, 68–70, 75, 77, 80, 124, 127–29, 137, 154, 156, 177–79, 185, 220–21, 227–29, 232
polyphonic, 11, 65
playful, 11–13, 65, 80, 107, 109, 178, 229
postcolonial, 7, 13, 24, 35, 68, 112, 118, 122, 126, 147, 150, 155, 159, 168
practice, 2, 4, 9, 11, 13, 18, 23–25, 30–32, 34, 42–43, 63–64, 71–72, 76, 78–80, 111, 114, 120, 129, 144–46, 156, 159, 175, 177, 190, 193, 196, 205, 227–28, 234

public apology, 16, 18, 23, 34, 88, 125

realism, 148–51, 165, 178
recognition, 1, 4, 9, 12, 14, 27–28, 38, 65, 67–68, 75, 80, 158–59
reconciliation, 1–10, 12, 14–16, 18, 22–29, 33–35, 37, 39–49, 59–60, 63–69, 71–72, 74–75, 77–82, 89–90, 93, 112–13, 118, 122, 124–28, 137–38, 154–56, 158–60, 167–68, 170, 175–79, 185–86, 200, 205–9, 212, 216–19, 221, 227–34
  reconcile, 18, 29, 79–80, 127, 186, 206, 231, 233
  reconciled, 9, 12, 45, 82, 103, 123, 158, 176, 185, 206–7, 211, 221, 229
redress, 6, 24, 42, 45, 66, 76, 228
reeducation, 37, 43, 59, 65, 68, 70–71, 74–75, 78, 80–82, 95, 129, 136, 138–39, 144, 146, 151–54, 156, 158, 160, 164, 168, 175, 177–79, 187, 206, 209, 229, 231
reeducate, 5, 35, 38, 75, 93, 139
reformulation, 13, 69
reparations, 34
representation, 2–4, 10–11, 13, 15–17, 25, 28–29, 31–33, 41–42, 48, 60, 63–65, 77, 81, 89, 92, 95, 99, 105–6, 112, 115, 118, 121, 124, 140, 148–50, 155, 157–60, 162–65, 167–68, 172, 174–79, 185, 189–91, 193–94, 197–204, 212, 217, 219–20, 229–30, 232
remembering, 43, 77, 88, 122, 142, 170–72, 199, 206, 232
remorse, 5, 12, 38, 43, 77, 80
residential schools, 5, 35–36, 39, 43, 48, 72–73, 76, 90, 160
responsibility, 4, 6, 34–36, 46, 69, 122, 156, 228
  responsible, 77, 113, 116, 172
restorative justice, 4
reversal, 2, 11–12, 28, 60, 62–63, 65–66, 68, 71, 80–82, 113, 115, 127, 151, 153, 164, 168, 178–79, 210–11, 228–29, 232
  reverse, 2, 3, 17, 70, 74, 78, 89, 99, 114, 117–19, 127, 139, 160–63, 165, 176, 179, 215, 221, 231, 233
  reversed, 2, 12, 60, 62, 66, 68, 77–78, 139, 151, 153, 155, 164, 211

rhetoric, 4, 8, 9, 12, 37, 60, 67, 70, 72, 74–76, 78, 80, 156, 158, 220, 228, 230
roles, 11, 14, 18, 61, 65–66, 80, 82, 155, 190, 198
Rudd, Kevin, 2, 5, 12, 33, 70, 72–73, 75–77,79–80, 88–89, 112, 206, 208

Scott, Kim, 16–17, 82, 136, 138, 141, 148, 165, 177, 179, 232
settlement, 5, 16, 18, 32, 38, 42, 71, 111–12, 114, 116–18, 127, 189, 191
settler colony, 5, 185
silence, 2–3, 10, 14, 25, 28, 31, 38, 43, 71, 89–90, 94, 111–12, 118, 121–22, 124–25, 127, 139, 148, 153–54, 215, 228, 231
  silencing 231
solidarity, 14, 76
South Africa, 7–8, 10, 18, 23–28, 34, 39–41, 46–47, 227
story, 7, 14, 17, 28–29, 33, 43, 59–60, 66, 79, 88, 91, 96, 98, 100–3, 110, 112, 121–25, 127, 140, 143–48, 154, 160–61, 166, 168, 173, 186, 192, 195, 202–3, 205, 207, 212, 214, 217–18, 220, 232
  storytelling, 2, 6, 8, 18, 22, 24–26, 29, 41, 44, 60, 63, 101, 159, 165, 142, 145, 194, 196, 199, 204, 210, 230, 232
subversive, 3, 15, 18, 60, 107, 150, 207–8, 214, 228, 230–31, 234
  subversion 16, 61
superior, 9, 62, 68, 111, 113–18, 126, 129, 188, 191–92, 209, 231
survivor, 1, 5–6, 10–11, 16, 22–23, 26, 30, 33–35, 39–41, 46, 65–66, 91, 123–24

temporariness, 14
  temporal, 11, 25, 28, 60, 62, 65, 68, 164, 196
testimony, 2, 7, 9, 24–25, 27, 92, 157, 159, 203, 211
  testify, 2, 27, 59
token, 4, 93, 96, 111, 115–16, 118, 126, 129, 157, 165, 167, 202, 204
toolbox, 4, 46
Transcultural, 3, 12–13, 15, 17–18, 27, 68, 70, 81–82, 88–90, 94, 99, 105, 107–8, 124, 126–29, 146–47, 151, 155, 157–59, 161–62, 164–65, 167–68, 170, 172, 175–77, 179, 185, 187–88, 197, 203, 205, 209, 217, 228, 231–34
transcultural identity, 17, 90, 94, 128–29, 156–57, 159, 161, 165, 177, 187, 194
transcultural identities, 16, 18, 60, 68, 71, 80, 89, 95, 121, 128–29, 150, 157–58, 167, 179, 185, 205, 212, 220, 229, 234
transgression, 13–14, 175, 230, 233
transitional Justice, 23, 27
transnational, 108
trauma, 2, 4, 10, 12, 14, 25, 34, 41–42, 47, 65, 74, 90–93, 95, 97, 110–11, 121–27, 129, 156, 158–59, 163, 168, 172–73, 177, 228, 231–32
trickster, 12, 16–17, 80, 95, 104–9, 128–29, 151, 157–59, 165, 167, 174, 176–77, 179, 203, 231–34
truth, 2–3, 5–8, 10, 13–15, 22–23, 25–28, 32, 34–35, 37, 39–41, 43–45, 59–61, 63–67, 78, 81, 106–7, 121, 128, 138, 145, 148, 152, 161, 163–64, 171–72, 192, 200, 202, 228, 230, 233
Truth and Reconciliation Commission, 2–3, 5, 7–8, 22–23, 25, 27–28, 34–35, 37, 39, 45, 59, 64
tundra, 186, 195, 197, 204, 220

victimhood, 3, 10, 18, 46–47, 59, 66, 68, 129, 137, 141, 155–57, 167–69, 172–73, 178, 205, 220, 228, 232
victimized, 27, 119
victim template, 228
victim paradigm, 4, 10, 22, 46, 59–60, 81–82, 129, 186, 232
violence, 4, 6, 13, 43–44, 77, 82, 92, 104, 125, 137, 147, 156, 159, 163, 167, 168, 227
voicing out, 6, 10, 41, 46, 124, 228, 230

witness, 5, 22, 44, 46, 62, 66, 73, 81, 90, 92, 115, 121, 125, 139, 140, 143, 153, 157, 168, 170, 172, 187–88, 192, 196, 203–6, 210, 231
World War I, 7, 23, 38, 69, 70, 88–89, 95–97, 99, 108, 110, 124, 188, 208, 231

www.ingramcontent.com/pod-product-compliance
Lightning Source LLC
Chambersburg PA
CBHW071336080526
44587CB00017B/2856